Security, Strategy, and Policy Responses in the Pacific Rim

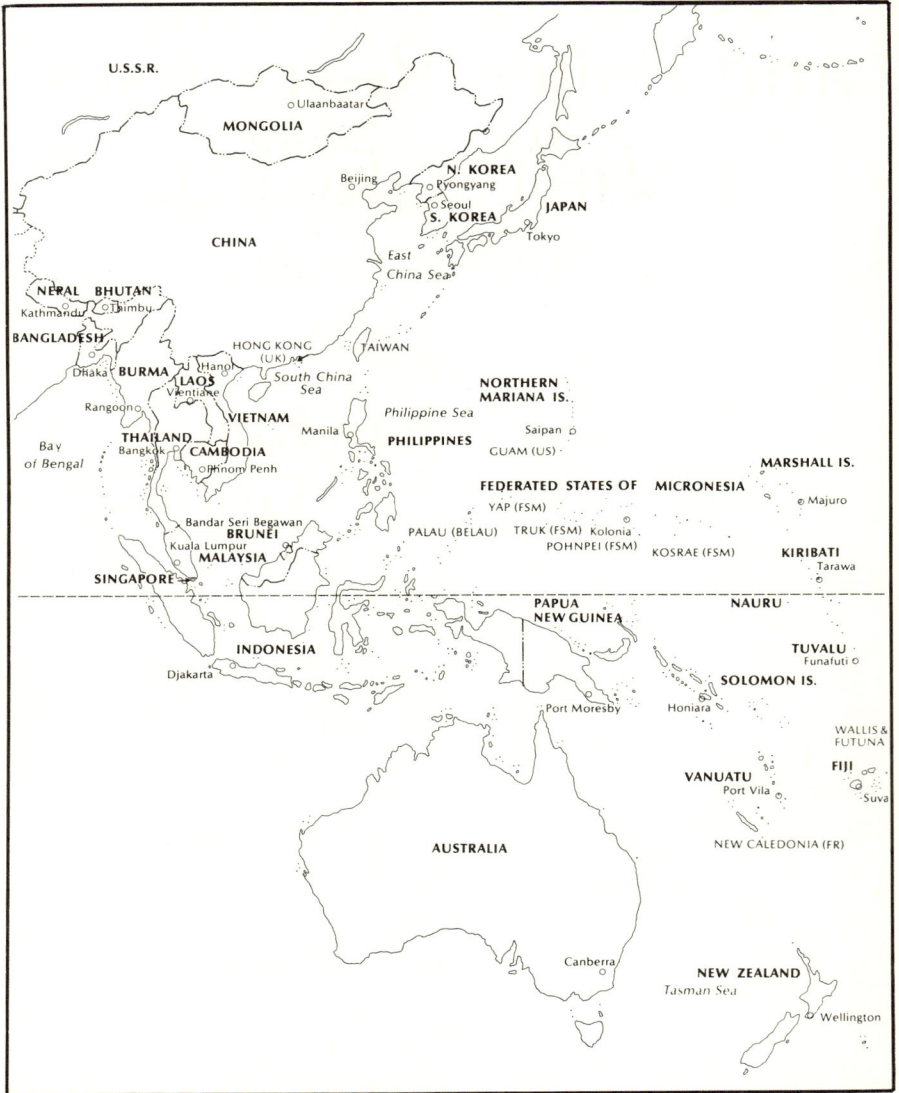

U.S.S.R.

MONGOLIA

Ulaanbaatar

CHINA

Beijing

N. KOREA
Pyongyang
Seoul
S. KOREA
JAPAN
Tokyo

East
China Sea

NEPAL BHUTAN
Kathmandu Thimbu

BANGLADESH
Dhaka BURMA
Rangoon

HONG KONG
(UK)
Hanoi
LAOS
Vientiane

TAIWAN

South China
Sea

VIETNAM

THAILAND
Bangkok CAMBODIA
Phnom Penh

Manila

Philippine Sea

PHILIPPINES

NORTHERN
MARIANA IS.

Saipan

GUAM (US)

MARSHALL IS.

Bay
of Bengal

Bandar Seri Begawan
BRUNEI
Kuala Lumpur
MALAYSIA

SINGAPORE

FEDERATED STATES OF MICRONESIA

YAP (FSM)

PALAU (BELAU)

TRUK (FSM) Kolonia
POHNPEI (FSM)

KOSRAE (FSM)

Majuro

KIRIBATI
Tarawa

PAPUA
NEW GUINEA

NAURU

INDONESIA

Djakarta

Port Moresby

TUVALU
Funafuti

SOLOMON IS.

Honiara

WALLIS &
FUTUNA

VANUATU
Port Vila

FIJI

Suva

AUSTRALIA

NEW CALEDONIA (FR)

Canberra

NEW ZEALAND
Tasman Sea

Wellington

Security, Strategy, and Policy Responses in the Pacific Rim

edited by
Young Whan Kihl
and Lawrence E. Grinter

Lynne Rienner Publishers • Boulder and London

Published in the United States of America in 1989 by
Lynne Rienner Publishers, Inc.
1800 30th Street, Boulder, Colorado 80301

and in the United Kingdom by
Lynne Rienner Publishers, Inc.
3 Henrietta Street, Covent Garden, London WC2E 8LU

Library of Congress Cataloging-in-Publication Data

Security, strategy, and policy responses in the
    Pacific rim.

    Bibliography: p.
    Includes index.
    1. East Asia—National security. 2. Oceania—
National security. 3. Pacific Area—National
security. I. Kihl, Young W., 1932–
II. Grinter, Lawrence E.
UA830.S366 1989   355'.03305   88-30611
ISBN 1-55587-131-3 (alk. paper)

British Cataloguing in Publication Data
A Cataloguing in Publication record for this book
is available from the British Library.

Printed and bound in the United States of America

The paper used in this publication meets the requirements of
the American National Standard for Permanence of Paper for
Printed Library Materials Z39.48-1984.

To a safer world
for this and future generations

Contents

Acronyms

AAA	Anti-Aircraft Artillery
ABRI	Angkatan Bersenjata Republik Indonesia (Indonesian Armed Forces)
AFP	Armed Forces of the Philippines
ALP	Australian Labour party
ALRI	Angkatan Laut Republik Indonesia (Navy)
ANZAC	Australia–New Zealand Army Corps
ANZUS	Australia–New Zealand–United States
APCs/IFVs	Armored Personnel Carriers/Infantry Fighting Vehicles
ASDF	Air Self-Defense Force (Japan)
ASEAN	Association of Southeast Asian Nations
ASW	antisubmarine warfare
AURI	Angkatan Udora Republik Indonesia (Indonesian Air Force)
BAM	Baikal-Amur Mainline
CAR	closer ANZAC relations
CBM	Confidence-Building Measures
CENTCOM	U.S. Central Command
CINCPAC	Commander-in-Chief, Pacific
CITUU	Committee for International Trade Union Unity
CMEA	Council for Mutual Economic Assistance
COIN	counterinsurgency
COMECON	Council for Mutual Economic Assistance
CPP	Communist party of the Philippines
CSBM	Confidence-Security and Confidence-Building Measures
CSDE	Conference on Security and Disarmament in Europe
CSIS	Comprehensive System of International Security

DCRK	Democratic Confederal Republic of Koryo
DEFCON	defense readiness condition
DMZ	Demilitarized Zone
DPRK	Democratic People's Republic of Korea
DSP	Democratic Socialist party
ECM	Electronic Counter Measures
EEZ	exclusive economic zone
FIP	Force Improvement Plan
GATT	general agreement on trade and tariff
GDP	gross domestic product
GNP	gross national product
GSDF	Ground Self-Defense Force
HF-DF	high frequency direction finding
IADS	Integrated Air Defense System
ICBM	Intercontinental ballistic missiles
ICP	Indochina Communist party
INF	Intermediate Nuclear Forces
JDA	Japan Defense Agency
JSDF	Japan's Self-Defense Forces
JSP	Japanese Socialist party
KODAL	Komando Daerah Angkatan Laut (Navy Area Command)
KODAM	Komando Daerah Militer (Military Area Command)
KOSTRAD	Komando Strategic Angkatan Darat (Indonesian Army Strategic Command)
KOWILHAN	Komando Wilayah Pertahanan (Defense Regional Command)
KPNLF	Khmer People's National Liberation Front
KWP	Korean Workers' party
LDP	Liberal Democratic party
MAF	Malaysian Armed Forces
MBFR	Mutual Balanced Force Reduction
MDB	Mutual Defense Board
MR/IRBM	Medium Range/Intermediate Range Ballistic Missiles
MSDF	Maritime Self-Defense Force (Japan)

NATO	North Atlantic Treaty Organization
NIC	newly industrialized country
NOIC	Naval Operational Intelligence Center
NOSIC	Naval Ocean Surveillance Center
NPA	New People's Army
NWFZ	Nuclear-Weapon-Free Zone
OECD	Organization of Economic Cooperation and Development
PAVN	People's Army of Vietnam
PKP	Philippine Communist party
PLA	People's Liberation Army
PRC	People's Republic of China
PTUF	Pacific Trade Union Forum
RAAF	Royal Australian Air Force
RAN	Royal Australian Navy
RBAF	Royal Brunei Air Force
RIMPAC	Rim of the Pacific naval exercises
RNZAF	Royal New Zealand Air Force
RNZN	Royal New Zealand Navy
ROK	Republic of Korea
RTA	Royal Thai Army
SA5	Soviet surface-to-air missile
SA10	Soviet surface-to-air missile
SAF	Singapore Armed Forces
SDF	Self-Defense Forces
SDI	Strategic Defense Initiative
SEANFZ	Southeast Asian Nuclear Weapons Free Zone
SEATO	Southeast Asia Treaty Organization
SIGINT	signals intelligence
SLOC	sea-lanes of communication
SPNFZ	South Pacific Nuclear-Free Zone
SRV	Socialist Republic of Vietnam
SSB/SSBN	ballistic missile-firing submarines
STOL	short-takeoff-and-landing
USFJ	U.S. Forces, Japan
VCP	Vietnam Communist party
WFTU	World Federation of Trade Unions

WPC   World Peace Council
WTO   Warsaw Treaty Organization

ZOPFAN   Zone of Peace, Freedom, and Neutrality

Preface

The Pacific Ocean, the world's largest hydrosphere (with some 64 million square miles and 170 million cubic miles of water—twice the size of the Atlantic Ocean) is no longer the physical barrier it once was. This vast water space has become a "common lake" for those countries bordering it. Travel among the Pacific Rim nations has become easy, and electronic communication is almost instantaneous.

The Western Pacific—or Asia Pacific—region is an arena in world politics where the major powers and their allies are constantly in competition. The region is conflict-ridden politically, heavily armed, and economically dynamic. And it is in this region that the two major socioeconomic systems, socialism and capitalism, have clashed ideologically in the mid-twentieth century—with the outcome far from clear.

Security is a serious concern of the nations and people of the Pacific Rim. Addressing that concern in this book, some of the leading analysts of Western Pacific affairs identify the region's emerging security trends and challenges—and their views regarding policy measures necessary to cope with those challenges. The book began as a revised edition of the 1986 publication, *Asian-Pacific Security: Emerging Challenges and Responses*. In the process of revision, however, the authors realized how rapidly regional security dynamics had changed, and the momentum of updating carried each of us beyond our initial expectations. Thus, this book is very different from its predecessor. The basic framework outlined in the original Chapter 1 remains, but there is new focus on strategy and policy responses in terms of new security realities and changing security requirements in the region. The following chapters are entirely new material: 3, 4, 6, 7, 10, and 11; other chapters have been extensively updated and revised.

We decided to use the broad term, "the Pacific Rim" (which encompasses several subregions) in the book's title because it connotes a futuristic concept, one that challenges the imagination as much as it reflects the present and past situations in the Pacific Basin. It is the Western Pacific Rim—or Pacific Asia—though, that is the focus of this book. This region is more active economically and more security-sensitive than are the regions of the Eastern or Southern Pacific Rim. The latter have yet to acquire the intensity of Pacific Asia, though we can anticipate that development under an altered global security environment in the twenty-first century.

Professors Kihl and Grinter have given equal time and effort to complete this project. They wish to thank Lynne Rienner and her editorial staff for their professional guidance, and also the contributors to the book for their unflagging support and cooperation in meeting deadlines. Young Whan Kihl wishes to thank his colleagues at Iowa State University and his students taking political science courses, especially one entitled "Asia in World Politics," where some of his ideas reflected in this book were tested. Professor Kihl also acknowledges the receipt of 1988 summer research support from MATRIC (Midwest Agricultural Trade Research and Information Center) of Iowa State University. The following graduate students assisted Dr. Kihl in preparing and updating the bibliography: Jeffrey Lee Beatty, Sung-Gol Hong, Tom Jacobsen, Byoung-ki Park, and David Rank. Lawrence E. Grinter wishes to thank his colleagues and students at Maxwell Air Force Base, Alabama, whose valuable comments and support over the years have sharpened his appreciation of the Pacific Rim security issues. He also is most appreciative for recent time spent in Asia and support provided by the Center for Aerospace Doctrine, Research and Education at Maxwell Air Force Base, and the National Council of World Affairs Organization.

About the Contributors

Lawrence E. Grinter is professor of Asian studies at the Air University, Maxwell Air Force Base, Alabama. He has also been a faculty member at the National War College and the Air War College. Among his publications are *Asian-Pacific Security* and *East Asian Conflict Zones* (both coedited with Young Whan Kihl).

Young Whan Kihl is professor of political science at Iowa State University, Ames. A specialist in international and comparative (Asian) politics, his most recent books include *Political Changes in South Korea* (coedited with Ilpyong J. Kim), *East Asian Conflict Zones* and *Asian-Pacific Security* (both coedited with Lawrence Grinter), and *Politics and Policies in Divided Korea*.

Marian Leighton is a foreign policy analyst with the Defense Intelligence Agency. She has written widely on Soviet foreign policy, including policy toward Asia; her recent publications include *The Soviet Threat to NATO's Northern Flank; The Deceptive Lure of Détente* is forthcoming.

Michael McKinley, previously lecturer in the Department of Politics at the University of Western Australia, has joined the faculty of the Department of Political Science at Australian National University, Canberra. He has published widely on the subjects of international relations and strategic studies on South Pacific and Indian Ocean affairs.

Edward A. Olsen is professor of national security affairs at the Naval Postgraduate School, Monterey, California. A specialist in Japanese and Korean affairs, he formerly served as a northeast Asian intelligence officer with the U.S. Department of State. He is the author of numerous books and articles, including *U.S.-Japan Strategic Reciprocity, The Armed Forces in*

Contemporary Asian Societies, and *The Two Koreas and U.S. Policies.*

Leif Rosenberger is senior analyst in the Strategic Studies Institute at the U.S. Army War College. He was a specialist in Soviet foreign affairs and counterterrorism with U.S. government agencies, and also taught at Providence College, Rhode Island. His articles on international communism have appeared in *Problems of Communism, Survey,* and the Hoover Institution's *Yearbook on International Affairs.*

Sheldon W. Simon is professor of political science and director of the Center for Asian Studies at Arizona State University in Tempe. He has also served as a consultant to the U.S. Information Agency, Department of State, and Department of Defense. He has published widely on Southeast Asian regional politics; his most recent book is *The Future of Asian-Pacific Security Collaboration.*

Robert Sutter is a specialist in Asian affairs with the Congressional Research Service of the Library of Congress. He has held assignments with the Department of State, the Senate Foreign Relations Committee, and the Central Intelligence Agency. He has published widely on Asian affairs and Chinese politics, including his most recent book, *Chinese Foreign Policy: Developments After Mao.*

William S. Turley is professor of political science at Southern Illinois University in Carbondale. He was Fulbright-Hayes Visiting Professor at Chulalongkorn University, Bangkok, Thailand, from 1982 to 1984. He is the author of numerous studies on Vietnamese affairs, including *The Second Indochina War 1954–1975;* and editor of *Confrontation or Coexistence: The Future of ASEAN-Vietnam Relations.*

Donald E. Weatherbee is the Donald S. Russell Professor of Contemporary Foreign Policy at the University of South Carolina, Columbia. He also taught at the University of Rhode Island and the U.S. Army War College, and was a Fulbright Fellow at the Institute of Southeast Asian Studies, Singapore, from 1981 to 1982. He has published widely on Southeast Asian affairs, including *Southeast Asia Divided: The ASEAN Indochina Crisis.*

1

Changing Security Requirements in Pacific Asia

YOUNG WHAN KIHL
LAWRENCE E. GRINTER

The Asian-Pacific area, also known here as the Western Pacific, is one of the most dynamic regions in the world. It is a conflict-ridden region, both politically and militarily, where the interests of four major world powers—the United States, the Soviet Union, China, and Japan—intersect. It is also the site of the United States' last three major military conflicts (World War II, the Korean War, and the Vietnam War). Yet, the Asian Pacific is growing rapidly economically and in world trade and investment, and it has grown in the 1970s and 1980s at rates not experienced elsewhere in the world. The Asian-Pacific region could become the world's most viable economic center in the not-so-distant future. Many pundits have recently predicted, in fact, that the twenty-first century will become the century of the Pacific Rim, with the center of the world's economic activities gradually shifting away from the North Atlantic to the Pacific Basin.[1]

The Pacific Basin region, defined broadly, includes the countries bordering on the Pacific: Australia, New Zealand, the United States, Canada, the ministates of the South Pacific, the Latin American states, and the East Asian and Southeast Asian nations. A subarea of the Pacific Basin is the Western or Asian Pacific, which for the purpose of the present study consists of three main areas—Northeast Asia, Southeast Asia, and Oceania—including Australia; New Zealand; Japan; the People's Republic of China (PRC); South and North Korea; Taiwan; Hong Kong; the three Indo-Chinese states of Vietnam, Laos, and Cambodia; and the six Association of South East Asian Nations (ASEAN) of Indonesia, Malaysia, the Philippines, Singapore, Thailand, and Brunei (the latter joined the organization in 1984).[2] The United States and the Soviet Union, which possess considerable regional ties and interests, are also included in the scope of this study. Soviet leader Mikhail Gorbachev, in his Vladivostok speech of July 28, 1986, reaffirmed the Soviet Union's legitimate claim as an Asian-Pacific country. U.S. leaders, including

1

Presidents Ford, Carter, and Reagan, have also repeatedly emphasized their country's role as a Pacific nation.

SECURITY ENVIRONMENT AND
THE SHIFTING POWER BALANCE

The Asian-Pacific area is one of the most heavily armed regions in the world, and regional peace and security are still marred by continuing political and military conflicts. Since 1945, East Asia (or the Far East) has been a center of the world struggle between the dominant adversarial socioeconomic systems of capitalism and socialism; the Asian-Pacific region today continues to be a prime conflict zone for critical countries in the global power struggle.[3] East Asia has witnessed not only communist revolutions after World War II in China, North Korea, and Indochina, following prolonged civil and international wars, but conversely also some of the most impressive capitalist achievements in the postwar era, in Japan, South Korea, Taiwan, Hong Kong, and Singapore. The economic "miracles" of the latter category have been credited to the dynamic forces of market-oriented capitalist economies.

The Asian Pacific is a region in search of peace and stability. The Korean Peninsula remains an armed camp where a combined total of 1.5 million troops are stationed face-to-face across the 155-mile-long Demilitarized Zone that separates the land into the communist North and the noncommunist South. In the Indo-Chinese countries of Vietnam, Cambodia, and Laos, some 1.3 million men are now under arms, and Vietnamese forces are face-to-face with Chinese forces across the Sino-Vietnamese border at the same time as Vietnamese forces also still occupy Cambodia and Laos. About one-third of the three million men in uniform in China confront Soviet troops across the Sino-Soviet frontier, and approximately one-third of the Soviet ground forces—some fifty-two divisions—are garrisoned in the Soviet Far East.

The increase in Soviet theater forces in the Far East since the U.S. withdrawal from Indochina and Thailand in 1974 and 1975 has been a major source of external threat perception shared by most of the region's governments. The Soviet Pacific Fleet is now at its largest, and Soviet air power, both tactical and strategic, is the largest in the region. About one-third of the Soviet SS-20 intermediate-range ballistic missile battalions have been stationed in the Asian-Pacific region, although the Soviet Union has pledged to remove them as part of the newly negotiated 1988 INF [Intermediate Nuclear Forces] Reduction Treaty with the United States.[4] The concentration of Soviet military forces in the Far East has been a source of considerable concern, given the demonstrated willingness of the Soviet Union and its allies—in Afghanistan and Cambodia and on the Korean Peninsula—to use military power for political ends.

Fortunately, the Soviet Union has not been able to translate this growing military power into equivalent political influence. Its ideological appeal in the Asian Pacific has been limited, and its economic leverage miniscule. Territorial disputes with Japan and China also have limited prospects for accommodation with these most important Asian neighbors, and Soviet support for Vietnam has fueled the suspicion with which all ASEAN states regard Moscow. It is to overcome these sterile policies that Mr. Gorbachev, with the July 1986 Vladivostok speech as his centerpiece, created a new Eastern policy designed to enhance Soviet appeal and influence in the region.

The recent U.S.-Soviet accommodation on intermediate nuclear weapons, however, has also impacted the region. The signing of the INF reduction treaty in December 1987 and its ratification timed with the Reagan-Gorbachev summit in May 1988 moderated the perception of the Soviet threat in the region by beginning the removal of the 150 SS-20s targeted on Asia. Soviet troop withdrawal from Afghanistan, already initiated as part of the Geneva agreement in 1988, combined with further reduction of the Soviet divisions along the Sino-Soviet border and the evident Vietnamese disengagement from Kampuchea, is also fostering a more favorable environment for a Sino-Soviet accommodation. Except for the Korean Peninsula zone of conflict, active debate and dialogue is now underway regarding the possible reduction of border tensions and conflicts among the critical countries in the region. The net result of these new initiatives and changes in regional security may be to usher in a new era of deescalation and stability among many nations in the Asian-Pacific region.[5]

REGIONAL DIVERSITY AND COMMONALITY

The Western or Asian Pacific is a region characterized by great diversity of population size, economic wealth, and cultural tradition. Populations range from the world's largest, China (with over 1.2 billion people and almost four million square miles), to the world's smallest independent state, Nauru, in the South Pacific (with a population of 8,000 in eight square miles). Economic size and influence also range from oil-rich Brunei (which gained independence in 1984), with a per capita GNP (gross national product) of over $20,000, to some of the island nations, with per capita GNPs of less than $180. Cultural, religious, and philosophical traditions reflect the world's great heritages, ranging from Confucianism, Buddhism, Hinduism, and Islam to Christianity.

The Asian-Pacific region is also noted for a variety of shared aspirations and attributes. Most of the countries in the region desire peace and stability, especially for economic growth and development. Human resources in the region are abundant and, given proper education and training, can be a productive force. The countries in the region with market-oriented systems have exhibited dynamic economic growth, aided by access to foreign markets, particularly the U.S. market. The Asian-Pacific economies have displayed the greatest resilience and the world's highest rates of growth. U.S. two-way trade with the region is growing, and by late 1988 was about $230 billion, although the U.S. deficit was over $100 billion.[6]

NEW REALITIES: THREE DIMENSIONS

Three dimensions of the new realities in the Asian-Pacific region are particularly noteworthy. These are: (1) the coupling of Soviet and Soviet client power projection with Gorbachev's new Eastern policies, (2) U.S. alliance dilemmas, and (3) noncommunist Asia's economic growth. For example, the Soviet Union has projected military forces and infrastructure into the area at a rapid pace. China, an adversary of the Soviet Union, has introduced a market economy into its countryside as well as into the cities, while also shopping for Western military equipment. Japan, totally defeated in World War II, has risen to possess the world's second largest GNP and has become East Asia's economic powerhouse. Other American friends, such as South Korea, Taiwan, and Singapore, have vibrant economies and are running trade surpluses with the United States. Overall U.S. two-way trade with East Asia and the Pacific long ago surpassed U.S. trade with Western Europe. But the United States stations fewer combat troops in the Asian-Pacific area today—only about 160,000 on shore and afloat—than in the last forty years, with the exception of the low point (about 140,000) under the Carter administration.

Dimension One: Soviet and Soviet Client
Power Projection in the Gorbachev Era

Beginning in 1965, the Soviet Union steadily and conspicuously increased its military capabilities and logistical infrastructure in the Asian-Pacific region. By the early 1980s, Moscow's Far Eastern forces were second in size and quality only to the forces it positioned opposite NATO. In the late 1980s, the USSR positioned about 480,000 troops on China's northern frontier and had 110,000 troops on China's western flank in Afghanistan until the 1988 pullouts began. The Soviets' largest fleet operates out of Vladivostok, Petropavlovsk, and Sovetskaya Garan to China's northeast. To the south, a squadron of, and Sovetskaya Garan twenty to twenty-six Russian warships and auxiliaries operates out of Vietnam's Cam Ranh Bay. In its eastern territories, the Soviet Union also deploys about two-fifths of its ICBMs (intercontinental ballistic missiles) and ballistic-missile-firing submarines, one-quarter of its tactical fighter aircraft, more than one-third of its strategic bombers, and one-third of its general-purpose forces. This enormous catalog of modern military forces made the Soviet Union East Asia's predominant in sheer numbers alone, although geostrategic disadvantages reduced its effectiveness.[7]

In geopolitical terms, it is perhaps not surprising that the Soviets have chosen to heavily arm their Asian territories. History and warfare have left a deep imprint on the Russian view of East Asia. The Soviet Union is an Asian state, as well as a European one, as three-quarters of Soviet territory lies east of the Ural mountains and 80 percent of Soviet energy is produced east of the Urals. Siberia holds up to one-fifth of the world's coal, a virtually untapped storehouse of lumber, and a huge stockpile of strategic minerals. However, Siberia, as distinct from Central Asia, is also a population vacuum, with only about twenty million Soviet citizens living in Western Siberia, Eastern Siberia, and the Far Eastern territories. In short, the USSR east of the Urals has a security problem: It pushes up against one billion Chinese and other armed adversaries. For a variety of reasons, therefore, Moscow has approached Asia and the Pacific from a position of psychological insecurity compensated by territorial expansion. Now with Gorbachev, more than ever, Asia occupies a central position in Moscow's geopolitical priorities.[8]

The growth of Soviet military power on the Sino-Soviet border was steady until 1987. The Chinese sought to oppose it with approximately one hundred much less well equipped divisions. Over 2,400 Soviet combat aircraft remain in the Far East, including 1,700 strike aircraft and 400 bombers, most of them highly modern. By late 1981, seeking to head off more tension, the Chinese and the Russians sought ways of improving their strained relationship. In 1982, a limited rapprochement began, one result being an increase in bilateral trade which has grown recently to about U.S. $2.5 billion. A slowly improving, more stable, and less polemical relationship between Moscow and Beijing has occurred, but distrust and negativism between the two are not likely to dissipate completely.[9]

As a complement to the Sino-Soviet deescalation and related border negotiations, the Soviets finally called it quits on China's western flank in Afghanistan. At the height of the violence, 110,000 Soviet troops plus about 30,000 Kabul soldiers were fighting between 80,000 and 100,000 *mujahedin*—to a stalemate. The Russians tested a variety of weapons in Afghanistan, some quite gruesome, against rebel personnel, encampments, and livestock. Over three million Afghans left their country (one-fifth of the population), most of them crammed into dismal refugee camps in western Pakistan; Soviet casualties became about 35,000 killed in action. This vicious war, one whose costs seemed tolerable to both Moscow and the *mujahedin*, finally became too much for the Soviets and their pullout began in May 1988.

In Northeast Asia, the Soviet Pacific Fleet remains now the largest of the Soviet Union's four fleets, exhibiting about ninety major surface combatants and 120 submarines. Overall Soviet naval tonnage in the Western

Pacific is twice that of the United States. One of the principal objects of this enormous naval buildup was Japan, Washington's main ally in the Asian-Pacific region and historically a Russian enemy. Prevented from occupying Hokkaido at the end of World War II by U.S. policy, the Russians settled for taking all of Sakhalin Island, occupying the northern half of Korea, and taking the southern Kuriles immediately adjacent to Hokkaido—what Japan calls the "Northern Territories" and has steadfastly continued to claim as its own. Deflecting attention from its 10,000 troops on these islands, Moscow has kept up an endless barrage of communication about the alleged "remilitarization" of Japan.[10] Then came Gorbachev's and Foreign Minister Edward Shevardnadze's new policy toward Japan as they attempted to charm Tokyo into weakening its links with Washington. On the Korean Peninsula, North Korea is allied with the Soviet Union; equipped largely by the latter. North Korea still shows no fundamental change in its announced objective of reunifying the divided land, by force if necessary.

In Southeast Asia, the Soviets continue to operate a naval squadron out of Vietnam's Cam Ranh Bay, part of a large naval-air-intelligence complex eight hundred miles across the South China Sea from United States assets in the Philippine bases of Subic Bay and Clark Air Base. At last count, twenty to twenty-six Soviet surface ships and four to six submarines use Cam Ranh Bay. Bear and Badger aircraft also deploy out of Vietnam.[11] Vietnam's dependency on the Soviet Union became striking—Hanoi's reliance on the 1978 treaty with Moscow and membership in the Soviet-bloc Council for Mutual Economic Assistance (COMECON) has entered its tenth year. All gasoline, oil, major weapons, logistics, and high technology in Indochina are of Soviet or East European origin. Inside Indochina, the Soviets may be spending $3 to $4 billion a year to prop up the local economies and to fuel Vietnam's militarism. The relationship between Hanoi and Moscow shows evidence of strain.[12] Vietnamese/Soviet militarism, in turn, produced reaction among the ASEAN countries, which, together with that of the United Nations, the United States and China, has evidently succeeded (along with Vietnam's bankrupt economy) in convincing Vietnam to significantly lower its costs in Kampuchea.

In short, Soviet military power projection did not translate into equivalent political influence in the Asian-Pacific region. The backlashes and policy sterility convinced Gorbachev to try new policies. As he and Shevardnadze implement the Vladivostok initiatives, a variety of energetic Soviet diplomats are now stationed in Asia. However, to date there is no evidence of significant Soviet military reductions in East Asia other than the SS-20s.

Dimension Two: U.S. Alliance Dilemmas

The second critical dimension of change involves American military force levels and basing arrangements in the Asian-Pacific region: U.S. forces continue at one of their lower points in the last forty years, and arrangements for their continued basing are in jeopardy. With about 160,000 U.S. combat forces on shore and afloat in the region, only Brunei, Singapore, Laos, Kampuchea, Malaysia, New Zealand, and Australia have fewer forces in East Asia and the Western Pacific.[13] However, under the Reagan administration, there was a sustained effort to modernize U.S. Pacific forces. These initiatives included introducing F-16s into Japan and replacing F-4s assigned to Okinawa and South Korea with F-15s and F-16s. The Seventh Fleet has also received more F-14s, and the aircraft carrier Carl Vinson and the battleship Missouri are now with the fleet. B-52s on Guam are being upgraded with air-launched cruise missiles.[14] Nevertheless, as a relative military lightweight, in terms of manpower, it is difficult to speak of the United States maintaining a "balance of power" in East Asia and the Pacific—unless its ability to counter manpower with firepower, or rapidly deploy more troops into the area, or see its allies undertake substantially increased efforts makes the difference. As we shall see, there are problems with all of these assumptions.

The baseline for U.S. forward deployed manpower in the Asian-Pacific area has tended to be about 180,000 personnel. That is 20,000 more than the current levels. At the time of the Japanese attack on Pearl Harbor, the United States had approximately 160,000 troops in East Asia. By the end of World War II, the figure was over three million (not counting the China-Burma-India theater). After demobilization, force levels quickly fell, only to rise by the end of the Korean War to 650,000. At the start of the Kennedy administration's Vietnam involvement, total U.S. forces in East Asia were back at about 185,000. With escalation in Vietnam, U.S. force levels rose to over 855,000, peaking just after the 1968 Tet Offensive. By mid-1975, the total U.S. force figure had dropped to 175,000. Additional withdrawals from Thailand, Korea, and Taiwan and some reduction in Seventh Fleet personnel reduced these forces by early 1979 to less than 140,000.[15] The Reagan administration sought to overcome some of these disadvantages with force modernization.

The fluctuating U.S. force presence in the Asian-Pacific area contrasts sharply with Soviet force deployments for the past twenty years. Until 1987, they were in only one direction: up. The numbers, an important measure of strength, are impressive. As of 1983, the Soviets had over 2,000 aircraft, including approximately 1,600 tactical aircraft and over 400 bombers in the area, while the United States had less than one-fourth of this amount—about 500. The Soviet surface navy outnumbered the U.S. surface navy in East Asia by a figure of 84 to 39. Soviet submarines totaled 122 compared to 13 for the United States. In the past three years, these Soviet advantages have stayed about the same. Finally, in addition to the massive Soviet force advantages in the region, there are the huge armed forces that North Korea and Vietnam bring to bear—785,000 and 1,227,000 active duty troops, respectively. Accordingly, to try to rebalance the scales, the United States must rely on the contributions of Asian allies and friends, in particular Japan's forces of 245,000, South Korea's 620,000 troops, and in Southeast Asia, Thailand's armed forces of 235,000.[16]

To maintain its forward presence in the Asian-Pacific region, even at reduced force levels, the United States depends on critical host country bases in Northeast Asia, Southeast Asia, and in special areas such as Australia. Backup and support bases are located on Guam and in Hawaii, Alaska, and the western states of the United States. In mainland Japan, these facilities include the U.S. Seventh Fleet headquarters at the Yokosuka-Yokohama naval complex. U.S. Fifth Air Force headquarters are at Yokota Air Base. On Okinawa, the United States relies principally on air bases and facilities at Kadena and Futema. In the Republic of Korea, the U.S. Second Infantry Division is headquartered at Camp Casey, the Seventh Air Force is at Osan, and the U.S.-ROK (Republic of Korea) Joint Command is headquartered in Seoul. In the Philippines, the United States relies principally on Subic Bay Naval Base and Clark Air Base.[17] The bases in the Philippines have become the subject of drawn-out and sharp negotiations in recent years. In the midst of rising Filipino nationalism, a formal review begun in April 1988 culminated in a new basing agreement in October 1988.

In addition to these basing arrangements, the United States also maintains defense treaties with the countries whose military facilities it utilizes. The United States originally signed bilateral defense pacts with the Philippines, Japan, the Republic of Korea, and the Republic of China of Taiwan. The Australia-New Zealand-U.S. (ANZUS) pact was signed in September 1951. The Manila Pact, by which Thailand comes under U.S. protection, was signed in September 1954; the Southeast Asia Treaty Organization (SEATO) was established shortly thereafter (SEATO has since been disbanded). The U.S.-ROK treaty was unilaterally abrogated in January 1979 by the Carter administration. New Zealand opted out of military cooperation with the United States, via ANZUS, when it enacted a ban on U.S. nuclear-power or nuclear-armed ships in 1984. Each of the remaining bilateral and multilateral treaties stipulated that an armed attack on any of the parties would endanger the United States' own peace and safety and that each party was obligated to "act to meet the common danger in accordance with its constitutional processes."[18]

With the collapse of the Marcos government in the Philippines in early 1986 and the 1987 changes in South Korea from authoritarianism to a democratic political system, the security or longevity of U.S. basing rights in Southeast Asia and Northeast Asia is no longer assured. Rising nationalism and anti-Americanism are evident in both Manila and Seoul. Whereas the outcome of the bases renegotiation in Manila was successful, in South Korea, even moderate opinion leaders now talk of the possibility of asking U.S. forces to leave in the next few years. Thus, alliance dilemmas, rather than the Soviet threat, are the most pressing challenges to U.S. security policy in East Asia.

Dimension Three: Noncommunist Asia's Economic Growth

The stunning economic growth of East Asia's noncommunist societies is the third critical dimension. Led by the "Gang of Five" (Japan, South Korea, Taiwan, Hong Kong, and Singapore), East Asia is the fastest-growing and most resilient trade region in the world. It is also the fastest-growing investment area. Add in the impact of the United States, and the Asian-Pacific region also becomes the "high technology" center of the world, bounded by Silicon Valley on the U.S. West Coast; Japan, Taiwan, and Hong Kong in Northeast Asia; and Singapore in Southeast Asia. Total U.S. two-way trade with East Asia and the Pacific in 1988 was in the vicinity of $235 billion—greater than U.S. trade with the European Common Market and almost one-third of total U.S. trade. But the United States is also running a serious trade deficit with the area—over $100 billion, more than half of that with Japan.

U.S.-Japanese two-way trade alone was over $110 billion in 1988. Japan now has the world's second largest GNP, $2.7 trillion.[19] Together, the United States and Japan account for almost one-third of all global economic productivity. Their combined share of world trade is about 22 percent. In Southeast Asia, the ASEAN countries also generally show remarkable progress. Their combined exports were over $70 billion in 1984, and their per capita income growth has been very impressive. For example, compared to Vietnam's meager $180 annual per capita income, Thailand's is $800. Singapore's is over $5,000, and oil-rich Brunei's may be pushing $20,000. ASEAN's combined population is almost five times that of Vietnam. The Association's combined GNP is over $210 billion, more than fifteen times that of Vietnam.[20] Finally, as a group, the ASEAN countries now form the United States' fifth largest trade partner, and new reciprocal trade arrangements are under consideration. U.S. markets have opened liberally to ASEAN products in the past few years.

These developments add up to something quite profound for the Asian-Pacific region's future: Economically and politically, the noncommunist countries (whether democratic, socialist, or authoritarian) are dramatically outstripping most of the communist countries. By contrast, the economies of the USSR, Mongolia, North Korea, Vietnam, Kampuchea, and Laos pale in comparison to the rest of East Asia. The region's two harshest regimes, Pyongyang and Hanoi, cannot hope to effectively develop as long as they rely on the Soviet Union, make war on their neighbors or spread terrorism, and divert 20 percent of more of their GNP to armament. Fortunately, China no longer belongs to this mold and is modernizing its economy through programs of economic reform, free market incentives, and external trade. U.S. trade with the PRC went from $1 billion in 1978 to about $4 billion in

1983; it reached $5.5 billion in 1984 and was at about $8.5 billion in 1988.[21] Having engaged with the West, China now has the chance to complete a new Long March—this time to economic maturity—if it can control its tendency toward political instability. In short, noncommunist Asia, plus China, is making extraordinary economic progress.

THE SOVIET CHALLENGE IN PERSPECTIVE

The rapid Soviet military buildup in the post-Vietnam War era did not translate into a strategic dominance by the Soviet Union. While Moscow maintains its forces and logistical infrastructure in the region, it has had minimal politicoeconomic success. Gorbachev's new Eastern policies are trying to change this.

Several factors were responsible for the failure of the Soviet policy. One astute observer of Soviet strategy has cited numerous regional developments as contributing to the Soviet problems: (1) the new Cold War between the communist states; (2) China's dramatic turn to the West; (3) the gradual reassertion of Japan; (4) the end of the period of American drift; (5) the development of ASEAN; (6) the Korean standoff; and (7) the dynamic economic growth in the region.[22] To this we must also add another factor: the failure of the Soviet economy.

The possibilities for a Soviet comeback in the Asian-Pacific area cannot be ruled out. A variety of possible developments and scenarios could facilitate a Soviet comeback in the region, such as: (1) instability among the noncommunist states; (2) shifts in the military balance back to Moscow's favor; (3) the unraveling of U.S. relations with China, Japan, or ASEAN members; (4) a Soviet détente with Japan; and (5) an accelerated Soviet reconciliation with China.[23]

Ultimately, however, it is an interplay of the forces both within each country and between the major regional actors that will provide the stimulus for change and stability in the region. Domestic political trends and foreign policy directions of each regional major country will thus need to be surveyed with a view to determining the shape of the emerging pattern of regional developments in the Asian Pacific. The policymakers' perceptions of the external environment are particularly important in determining the pattern of policy response by individual countries in the region.

As the Soviet Union pursues its new Eastern policies, it is likely that it will remain militarily engaged with the region because of its previous heavy infrastructure, investment, and military commitments. The Soviet troop withdrawal from Afghanistan initiated in 1988, welcome as it is, must thus be placed in its proper perspective of the Soviet long-term geostrategic calculus and geopolitical considerations. Gorbachev's 1986 Vladivostok initiative on Asia acquires special meaning and historical significance in the sense of the Soviet Union proclaiming itself a legitimate Asian-Pacific power. In fact, it is more likely that the Soviets are here to stay in the Asian-Pacific region for the foreseeable future. After all, the Soviet Union has longer coastlines along the Pacific Ocean and more mineral resources in Asia than any Asian-Pacific state.

The implications of the new Soviet policy and continuing presence in the region in terms of impact on individual countries and the region as a whole receives further analysis and interpretation in individual chapters of this volume. The significance of U.S. military basing and leadership dilemmas vis-à-vis the Soviet Union in the Asian-Pacific region also is analyzed. Throughout, these trends and others are discussed within the larger importance and prospects of Asia's economic growth as it bears on regional stability and the power balance.

POLICY RESPONSES AND NEW U.S. ASIAN-PACIFIC POLICY

The Asian-Pacific area is thus a region of challenge and diversity that requires comprehensive policy frameworks that elicit creative responses by the various governments with regard to regional security and welfare. The United States, for instance, was responsible for shifts in policy emphasis and attention in the 1970s which, after Vietnam, were reinforced by the Carter administration's initial decision to withdraw U.S. ground combat forces from South Korea. The move generated confusion and concern among U.S. Asian allies and friends, including Japan.[24]

By contrast, President Reagan's unswerving support and shared optimism for the future of the Asian-Pacific area was manifested in a series of unambiguous statements and acts. These included President Reagan's addresses in November 1983 before the Japanese Diet in Tokyo and the South Korean National Assembly in Seoul and his talks with Chinese leaders during his visit to Beijing in April 1984. The policy agenda for promoting "a Pacific era" was also put into effect in September 1984 when President Reagan, during White House ceremonies, demonstrated his commitment to the future of Pacific cooperation by inaugurating the United States National Committee for Pacific Economic Cooperation.

One U.S. government official, at the outset of President Reagan's second term in office, perceived that changes in the Asian-Pacific security environment and regional development would offer the United States both opportunities and risks in the future. He defined U.S. opportunities in the region as follows: (1) expanding commercial and investment opportunities; (2) associating Japan even more closely with the West; (3) propelling China toward closer cooperation with the United States; (4) working constructively with regional groupings in the area, particularly ASEAN; and (5) fostering a North-South dialogue on the Korean Peninsula. Included in the list of potential risks are: (1) burgeoning trade deficits that will stimulate increased protectionist sentiment and protectionist trade measures in the U.S. Congress; (2) succession crises in several Asian-Pacific countries that could lead to political instability adversely affecting U.S. financial flows, economic development, and strategic interests; (3) antinuclear sentiment that could check U.S. naval access to New Zealand and vitiate a key alliance; (4) failure to address the imbalance within the Cambodian resistance that would undermine future possibilities for a political solution; and (5) a Soviet policy that will continue to build its military strength in Asia and play for any diplomatic and political breaks that may come along.[25]

THE U.S. ROLE IN PACIFIC DEVELOPMENT

The United States must continue to evolve an Asian-Pacific strategy for regional security and development by articulating its current policy agenda and responding to new and anticipatory situations in the future. In 1945, the Western Rim of the Pacific was anything but "pacific" as the United States was faced with Asian nations in debilitating political turmoil and internal wars. China, for instance, became communist after the prolonged civil war, with the newly victorious communist regime in 1949 and the Sino-Soviet alliance in 1951. This was followed by similar civil wars in Korea in 1950 and Vietnam in the sixties and seventies.

An end to the Vietnam conflict in 1975, however, restored a modicum of peace and prosperity to the Western Rim of the Pacific. The Asian-Pacific region has begun to go through rapid economic growth, first in Japan and later in newly industrializing countries—the "little dragons" of South Korea, Taiwan, Hong Kong, and Singapore. Future U.S. strategy and current policies must maximally exploit and utilize this newly acquired opportunity for regionwide trade and investment in the Pacific Rim.

In the late 1980s, the United States had become truly a Pacific country. The United States has participated in the growing economic prosperity of the region, which is generated by the capitalist, market-oriented economies of East Asian countries. U.S. trade with countries across the Pacific, for instance, has now surpassed that with European countries across the Atlantic. With the dawning of a new Pacific era, America is no longer an island country apart from the rest of the Eurasian continent that links the two great oceans, the Atlantic and the Pacific. As such, the United States cannot afford to pursue Pacific interests at the expense of those across the Atlantic, or vice versa.

As a global power, the United States cannot ignore or overlook the importance of Asia over Europe, or vice versa. In the age of shrinking resources and escalating expenditures, however, the United States must learn to balance its interests and power by adjusting to changing circumstances and environments outside. Otherwise, the United States could end up with the self-fulfilling prophesy of the modern-day Cassandra, such as Paul Kennedy's recent prediction of an impending doom for America as an empire.[26]

As long as the United States is capable of controlling its own destiny, learning from its past mistakes and accommodating the new challenges, perhaps there is hope for the United States to prevail through the twenty-first "Pacific" century.

In the immediate future (beyond 1988), several critical challenges regarding Pacific development await the United States. In the opinion of one official, these challenges are the following four: (1) structural adjustments in a global economy that is being transformed in part by new technologies, and the challenge of trade imbalances reflecting this transformation; (2) the surge of democracy in the Pacific and the tasks the United States faces in helping the Philippines and South Korea to consolidate their more open political systems; (3) the unique, outward-looking regionalism of the Pacific and problems of linking the region to the global system; and (4) the security challenges that remain, especially the issue of how to deal with the communist countries as they struggle to keep pace with the market-oriented economies of the Asian-Pacific region.[27]

ORGANIZATION OF THIS BOOK

Security, Strategy, and Policy Responses in the Pacific Rim reflects varying national views regarding changing security requirements in the Western Pacific expressed in terms of each country's or subregion's perception of and response to the emerging security environment in the late 1980s and beyond. Policy implications for the region, and especially for the United States, are then discussed in terms of past commitments, alliances, and treaties as contrasted with the current security realities and changing relationships. Each contributor's chapter has been organized according to three concerns: (1) the country's (or subregion's) perceived security threats or challenges; (2) the country's (subregion's) emerging security policy responses in the late 1980s; and (3) national interests of the countries in the region and especially of the United States.

Although not all countries in the region (e.g., Taiwan) are included, most of the important regional actors are represented. This introductory chapter presents an overview of regional security realities and emerging patterns as well as a framework for the subsequent individual analyses. Under the rubric of "the region-wide focus" in Part 1, three separate chapters are included. The two superpowers, the United States and the Soviet Union, are examined separately in Chapters 2 and 3. The Western Pacific countries' response and reaction to U.S. military strategy toward Asia are examined in Chapter 4.

In Part 2, the Northeast Asia subregion, whose major regional actors are China, Japan, and the two Koreas, is examined in terms of each country's security role and defense policies. China's perception of the changing strategic environment and its diplomatic policy are discussed in Chapter 5. Japan's perception of its security role and policy options are examined in Chapter 6. North and South Korea's military balance and the security dilemma in the Korean Peninsula are examined in Chapter 7.

In Part 3, the Southeast Asia and Oceania subregions, whose main regional actors are Vietnam, ASEAN and ANZUS, are examined. Vietnam's challenge to regional security in Southeast Asia in terms of Hanoi's perception and ideological stands is examined in Chapter 8. The military and security policies of each ASEAN member state are examined in Chapter 9; divergence in ANZUS relations since the time of New Zealand's intransigent behavior is examined in Chapter 10.

In Part 4, the concluding chapter discusses the prospects of Western Pacific security and strategy. The emerging regional trends are highlighted, and the policy responses and implications are discussed for the region and for the United States. Both short-term and long-range prospects are introduced as probable future trends, and policy options are examined. This chapter closes with recommendations for U.S. policy.

NOTES

1. See, for instance, February 22, 1988, issue of *Newsweek*, "Special Report on The Pacific Century: Is America in Decline?"

2. Excluded from the scope of the present study are Mongolia, Burma, Papua-New Guinea, and some island countries in the Pacific, such as Western Samoa, Tonga and Fiji, and a large number of dependencies of the United States, France, and New Zealand in Oceania.

3. See Lawrence E. Grinter and Young Whan Kihl, eds., *East Asian Conflict Zones* (New York: St. Martin's Press, 1987).

4. Department of Defense, *Soviet Military Power 1984* (Washington, D.C.: U.S. Government Printing Office, 1984). Also, see U.S. Department of Defense, *Annual Report To The Congress for Fiscal Year 1989*, Executive Summary (Washington, D.C.: U.S. Government Printing Office, 1988), pp. 9–10.

5. Grinter and Kihl, *East Asian Conflict Zones*.

6. These estimates are based on 1987 projections. See, for example, the data in Donald S. Zagoria's paper, "The Soviet Peace Offensive in the Pacific Basin," given at the National Defense University Pacific Basin Security Symposium, Honolulu, Hawaii, 27 February 1987.

7. Details are in Paul F. Langer, "Soviet Military Power in Asia," in Donald S. Zagoria, ed., *Soviet Policy In East Asia* (New Haven and London: Yale University Press, 1982), pp. 269–271; Patrick J. Garrity, "Soviet Policy in the Far East," *Asia-Pacific Defense Forum*, Summer 1983, pp. 14–20; and

Peter Polomka, "The Security of the Western Pacific: the Price of Burden Sharing," *Survival*, January–February 1984, p. 4.

8. An insightful presentation is in John J. Stephen, "Asia in the Soviet Conception," in Zagoria, *Soviet Policy*, pp. 29–56.

9. See Chi Su, "China and the Soviet Union: 'Principled, Salutary, and Tempered' Management of Conflict," in Samuel S. Kim, ed., *China and The World: Chinese Foreign Policy in The Post-Mao Era* (Boulder, CO: and London: Westview Press, 1984), pp. 155–156. Also see Steven Levine, "Sino-Soviet Relations in the Late 1980s and an End to Estrangement?" in Grinter and Kihl, *East Asian Conflict Zones*, pp. 29–46.

10. Details are in Peggy L. Falkenheim, "Japan, the Soviet Union, and the Northern Territories: Prospects for Accommodation," in Grinter and Kihl, pp. 47–69.

11. Donald S. Zagoria, "The USSR and Asia in 1984," *Asian Survey*, January 1985, p. 27.

12. Donald S. Zagoria and Sheldon W. Simon, "Soviet Policy in Southeast Asia," in Zagoria, *Soviet Policy*, pp. 164–166.

13. *The Military Balance 1984–1985*, as reprinted in *Pacific Defense Reporter*, 1985 Annual Reference Edition, December 1984/January 1985, pp. 137–147. The 160,000 U.S. combat or combat support troops in the Asian-Pacific are composed mainly of Army divisions in Korea and Hawaii, a Marine division and brigade in Okinawa and Hawaii, 7th Fleet assets, and U.S. Air Force strategic and tactical fighter squadrons. See Secretary of Defense Casper W. Weinberger, Annual Report to the Congress, Fiscal Year 1986 (Washington, D.C.: U.S. Government Printing Office, 4 February 1985), pp. 237–240.

14. Jonathan D. Pollack, "East Asia: A Positive Example for U.S. Interest," in Barry M. Blechman and Edward N. Luttwak, *International Security Yearbook 1984/85* (Boulder, CO, and London: Westview Press, 1985), pp. 172–173.

15. Details are in Lawrence E. Grinter, *The Philippine Bases: Continuing Utility in a Changing Strategic Context*, National Security Affairs Monograph 80–2 (Washington, D.C.: National Defense University, 1980), p. 4.

16. Armed forces numbers come from *The Military Balance 1984–1985*, pp. 139–147.

17. Details of all U.S. basing arrangements in East Asia and the Western and Eastern Pacific are in William R. Feeney, "The Pacific Basing System and U.S. Security," in William T. Tow and William R. Feeney, eds., *U.S. Foreign Policy and Asian-Pacific Security: A Transregional Approach* (Boulder, CO: Westview Press, 1982), pp. 174–187.

18. A protocol of the Manila Pact defines "aggression by means of armed attack" as limited "only to Communist aggression." Article II of the 1954 U.S. ROK Mutual Defense Treaty stipulated that the two "will maintain and develop their individual and collective capacity to resist armed attack and Communist subversive activities directed from without against their territorial integrity and political stability." The U.S. Japanese Security Treaty of 1951 stipulated the United States would help defend Japan from both external attack and "largescale internal riots and disturbances." The subsequent U.S.-Japanese

Mutual Cooperation and Security Treaty of 1960 refers only to an "armed attack" against territory. Neither of the Japanese treaties, nor the Korean or Philippine treaties, specified Communist aggression. Nor does the ANZUS treaty. See U.S. Department of State, *United States Treaties and Other International Agreements*, Vol. 6, Part 1, 1955, pp. 81–89, 322–343; Vol. 3, Part 3, 1952, pp. 3329–3340; Vol. 2, Part 2, pp. 1632–1635; Vol. 5, Part 3, 1954, pp. 2368–2376; Vol. 3, Part 3 1952, pp. 3947–3951 and 3421–3425, published, respectively, in 1956, 1953, 1960, 1955, and 1953 by the U.S. Government Printing Office, Washington, D.C.

19. See Undersecretary for Economic Affairs, Allen Wallis, "The U.S. and Japan: Partners in Global Economic Leadership," U.S. Department of State, Current Policy No. 1072, 19 April 1988.

20. Population and GNP figures are taken from *The Military Balance 1984–1985*.

21. Lawrence Grinter's interviews at U.S. Embassy, Beijing, March 1988.

22. Zagoria, *Soviet Policy*, p. 5.

23. *Ibid.*

24. See, for instance, Franklin B. Weinstein and Fuji Kamiya, eds., *The Security of Korea: U.S. and Japanese Perspectives in the 1980s* (Boulder, CO: Westview Press, 1980).

25. Michael H. Armacost, "The Asian-Pacific Region: A Forward Look," Current Policy No. 653, U.S. Department of State, Washington, D.C., 29 January 1985.

26. Paul Kennedy, *The Rise and Fall of the Great Powers* (New York: Random House, 1987).

27. Richard H. Solomon, "Pacific Development and the New Internationalism," Current Policy No. 1060, U.S. Department of State, Washington, D.C., 15 March 1988.

Part 1
Region-Wide Focus

2

Policy of the United States Toward East Asia: Tough Adjustments

LAWRENCE E. GRINTER

The changing political, military, and economic landscapes of East Asia and the Western Pacific are creating new dilemmas and difficulties for U.S. policy. Whereas anti-Sovietism and trade liberalization were simple and logical U.S. priorities in Asia in the first six years of the Reagan administration, by the late 1980s some traditional U.S. military and economic premises about the region were beginning to crumble. One result is that a new political agenda has surfaced. In short, U.S. allies have become increasingly skeptical about, or bored with, U.S. security premises, and the principal adversary of the United States in East Asia, the Soviet Union, is operating a new peace diplomacy seeking to exploit U.S.-allied dilemmas.

Soviet leader Mikhail Gorbachev's July 1986 Vladivostok and September 1988 Krasnoyarsk speeches and Philippine Foreign Minister Manglapus' March 1988 Manila speech regarding military bases symbolize much that is new, and difficult, for U.S. policy in East Asia. They establish the main challenges ahead: factoring the Soviet's new détente policies into our traditional security assumptions, and redistributing defense and economic responsibilities more equitably among our allies and friends.

Through 1986, the Reagan administration had based its policy assumptions in East Asia on two fundamental trends: (1) the vibrant economic growth of the noncommunist countries whose leader, Japan, was nevertheless seriously complicating the U.S. trade profile with the area and (2) the growing Soviet and Soviet client military buildup in the region. In February 1985, Secretary of State George Shultz affirmed both perceptions when he commented:

> In economic development, in the growth of free institutions, and in growing global influence, the Pacific region has rapidly emerged as a leading force on the world stage. Its economic dynamism has become

a model for the developing world and offers a unique and attractive vision of the future.[1]

Shultz continued:

While the prospects for the nations and people of the Pacific Basin are bright, politically and economically, we must bear in mind that this is now one of the most heavily armed regions in the world, and Asian peace is still marred by continuing and tragic conflicts. In Vietnam, Cambodia, and Laos, some 1.1 million men are now under arms, while on the Korean Peninsula there is a combined total of 1.5 million troops. In addition to 4.4 million men in uniform in China, approximately one-third to one-half of the USSR's ground forces— some 52 divisions—are garrisoned in the Soviet Far East. Soviet air power, both tactical and strategic, continues to grow; the Soviet Pacific Fleet is now their largest; and about one-third of the Soviet SS-20 intermediate range ballistic missile battalions overshadow much of the population of the region. This concentration of military forces is of considerable concern given the demonstrated willingness of the Soviet Union and its proxies—in Afghanistan, Cambodia, and Korea—to use their military power for their political ends.[2]

These twin perceptions and concerns were evident in the Reagan administration's views of Asia and the Pacific from the start, in 1981. However, by 1984, as the Japanese trade surplus with the United States really escalated, economic competition and other alliance difficulties began to occupy more attention than the Soviet threat. By 1985, the Newly Industrialized Countries (NICs) of East Asia (South Korea, Taiwan, Singapore, and Hong Kong), like Japan, were all running trade surpluses with the United States. In 1986, Gorbachev and his foreign minister, Shevardnadze, began to exploit these frictions as part of Moscow's new Eastern policy, bent on better relationships with China, Japan, Southeast Asia, and the South Pacific. U.S. policy was slow to react. Gorbachev's subsequent Afghanistan policies were first seen in Washington as transparent. His openings to China and Japan were labeled as ploys. U.S. allies were assumed to be safely uninterested. Basing arrangements would continue. But Gorbachev's initiatives began to create questions in Asian minds about the old premises. Burden-sharing dilemmas between the United States and its allies and friends became pronounced. As Gaston Sigur, assistant secretary of state for East Asian and Pacific affairs in the last three years of the Reagan administration, stated:

Among democratic allies, it is a delusion to think that sacrifices can be safely deferred. For whenever partners do not reinforce one another, the safety and unity of the entire alliance is jeopardized . . . if one partner is unwilling to bear the burdens of defense, why should other partner's make sacrifices?[3]

Prior to Gorbachev's Vladivostok speech, U.S. policy toward East Asia had focused on a mix of old commitments and new problems. For example, in April 1981, Under Secretary of State for Political Affairs, Walter Stoessel, concentrating on U.S. allies, assured South Korea that the new administration would not reinitiate the Carter withdrawal plan; said that U.S.-Japanese trade problems could be handled; and backed ASEAN's stand to get Vietnam out of Kampuchea. The Soviet Union's military buildup was mentioned in passing.[4] In June 1982, Soviet activities and vast military buildup got additional attention. To counter Soviet activities, Under Secretary Stoessel argued that U.S. policy should: urge Japan to do more defense (especially in "air defense, antisubmarine warfare, logistics, and communications"); continue to rely on Australia's and New Zealand's role in standing "guard over a secure, if lengthy, line of communication between the Pacific and Indian Oceans"; continue U.S. assistance to South Korea; and be encouraged by China's "common perception [with the United States] of threatening Soviet ambitions worldwide. . . . China's opposition to Soviet and Soviet proxy aggression is an important factor in maintaining regional and global peace and stability."[5] Stoessel concluded with remarks about burden-sharing:

> In summary, while our defense burdens are heavy and we continue by necessity to make the largest single contribution of any country, our allies and friends are continuing to assume on ever-increasing share of the burden. Given the increasing Soviet threat to our common interests, it is essential that we, our allies, and our friends transmit an unremitting signal of resolve to protect these interests for so long as they continue to be threatened.[6]

Thus, eighteen months into its first term in office, four priorities had emerged in the Reagan administration's Asian-Pacific policy: counting on Japan's increased security role, relying on Australia's and New Zealand's security contributions, acknowledging South Korea's critical military role, and depending on China as a "friendly, nonaligned country" with "parallel" strategic interests.

By 1984, these four priorities had enlarged to take into account ASEAN and U.S. problems with the Philippines and New Zealand.[7] In April 1985, Assistant Secretary Paul Wolfowitz addressed the Philippines and commented that the U.S. favored "free and fair local elections in 1986 and Presidential elections in 1987," backed "efforts to restore a free-market orientation in the economy," and would provide "enhanced military assistance in the expectation that reforms already begun will continue and expand."[8] In February 1985, President Reagan spoke of the strains within ANZUS:

> We deeply regret the decision by the New Zealand Government to deny port access to our ships. . . . It's our deepest hope that New

Zealand will restore the traditional cooperation that has existed between our two countries.[9]

Just prior to Gorbachev taking office, the Reagan administration broadened its priorities once again in Asia. In early 1985, Secretary of Defense Caspar Weinberger signed an article entitled "The Five Pillars of our Defense Policy in East Asia and the Pacific." Now five "foundations stones" underpinned U.S. Asia policy:

- The key importance of the U.S.-Japanese security relationship;
- The U.S. commitment to stability on the Korean Peninsula;
- U.S. efforts to build an enduring relationship with China;
- U.S. support for ASEAN; and
- The long-standing U.S. partnership with Australia and New Zealand.[10]

With these five policy pillars as its pre-Vladivostok priorities, the Reagan administration was acknowledging Washington's dependency on Asian-Pacific countries to help deter the Soviets and their allies.

Then came the Vladivostok speech. While Asia took note, the U.S. government downplayed it, conducting very limited analysis. With one prominent exception, Assistant Secretary of Defense Richard Armitage's February 1987 Honolulu speech, there was almost no U.S. reaction. But by 1987, the effects of Moscow's new Eastern policy and the difficulties in the U.S. alliance system were impacting the political context of the Washington-East Asian relationship. The rest of this chapter examines those five policy pillars, the impact the changes are making on them, and the tough adjustments underway.

U.S.-JAPAN RELATIONS: WHO LEADS, WHO FOLLOWS?

In 1984, U.S.-Japanese relations, troubled by the growing trade imbalance between the two partners (the U.S. deficit was $37 billion in 1984 and approached $50 billion in 1985), became the single most-commented-upon aspect of United States policy toward East Asia. Things did not start out this way. In October 1981, the newly appointed assistant secretary of state for East Asian and Pacific affairs, John Holdridge, concluded that, despite the burgeoning trade imbalance (about $15 billion in 1981),

a continuing relationship of mutual confidence and credibility between Japan and the United States is essential to the maintenance of peace in East Asia. A solid foundation exists to sustain such a relationship.[11]

But three and one-half years later, in April 1985, the next East Asia assistant secretary of state, Paul Wolfowitz, spoke in very different terms:

The striking increase in our bilateral trade deficit with Japan last year has provoked strong concern in the Congress, our business community, and the popular press. Pressures for protectionist action, which could have a major detrimental impact on this relationship as well as on the global trading system, have mounted on a dangerous level. Our relations with Japan are too vital strategically, politically, and economically for us not to resolve current and underlying difficulties on an urgent basis.[12]

What happened to Japanese-U.S. relations—"The core element of our Asia policy"—in those four years? The answer is that U.S. consumers and industry bought about $100 billion more of Japanese goods than U.S. businesses sold to Japan, and a political backlash broke loose in the United States that became progressively more severe. By 1984, it was almost as though the executive branch of the U.S. government were acting as a referee between Tokyo and Congress. As congressional backlash mounted, the State Department acknowledged it:

In the view of many Americans, the U.S.-Japan relationship is not characterized by global partnership and potential but by divisive problems, especially in trade and security.[13]

In June 1984, the administration sought to convey a conciliatory and optimistic view. In a thoughtful statement, Assistant Secretary Wolfowitz argued:

When many people look at U.S.-Japan relations, the focus is on the problems in our relationship and not on its successes. But I believe that if we step back and take a look at our overall relationship, we would determine that it is the best that it has ever been and that the problems that we have are the exceptions and not the rule.

First of all . . . our defense relationship with Japan has never been better.

Second, we have with Japan one of the broadest and most diverse scientific relationships that we have with any country in the world—both in the private sector and between our governments.

Our educational and cultural relationship with Japan is another aspect of our relationship that we hear little about—again, because everything is going so smoothly.

Although the common perception is of a closed market, Japan actually is our largest overseas market. Last year, it bought $23 billion worth of American products, equal to our exports to France, West Germany, and Italy combined.[14]

However, by April 1985, the administration conceded that

Pressures [within the U.S. Congress and public] for protectionist action, which could have a major detrimental impact on this relationship as well as on the global trading system, have mounted to a dangerous level.[15]

The administration and the Nakasone government singled out four trade sectors for special attention: (1) telecommunications, (2) electronics, (3) forest products, and (4) medical/pharmaceutical products.[16] Prime Minister Yasuhiro Nakasone pledged to take "dramatic steps" to open Japan's markets; Japan must be "more like the world," he said.[17] The Reagan administration removed quotas on Japanese cars in April 1985, and the Japanese trade surplus with the United States went up again.

As the close of 1985, U.S.-Japanese two-way trade reached $94 billion, with a $50 billion U.S. deficit.[18] A year later, U.S.-Japanese trade was over $112 billion, with a U.S. deficit of $60 billion.[19] As 1987 came to a close, the bilateral trade profile was $116 billion, with the U.S. disadvantage at $65 billion.[20] In the spring of 1987 and again in 1988, Allen Wallis, the U.S. undersecretary of state for economic affairs, spoke about the extraordinary effects of Japan's protectionism *on the Japanese*:

> For beef the Japanese consumer pays three to five times the world price. The beef for which Japanese consumers pay $20 billion would cost them only $4 to $7 billion if they would buy beef at world prices. Rice prices are six times the world price and cost Japanese consumers another $10 billion extra. . . . Japanese consumers spend approximately 24% of their income on food, compared with 12% in the United States and 15% in the United Kingdom and the Netherlands.[21]

The undersecretary concluded with an admonition to the Japanese now heard for over fifteen years:

> It is time for Japan to eliminate [these] quotas and other aspects of the trade into conformance with GATT.[22]

Thus, without quite explicitly acknowledging it, in 1988 Washington had conceded the permanency of the U.S. trade deficit with Japan.

Turning to defense, a link between the economic and defense aspects of U.S. policy toward Japan is the military-burden-sharing problem. In a June 1988 trip to Japan, and in subsequent pronouncements U.S. Defense Secretary Frank Carlucci appealed to Japan to pay more of the costs of U.S. military forces operating in Japan.[23] However, by 1988 Japan was spending $30 billion on defense—more than North Korea's entire GNP—and also contributing more per capita to U.S. troop maintenance than any other ally. Since the Nixon-Laird initiatives of the early 1970s, successive American administrations have tried to prod Japan into substantial increases in their defense spending, capabilities, or both. Under Presidents Ford and Carter, defense spending was pushed. Under President Reagan, it was "roles and missions." It seems to have had little effect until Yasuhiro Nakasone became prime minister. The most hawkish post-war Japanese leader and former naval officer and Japanese Defense Agency (JDA) director, Nakasone referred to Japan as a "national unsinkable aircraft carrier." At his first news conference after his November 1982 election, Nakasone said:

> I believe that our country's defense efforts have not been adequate. And I understand the argument put forward by the U.S. and its European allies that Japan should increase its military spending now that it has become a great economic power.[24]

During his January 1983 visit to the United States, Nakasone talked about control of "the four straits that go through the Japanese islands so that there should be no passage of Soviet submarines," and he emphasized Japan's role in defending the sea-lanes out to one thousand miles.[25]

U.S. officials, in turn, were candid about Japan's minimal defense effort. In November 1982, Admiral Robert Long, commander-in-chief in the Pacific, stated:

> The Japanese are individually well-trained, well-disciplined and technically very competent. The major problem is that they lack adequate supplies of fuel, ammunition and missiles. In my judgment, they lack the ability to handle even a minor contingency.[26]

In March 1982, Francis West, an assistant secretary of defense in the first Reagan administration, testified before Congress:

> By its own public analysis, [Japan's] Self-Defense Forces [SDF] cannot sustain its army divisions, destroyers, and tactical aircraft in combat due to very limited supplies of ammunition, torpedoes, and missiles. The size and modernization of Japan's air and naval forces are not adequate to defend its air space and sea lanes to 1,000 miles against the Soviet force levels of the 1980's, which even the Japanese Government now identifies as potentially threatening.[27]

The inevitable U.S. congressional backlash on this issue also occurred: There were resolutions reintroduced into Congress demanding that the Japanese pay a $20 billion, or more, "security tax" to the United States.

All this controversy and push to adequately arm Japan stems in part from the stunning enlargement of Soviet military capabilities in Asia prior to Vladivostok 1986. The analysis of the Soviet Union's capabilities by the JDA was sobering.[28] Various initiatives have been discussed in U.S.-Japan defense circles. These include:

- Doubling Tokyo's defense expenditure from 1 to 2 percent of the GNP: this would raise the amount to about 60 billion in 1988 dollars. It would permit Japan a competent defense of the Sea of Japan's eastern reaches, including coordinated mining and blockade activity with the U.S.
- Replacing obsolescent equipment: despite current modernization efforts, too much Self Defense Forces (SDF) equipment remains

obsolescent. With ground forces, equipment may be 60 percent out-of-date.

- Improving training: training exercise areas and training funding for Japan's armed services are extremely limited.
- Increasing SDF manpower with an authorized manpower strength of some 272,000 men: the SDF is a relatively modest force, and its forces are actually manned below this level.
- Increasing ammunitions supplies and logistic support: U.S. estimates are that the SDF has about three to five days of ammunition and logistics stocks in the event of combat.
- Developing an integrated strategy and concept for operations: evidence indicates that Japan's armed forces have serious problems with a unified command system and a concept for integrated operations.
- Expanding transportation capabilities: Japan's transport capabilities for troops and supply movements are extremely limited. Even a limited engagement would be difficult to handle under these circumstances.[29]

Thus, U.S. policy toward Japan is caught in a variety of dilemmas. We are the traditional leader in this alliance, but Japan's economic policies are confounding that leadership. Having pushed the Japanese to take more of the defense burden, Japan is now on the threshold of upsetting its East Asian neighbors. Who leads and who follows in this relationship is no longer obvious. What is clear is the increasing constraints on U.S. ability to provide the *predominant* defense of the Sea of Japan in an era of East Asian affluence and U.S. indebtedness but continuing global commitments.

U.S.-CHINA RELATIONS IN A CHANGING STRATEGIC CLIMATE

In terms of the strategic interests of the United States and the West in the last quarter of the twentieth century, China may be the most important country in the world.   —*Alexander M. Haig, Jr.*

This was Alexander Haig's view while he was the Reagan administration's first secretary of state.[30] The view was not shared initially by President Reagan, and it seems to have taken over a year for a consistent China policy to emerge from the Reagan administration. Ronald Reagan held strong views about not "abandoning" Taiwan.[31] However, in June 1982, in a speech on Sino-U.S. relations, Deputy Secretary of State Walter Stoessel signaled new priorities in U.S.-PRC relations:

• A strong U.S.-China relationship is one of the highest goals of President Reagan's foreign policy.
• Strong U.S.-China relations are not only critical for our long-

term security but also contribute to Asian stability and global harmony.

   • We view China as a friendly country with which we are not allied but with which we share many common interests. Strategically, we have no fundamental conflicts of interest, and we face a common challenge from the Soviet Union.[32]

Between the campaign of 1980 and the summer of 1982, Mr. Reagan came around to the position that China should be viewed as a strategic partner of the United States. Secretary of State Haig did not last long enough to see much of the effects of his efforts (and those of others) in this regard, resigning in July 1982. Three years later, he wrote in his memoirs:

More than any other thing that happened in the eighteen months that I was Secretary of State, the China question convinced me that Reagan's world view was indeed different from my own, and that I could not serve him and my convictions at the same time.[33]

It was the question of Taiwan which most complicated early U.S.-China policy. After much debate within the administration and frustrating discussions with the Chinese ("an especially difficult and sensitive time for both sides"),[34] Washington and Beijing issued their joint communiqué of 17 August 1982. The document reflected the unresolved differences between the two countries—the ongoing U.S. "special relationship" (including arms sales) with the Republic of China government on Taiwan, and the PRC's denial of legitimacy to that government. A State Department appraisal noted:

Aware of our consistent and firm opposition to the use of force against Taiwan, the Chinese during these discussions agreed to state in very strong terms their policy of pursuing a peaceful resolution of the Taiwan issue and described this policy as "fundamental." The Chinese insisted, however, that we agree to the ultimate termination of arms sales [to Taiwan]. We refused.[35]

As finally hammered out, the communiqué reflected this U.S. position:

- The United States "has no intention of infringing on Chinese sovereignty."
- The United States "understands and appreciates the Chinese policy of striving for a peaceful resolution of the Taiwan question."
- The United States "does not seek to carry out a long-term policy of arms sales to Taiwan . . . its arms sales to Taiwan will not exceed, either in qualitative or in quantitative terms, the level of those supplied in recent years since the establishment of diplomatic relations between the United States and China, and that it intends to reduce gradually its sales of arms to Taiwan, leading over a period of time to a final resolution.[36]

This position on Taiwan was Reagan administration policy right up to the end, but U.S. policy grew to encompass arms sales *to Beijing*. Selling arms to both Chinas while still encouraging the peaceful resolution of their difficulties gave a Mideast quality to U.S.-China policy.

As part of the "realpolitik" conceptions of recent years, statesmen and analysts have seen advantages to a Sino-American "de facto strategic partnership in their parallel competition against the Soviet Union."[37] United by their ostensible anti-Sovietism, a Sino-American strategic engagement would indeed have been a critical world realignment.[38] Zbigniew Brzezinski, President Carter's national security advisor, expressed the idea during a May 1978 trip to the PRC: "We see our relations with China as a central facet of U.S. global policy. The United States and China share certain common interests and we have parallel, long-term strategic concerns. The most important of these is our common opposition to global or regional hegemony by any single power."[39] Even Vice President Walter Mondale, in Beijing in August 1979, told the Chinese:

> We are committed to joining with you to advance our many parallel strategic and bilateral interests. Thus any nation which seeks to weaken or isolate you in world affairs assumes a stance counter to American interests.[40]

However, during the 1980 election campaign, Ronald Reagan implied that he favored a return to a "Two Chinas" policy (giving Taiwan an "official" status), and he included several pro-Taiwan specialists among his advisors. The Chinese, touchy about Taiwan, found the initial Reagan position disappointing, and the U.S. faced "the threat of collapse of the entire structure [of Sino-U.S. relations.]"[41] Not surprisingly, reconciliation talks between Moscow and Beijing began in early 1983.[42] China evidently had concluded there was greater advantage for her to maneuver between the two superpowers. Although Beijing characterized the cooling with Washington as being due to American ties to Taiwan ("interference in China's internal affairs"), it is likely that the need to defuse the Soviet threat was equally acute in PRC thinking. Still touchy about shifts in the PRC's policies, Chinese spokesmen suggested to Americans that they not worry.[43] Sino-U.S. relations hit a low in 1982 and continued so into 1983. However, trips by Secretary of State Shultz and Secretary of Defense Weinberger helped to ease bad feelings on both sides, and the notion of strategic cooperation had never really died, as concurrent events revealed:

- The late 1979 Carter administration agreement to establish a joint U.S.-PRC landsat missile monitoring station in Xinjiang (run by Chinese technicians);
- Secretary of Defense Harold Brown's January 1980 visit to the PRC and the subsequent U.S. agreement to sell China "nonlethal" military equipment;
- Secretary of State Haig's June 1981 visit to the PRC and indications

that the United States would increase technology sales to China and
would consider defensive weapons sales on a "case-by-case" basis;
- The December 1981 U.S. lifting of barriers on munitions sales to
  the PRC;
- Secretary of State Shultz's February 1982 visit to China, seeking to
  put Sino-U.S. relations "back on a stable, realistic footing";
- Secretary of Commerce Baldridge's May 1983 visit to Beijing
  granting the Chinese liberalized dual-use technology access;
- In June 1983, the president amended U.S. export controls,
  recognizing China as a "friendly, non-aligned country."

With Secretary of Defense Weinberger's September 1983 visit, security
cooperation between the two countries was back on track. In November
1983, new guidelines regarding technology transfer allowed the Chinese
access to computers, scientific instruments, and microelectronic
manufacturing equipment. In January 1984, Chinese Premier Zhao Ziyang
signed a series of science, technology, and trade agreements with the United
States. Overall two-way trade had grown to the $4.4 billion level.[44] In April
1984 came President Reagan's lavishly publicized trip to the PRC, which
also resulted in the signing of a nuclear cooperation accord. In his 27 April
address to Chinese leaders in Beijing's Great Hall of the People, President
Reagan said:

> America and China both condemn military expansionism, the brutal
> occupation of Afghanistan, the crushing of Kampuchea; and we share
> a stake in preserving peace on the Korean Peninsula.[45]

Chinese Defense Minister Zhang Aiping came to the United States in
June 1984. That trip coincided with press indications that the Chinese had
received computers and radars for military use and that export licenses for
antitank and antiaircraft weapons had been granted to U.S. firms dealing with
China. Two months later, (August 1984) Secretary of the Navy John
Lehman toured China amid indications that U.S. ships would make port calls
in 1985. In January 1985, Chairman of the Joint Chiefs of Staff Vessey
made a widely publicized military tour of China. In the summer of 1985,
China and the United States finalized details of their nuclear cooperation
agreement.[46] In short, the United States and the People's Republic of China
became *de facto* security allies in the political-military containment of the
Soviet Union in the Asian-Pacific region, but rather than explicitly admit it,
they used terms like "parallel interests" and "neither is a threat to the
other."[47] Moscow's nightmare—a network of security relationships among
Beijing, Washington, and Tokyo, backed by the military-technological-
economic might of the United States—was occurring.[48] Then came
Gorbachev's July 1986 Vladivostok speech, and the premises of this strategic
triangle began to shake.

Regarding arms sales to the Chinese, Washington and other capitals[49] have acted to selectively modernize the PRC's huge and often outdated, ground, air, and naval forces with a variety of precision-guided weapons, missiles, radar systems, and training aids. In the unlikely event the Chinese were to try to counter the Soviets' much better equipped forces on the Sino-Soviet border, they would need quantum leaps in lethality and mobility.[50] Soviet forces on the border display three times as many tanks and ten times the armored fighting vehicles as China, and they also have assured air superiority given technology twenty to twenty-five years ahead of that of China.[51]

Specialists who track Chinese efforts to improve their armed forces have detected a variety of efforts aimed to improve capabilities in combined armed operations, to increase logistical and combat support proficiency, and to improve the officer corps. The PLA has conducted combined arms military exercises in northern China involving army, airborne, and air force units. There is also evidence that Beijing may be slowly developing tactical nuclear weapons in support of conventional forces.[52] Defense, however, is still one of the lowest priorities in China's national programs. The present military imbalance on the Sino-Soviet border is not likely to be dramatically altered,[53] except by arms-control efforts.

Thus, selective U.S. arming of China takes place within the realization that it is not going to make much difference unless the Chinese themselves upgrade their own defense commitment. Moreover, as the hostility between Moscow and Beijing reduces, U.S. arms sales to China are occurring within an altered strategic climate. Because air and naval forces would be the most likely Chinese instruments for use against Taiwan, restrictions on assisting Chinese amphibious or airborne units is prudent. Ground-force modernization is the most logical emphasis. Hawk ground-to-air missiles, antitank weapons, air-defense systems, anticruise missile defenses, attack helicopters, and armour-piercing ammunition have been previously mentioned in press reports.[54] A more questionable U.S. arms policy involves the large avionics package improving fifty-five PRC F-8 fighters (equivalent to MIG-23s). Nothing, then, prevents the PRC from targeting those fighters against Taiwan.

China became a *de facto* American partner in the politico-military containment of the Soviet Union. Then Gorbachev reduced the perceived threat to China with his Vladivostok initiatives. U.S. policy now has to adjust to an incipient reconciliation between Taiwan and China and an emerging normalization between China and the Soviet Union. Does continued U.S. arming of China make sense in these altered circumstances?

STABILITY IN KOREA: CHANGE AND CHALLENGE

> I think the time has come for a very careful, very orderly withdrawal over a period of four or five years of [U.S.] ground troops leaving intact an adequate degree of strength in the Republic of Korea to

withstand any foreseeable attack and making it clear to the North Koreans, the Chinese, and the Soviets, that our commitment to South Korea is undeviating and is staunch. *—President Jimmy Carter*
Press Conference 16 May 1977,
as reported in the Washington Post
27 May 1977

We have moved quickly to affirm our security commitment to the Republic of Korea and to lay to rest any notion that this Administration will contemplate withdrawing U.S. forces from South Korea in the foreseeable future.

—Undersecretary of State Walter Stoessel, Jr.
Foreign Policy Priorities in Asia,
U.S. Department of State, Current Policy No. 274
24 April 1981

The contrast between the Carter and Reagan administrations' perceptions of the importance of South Korea and how to ensure stability on the peninsula was striking. Four months into his administration, Jimmy Carter announced he would withdraw all U.S.ground combat forces from South Korea. He did this against the private and public advice of every senior U.S. commander involved in Asian-Pacific security.[55] A year later, following much national and international debate as leading congressional members of Mr. Carter's own Democratic Party worked to stop his plan, President Carter changed his mind. Eighteen months after his May 1977 announcement, Carter stated that new intelligence estimates of North Korea's strength had been a factor in reversing his decision. The withdrawal plan was shelved. Today, in the late 1980s, the possibility looms that in the not too distant future U.S. forces will again plan to leave South Korea—but in this case as a result of decisions by a new democratic government in South Korea.

The Korean Demilitarized Zone (DMZ) remains one of the most heavily armed places in the world. Behind it, on both sides, stand a total of 1.5 million armed men who, unlike 1950, are now equipped with the most modern conventional military weapons.[56] North Korea still devotes between 15 to 20 percent of its meager GNP to the military. Its approximately 840,000-man standing army is comprised of 13 percent of all North Korean males of military age (seventeen to forty-nine).[57] This force includes 100,000 commandos, the largest commando force in the world. Over 60 percent of the forces of the DPRK are deployed near the DMZ. By the mid-1980s, the DPRK was fielding over 2,600 tanks and 4,000 to 5,000 artillery guns and howitzers, perhaps three-fourths as many as the U.S. Army has world wide.[58] Compared to the South, the North has a 2-to-1 advantages in tanks, artillery, and armored personnel carriers. Russian-made Frog 5 and Frog 7 missiles close to the DMZ could hit Seoul, just thirty-five kilometers away, in a matter of seconds.

Unmistakable evidence of North Korea's hostility to peace on the peninsula continues: In October 1983, North Korean officers attempted to kill South Korea's president and cabinet. President Chun Doo Hwan escaped, but seventeen ROK officials, including four cabinet members, died. A few weeks later, North Korean agents resumed infiltration attempts against South Korea. In 1987, North Korean agents destroyed a South Korean airliner over Burma, killing over one hundred people.

Still governed by perhaps the harshest Stalinist regime in the world, most power in North Korea is concentrated in the hands of two men, Kim Il-Sung and his son, Kim Chong-Il. President Kim's cult of personality in North Korea is the most intense and bizarre of any in the world.[59] In the last few years, President Kim's son has emerged as his father's successor, handling a variety of activities. Accordingly, the younger Kim's own personality cult has appeared.[60] North Korea's economy has made remarkable progress since the Korean War's destruction, the war which Kim Il-Sung started. With most of the peninsula's heavy industry and mineral resources concentrated in the north, the DPRK's labor-deficient economy had to rely on massive foreign aid despite the regime's insistence on an independent self-reliant party ("Juche"). In the 1970s, the DPRK sought to modernize its economy with a sharp turn outward to Western markets, and particularly Japan. North Korea soon found, however, that the recessions in the West had shrunk the very markets it was counting on. One result was a serious DPRK hard currency debt.[61] Unable to earn its way out of debt, in 1979 the DPRK became the first communist country to default on loans from free-market countries. A new technocratic elite is gradually emerging in North Korea and is attempting to encourage limited foreign investment in the DRPK.[62]

South Korea, in turn, has experienced major political and economic changes. The assassination of ROK President Park Chung Hee in November 1979, while temporarily halting economic growth, was overcome by 1981 and 1982 as Park's successor, General Chun Doo Hwan, solidified his power due to substantial housecleaning. South Korea's extraordinary economic performance was renewed. By 1985, three venerable political competitors in South Korea—Kim Chong Pil, Kim Young Sam, and Kim Dae Jung—were challenging the political system. Increasing political agitation and demonstrations began to rock South Korea. By spring 1987, the situation was serious. That summer, during eighteen dramatic days, South Korean oppositionists and students demanded—and got—major changes in the ROK's political system: constitutional reform, direct presidential elections, and a promise by Chun Doo Hwan to step down. In the subsequent December 1987 election, the government party, led by Roh Tae Woo, won (but just barely), the opposition splitting between Kim Dae Jung and Kim Young Sam. Today, President Roh governs with the concurrence of the moderate opposition. Following half a year of poor economic performance, South Korea regained its surge, and by 1988 the GNP stood at almost $115 billion. Productivity, hard work, concentration of industrial capital, and technical ingenuity were demonstrating themselves in spite of a foreign debt that may be the fourth largest in the world.[63] Emerging into the middle ranks of the industrial powers, South Korea, with its Olympics prestige established, is a major trading nation, earning about 40 percent of its GNP through trade and doing close to $20 billion of trade with the United States alone.

The question of Korean unification has recently become even more crucial in both South and North Korea, and it impacts on the rest of Northeast Asia. Since 1972, Seoul and Pyongyang have been discussing reconciliation. North Korea has subscribed to three principles for Korean unification:

- Independent Korean efforts "without being subject to external imposition or interference";
- Peaceful means; that is, "not through the use of force against each other"; and
- A greater national unity "transcending differences in ideas, ideologies, and systems."[64]

Debunking gradualist approaches to reunification, DPRK spokesmen have proposed rapid reunification facilitated by the elimination of "external forces" (i.e., the U.S. Second Infantry Division, U.S. Seventh Air Force, and the United Nations Command), easing of tensions, and the "democratization" (i.e., radicalization) of South Korean society. Pyongyang has called for a "peace treaty" between the DPRK and the United States—thus dealing over Seoul's head.[65] By contrast, South Korea has favored an incremental, step-by-step unification strategy, allowing psychological adjustments by people on both sides to help reduce tensions prior to explicit unification measures. This basic ROK position of "unification preceded by peace" is cautious.

Thus, in the late 1980s, U.S. policy toward the Korean Peninsula encounters critical changes on both sides of the DMZ. There has been some progress recently on the diplomatic front between Seoul and Pyongyang.[66] However, the arms race on the peninsula continues: increased DPRK forward positioning near the DMZ, and ROK and DPRK acquisitions, respectively, of F-16s and MIG23s. Can the Korean situation be guided toward more stability? Should an international conference on Korea, with the objective of getting a general peace agreement, be convened? Probably not—as long as the two Koreas are themselves talking about a settlement. U.S. policy continues to emphasize direct North-South discussions, although the Reagan administration has indicated flexibility.[67]

Conventional arms reductions in the two Koreas seem to be a more logical and concrete problem on which to work. There is little sense in the two Koreas continuing to pile up arms in what is already the most heavily armed 155-mile zone in the world. In the late 1970s, in anticipation of U.S. ground combat force withdrawals, South Korea's government strengthened its defenses to catch up with the pace set by North Korea. These efforts in turn evidently triggered new defense spending by Pyongyang. Thus, the Carter withdrawal plan may have actually contributed to an arms race on the peninsula. Conceivably, there could come a point where the Korean arms race simply reaches saturation. It may already have done so. As chief weapons suppliers to the two Koreas, what is the responsibility of the United States and the Soviet Union in this regard? Should Washington and Moscow restrain, and then reduce, arms deliveries to control negotiations between Washington and Moscow? A variety of deescalation proposals and initiatives involving restraint by the superpowers, arms reductions by Seoul and Pyongyang, and a nonaggression pact or peace treaty have been proposed by scholars and analysts working on the problem.[68]

The question of nuclear weapons in or around the Korean Peninsula is also critical. With the three most powerful nuclear states operating at close proximity in and around the peninsula—which already contains the most intense concentration of conventional armaments anywhere—the risks to peace are obvious. The Soviet Union, the People's Republic of China, and North Korea have all asserted that the United States stations tactical nuclear weapons in South Korea. Yet in the past, Washington evidently has had to press the South Korean government away from what appeared to be pursuit of nuclear capabilities. Is North Korea, a terrorist state, attempting to gain nuclear weapons? Do the United States and the Soviet Union pay a price for nonproliferation by Seoul and Pyongyang? The answer to these questions might clarify the degree to which the United States, the Soviet Union, and China could possibly collaborate on a nuclear-free zone in and around Korea.

There continues to be the question of the admission of the two Koreas to the United Nations. Pyongyang has turned down proposals that would legally acknowledge what is completely obvious: There are two independent, sovereign, Korean states run by separate, recognized governments. Pyongyang's traditional "Koryo" confederal republic proposals based on a "Great National Congress composed of representatives of all people in the North and South" have not met with much sympathy from any corner, including the Soviets, who speak of "both Korean states" and invite South Korean athletic teams to Moscow, while the Chinese invite the teams to Beijing. Both communist giants attended the Seoul Olympics. Today, the two Koreas remain in diplomatic limbo at the United Nations, but both are recognized by a total of about ninety states (close to seventy of which recognize both South Korea and North Korea).

Ultimately, the key to peace on the Korean Peninsula rests with the two Koreas, not outside powers. Both Koreas are undergoing important political and economic transitions. The recent rounds of dialogue between Seoul and Pyongyang are encouraging. South Korea's new international stature is impressive. But, as always, the objectives of North Korea's ruling elite remain unknown. Whether Pyongyang may someday grant a fundamental accommodation with Seoul is the question; that it cannot be answered conditions the changing U.S.–South Korean relationship as well. While Washington and Seoul are moving from a "tutorial" relationship to a "partnership," vigilance and caution are still dictated by Pyongyang's enigmatic behavior.

U.S.-ASEAN RELATIONS: NEW RESILIENCE, NEW PROBLEMS

U.S. policy in Southeast Asia in the late 1980s encounters three critical developments:

- ASEAN's continuation as an economically dynamic, anticommunist regional association;
- A loosening of Vietnam's grip on Kampuchea, but no concurrent reduction of Soviet power projection from Vietnamese bases; and
- Political transitions bearing on U.S. military basing.

The Association of Southeast Asian Nations (ASEAN) has been one of the most encouraging regional developments among Asian-Pacific countries in the last twenty years. With six current members (Thailand, Malaysia, Singapore, Indonesia, Brunei, and the Philippines), ASEAN was founded in August 1967. The growth and strengthening of ASEAN has taken time; conflicting interests based on territorial, ethnic, and historical differences have produced problems, but the unstable and/or notoriously corrupt leaders of the past, like Sukarno and Marcos, are gone. With the exception of the Philippines, all ASEAN economies have experienced real GNP growth of between 6 and 9 percent in the last fifteen years.[69] Their combined GNPs are fifteen times that of Vietnam.

Secretary of State George Shultz noted ASEAN's remarkable progress in July 1984:

> The accomplishments of all the ASEAN countries, individually and as a group, have captured worldwide attention and admiration. . . . Through disciplined and creative economic management your real growth rate has averaged over 7% a year for the last decade. Through realism and courage you have forced the world to address the threat to regional and world peace posed by Vietnamese aggression in Kampuchea.[70]

Shultz further noted that U.S. investment in ASEAN countries was almost $8 billion and that the Association had become the fifth largest trading partner of the United States.[71] Like other noncommunist economies in East Asia, most ASEAN countries are running trade surpluses with the United States.

ASEAN's dramatic economic growth has occurred, however, in the midst of a variety of threats to the region. These include:

1. The establishment and expansion of a large Soviet military presence on the South China Sea—based out of Cam Ranh Bay and Da Nang—and diplomatically anchored in a twenty-five-year treaty with the Socialist Republic of Vietnam.
2. The peaking of Vietnamese military aggression. Exhausted by its ten-year occupation of Kampuchea, Hanoi is relaxing its grip on that unfortunate country.
3. Growing maritime security problems in the region. Offshore territorial claims and mineral deposits in the South China Sea, particularly among the Spratly Islands where Vietnam, Malaysia, China, Taiwan, and the Philippines have all staked claims, continue to produce tension.
4. The continuing patterns of insurgency and/or communal threats against existing ASEAN governments. These include the NPA (New People's Army) and Moro violence in the Philippines, the periodic appearance of communist cells in Indonesia, and communal/religious fundamentalist agitation in Malaysia and Indonesia.

The combined effects of these threats and changes have motivated ASEAN governments to take increased security measures.

The responses of the ASEAN governments to these multiple threats and challenges have been encouraging, although gradual and somewhat unfocused. As Donald Weatherbee has pointed out, over the last few years, ASEAN armed forces have been changing from an almost exclusively internal, counterinsurgency emphasis to conventional capabilities focused on external threats.[72] Substantial increases in defense expenditures have resulted. In 1980, ASEAN defense spending totaled about $5.5 billion, twice that of 1975. In 1983, it reached $8 billion; in 1984, it was estimated to have surpassed $8.25 billion.[73] Standardization of equipment also has occurred. All ASEAN countries, except Brunei, have U.S. F-5 fighter aircraft. Thailand and Singapore have bought U.S. F-16s. Great Britain equips the navies and coastal forces of Singapore, Malaysia, and Brunei. Thai and Philippine armed forces are largely U.S.-equipped.[74] Finally, bilateral and trilateral military cooperation occurs among ASEAN countries on a regular basis—joint infantry operations, joint border patrols, countersmuggling operations, and joint naval exercises. There is room to broaden the exercises to include all six members.

Regarding the war in Kampuchea, 1988 was the year of change. Exhausted by eleven years of border violence and warfare, 55,000 Vietnamese killed in action, and a bankrupt economy, Hanoi seemed to be following in Gorbachev's Afghan footsteps as it pulled troops out of Kampuchea in 1988.

Despite enormous sacrifice, Vietnam's army had not been able to destroy the Cambodian guerrilla resistance. Hanoi's client in Phnom Penh, the People's Republic of Kampuchea government and its armed forces, remained unable to cope with the resistance by itself, showing an unwillingness to fight unless prodded by the Vietnamese.

In turn, the resistance fighters, led by the opposition Coalition Government for Democratic Kampuchea, were still composed of a triad of Chinese-armed and fanatically led Khmer Rouge, a diplomatically influential and combat improving Moulinaka (Prince Norodum Sihanouk's group), and an ill-disciplined and struggling rightest faction, the Khmer People's National Liberation Front, led by Son Sann. Despite its problems, the resistance endured in this protracted struggle, and relations between the Khmer Rouge, the Sihanoukists, and Son Sann's people have become comparatively smooth.

Between 1986 and 1987, the fighting in Kampuchea was greatly reduced. Still, the Vietnamese chose not to respond to a variety of diplomatic offers, proposals, and pressures from ASEAN, Thailand, the United Nations, and the United States.[75] Then, in late 1987, the Vietnamese began using Khmer labor batallions to lay down millions of mines and booby traps along the borders with Thailand. Next, the Vietnamese army started pulling back from the borders and pushing Khmer troops onto the frontiers. Combat further dwindled. By early 1988, the war that had once existed in Kampuchea was over.

This has led to intense speculation regarding future outcomes. Hanoi, never a Southeast Asian capital to be easily led by the ideas of others, seemed to be recalibrating its security system inside Kampuchea for the endgame. Vietnamese diplomats talked energetically of removing all the *regular, uniformed* troops by 1990; that, however, left open to speculation the varieties of *irregular, quasimilitary* cadres that could be reinfiltrated or left in place (remember 1954 to 1955 in South Vietnam?).

What about the millions of mines and booby traps on the Thai borders? Not the kind of activity one would predict if Vietnam intended to forget Kampuchea. And what about those Vietnamese settlers? There are thousands of new Vietnamese settlers and farmers continuing to move into Kampuchea's Tonle Sap fishing preserves. What of the redeployment of Vietnamese troops behind Kampuchea's borders? The move cuts costs and signals restraint, but it keeps a security system inside Kampuchea that, at least, protects Vietnam's borders and maintains a Phnom Penh government that does not threaten Vietnam. Thus, the bottom line for Hanoi, so far as one can tell, is to reduce costs, redistribute security burdens, and carry out regular troop withdrawals, while making sure that a compliant government and security apparatus remain in Kampuchea. This does not look like a Russian-style cop-out as in Afghanistan.[76]

The future? Perhaps it will be politic for Hanoi to compromise a bit further as 1990 arrives and as Vietnam's population gets really hungry; one can imagine Prince Sihanouk back in Phnom Penh heading up some kind of ramshackle coalition government. But will he do so with Khmer Rouge *military* participation? No way. Not as long as Vietnam's archenemies—Pol Pot, Ieng Sary, Khieu Sampan, and the other bizarre Khmer Rouge gang leaders—remain in control. Hanoi won't stand for it. Moreover, if Vietnam insists on secure western borders and a compliant government in Phnom Penh, then certainly Thailand has an equal right to secure southeastern borders and a Phnom Penh government that does not threaten Thailand or drive new waves of Kampucheans across the border. Therein lies an emerging basis for peace in Kampuchea: an understanding, however informal, between Bangkok and Hanoi to stop supporting those activities that threaten each other. In other words, Vietnam ends all Vietnamese and Kampuchean thrusts near the borders, and Thailand (with Chinese connivance, of course) disarms the Khmer Rouge. Enter Sihanouk.

Finally, there are political transitions in Southeast Asia which bear on U.S. military basing and this, of course, points up the problems in the Philippines. It is from Subic Bay Naval Base and Clark Air Base—prime pieces of Asian military real estate—that American power has protected the interests of our country and the Philippines, and helped keep the strategic balance in Southeast Asia.

Eight hundred miles west of Subic Bay, at Vietnam's Cam Ranh Bay in the geographic heart of Southeast Asia, is the Soviet naval, air, and intelligence complex. American critics of U.S. policy in the Philippines have been curiously silent about the Soviets and Cam Ranh Bay.[77] But ASEAN countries, as we have seen, began beefing up their defenses years ago. Subic Bay and Clark Field cannot simply be packed up and reassembled in some less objectionable part of Asia and the Pacific. Such recommendations are not based on a competent understanding of the strategic realities in the Asian-Pacific region, nor ASEAN's desires, nor the requirements of projecting and sustaining modern military power ten thousand miles from U.S. shores. And yet radical Filipino nationalism under the Aquino administration has been, if anything, even more critical of the U.S. than during the Marcos administration.

Subic Bay remains one of the finest deep water ports in the entire Asian/Pacific/Indian Ocean region. With over sixty thousand acres of land and water, Subic is the major U.S. ship repair and storage facility west of Hawaii. Guam, Palau, and Singapore are sometimes mentioned as alternatives. But neither the small Apra harbor at Guam, nor the primitive Malakal or Babelthuap harbors in the Palau Republic, nor Singapore's commercial harbor can become military substitutes for Subic Bay. Guam is four steaming days from the Philippines, another two days from the Malacca Straits. Guam's harbor has one-quarter of the ship berthing capacity of Subic. Harbors in the Palau Islands are small, poorly developed, and without trained labor. Singapore's teeming harbor has large capacity, but the United States (if asked to come to Singapore) would have to share the harbor's crowded space and high labor costs with many other countries, a questionable security practice.

Clark Air Base is the largest air complex in the Asian-Pacific region. With 130,000 acres of land, all-weather runways, and satellited electronic warfare and gunnery training ranges, Thirteenth Air Force headquarters is the major military communications center, air training and transit hub west of Hawaii (although the U.S. facility within Clark occupies only 7 percent of Clark's total land area). Are there alternatives? Tinian Island in the northern Marianas is actually closer to Japan than to the Philippines. Tinian has some training areas and several primitive runways. The price tag to modernize Tinian begins at one billion dollars. Andersen Air Force Base on Guam is more promising. On secure U.S. territory and B-52 capable, Andersen could absorb some traffic coming off Clark. The rest would have to relocate to other parts of the region. The superb Philippine training ranges would be lost, and thirteenth Air Force headquarters would be nine hundred miles farther away from the South China Sea, the oil flow, and Soviet power. In a word, Subic and Clark remain extremely valuable.[78]

Whether these strategic facts enjoy much real appreciation within the upper levels of the Aquino administration is not evident to this writer. The Philippines has moved from one-man authoritarian rule to a democratic and less centralized system. But as Mrs. Aquino's questionable leadership has shown, there is no formula for this process: Like many developing countries, the Philippines has a weak government, immature institutions of democracy, a tradition of political violence, extremely serious imbalances in wealth, armed minorities and Marxist insurgents, and—continuing to sour the whole process—an economy that flounders. Analysts at the U.S. Embassy in Manila estimate that President Marcos and his cronies may have deposited the equivalent of one-third or more of the Philippine GNP offshore in the last six years of Marcos rule.[79]

The Communist CPP/NPA (Communist Party of the Philippines/New People's Army) challenge is shifting in tactics and targeting. U.S. and Philippine estimates are that by mid-1988, the NPA/CPP had about 26,000 full-time active members, about half of them armed with automatic weapons (counting handguns, 75 percent of the NPA may be armed). The active support structure sustaining these people is estimated to be ten to fifteen times as large, with communist influence possibly extending into 12 percent of the Philippine population (or seven million people out of fifth-eight million). The *total* AFP (Armed Forces of the Philippines) plus national police forces add up to 250,000 personnel, of which less than one-third (or 80,000) are estimated to be carrying weapons in active pursuit or surveillance of the insurgents or urban terrorists.[80]

Regarding NPA/CPP operations, the "urban laboratory" experiment begun in Davao City in Mindanao in 1983 was transferred to Cebu and Metro Manila. Since February 1987, when the Aquino-NPA cease-fire ended, the migration of NPA "Sparrow Squad" teams into the first and second largest cities of the Philippines produced a serious, although still containable, urban siege. In a maximum counter effort on 28 to 30 March 1988, the Manila police and armed forces captured Raphael Baylosis and Romulo Kintanar, reputed to be two of the top seven CPP/NPA leaders, but there is skepticism that those captures made a fundamental difference. The Party lost some momentum and assets in the capital, but the organization seems too resilient and well resourced. The total NPA "Sparrow Squad" structure in the capital region that can be brought into play may be between 1,500 and 2,000 personnel—hit men, intelligence and counterintelligence people, safe-house operators, runners, drivers, finance collectors, weapons buyers, and others.

The problems of disunity and mediocrity in the armed forces of the Philippines also remain critical. There were five major rumbles in the AFP during the first two years of Mrs. Aquino's administration, the worst being Honasan's August 1987 coup attempt that nearly toppled the government. Honasan was jailed, escaped, and remains at large. Mrs. Aquino and General (now Defense Secretary) Ramos have put loyal officers in a variety of positions, but the demoralization of the armed forces and its low resources, training, and support are only gradually being overcome. A decentralization of the AFP effort and truly aggressive local strategies have yet to be accomplished.[81] In trying to combat the NPA's rural strategy, the Aquino government accommodated to vigilante forces in Negros, Mindanao, and other outlying areas. Given the inability of the AFP or reserve groups to extend deeply into communist affected areas, and lacking sufficient intelligence about NPA/CPP movements, the AFP has chosen to rely on local vigilantes and infrastructure. The effect was to create vigilante pressure against the NPA, but vigilantes also drew on AFP resources without coming under full or, in some instances, even marginal government control. The Aquino government is "riding a tiger."

It is from this unfortunate background that the formal "review" of the Military Basing Agreement between the Philippine and U.S. governments began on 5 April 1988. Prior to the review, the Filipino media, congress, and executive branch officials made a variety of statements about how the U.S. facilities on the bases were an "affront to Philippine dignity," that U.S. use of the bases "invites nuclear attack," how the bases ought to be converted to commercial activity, how the United States does not "pay the Philippines enough" for use of the facilities, how the United States cannot do without them (and, therefore, are worth "hundreds of billions" to the United States), and so forth. Most of these arguments have been heard for the past twenty years.

However, some facts surrounding the bases tell a different story:[82]

- The U.S. facilities inside Subic and Clark occupy no more than 40 percent and 7 percent, respectively, of the actual base territory.

- Filipino (not U.S.) flags and base commanders demonstrate Philippine control and sovereignty.
- Direct U.S. spending injected into the Philippine economy by Subic and Clark is over $500 million per year. When added to U.S. military and economic assistance, the yearly figure approaches $1 billion per year, or about 3.5 percent of the Philippine GNP.
- Next to the Philippine government, the U.S. government is the second largest employer in the Philippines, affecting about 68,000 Filipinos directly or indirectly.
- U.S. operations out of Subic and Clark are very valuable in terms of resupply and power projection. The ship repair facility at Subic has three floating dry docks which can handle anything below an aircraft carrier.
- U.S. estimates are that if all U.S. military facilities and spending were withdrawn from the Philippines and the Philippine government converted the space to agricultural or commercial use, it might generate one-twentieth to one-tenth of the income that U.S. military spending generates.
- U.S.military forces in the Philippines provide Filipinos almost the entire defense shield against external attack. Trying to rebuild the Philippine armed forces so they could conduct a reasonably effective external defense might require five to ten times the current Philippine defense budget for many years.

The recent outcome of the bases negotiation between Manila and Washington was only a temporary solution. New negotiations will start in 1990, giving more opportunity for vitriolic Filipino public opinion, exacerbated by the CPP/NPA, making it more difficult to reach a sensible agreement. The problems of the Philippines are largely of its own making. By trying to extract larger and larger sums from the United States for the privilege of allowing Washington to protect it, Manila may price itself out of the market.

THE ANZUS ALLIANCE: NEW ZEALAND OUT

The importance of Australia and New Zealand to the United States' Asian-Pacific policies is derived from shared democratic traditions, common ancestral roots, and critical geographic positioning. Protected by the U.S. nuclear guarantee, Australia and to a lesser extent New Zealand have granted the United States access to important military facilities, enabling U.S. military projection and secure communications across the southern zones of the Pacific and out into the Indian Ocean.

The ANZUS alliance (Security Treaty Between Australia, New Zealand

and the United States) was founded in 1951. Originally sought by Australia and New Zealand, ANZUS has subsequently evolved into an integral part of the Western security system. The alliance provides benefits to each member. There are, however, inevitable problems of "proportionality" in the triangle. Neither the obligations nor the interdependencies have ever been equally distributed. Sensitivity to these points of difference, and policy shifts, have periodically disturbed the generally high quality of the alliance's partnership. The most recent and serious example has been the New Zealand Labor government's policy of banning U.S. nuclear-armed or nuclear-powered vessels from New Zealand's ports despite the fact that allowing U.S. ships to dock in New Zealand is one of the very few obligations Wellington undertook as part of ANZUS.

Although each country had critical leadership changes in the last fifteen years, a similarity of U.S., Australian, and New Zealand perceptions of global and regional developments and the required policies and capabilities to respond has been the norm. "This includes," writes Henry Albinski,

> views about the interregional significance of rivalry between great powers, the ascription of mischievous motives to the USSR, and the need to appreciate the varieties and sensibilities of individual and regionally associated states that are not in direct line of First and Second World conflicts, as within the ASEAN community and in the South Pacific. Both Australia and New Zealand place a high premium on an effective and credible American presence in the region. Both feel that the United States should be encouraged and supported.[83]

Such views were less firmly held among the Labor parties and the Democratic party in the United States. Indeed, Labor in New Zealand has advocated barring visits by nuclear-powered vessels for many years. There are differences as well between New Zealand's and Australia's labor parties—the New Zealanders regarding themselves

> as less centrally placed, less vulnerable, and less threatened by great or intermediate powers than Australians do. New Zealanders also feel that they can do less about what happens overseas with the special exception of the neighboring South Pacific Community.[84]

New Zealand's secondary role in the alliance, compared to the United States and Australia, was frequently mentioned by Australian commentators.[85] And, or course, arrangements between Australia and the United States for jointly managed defense facilities in Australia (particularly Pine Gap, Nurrungar, and North West Cape) have made very valuable contributions to allied communications, navigation, satellite tracking, and intelligence acquisition. Prime Minister Lange's position on nuclear-ship visits has been generally popular in the pastoral country of New Zealand, but Lange also admits that he comes from a generation which did not fight side by side with the United States and Australia in World War II. Lange calls his policy "anti-nuclear, not anti-American or anti-ANZUS." U.S. and Australian authorities did not, and do not, agree.

In a speech in June 1984 (just before the election of the Lange government in New Zealand that July), U.S. Assistant Secretary of State Paul Wolfowitz stated:

> For alliance managers, the essential task, whether in Washington, Canberra, or Wellington, is to maximize cooperation to mutual advantage when we are on common ground and to contain differences—legitimate though they may be—through the kinds of compromises necessary in an effective working partnership. By so doing, we can assure that competition in commerce and differences in other areas do not threaten cooperation linked to our most fundamental shared interest—mutual national survival.[86]

By the spring of 1985, with the effects of the Lange government's nuclear ban policy in full view, the Reagan administration told Wellington that the United States, unlike New Zealand, has global responsibilities and has only one navy—not one conventional navy and one nuclear navy; not one navy to accommodate one country's policy and another navy for the rest of the world.[87] The United States further indicated it would not weaken its deterrent posture by advertising to potential adversaries which American ships are, and are not, carrying nuclear weapons. Assistant Secretary of State Wolfowitz states:

> In sum, we believe that New Zealand's policy, whatever its intentions, is not good for the alliance or for the cause of peace. While we do not exaggerate the effect of that policy, we cannot ignore it.
>
> With words New Zealand assures us that it remains committed to ANZUS; but by its deeds New Zealand has effectively curtailed its operational role in ANZUS. A military alliance has little meaning without military cooperation—without some equity in sharing both the burdens and the rewards. New Zealand can't have it both ways.
>
> In light of New Zealand's diminution of cooperation with us, we have reduced our own military and security cooperation with New Zealand. We have made these reductions with regret given New Zealand's history as an ally—one that has fought with us in four wars in this century. But unless our alliance partners bear a commensurate share of military cooperation essential to the alliance, our partnership cannot be sustained practically or politically.[88]

And so the United States and New Zealand parted company and military cooperation over this issue. In the process, Australia and the United States seem to have become even stronger allies. Before the U.S. Congress in June 1988, Australian Prime Minister Bob Hawke stated:

> I wish to state clearly that Australia and the United States are not just friends; we are allies. . . . That alliance is stronger, and the

commitment of Australians to it greater, for its having been thought about rather than merely assumed. . . . The United States has every right to see alliances as two-way streets, to expect that allies will carry their weight. I assure you that Australia is and will remain such an ally. We welcome your ships and aircraft to our ports and airfields.[89]

Other effects of the ANZUS breakdown were negative. The New Zealand nuclear ban influenced the Philippines, where a nationalistic and liberal senate voted to ban U.S. nuclear-powered or nuclear-armed naval vessels. The Soviets reacted by complementing and courting these attitudes, implying a vague reciprocity should the United States be required to leave the Philippines. Nevertheless, Australia and the United States, as the core of ANZUS, seemed to have gained a clearer definition and integration of their interests as a result of the New Zealand ban.

CONCLUSION

What is striking about the position of the United States in the Asian-Pacific region in the late 1980s is the extent to which the United States has become dependent on countries in the area to maintain the region's security and prosperity. Moreover, the old threat premises which supported our traditional forward basing strategy are being challenged by the Soviet Union's new détente policies and the skepticism of our allies.

By the mid-1980s, the USSR had become the strongest conventional military power in East Asia and the Western Pacific, piling up armaments in redundant quantities and surrounding China with military forces—some of them in combat as the Russians' largest fleet patrolled the Sea of Japan. However, Moscow was not able to translate that determined military growth into equivalent political-economic influence and, with the rise of Gorbachev, the USSR is now seeking to mend fences in Asia so as to handle internal reform. Japan, the most important ally of the United States in the Asian-Pacific region, has grown to dominate the area's trade and investment. Japan and the NICs of East Asia run mounting and troublesome trade surpluses with the United States. China, in turn, continues to be open to Western economic and technical assistance but, unlike Japan, the PRC's future political stability cannot be assumed. The two Koreas are talking about a new thaw on the peninsula. Southeast Asia seems to be growing tired of military confrontation.

In the early 1980s, changes and complications in the U.S.-sponsored security system in Asia and the Pacific reduced United States dominance without altering the main goal of the system—containing and deterring the Soviet Union and its allies. But with Gorbachev's new policies, threat perceptions are changing and so is the conservative consensus that once allowed the United States to take its basing arrangements in Asia for granted. Among U.S. allies in the region, the Japanese economic challenge and the unpredictable effects of Philippine nationalism are creating the most serious consequences for U.S. interests. Gradually, inexorably, they are, along with Gorbachev's new Eastern policies, weakening traditional U.S. security leadership. On the Korean Peninsula, the political transitions underway in both South and North Korea are encouraging; but they, too, are complicating U.S. security policy premises. Regarding China, U.S. security assistance to both China and Taiwan takes place within a changing strategic context for both countries. In Southeast Asia, assisting ASEAN as the principal stabilizer in that subregion continues to be an intelligent U.S. policy, and ASEAN diplomats want us there. But Philippine nationalism may unfortunately be the ultimate arbiter of U.S. basing in the Southeast Asia. ANZUS is holding together despite policy variations by its three partners.

Thus, as threat perceptions change and power redistributes within the security arrangements of East Asia and the Western Pacific, tough adjustments lie ahead for the United States. Will the United States and its Asian partners find new and more equitable ways to redistribute and rationalize the security burden in the years ahead? Or will U.S. military forces increasingly become the "Hessians" of East Asia, hired out by our prosperous allies to protect their affluence as our own economy becomes hollow with debt and liability?

NOTES

Opinions, conclusions, and recommendations expressed or implied in this chapter are solely those of the author, and do not necessarily represent the views of the Department of the Air Force, the Department of Defense, or any other government agency.

1. Secretary of State George P. Shultz, "Economic Cooperation in the Pacific Basin," Current Policy No. 658, U.S. Department of State, Washington D.C., 21 February 1985.

2. *Ibid.*

3. Assistant Secretary of State for East Asian and Pacific Affairs, Gaston J.Sigur, Jr., "The U.S. and East Asia: Meeting the Challenge of Change." Current Policy No. 821, U.S. Department of State, Washington D.C., 18 April 1986.

4. Under Secretary of State for Political Affairs Walter T. Stoessel, Jr., "Foreign Policy Priorities in Asia," Current Policy No. 274, U.S. Department of State, Washington D.C., 24 April 1981.

5. Deputy Secretary of State Walter T. Stoessel, Jr., "Allied Responses to the Soviet Challenge in East Asia and the Pacific," Current Policy No. 403, U.S. Department of State, Washington D.C., 10 June 1982.

6. *Ibid.*

7. Secretary of State George P. Shultz, "Challenges Facing the U.S. and ASEAN," Current Policy No. 597, U.S. Department of State, Washington D.C., 13 July 1984.

8. From a speech by Assistant Secretary of State for East Asia and the Pacific Paul D. Wolfowitz, as reprinted in *Wall Street Journal*, 15 April 1985, p. 29.

9. President Reagan is cited by Assistant Secretary of State Paul D. Wolfowitz in "The ANZUS Alliance," U.S. Department of State, Current Policy No. 674, 18 March 1985.

10. Secretary of Defense Caspar W. Weinberger, "The Fiver Pillars of Our Defense Policy in East Asia and the Pacific," in *Asia-Pacific Defense Forum*, Winter 1984–1985, pp. 2–8.

11. Assistant Secretary of State John H. Holdridge, "Japan and the United States: A Durable Relationship," U.S. Department of State, Current Policy No. 337, 28 October 1981.

12. Assistant Secretary of State Paul D. Wolfowitz, "Protectionism and U.S.-Japan Trade," U.S. Department of State, Current Policy No. 689, 17 April 1985.

13. Deputy Secretary of State Kenneth W. Dam, "U.S.-Japan Relations in Perspective," U.S. Department of State, Current Policy No. 547, 6 February 1984.

14. Assistant Secretary of State, Paul D. Wolfowitz, "Taking Stock of U.S.-Japan Relations," U.S. Department of State, Current Policy No. 593, 12 June 1984.

15. Assistant Secretary of State Paul D. Wolfowitz, "Protectionism and U.S.-Japan Trade," U.S. Department of State, Current Policy No. 689, 17 April 1985.

16. Assistant Secretary of State Paul D. Wolfowitz, "U.S.-Japan Relations: Dangers and Opportunities, Myths and Realities," U.S. Department of State, Current Policy No. 714, 13 June 1985.

17. Frank Langdon, "Japan and North America," in Robert S. Ozaki and Walter Arnold, eds., *Japan's Foreign Relations* (Boulder, CO: Westview Press, 1985) p. 23.

18. "U.S.-Japan Trade" *gist*, U.S. Department of State, April 1986.

19. Assistant Secretary of State Gaston J. Sigur, "Current Reflections on U.S.-Japan Relations," U.S. Department of State, Current Policy No. 1056, 16 March 1988.

20. Under Secretary for Economic Affairs, Allen Wallis, "The U.S. and Japan: Partners in Global Economic Leadership," U.S. Department of State, Current Policy No. 1072, 19 April 1988.

21. *Ibid.*

22. *Ibid.*

23. *New York Times*, 7 June 1988, p. 5. Also see Frank C. Carlucci, "Japan and the Enduring Importance of Mutual Security," *Pacific Stars and Stripes* 10 September 1988 p. 9.

24. Nakasone cited in Steve Lohr, "Japanese Premier Urges an Increase in Armed Strength," *New York Times*, 28 November 1982, p. 1.

25. Nakasone's interview with the *Washington Post* is summarized in the

Far Eastern Economic Review, 15 December 1983, p. 30–31. Recall that it was Prime Minister Suzuki who first proposed the sea lanes mission in May 1981.

26. Long interviewed in Niel Ulman and Urban C. Lehner, "Tokyo's Buildup," *Wall Street Journal*, 22 November 1982, p. 1.

27. Francis J. West, Jr., "US-Japan Defense Cooperation and US Policy," testimony before the House Foreign Affairs Committee, March 1982, pp. 7–8.

28. See, for example, Japanese Defense Agency, *Defense of Japan, 1984* (Tokyo: The Japan Times, Ltd., 1984), pp. 31–37, and *The Military Balance 1984–1985*, p. 142.

29. The author is grateful to Major John Ebinger, U.S. Air Force, for ideas concerning the issues which appear below. See his "Sharing the Defense Burden in East Asia: Japanese Defense Capabilities in the 1990s," *ACSC Student Report* 85–0735, April 1985, Maxwell AFB, Alabama.

30. Alexander M. Haig, Jr., *Caveat: Realism, Reagan, and Foreign Policy* (New York: Macmillan Publishing Company, 1984), pp. 194–217.

31. Haig: "Taiwan was a difficult question for Ronald Reagan. he is an anti-communist. Reagan's emotions were deeply engaged in this question, and so was his sense of honor" (p. 189 of *Caveat*). Haig continued: "As late as March 1982, the President took the stance that we were going to sell spare parts to Taiwan whether the Chinese liked it or not; if they wanted to talk, then we would accommodate them, and if they did not, then there was nothing to talk about" (p. 213).

32. Deputy Secretary of State Walter J. Stoessel, Jr., "Developing Lasting U.S.-China Relations," U.S. Department of State, Current Policy No. 398, 1 June 1982.

33. Haig, *Caveat*, p. 195. However, when I discussed Haig's position and other aspects of the Reagan administration's China policy with senior U.S. officials in Beijing in June 1984, I found a genuine belief that it was Haig, more than anyone else, who had ultimately turned the president around on this issue.

34. Assistant Secretary of State John H. Holdridge, "Assessment of U.S. Relations with China," U.S. Department of State, Current Policy No. 444, 13 December 1982.

35. Assistant Secretary of State John H. Holdridge, "U.S.-China Joint Communique" U.S. Department of State, Current Policy No. 413, 18 August 1982.

36. "U.S.-China Joint Communique," 17 August 1982.

37. Steven I. Levine, "China and the United States: The Limits of Interaction," in *China and the World: Chinese Foreign Policy in the Post-Mao Era*, Samuel S. Kim, ed. (Boulder, CO and London: Westview Press, 1984) p. 113.

38. See, for example, comparisons of the original Nixon-Kissinger position with those of Carter and Reagan in Henry B. Gass, *Sino-American Security Relations: Expectations and Realities*, National Defense University Essay 84–2, Washington D.C., 1984, pp. 1–11.

39. Brzezinski cited by Levine in Kim, *China and the World*, p. 113.

40. Mondale cited by Levine in Kim, *China and the World*, p. 116.

41. Holdridge, "Assessment of U.S. Relations with China."

42. The details are tracked in Chi Su, "China and the Soviet Union: 'Principled, Salutory, and Tempered' Management of Conflict," in Kim, *China and the World*, pp. 136–141.

43. See, for example, the argument in Zhang Jia-Lin, "The New Romanticism in the Reagan Administration's Asian Policy: Illusion and Reality," *Asian Survey*, October 1984, pp. 1007–1009.

44. Assistant Secretary of State Paul D. Wolfowitz, "The U.S.-China Trade Relationship," Current Policy No. 594, U.S. Department of State, 31 May 1984.

45. President Ronald Reagan, "A Historic Opportunity for the U.S. and China," U.S Department of State, Current Policy No. 574, 27 April 1984.

46. Director of the Arms Control and Disarmament Agency, "U.S.-China Nuclear Cooperation Agreement," U.S Department of State, Current Policy No. 729, 31 July 1985.

47. Assistant Secretary of State Gaston J. Sigur, Jr., "China Policy Today: Consensus, Consistence, Stability," U.S. Department of State, Current Policy No. 901, 11 December 1986.

48. Burgeoning China-U.S. trade continued; in 1985 and 1986, it was over $8 billion each year (lest this appear too extraordinary, however, U.S.-Taiwan trade in 1986 was over $25 billion). See Secretary of State George P. Shultz, "China and the U.S.: Facing the Economic Challenges of the Future." U.S. Department of State, Current Policy No. 930, 3 March 1987.

49. Evidently, Israeli advisors and weapons systems have entered the PRC through Hong Kong. Press reports indicate equipment supplied is believed to include "air-to-air missiles, surface-to-air missiles, sensors, locating radar, head-up displays for fighter pilots cockpits, and possibly a point defense alert radar system." Israel, which has diplomatic relations with Taiwan, also supplies Taipei with a variety of military items (*Washington Times*, 24 January 1985, p. 1).

50. When I suggested such a policy to my Chinese hosts in Beijing in March 1988, they laughed, explaining there was no way China could match Soviet force deployments on the Sino-Soviet border.

51. A. James Gregor, "The Military Potential of the People's Republic of China and Western security Interests," *Asian Affairs*, Spring 1985, pp. 1–24. Estimates of the cost to modernize China's three hundred divisions range from 200 to 300 billion U.S. dollars. Purchases abroad could require another $60 billion before a confident defense against the Soviets existed. Gass, *Sino-American-Security Relations*, p. 31.

52. Robert S. Wang, "China's Evolving Strategic Doctrine," *Asian Survey*, October 1984, pp. 1044–1045.

53. Details of China's severely handicapped defense capabilities vis-à-vis the Soviets are in Gass, pp. 31–39.

54. See, for example, *Far Eastern Economic Review*, 8 March 1984, pp. 12, 13 and 28 June, pp. 1–13, *and Christian Science monitor*, 14 January 1985, pp. 9–10.

55. On 8 January 1977, General John W. Vessey, Jr., Command-in-Chief of U.N., U.S., and ROK forces in South Korea, stated that removal of the remaining U.S. combat forces from South Korea would "increase considerably"

the risk of war. "It's the one clear signal to Kim Il-Sung that if he starts a war, he fights both the U.S. and the ROK armies" (*Washington Post*, 9 January 1977, p. A–20).

In May, General Vessey told reporters, on record: "I have told my superiors that no one here who is concerned with the military situation in Korea is in favor of a U.S. troop withdrawal" (*Far Eastern Economic Review*, 20 May 1977, p. 28.

On 11 March, Admiral Maurice Wisner, Command-in-Chief, Pacific, told the U.S. Senate Foreign Relations Committee that "from a purely military" standpoint, a withdrawal would "reduce the deterrent" to an invasion from the North [Marc Leepson, "Relations with South Korea," Editorial Research Report, Vol. II, No. 6 *Congressional Quarterly* (Washington, D.C.) 12 August 1977, p. 608].

Later that year, the new CIA Director, Stansfield Turner, choosing his words carefully, stated: "My position is that we have a balance of deterrence (between the ROK and the DPRK) today; when you withdraw forces, that in some measures diminishes it." (As cited in Donald S. Zagoria, "Why We Can't Leave Korea," *New York Times Magazine*, 20 October 1977, p. 18). On 18 May 1977, major General John Singlaub said that a U.S. force withdrawal "would lead to war"—a statement which led President Carter to relieve him of command (*Washington Post*, 19 May 1977, pp. A–1).

56. See Young Whan Kihl, "The Korean Peninsula Conflict: Equilibrium or Deescalation?" in Lawrence E. Grinter and Young Whan Kihl, eds., *East Asian Conflict Zones* (New York: St. Martin's Press, 1987), pp. 104–106, 108–110.

57. Tai Sung An, *North Korea in Transition: From Dictatorship to Dynasty* (London: Greenwood press, 1983), p. 81.

58. C.I.Eugene Kim, "Civil-Military Relations in the Two Koreas," *Armed Forces and Society*, Fall 1984, p. 12.

59. See B.C. Koh, "The Cult of Personality and the Succession Idea," in C.I.Eugene Kim and B.C. Koh, eds., *Journey to North Korea: Personal Perceptions* (Berkeley: University of California, 1983), pp. 25–41, and Tai Sung An, *North Korea in Transition*, pp. 129–148.

60. Koh, p. 27; An, pp. 149–157, and Bruce Cumings, *The Two Koreas*, Headline Series No. 69 (new York: Foreign Policy Association, 1984), p. 57.

61. "North Korea," DOS Background Notes, April 1985, p. 6, and Chae-Jin Lee, "Economic Aspects of Life in North Korea," in Kim and Koh, *Journey to North Korea*, pp. 55–61.

62. Young Whan Kihl, "North Korea in 1984: The Hermit Kingdom Turns Outward!" *Asian Survey*, January 1985, pp. 67–70.

63. Chae-Jin Lee, "South Korea in 1984: Seeking Peace and Stability," *Asian Survey*, January 1985, p. 83.

64. Young Whan Kihl, "The Issue of Korean Unification: North Korea's Policy and Perception," in Kim and Koh, *Journey to North Korea*, p. 99.

65. Kihl, pp. 103–104, and Young Whan Kihl, *Politics and Policies in Divided Korea: Regimes in Contest* (Boulder, CO: Westview Press, 1984), pp. 204–212.

66. President Roh Tae Woo made well publicized conciliatory offers to North Korea in July and October 1988. In September 1988 North and South Korean delegates met to discuss a non-aggression pact.

67. Assistant Secretary of State for East Asian and Pacific Affairs Paul D. Wolfowitz, "The U.S. and Korea: Auspicious Prospects," Current Policy No. 543, Washington, D.C.: U.S. Department of State, 31 January 1984. Secretary of State Shultz, in Seoul in July 1988, also indicated an easing of U.S. visa requirements for North Koreans to enter the United States.

68. See, for example, "Conclusion: Opportunities for Deescalating East Asia's Conflict," in Grinter and Kihl, *East Asian Conflict Zones*, pp. 211–212.

68. ASEAN, Department of State Background Note, Washington, D.C. November 1983, relying on International Monetary Fund data.

70. Secretary of State George P. Shultz, "Challenges Facing the U.S. and ASEAN," Current Policy No. 597, U.S. Department of State, Washington, D.C. 13 July 1984.

71. *Ibid.*

72. See Donald E. Weatherbee, "ASEAN: Patterns of National and Regional Resilience" in Kihl and Grinter, *Asian-Pacific Security*, pp. 201–204. Also, see Dr. Weatherbee's chapter in this book.

73. Sheldon W. Simon, "U.S. Security Interests in Southeast Asia," in William T. Tow and William R. Feeney, eds., *U.S. Foreign Policy and Asian-Pacific Security*, p. 125; *Asia 1984 Yearbook* (Hong Kong: Far Eastern Economic Review, 30 November 1983) p. 20; and *The Military Balance*, 1984–1985.

74. *The Military Balance 1984–1985*, as reprinted in *Pacific Defense Reporter*, 1985 Annual Reference Edition, December 1984/January 1985, pp. 137–147.

75. See proposals in Assistant Secretary of State for East Asian and Pacific Affairs Paul D. Wolfowitz, "Cambodia: The Search for Peace," Current Policy No. 613, U.S. Department of State, Washington, D.C., 11 September 1984; also see Deputy Assistant Secretary of State for East Asian and Pacific Affairs John C. Munjo, "Kampuchea After Five Years of Vietnamese occupation," Current Policy No. 514, U.S. Department of State, Washington, D.C., 15 September 1983.. Also relevant is Sukhambhand Paribatra, *Kampuchea Without Delusion* (Kuala Lumpur, Institute of Statategic and International Studies, 1986).

76. Lawrence E. Grinter, "Developments in Kampuchea Paving Way for Possible Quasi-Peace in Future," *The Atlanta Constitution*, 28 June 1988, p. 13–A. Also, see Keith B. Richburg, "Hanoi Cuts War Role in Cambodia," *Washington Post*, 1 July 1988, p. 1, and Clayton Jones, "West, Asians Aim to Rein in Khmer Rouge," *The Christian Science Monitor*, 8 July 1988, p. 8. In September 1988, Hanoi moved some Vietnamese troops back into border areas.

77. See, for example, George McT. Kahin, "Remove the Bases from the Philippines," *New York Times*, 1 October 1983.

78. The details are in Lawrence E. Grinter, *The Philippine Bases: Continuing Utility in a Changing Strategic Context*, National Security Affairs Monograph 80–2 (Washington, D.C.: National Defense University, 1980).

Also relevant is Francisco S. Tada, "Keeping Philippine Bases," *Washington Quarterly*, Winter 1984; William H. Sullivan, "Relocating the Bases in the Philippines," *Washington Quarterly*, Spring 1984; and Lawrence E. Grinter, "Pacific Military Installations Vital to U.S. Defense," *Human Events*, 4 August 1984, and "Philippine bases are critical for maintaining U.S. power in Far East," *The Atlanta Constitution*, 23 October, 1985, p. 15–A.

79. Author's discussions at U.S. Embassy, Manila, March and September 1988. Also see Lawrence E. Grinter, "Taiwan and Philippines Tell a Tale of Two Nations," *Montgomery Advertiser and Alabama Journal*, October 2, 1988, p. 38.

80. Author's discussions at U.S. Defense Attaché Office and Joint U.S.-Philippine Military Advisory Group, Manila, March 1988.

81. Richard G. Stilwell, "Averting Disaster in the Philippines," *Policy Review*, Winter 1988, pp. 20–24.

82. See, for example, "Background on the Bases: American Military Facilities in the Philippines," United States Information Service, second edition, 1987, Manila.

83. Henry Albinski, "The U.S. Position in Asia and the Pacific: The Relevance of Australia and New Zealand," in Ramon H. Myers, ed., *A U.S. Foreign Policy for Asia: The 1980s and Beyond* (Standford: Hoover Institution Press, 1982), p. 90.

84. Albinski, p. 91.

85. See, for example, F.A. Mediansky, "ANZUS: An Alliance Beyond the Treaty," *Australian Outlook*, December 1984, pp. 178–183, and Desmond Ball, *The Anzus Connection: The Security Relationship Between Australia, New Zealand and the United States* (SDSC Reference Paper No. 105, RSPS Australian National University, Canberra, 1983), p. 2.

86. Assistant Secretary of State for East Asian and Pacific Affairs Paul D. Wolfowitz, "The ANZUS Relationship: Alliance Management," Current Policy No. 592, Washington, D.C., U.S. Department of State, 24 June 1984.

87. Australia's Labor Prime Minister Robert Hawke also told Lange, "We could not accept . . . that the ANZUS alliance had a different meaning and entailed different obligations for different members." *Wall Street Journal*, 6 February 1985, p. 26.

88. Assistant Secretary of State for East Asian and Pacific Affairs Paul D. Wolfowitz, "The ANZUS Alliance," Current Policy No. 674, U.S. Department of State, Washington, D.C., 18 March 1985.

89. Speech by Prime Minister R. J. L. Hawke before joint meeting of the U.S. Congress, 23 June 1988.

3

Gorbachev's New Strategic Designs for Asia

LEIF ROSENBERGER
MARIAN LEIGHTON

During the Brezhnev era, Soviet Policy in Asia, as elsewhere, placed primary emphasis on the military dimension. The unattractiveness of the USSR as an economic model for Asian countries and the lack of appeal of Communist ideology left the military option as the only available means of enhancing the Soviet presence and influence in Asia. Thus, the USSR engaged in a military buildup of unprecedented proportions, with the aims of reducing United States influence in the Asian-Pacific region, surrounding and isolating China, and intimidating pro-Western Asian states. The Soviets also forged an alliance with Vietnam that was based on military cooperation; in return for weapons to Hanoi and support for the Vietnamese invasion and occupation of Cambodia, the USSR obtained basing rights at Cam Ranh Bay. That U.S.-built facility and other Vietnamese bases became the most important Soviet military installations outside the USSR itself and a key forward base complex for Soviet naval and air power. Finally, by invading Afghanistan, the Soviets demonstrated their military muscle by sending troops beyond the recognized boundaries of the Communist bloc for the first time since World War II.

General Secretary Mikhail Gorbachev has deemphasized the military element of Soviet foreign policy in favor of advocating political and economic cooperation with other nations. Gone is the crude Brezhnev approach, with its lopsided reliance on military expansion, bluff, and intimidation. In its place is a sophisticated strategy that seems to owe more to Madison Avenue than to Muscovite tradition. However, Gorbachev certainly does not seem inclined to transform the USSR into a status quo power or to preside over the liquidation of the Soviet empire. The hallowed Leninist axiom, *Kto kovo*? (Who defeats whom?), is alive and well in Gorbachev's Kremlin. Nevertheless, the new general secretary is also pursuing Soviet goals through a strategy of denial. His objective is to isolate the United States and inhibit U.S. forward deployments around the globe by fanning peace movements, advocating nuclear-free zones, and encouraging neutralism and nonalignment among pro-Western states. He is also attempting to insert the Soviet Union's presence abroad as a partner in regional security and economic development programs of the type in which the United States and other Western powers traditionally have played the leading role.

Gorbachev apparently perceives the Asian-Pacific region as a promising field for his "new thinking" in foreign policy. Gorbachev's "new look" in Asia was most clearly enunciated in his Vladivostok speech of 28 July 1986 (a speech that had its northern analogue in Murmansk in October 1987 and its Mediterranean parallel in Belgrade, Yugoslavia, in March 1988).[1] Starting from the well-established premise that "the Soviet Union is . . . an Asian and Pacific country" that "is directly touched by this vast region's complex problems," Gorbachev proposed the establishment of a cooperative framework along the lines created by the "Helsinki process" in Europe. Specifically, he offered closer bilateral relations with China, Japan, individual members of the Association of Southeast Asian Nations (ASEAN); support for a reduction of naval activity and antisubmarine capabilities in Asian and Pacific waters; creation of nuclear-free zones and other "confidence-building measures"; and Soviet leadership in convening an Asian and Pacific conference as a step toward forging a regional security system. He envisioned such a system, in turn, as a component of what Moscow calls a "Comprehensive System of International Security" (CSIS).

Gorbachev's proposals have been designed to undermine Western military strategy and deployments in the Asian-Pacific theater while protecting Soviet strategic requirements. For example, Gorbachev's calls for naval arms-control measures have pointedly excluded the Sea of Okhotsk, a key bastion and patrol area for Soviet nuclear submarines. Similarly, his advocacy of nuclear-free zones has focused on Southeast Asia and the South Pacific—areas where U.S. naval power is predominant—and on the Korean Peninsula, where Moscow has accused Washington of storing nuclear weapons. Meanwhile, the Soviet Union works to "de-couple" South Korea from the United States while building up its own military relations with North Korea. This relationship, dating from the visit of North Korean leader Kim Il-Sung to Moscow in 1984 (his first such visit in twenty-three years) essentially involves the delivery of MiG-23 fighter aircraft and other sophisticated arms in return for Soviet permission to overfly North Korea en route to Vietnam and points south and to make naval ship visits to North Korean ports.

Gorbachev's 1986 Vladivostok speech came at the conclusion of a twenty-year Soviet military buildup in Asia. From the 1966 signing of a Soviet-Mongolian friendship treaty, the deployment of five divisions of Soviet troops in Mongolia, and a steady augmentation of Soviet forces along the Sino-Soviet frontier, the USSR introduced land, naval, and air power to

Asia that made it the greatest military threat to the region by the end of Brezhnev's rule. Unlike the half-million troops now stationed along the Sino-Soviet border (troops equipped to wage an air-land war with China), more recent deployments in the Soviet Far East denote a strategy to take on U.S. forces in the Pacific, neutralizing Japan in the process. In 1978, a new theater high command was created for the Far East, and the same period witnessed the siting of SS-20 intermediate-range mobile missiles aimed at targets in Asia. The quantitative and qualitative strength of the Soviet Pacific Fleet continues to grow, and the enhancement of Soviet air power in the region is symbolized by the nuclear-capable Backfire and the impending introduction of the Blackjack aircraft.

A Soviet strategic bastion has developed north of Japan on the Sea of Okhotsk and the Kamchatka Peninsula. The Sea of Okhotsk, virtually encircled by Soviet territory, makes a natural strategic sanctuary and protective barrier for the USSR's Asian landmass and is blanketed with an air-defense network of radars, missiles, guns, and interceptor aircraft. It was here in 1983 that the Soviets shot down a South Korean civilian jetliner with 269 passengers aboard when it strayed off course en route from Alaska to Japan.

The Soviet ring around the Sea of Okhotsk has been closed with the fortification of the southern Kurile Islands, which control passage from the Pacific to the Sea of Okhotsk. These islands, which Japan claims as its Northern Territories, were seized by the USSR at the end of World War II and have been a major bone of contention in Soviet-Japanese relations ever since. In 1983, Moscow deployed a squadron of supersonic MiG-23 fighter-bombers on Etorofu, one of the islands—a deployment that gave a strong signal that the Soviets intend to occupy the Northern Territories permanently.[2]

Moscow's use of the base at Cam Ranh Bay, Vietnam, enables it to project power far to the southwest of Japan and to pose a threat to the vital sea-lanes and choke points linking the Pacific and Indian oceans.[3] The Soviets also use the Vietnamese air base at Da Nang and the Cambodian port of Kompong Som on the Gulf of Thailand. Bear-D long-range reconnaissance aircraft and Bear-F antisubmarine warfare planes operate out of Vietnamese bases; they enhance Soviet operational and intelligence-gathering activities and power projection into maritime Southeast Asia. In the spring of 1984, Soviet and Vietnamese naval infantry forces staged an unprecedented joint amphibious exercise off the coast of northern Vietnam in the Gulf of Tonkin.[4] The Soviet Union's deployment of a permanent naval contingent in the South China Sea at a time when U.S. prospects for retaining use of military bases in the Philippines are questionable constitutes another ominous portent for the Asian-Pacific region. Gorbachev declared at Vladivostok that "if the United States were to renounce a military presence, say in the Philippines, we should not be found wanting of any response."

The Soviets traditionally have feared a two-front war, in Europe and Asia. Their strategic nightmare in the latter theater is the formation of an alliance among the United States, China, Japan, and perhaps South Korea. However, the thrust of the Kremlin's Asian policy under Brezhnev had the effect of a self-fulfilling prophecy. Its intransigence toward Japan and China left those countries virtually no alternative but to recoil from the USSR and seek closer links with each other, with the United States, and with ASEAN. In short, the Soviet Union created a situation in which its provocative behavior was the catalyst for the moves toward "collusion" among its foes that it professed to recognize and deplore. The Brezhnev legacy included an overextended empire, an economy in decay, a heavily militarized foreign policy, and uneasy political relations along Soviet borders—not least in Asia.

By contrast, Gorbachev's emerging foreign policy toward Asia is part of a broader strategy to undo the Brezhnev legacy. His major goals evidently are to create a more benign strategic environment in Asia and the Pacific for Soviet strategic interests, to transform the USSR into a legitimate power player in the region, and to carve out a stake for Moscow in Asia's dynamic economy. A brief glance at Moscow's geopolitical status vis-à-vis Asia and the Pacific helps to place the Gorbachevian policy in perspective.

With two-thirds of its landmass and the bulk of its mineral and energy resources in Asia, the USSR is increasingly focusing eastward. Gorbachev declared that "Vladivostok could become a major international center, a seat of trade and culture, a city of festivals, sports meetings, congresses and scientific symposia. We should like to see it as our open window to the East." Gorbachev's optimism contrasts sharply with the Soviet Union's traditionally pessimistic outlook that has stemmed from fears of "capitalist encirclement" from the West and the "Yellow Peril" in the East.

The fact that the Soviet Union lacked friendly and allied states along its Asian periphery contributed heavily to its sense of insecurity and vulnerability:

> Asia's spatial interpenetration with the Soviet Union is symbolized by the vast European plain, which stretches from the Urals to Mongolia. In the absence of major barriers, waves of migrations have moved across the plain for centuries, displacing or absorbing earlier inhabitants. . . . An awareness of the plain's permeability and ethnic evanescence leaves many Russians with a half-formed sense of territorial insecurity that manifests itself not only in the predilection for strong central authority but in what amounts to a national fixation on frontier defense.[5]

Moscow's concern about security is especially pronounced in Asia because of the peculiar geopolitical and demographic vulnerabilities that shape Soviet threat perceptions there. In sharp contrast with the United States, which looks out on vast expanses of ocean on its eastern and western flanks and friendly countries to the north and south of its borders, the Soviet empire is surrounded in most directions by hostile neighbors.

Logistical problems plague the Soviet military position in the East Asian-Pacific arena. Enormous distances separate the resource-rich but sparsely populated Soviet Far East from the major industrial and population centers of European Russia. The Trans-Siberian Railway constituted virtually the only link between the two areas until the recent completion of sections of the Baikal-Amur Mainline (BAM). The BAM runs parallel to and a few hundred miles south of the Trans-Sib and would be almost equally vulnerable to Chinese sabotage during a Sino-Soviet war.

Soviet logistic vulnerabilities pertain to the sea as well as the land. Siberian ports are limited in number and are very congested. A new port at Nakhodka is designed to handle civilian cargo so that Vladivostok can be reserved strictly for military use. Although icebreakers (some of them nuclear-powered) have helped keep open the Arctic sea-lanes to the Soviet Far East, use of that route to supply coastal villages (not to mention such vital military installations as Vladivostok) remains time-consuming, extremely expensive, and ultimately unreliable. Vladivostok and Petropavlovsk, the two principal bases for the Soviet Pacific Fleet, both suffer from highly unfavorable weather conditions. Even more importantly, Vladivostok has no direct access to the open ocean. Naval vessels based there must transit one of the three narrow chokepoints—the straits of Tsushima, Tsugaru, or Soya— from the Sea of Japan to the Pacific. Petropavlovsk faces the open sea but is too far north to be supplied by land from Soviet territory.

In summing up the USSR's logistical difficulties as they relate to potential military operations in Asia, one scholar has pointed out that:

> These logistical problems do not [pose] major constraints on Soviet military power in East Asia, so long as any future conflict is geographically limited and of short duration. . . . Thus, a quick offensive action against a regional East Asian country in pursuit of a limited military objective along the Soviet periphery is possible. But Soviet logistical constraints mean that Moscow would experience extreme difficulty in any large-scale military involvement over a longer period of time outside the immediate Soviet periphery.[6]

This problem for the Soviet Union is compounded by the fact that the Soviet Pacific Fleet is deficient in afloat replenishment, supply capabilities, and sea-based tactical air power. The fleet would have to rely on shore-based air cover in order to sustain a conventional conflict with U.S. naval forces in the Pacific. Soviet acquisition of a naval base in Vietnam and the construction of aircraft and helicopter carriers are helping to remedy these deficiencies, as is a recent Soviet focus on amphibious landing capability in the Pacific area—reflected in the joint Soviet-Vietnamese naval infantry landing exercise off the Vietnamese coast in 1984.[7]

While continuing to modernize its military arsenal, the Soviet Union is seeking to compete with the United States in Asia through other means as well:

Even though two thirds of the USSR lives in Asia, the Soviets have never enjoyed significant influence there. Through neglect, economic isolationism, and political brutishness, Russian leaders have alienated most Asian capitals. Now, in a historic turnabout, Mikhail Gorbachev has discovered the importance of Asia; his decision to eliminate all medium- and short-range missiles from Soviet Asia was only the latest in a series of eastward steps designed to bring the Soviet Union closer to the flourishing economies of the Far East.[8]

Among other things, Gorbachev seeks joint ventures with Asian countries for the development of the Asian and Far Eastern portions of the USSR. In the past, the Soviet Union has obtained most "turnkey projects" from the West and has proved unable to manage the enterprises or maintain their Western equipment and technology. Now the Kremlin seeks joint ventures (from both Western and Asian sources) in which managerial talent as well as capital and technology would be supplied. Gorbachev, however, must overcome a great deal of skepticism in Asia about Soviet motives. His approach is to project an image of the USSR as a potential economic and security partner in Asia. He plays upon widespread anti-nuclear sentiment and other contradictions among the capitalist partners of the United States, hoping the net effect will be to undermine U.S. influence.

Since the 1986 Vladivostok speech, the Soviets have made a virtue of necessity by portraying the impending removal of their SS-20 missile force from Asia as an earnest sign of their commitment to peace. The Soviets also are pressing further ahead on denuclearization by advocating restrictions on naval movements in Asian-Pacific waters, the creation of nuclear-free zones, and other measures that would redound against the United States, the region's predominant naval power. Gorbachev also has called for an Asian-Pacific Disarmament Conference to bring about a reduction in naval forces, the removal of foreign (read: U.S.) bases, and a limitation on nuclear weapons in the region. In general, Gorbachev's arms-control policies are designed to alleviate the arms race, on earth as well as in space, until the Soviet economy is ready to compete more credibly with the United States on the technological level. During this "breathing space" (*peredyshka*) that Gorbachev seeks for his game of economic catch-up, the Soviet leader can be expected to conduct his political and diplomatic offensive in Asia with as much imagination as he can muster.

NORTHEAST ASIA: SOVIET RELATIONS WITH CHINA, JAPAN, AND KOREA

Moscow's chief security concern in Northeast Asia is the possibility of closer military cooperation among Japan, China, and the United States. As one scholar has aptly pointed out:

> What the Soviets fear is a China industrialized and given military technology and assistance by Tokyo and Washington. . . . The Soviets are conscious of the high level of Japanese technology and of the danger that it might be applied to military ends. . . . Even if Japanese technological cooperation should remain outside the military sector, it could produce a quantum jump in Chinese industrial-military capabilities.[9]

During an international crisis, the Japanese might mine the three straits through which the Soviet Pacific Fleet must exit the Sea of Japan into the open ocean, and the Chinese might align themselves actively with the United States and Japan in a superpower conflict. Moreover, as one scholar has stated, "Although China is no match for the Soviets in a frontal, one-on-one conflict, its relatively obsolete weapons could turn into a formidable factor if the Soviet Union were to exhaust itself in a major conflict with the United States in East Asia."[10]

Moscow's concerns should be viewed against the backdrop of the Sino-Soviet dispute, which, in turn, evolved out of a long historical legacy:

> The Soviet security perspective in Asia and worldwide . . . bears the imprint of years of confrontation with the world's most populous, and Asia's largest, nation. The two countries share a border that stretches for more than 4,000 miles across Asia. Bitter ideological-political and territorial conflicts rooted in history going back to Czarist times have envenomed the . . . relationship. . . . Chinese military inferiority and technological backwardness are to some extent compensated for by China's enormous manpower resources, its proved tenacity in resisting foreign invaders, and the vastness of the country, where invading armies tend to bog down, as did those of the Japanese in the 1930's and early 1940's.[11]

Moscow's attitude toward Sino-U.S. relations remains cautious. Until recently, Soviet propaganda has lambasted Beijing and Washington for alleged collusion against Moscow; at the same time, Soviet spokesmen profess to be unconcerned about a Sino-U.S. rapprochement because the ideological gap between the two nations seems unbridgeable.

During the early and mid-1980s, despite China's assertions that it was pursuing an "evenhanded" policy equally critical of both superpowers, Soviet media accused Beijing of a pro-U.S. bias. For example, a December 1983 publication charged China of complicity with U.S. "imperialism." It also chided the Chinese for "forgetting" that "the entire Asian continent is surrounded by U.S. military bases."[12] One could spot traces of Soviet concern about Sino-U.S. security ties in the wake of Premier Zhao Ziyang's U.S. visit in January 1984. Nevertheless, Soviet statements expressed relative optimism that the underlying differences between the United States and China would preclude "a comprehensive Sino-U.S. strategic agreement."[13]

A short time later, Moscow's optimism gave way to a more pessimistic outlook as a result of President Ronald Reagan's April 1984 official visit to China. Tass, for example, denounced Chinese leader Deng Xiaoping for reportedly stating that "China is not opposed" to a U.S. arms buildup.[14] Soviet policymakers and academics alike have periodically accused Beijing of "tilting" toward Washington. The Soviets undoubtedly were relieved by Beijing's rejection of Sino-U.S. strategic cooperation, but they remain concerned about the possibility that secret accords were signed during Reagan's visit.

The year 1984 was notable for the number of high-level Sino-U.S. exchanges.[15] In January, Premier Zhao visited the United States, and in March a group of Chinese defense industry specialists—reportedly including Defense Minister Zhang Aiping's sons—paid a visit. The following month, President Reagan journeyed to Beijing. Although Reagan received a warm welcome, the Chinese media deleted some of his strongest anti-Soviet statements,[16] presumably reflecting China's desire to avoid offending the Kremlin on the eve of a planned visit by First Deputy Prime Minister Ivan Arkhipov (who served as Moscow's chief economic advisor in China during the Sino-Soviet honeymoon of the 1950s). However, the Soviets postponed Arkhipov's visit as border clashes escalated between Chinese and Vietnamese armed forces. Moscow warned Beijing against attempting to "teach Vietnam a second lesson," for its invasion of Cambodia, while Beijing reiterated its three preconditions for a full normalization of Sino-Soviet relations: a Soviet drawdown of troops on the Sino-Soviet border and in Mongolia; Soviet withdrawal from Afghanistan; and cessation of Soviet support for Vietnam's occupation of Cambodia. China tried to reassure the Kremlin that "China is not entering and will never enter into any alliance with the United States against the USSR. Never."[17]

Arkhipov finally visited Beijing in December 1984. The highest ranking Soviet official to come to China in fifteen years, he negotiated a five-year trade accord and an agreement providing for Soviet assistance in the modernization of Soviet-financed industrial projects dating from the 1950s. The trade agreement was particularly significant because it represented the first time in many years that bilateral trade was placed on a long-term rather than an annual basis.

In the period following Arkhipov's visit, Sino-Soviet trade increased markedly, particularly in the border regions, and numerous additional economic projects were proposed. As *The Far Eastern Economic Review* pointed out,

> The two Socialist countries are natural trading partners to a certain extent because of proximity, historical ties, and supplementary economic structures. Soviet timber and steel are raw materials which China is short of, while Chinese light-industrial projects and foodstuffs, which are not competitive enough for other markets, are

welcomed by eager Soviet consumers, especially in the Soviet Far East.[18]

Gorbachev's 1986 Vladivostok speech contained a number of initiatives aimed at cultivating friendship with China; but his effort to resolve the three major obstacles preventing reconciliation appeared more symbolic than real. Gorbachev announced that six Soviet regiments would be withdrawn from Afghanistan before the end of 1986. However, the USSR sent new regiments into the country with the express purpose of withdrawing them in a glare of publicity. Moreover, the regiments included air defense troops that obviously had no relevance against Afghan insurgents who lacked an air force. With regard to Soviet troops along the Sino-Soviet border and in Mongolia, Gorbachev expressed readiness to discuss "commensurate lowering of the level of land forces" and stated that Soviet forces in Mongolia would be thinned out. A withdrawal of 11,000 soldiers from the Soviet Union's five-division, 65,000-man contingent in Mongolia subsequently occurred. Gorbachev ducked the issue of Cambodia, however, contending that "it is unacceptable to draw out its tragic past and decide the future fate of this state in distant capitals." He also indicated that a Cambodian settlement would have to be preceded by an improvement in Sino-Vietnamese relations, an approach diametrically opposite to that of China.

In mid-August 1986, two weeks after the Vladivostok speech, Chinese leader Deng Xiaoping's rejoinder to Gorbachev came during a television interview with U.S. journalist Mike Wallace. "Among the three major obstacles [to Sino-Soviet reconciliation], the main one is the Vietnamese aggression against Cambodia," said Deng, "for China and the Soviet Union are actually in a state of confrontation . . . which takes the form of pitting Vietnamese armed forces against China."[19]

On 2 September, Deng announced that he would travel to the USSR for a summit with Gorbachev *if* the Soviet-backed Vietnamese occupation of Cambodia were terminated. The following day, Deng told a Japanese delegation that Gorbachev's proposals for troop withdrawals from Mongolia were inadequate, since Soviet bases and facilities in Mongolia would remain and the forces could be reintroduced quickly.

Prospects for a resolution of the Sino-Soviet border dispute appeared brighter in the wake of the Vladivostok speech. For the first time, Gorbachev concurred with China's position that the main ship channel of the Amur River should serve as the boundary between the two countries. Border talks resumed in Beijing at the vice-ministerial level in February 1987 after a nine-year hiatus. Gorbachev also suggested "the acceleration of socioeconomic development" as a common priority of the two states and offered support for the construction of a railway linking the Xinjiang Uigur Autonomous Region of China with the Soviet Republic of Kazakhstan.

In an interview with the Chinese weekly magazine *Liaowang* on 10 January 1988, Gorbachev again offered to meet Chinese leaders at a summit.

This interview, the first by a Soviet leader with a Chinese periodical in nearly three decades, represented a public affirmation of earlier summit proposals by Gorbachev. Deng reiterated his December 1987 position that "my proposal [for a top-level Sino-Soviet meeting] does contain a precondition: that is, the Soviet Union must urge Vietnam to pull out its troops from Cambodia."[20] This formulation appeared to be a dilution of Beijing's hardline stance in that it did not even specify that an actual Vietnamese pullback would have to precede a Sino-Soviet summit. Another possible indication of movement in Sino-Soviet relations was the visit to Beijing in December 1987 of Soviet Deputy Foreign Minister Igor A. Rogachev, who briefed Chinese officials on the Washington summit meeting between Gorbachev and Ronald Reagan. This evidently was the first time a senior Soviet official has given such a briefing to the Chinese.[21] However these recent improvements in Sino-Soviet government relations have not been matched in the party-to-party sphere.

Moscow traditionally has regarded Japan, like China, a potentially serious threat to its security. As a 1982 Soviet commentary stated: "It is well known that it is primarily a country's industrial base and . . . skilled manpower which constitute the foundation of military industry. Both these factors are present in Japan."[22] Under Prime Ministers Yasuhiro Nakasone and Noburo Takeshita, Japan has continued to increase its military expenditures, and the Kremlin has displayed concern that Tokyo will harness its economic and technological prowess militarily to undermine Soviet security interests in Asia.

The uneasy relationship between the USSR and Japan, like that between the USSR and China, has deep historical roots.

> The two powers have faced each other on the Korean Peninsula, on Chinese territory, and in areas traditionally included in the Chinese zone of influence. They have clashed repeatedly in enormously costly and bloody land and sea battles: in the Russo-Japanese War, in confrontations triggered by the spread of the Bolshevik Revolution into the Far East and leading to the Japanese armies' attempted occupation of Siberia, in the large-scale Soviet-Japanese tank battles of the 1930s, and in the sudden thrust of the Soviet armed forces into Japanese-occupied Manchuria during the closing days of World War II, a military operation that led to the capture and abduction of hundreds of thousands of Japanese into Siberian labor camps. . . . History has left in both nations a residue of psychological attitudes that can be described only as dark suspicions of the neighbor's intentions.[23]

Although Japan represents an attractive trade and economic partner for the USSR, the Soviets have focused primarily on the military threat that they perceive in the U.S. security treaty and the U.S. nuclear umbrella over Japan. In recent years, both Moscow and now China have expressed alarm over the Japanese defense buildup, although the Soviets have worked to break up close defense cooperation between Tokyo and Washington. U.S. and Japanese military staffs have conducted joint planning, and Tokyo has agreed to defend its sea-lanes out to 1000 miles and to export advanced military technology to the United States and to increase its financial support for the maintenance of the 45,000 U.S. troops stationed in Japan.

Gorbachev's new approach toward Japan is in marked contrast to the policies of Brezhnev and Gromyko. For example, during a journey to the United States in January 1983, Prime Minister Yasuhiro Nakasone told a *Washington Post* interviewer that Japan should become "an unsinkable aircraft carrier" against Soviet Backfire bombers and should control the straits around the Sea of Japan to prevent Soviet warships from crossing between Vladivostok and the open Pacific. The following day, Tass declared:

> Is is not clear that in the present nuclear age there can be no "unsinkable aircraft carrier" and that by deploying "onboard the carrier" arsenals of armaments, including American [arms], the authors of such plans make Japan a likely target for a response strike? And for such a densely populated, insular country as Japan, this could spell a national disaster more serious than the one that befell it 37 years ago.[24]

Moscow's propaganda offensive against Japanese military policies intensified markedly after the March 1983 arrival of the U.S. nuclear-powered aircraft carrier *Enterprise* at the port of Sasebo. On 25 March, Radio Moscow warned that "Japan will be the first victim in all disputes that arise in the Far East." On 5 April, Tass thundered that Japan's increasing military cooperation with the United States "threatens to transform Japan into an arena of nuclear combat and, in the final analysis, to bring about the country's destruction."[25] Soviet Foreign Minister Andrei Gromyko charged that Japan was already "bristling with nuclear missiles."[26] Even more disturbing from Moscow's viewpoint, however, was the belief that Japan might become a *de facto* member of the North Atlantic Treaty Organization (NATO). According to an article on 11 March 1983 in *Le Monde*:

> Through various channels, with the active support of their American allies, the Japanese sounded out the members of the Atlantic Alliance early this year with a view to obtaining the status of "external associate," which would have enabled them to participate . . . in the operations and discussions of the regional organization which relate to East-West economic relations. . . . The French government . . . cut short the initiative, vetoing in principle any expansion or globalization of NATO.[27]

In seeking to further complicate Japan's relations with the West, Soviet propaganda has continued to exploit Japan's "nuclear allergy" to the hilt. Tokyo adheres to a self-restraining policy in the form of the "three non-nuclear principles"—no manufacture, possession, or introduction of nuclear weapons into the country. In June 1984, when Prime Minister David Lange of New Zealand prohibited the entry of U.S. nuclear-armed ships into his country's waters, the reverberations were felt throughout Asia; however, the Japanese government to date has not challenged the movements of U.S. warships in Japan's waters. (Moscow presumably would welcome a U.S.-Japanese crisis over this delicate issue and has spared no effort in praising Wellington's antinuclear stance.)

The Soviets have not confined themselves to propaganda in attempting to ward off what they view as a potential military challenge from Japan. Russian military forces in Northeast Asia patrol in an offensive and aggressive posture. Soviet surface combatants and submarines sail along the very edges of Japanese territorial waters. Soviet minisubmarines of the type that have penetrated deep into Swedish waters now have appeared off Japan's coasts. They are capable of demolition, agent insertion, and other sabotage operations. Soviet intelligence-gathering vessels (AGIs) ply constantly along Japanese shores. Soviet reconnaissance planes frequently appear simultaneously on both sides of the Japanese archipelago and approach perilously close to Japan's airspace. The regular flights of Bear reconnaissance planes near Japan en route from the USSR to Vietnam have come to be dubbed the "Tokyo Express."[28]

Regarding the Northern Territories issue, Aleksandr Bovin, a political commentator for *Izvestia*, laid out the Soviet policy, a policy that has not changed for years:

> It is a principled position of the Soviet Union that it will reject any proposal aimed at readjusting territorial delineations reached as a result of the Second World War. It took us 30 years to make Europe understand this position, which was at last recognized at the Helsinki Conference. . . . Our position of preserving political and geographical borders delineated after the Second World War is also applicable to Asia.[29]

Perhaps the underlying factor in Moscow's traditional refusal to discuss the return of the Northern Territories, however, is its fear of creating a precedent for concessions on other significant territorial issues, particularly those involving the huge tracts of land that China claims were seized illegally in the nineteenth century.

Against this background of enmity between the USSR and Japan, Gorbachev had his work cut out for him in seeking improved relations. The close personal rapport between President Reagan and Prime Minister Nakasone constituted a further obstacle to Moscow's inroads into Tokyo. A Japanese academic has pointed out quite rightly the following:

> Like his predecessors, Gorbachev faces a serious dilemma in Soviet policy toward Japan. The Soviet Union needs sophisticated economic

management, know how, and technology from Japan more than ever before. In spite of this, the Gorbachev government is not yet ready to pay the price: concessions on the issue of what the Japanese call the "Northern Territories."[30]

In January 1986, Eduard Shevardnadze became the first Soviet foreign minister to visit Japan in ten years. His Japanese counterpart, Shintaro Abe, returned the visit four months later and was received by Gorbachev in the Kremlin. A series of agreements reactivated or expanded Soviet-Japanese relations in the areas of scientific and technical cooperation, cultural exchanges, and trade. Of particular symbolic importance was an accord permitting Japanese visits to family graves in the Northern Territories. The USSR, however, continued to regard the question of returning the Northern Territories as nonnegotiable. As the aforementioned Japanese professor wrote: "The Soviets, at least for the time being, are prepared to make almost any concession short of showing a willingness to return these four islands. Japan cannot accept this policy."[31]

The relative lack of progress in Soviet-Japanese relations stands in sharp contrast with the continuing improvement in ties between the Soviet Union and North Korea. The Kremlin has been so successful in wooing North Korea away from the Chinese orbit that the emerging Moscow-Pyongyang axis could become the "fourth obstacle" to Sino-Soviet reconciliation.

In May 1984, Kim Il-Sung paid his first official visit to the Soviet Union in twenty-three years. He was accompanied by a high-ranking party and state delegation. From Moscow, he traveled to a number of East European countries. Soviet statements and actions during Kim's visit suggested an effort to draw the Asian communist countries (notably North Korea and Vietnam) closer to the USSR and the East European bloc as part of a campaign to reinvigorate the international communist movement and to gain support for Soviet security objectives in Asia. Pyongyang reportedly is reluctant to strain its friendship with Beijing, however, and retains its treaties of friendship, cooperation, and mutual assistance with both the USSR and China dating from 1961.

Kim's 1984 sojourn to Moscow was marked by expressions of desire for closer bilateral relations and cooperation in the global arena. He referred to the USSR and North Korea's relationship as an "alliance" (a surprising term in view of the DPRK's self-proclaimed nonalignment). During a Kremlin banquet in his honor, Kim evinced a wish to learn from the success and advanced experience of the Soviet people and to extend cooperation between the two countries. In addition, he invoked "proletarian internationalism" (the code word for joint action by communist nations in support of "fraternal" states and revolutionary movements worldwide). In the latter context, North Korea, although not a Soviet proxy, "objectively" serves Moscow's interests by rendering military and propaganda assistance to the Sandinistas in Nicaragua, the communist regime in Ethiopia, the Tamil rebels in Sri Lanka, and various anti-Western groups in the Middle East and Africa. North Korea also maintains friendly relations with Afghanistan.

According to reports following Kim's visit to Moscow, special emphasis was placed on questions of strengthening security in the Far East and the Pacific. The Soviet-North Korean summit laid the groundwork for the delivery of MiG-23 fighter planes and other sophisticated equipment to North Korea, thus reversing a decade-old policy of withholding offensive weapons from Kim's militant regime. In exchange, the USSR evidently obtained permission for military overflights over North Korean territory.[32] These flights shorten the transit time between bases in the USSR and Vietnam and also enable the Soviets to conduct surveillance along the Chinese and Japanese coasts.

In November 1984, Soviet Deputy Foreign Minister Mikhail Kapitsa visited Pyongyang. As was the case after Kim's Moscow visit, no formal military or economic agreements were announced, but the existence of secret accords cannot be precluded. The first shipment of MiG-23s arrived in North Korea in mid-1985. Soviet Foreign Minister Shevardnadze traveled to Pyongyang in January 1986. In July, Yuri Solovyev, a candidate member of the Politburo, led a delegation there to commemorate the twenty-fifth anniversary of the Soviet-Korean Treaty of Friendship and Cooperation. High-level delegations from the Soviet navy and air force also attended the celebrations.[33]

During his July 1986 Vladivostok speech, Gorbachev expressed Soviet support for "the serious dialogue being proposed by the Democratic People's Republic of Korea (DPRK)" to bring about peace between North and South Korea. He also endorsed the DPRK's proposal for the creation of a nuclear-free zone in the Korean Peninsula. Kim Il-Sung made a five-day trip to Moscow in October 1986 that was shrouded in mystery. No joint communiqué was published at the end of the visit. Military matters almost certainly topped the agenda, however, because by November there was a visible increase in Soviet military utilization of North Korean airfields and ports.[34] Admiral Ronald Hays, commander-in-chief of the U.S. Pacific Command, remarked at the time:

> Just this last week, we saw for the first time ever, I believe, a major naval exercise . . . between the North Koreans and the Soviet Union just off the North Korean coast in the Sea of Japan, an exercise of a size that we have not seen before."[35]

If the USSR obtains regular access to North Korean naval and air bases, the Soviets would be able to thwart U.S.-Japanese control of the Sea of Japan in a crisis situation.[36]

Regarding North Korea's internal developments, Moscow seems to have abandoned its strong resistance to the transfer of power from Kim Il-Sung to his son, Kim Chung-Il—a dynastic succession at odds with Marxist-Leninist precepts (if not Korean customs). Befriending the younger Kim smooths Soviet political relations with North Korea but is unlikely to temper the new leader's aggressive and independent nature. Kim Chung-Il, who is said to have masterminded the 1983 Rangoon bombing incident that killed several South Korean government officials and narrowly missed the president, reportedly is committed to the reunification of Korea—through military action if necessary. A new Korean war would plunge Northeast Asia into a crisis and almost certainly would lead to a direct U.S.-Soviet military confrontation. Thus, although Moscow would like to incorporate North Korea into a glacis of friendly communist states on the USSR's Asian border, it would be loathe to endorse a new militant foreign policy of the Pyongyang regime. A MiGs-for-bases agreement could be the initial step in destabilizing Northeast Asia. Whether the USSR can influence North Korea sufficiently to prevent the senior or junior Kim from provoking a crisis that would destroy Gorbachev's new peaceful image in Asia remains a major unanswered question.

Soviet policies in Northeast Asia have been designed primarily to bolster the security of the USSR against real and potential challenges Moscow perceives to exist from the United States, Japan, and China. By his new policies in Northeast Asia, Gorbachev is seeking to neutralize those challenges. In Southeast Asia, on the other hand, the Soviets view the security environment more in terms of opportunities than of challenges, and their recent offensive is a low-risk one that is opportunist in character.

SOVIET OPPORTUNITIES IN SOUTHEAST ASIA

During the Brezhnev era, the Soviets were successful in establishing a strong presence in Indochina. The U.S. withdrawal from Vietnam left the Soviet Union with an irresistible opportunity to acquire the former U.S. base at Cam Ranh Bay. Although both Moscow and Hanoi vehemently denied that the Soviets enjoyed unrestricted use of the base, this fiction became increasingly difficult to sustain in the wake of the signing of the Soviet-Vietnamese friendship treaty on 3 November 1978, followed by the Soviet-backed Vietnamese invasion of Cambodia. The quantity and quality of Soviet arms and equipment at Cam Ranh Bay have risen steadily. A squadron of TU-16 Badger bombers and a contingent of MiG-23 fighter bombers are among the weapons systems deployed there—evidently on a permanent basis.

Cam Ranh Bay serves the USSR admirably both as a means of projecting Soviet power into Southeast Asia and as a component of a worldwide network of staging areas for potential wartime use. Southeast Asia may be regarded as a missing link in the chain of military strong points with which the Soviet Union aspires to gird the globe. Soviet control of access to the Strait of Malacca, in particular, would round off an arc of military facilities stretching from Murmansk to Vladivostok (across the northern sea route, which is kept open by icebreakers) to Indochina and southward through the Pacific into the Indian Ocean and across toward Soviet facilities in South Yemen and Ethiopia.

Pointing to Southeast Asia as a vital arena in Moscow's quest for global hegemony, a 1985 article in the Chinese Communist Party's theoretical journal *Red Flag* contended that the Soviets sought to create a "bow-shaped navigation line" connecting the Mediterranean, the Red Sea, the Indian Ocean, the southwest Pacific, the Sea of Japan, and the continents of Europe, Asia, and Africa. According to the Chinese, such a navigation line would (1) enable the Soviet Pacific and Black Sea fleets to conduct mutual support operations; (2) permit the Soviets to impede the U.S. Seventh Fleet's entry into the Indian Ocean; (3) threaten China from the seas; and (4) would leave the Soviet Navy poised to cut off maritime ties between the Far East and Europe, thus choking off Japan's commercial lifeline (and wartime resupply route).[37]

Aside from positioning itself for a number of wartime scenarios, the USSR has sought to exploit its growing military prowess in Asia for peacetime advantage. The *Wall Street Journal* aptly summed up this phenomenon in an editorial entitled "Ivan Knocking." The *Journal* wrote: "The strategy is to build up armed strength, deploy those arms in threatening numbers, and then make an offer your 'partners' are afraid to refuse. In the gangster world, this is called a protection racket."[38]

Insofar as Vietnam remains a pivotal player in the Soviet Union's response to challenges and opportunities in Southeast Asia, the nature of the Soviet-Vietnamese alliance must be examined and its prospects assessed. The *raison d'tre* of the alliance, which dates officially from the signing of the Treaty of Friendship and Cooperation on 3 November 1978, is mutual hostility toward China. Within weeks of the treaty's signing, Vietnam, bankrolled and supported materially and logistically by the Kremlin, invaded Cambodia and installed a puppet regime under Heng Samrin in Phnom Penh. In February 1979, Chinese forces launched an attack across the Sino-Vietnamese border—an attack for which Moscow claimed Beijing got the green light during Deng Xiaoping's visit to Washington at the end of 1978. In the aftermath of the invasion, which China claimed was designed to "teach Vietnam a lesson" about Cambodia, the Soviet Union sent military equipment that enabled Hanoi to bolster substantially the quantity and quality of its troops along the Sino-Vietnamese frontier. Moscow also warned Beijing against any attempt to administer a second lesson to Vietnam.

The Vietnamese have sought to straddle the fence in the Sino-Soviet dispute in order to enjoy the greatest potential for foreign policy maneuvering. Thus, Hanoi presumably applauded when the Sino-Soviet treaty expired in 1980 at China's initiative; by the same token, however, the initiation of normalization talks between the USSR and China in October 1982 was cause for Vietnamese concern. Although the Soviets to date have indicated little receptivity to a settlement of the Cambodian issue on terms acceptable to China, reiterating that improvement in Sino-Soviet relations would not come at the expense of third countries, Hanoi recalls past occasions in which Moscow sacrificed its interests on the altar of superpower politics.

As an insurance policy, Vietnam has tried on a number of occasions to mend its relations with China. In turn, Moscow's concern that Hanoi might seek a deal with the Chinese behind its back evidently has induced the Soviet Union to remain inflexible on the Cambodian issue and not deviate from the Vietnamese position. To reassure Vietnam of continuing Soviet support, a delegation led by Politburo member Geidar Aliyev arrived in Hanoi in October 1983 to sign a new agreement updating the Soviet-Vietnamese friendship treaty. The new declaration (signed on 4 November 1983 and published in *Pravda* the following day) restated Soviet support for the Vietnamese communist regime. It stressed "the unchanged principled line of the USSR to provide support and assistance to fraternal Vietnam." In addition, it asserted that the Communist party of Vietnam "completely supports the principled line of the Soviet Union to normalize relations with the People's Republic of China." However, this assertion was accompanied by the contention that the existing government in Kampuchea (Cambodia) is the only legal one and the "the basic cause of the still existing tensions in the region is the hostile policy for the forces of hegemonism and imperialism which threaten the sovereignty and the territorial integrity of Vietnam, Laos, and Kampuchea." Hegemonism is a Soviet code word for Chinese policy.[39]

Although the declaration seemed to reflect Soviet-Vietnamese harmony, the speeches delivered by Aliyev and Vietnamese Prime Minister Pham Van Dong on the occasion of its signing indicated that friction between the two allies persisted. Aliyev downplayed the Chinese threat and presented the United States as the greatest threat to world peace. He called on Vietnam to coordinate its policies with Moscow in facing the U.S. challenge. Dong, on the other hand, emphasized the Chinese peril.[40]

Yuri Andropov's death in February 1984 and Konstantin Chernenko's accession to the top Soviet leadership post lead to changes in the Kremlin's posture toward Vietnam and China. Unlike Andropov, Chernenko seemed strongly in favor of strengthening Moscow's relationship with Hanoi and using that relationship as a strategic asset against what the Soviets regarded as Sino-U.S. military collusion. Chernenko was particularly vehement in accusing China of aggressive activities in Afghanistan and elsewhere in Asia.

In the spring of 1984, worsening Sino-Vietnamese border tensions, increasing Soviet-Vietnamese military and naval cooperation, and Chinese naval maneuvers constituted both a cause and a symbol of deteriorating relations between Moscow and Beijing. In an unequivocal gesture of militant solidarity, the Soviets and Vietnamese staged an amphibious exercise highlighted by the landing of some four hundred Soviet naval infantrymen (marines) at Haiphong.[41] In May, the Chinese countered with their own naval exercises in the South China Sea. Moscow canceled Arkhipov's May visit to China.

The year 1985 witnessed a noticeable improvement in Sino-Soviet relations. Vietnamese President Troung Chinh, reputed to be the leader of the pro-Chinese faction in Hanoi, journeyed to Moscow in March for talks with new Soviet party chief Mikhail Gorbachev. A Radio Moscow broadcast of 14 March lauded the "unshakeable cohesion" between the Soviet Union and Vietnam. The two countries were said to share a "complete identity of views," a formulation generally applied only to relations between the USSR and its Warsaw Pact allies.

Nevertheless, strains persisted in the Soviet-Vietnamese relationship, and Chinese policy sought to exploit them. In May 1985, Deng Xiaoping averred that Beijing would tolerate a continuation of the Soviet military presence at Cam Ranh Bay if Moscow would halt its support for the Vietnamese war effort in Cambodia. Deng seemed to be offering the Kremlin an opportunity to accede to one of China's principal conditions for a normalization of Sino-Soviet relations (an end to Soviet support for the conflict in Cambodia) and maintain the strategic presence in Vietnam that enhances the USSR's capabilities in its global military competition with the United States. At the same time, Deng's statement provided the Soviets with an opportunity to curry favor with the ASEAN states, which strongly demand a Vietnamese withdrawal from Cambodia.

The USSR's impressive naval and air presence in Southeast Asia, its power-projection capabilities, and its alliance with Vietnam have created the preconditions for substantial forms of "fraternal" assistance to communist insurrections in the area. Although Moscow's objectives in Southeast Asia do not necessarily entail the installation of communist regimes, the destabilization of pro-Western governments would add immeasurably to Soviet security goals in the region.

Like his predecessors, Mikhail Gorbachev needs a strong military to counter U.S. naval and air muscle in Southeast Asia. But Gorbachev is a much more skilled diplomat than his predecessors, and his strategy in the region is really one of denial rather than intimidation. He wants to see the United States denied use of bases at Clark and Subic in the Philippines; therefore, Gorbachev and his diplomats are aggressively fanning antinuclear sentiment in ASEAN. Instead of military intimidation, Gorbachev is trying to politically isolate the United States. Soviet naval activity in the Asian-Pacific region showed some reductions in 1987, although modernization continues.[42] The New Zealand decision to prohibit U.S. warships is something the USSR would love to see duplicated in ASEAN. The New Zealand action is not something the Soviets created, but Gorbachev regards this development as an implicit strategic victory for the Soviet Union. Certainly the Soviet Pacific Fleet was the prime beneficiary.

Gorbachev is also a shrewd public-relations specialist. He plays on the simple message that nuclear weapons are "bad," the Soviet desire to get rid of them is "good," and the American reluctance to see the nuclear weapons leave the region is "proof" of "U.S. Militarism." Beneath this seemingly persuasive propaganda is found Moscow's hidden agenda. For if U.S. warships were to leave Southeast Asia, then the ASEAN military forces would have to fill the vacuum. That means more money devoted by ASEAN governments to arms and less money toward social-economic development. This arguably sows the seeds of discontent and improves the revolutionary conditions for radicals to exploit.

While U.S.-Soviet relations are the top priority for Moscow under Gorbachev, China is his top concern in Asia. Gorbachev appears to be doing whatever he can to satisfy China, including sizable concessions on the three obstacles impeding closer Soviet-Chinese relations (removing large numbers of troops from the Sino-Soviet border and Mongolia, pulling out of Afghanistan, and moving toward a settlement in Kampuchea).

For Southeast Asia, Soviet support for a Kampuchean settlement is the most recent and significant Soviet concession. While not all the information is clear, Gorbachev plans to try to reunify the Cambodian communists are receiving lots of interest in ASEAN capitals.[43] Of course, unifying the two communist groups (the Khmer Rouge and the Phnom Penh government) that have been fighting each other for years is a herculean task. But Gorbachev evidently hopes to pull it off. He sees Prince Sihanouk as a nominal leader of the coalition. Unfortunately for Gorbachev, so far the Khmer Rouge (as well as the KPNLF) has refused to join the ongoing Cambodian peace talks. The Soviets are working behind the scenes, however, to try to get the other two parties (especially the Khmer Rouge) to join the negotiations and be part of any future coalition government.

Of course, any agreement in Kampuchea must have the support of Hanoi as well as Moscow. Gorbachev has urged the Vietnamese to concentrate on reforming and improving their economy. Pressure on the Vietnamese to reach a settlement regarding Kampuchea is part of Soviet activity.[44] In order to facilitate this, Gorbachev has strongly encouraged the Vietnamese to normalize relations with China. The Vietnamese have responded by sending conciliatory signals to China for the last two years (this was interrupted in March 1988 when both China and Vietnam were claiming portions of the Spritley Islands, and naval gunboat firefights broke out between them in the South China Sea). Moscow is also strongly encouraging the Vietnamese to honor their declaration to pull all their troops out of Kampuchea in 1990.

Within ASEAN, the Philippines has received the lion's share of Soviet attention. Under Gorbachev, the Soviets have increased their fanning of Philippine nationalism and are encouraging Manila to get rid of U.S. military facilities at Clark and Subic, which again would be a tremendous Soviet strategic victory.

At the same time that Gorbachev is trying to influence the Aquino government to move in anti-American directions, he has continued the policy set in motion by his predecessors of supporting the militant Communist Party of the Philippines (CPP) and its New People's Army (NPA). Soviet support for the communist insurgency in the Philippines—a subject that has been virtually ignored by scholars and journalists alike—enables the Kremlin to promote two of its principal security objectives in Asia.[45] One is to fuel the campaign for the removal of U.S. military facilities from the Philippines, thus allowing the Soviets, through their Vietnamese bases, to acquire hegemony in the South China Sea and adjacent strategic areas. The other objective is to recapture the allegiance of Southeast Asian communist parties and movements that fell under China's sway during the Sino-Soviet schism. If the Philippine Communists win a military victory or a dominant place in a coalition government, both the U.S.-Philippine alliance and ASEAN will be damaged irreparably, and the "correlation of forces" in Southeast Asia will swing heavily in favor of the Soviet Union. Thus, Soviet strategy in Southeast Asia combines minimal risks with the possibility of dramatic gains.

When a new Soviet ambassador appeared in the Philippines in the summer of 1987, it was time to take stock once again of Soviet activities in the Philippines. Indeed, the commander of the U.S. Pacific Fleet, Admiral James A. Lyons, suggested that the Soviets have more than a diplomatic interest in the Philippines. While in Manila in March 1987, he told reporters bluntly that "there is no question" Moscow is supporting the New People's Army insurgency.[46]

True enough, there is no "smoking gun" of Soviet support. But if one can understand how the U.S. government could use private surrogates, CIA fronts, and Swiss bank accounts to fund the Nicaraguan Contras, you can understand the relationship the Soviets have with the Communist party of the Philippines. Not only are the Soviets much better at covert operations than are Americans, their support for Philippine insurgents is consistent with past help for budding communist revolutions in El Salvador, Nicaragua, Ethiopia, and Yemen.

While precise dates of demarcation are difficult to assess, Soviet policy toward the CPP can be broken down into roughly four stages:[47]

1. *Stage One: 1969–1973.* Moscow had no real links to the CPP, a Maoist party dependent upon Chinese material assistance. Following unsuccessful armed struggle against the Marcos government, the CPP reassessed its revolutionary strategy and began to look to the USSR.

2. *Stage Two: 1974–1979.* Moscow refused to provide any appreciable material assistance to the CPP, offering political guidance instead. The Soviets promised material assistance only after nationwide organizational infrastructure of Leninist party cells was in place.

3. *Stage Three: 1979–1984.* Publicly, the CPP remained anti-Soviet, but privately it cemented links with the Kremlin. The Soviets, however, were extremely cautious, and their number-one rule was "no blow-backs"—i.e., don't let an operation be traced back to the Kremlin. Most meetings were conducted outside the Philippines and the Soviet Union via middlemen or surrogates in such places as South Yemen, Western Europe, Australia, and Japan.[48] Soviet-bloc financing in turn found its way into National Democratic Front offices in Rome, Stockholm, and Amsterdam. Soviet and East European money is also passed to the CPP and NDF in Western Europe through a maze of religious groups, human rights groups and solidarity organizations.

4. *Stage Four: 1984–present.* The apparent debate with the Kremlin between those advocating caution and those who wanted a more aggressive, Cuban-style approach toward other revolutions has led to a new stage vis-à-vis the CPP. In 1984, while Secretary General Konstantin Chernenko was still in power, the Kremlin decided to provide direct support to the CPP. When Mikhail Gorbachev took power in March 1985, the policy direction was already in place, but he and his new International Department Chief, Anatoli Dobrynin, gave the policy more life.

Because of his long tenure as Soviet ambassador to the United States, Mr. Dobrynin was sensitive to the foreign-policy debate in Washington and knew that Philippine policy was being run by officials with no appreciation of the nature and extent of Soviet links to the CPP. Thus, he probably argued that the Kremlin could do a lot more without alarming Washington.

Some of the best information regarding Soviet activity in the Philippines came from the insurgents' top man, Rodolfo Salas, captured by Philippine authorities in September 1986. In January 1987, he told a Japanese newspaper that the Soviets and the Vietnamese began direct negotiations with the CPP in 1984 and 1985.[49] According to Salas, during these negotiations Moscow and Hanoi made proposals to give direct material assistance to the insurgents. At the December 1985 CPP party congress, for example, a Soviet representative offered direct financial and propaganda support.[50] In early 1986, Moscow began direct negotiations with the CPP in Australia at the Soviet Consulate in Sydney and the Soviet Embassy in Canberra.[51]

Then, in October 1986, a former CPP leader, identified by Philippine intelligence officials as Ka (Commander) Temyong, revealed that the Soviets were using both Vietnamese and Japanese communists as surrogates.[52] Japanese communists, for example, were said to have financed a shipment of Soviet arms from Vietnam to the Philippines via Malaysia. Commander Temyong also referred to the Vietnam supply line as the Soviet connection to the insurgents and said a huge shipment of Soviet arms was in the pipeline.

KGB operatives took advantage of the sixty-day cease-fire in early 1987, reportedly infiltrating one hundred agents into insurgent strongholds.[53] With this KGB infrastructure in place, Soviet weapons were successfully smuggled into the Philippines, apparently from Vietnam's Cam Ranh Bay, only seven hundred miles away. KGB operatives are now solidly entrenched in such places as Mindanao and Cebu, posing as tourists, businessmen, and even gold panners.

The Soviets have pressed Mrs. Aquino to let more Soviet ships into Philippine waters, allow more Soviet ships to dock at Philippine ports and let more Soviet ships undergo repairs in Philippine ports.[54] Moscow continues to press the Philippine government to increase the official Soviet diplomatic presence, for example, by opening consulates in Cebu and Mindanao.[55]

Perhaps the most telling sign of Moscow's intentions is its construction of an $800,000 three-story building overlooking a Philippine army post at Fort Bonafacio in Manila.[56] As they do elsewhere, the Soviets will doubtless install listening devices and probably relay information regarding Philippine army operations to the insurgents.

Because of the more open nature of Soviet support, Moscow and the CPP are giving up the fiction that the CPP is "independent." At the last CPP congress in December 1986, Moscow sent official greetings.[57] In January 1987, Richardo Silvestre and Javier Domingo, both Philippine communists, admitted the insurgency was getting support from "foreign governments" and that the Soviets offered "all the arms and money it needed."[58]

All this Soviet activity finally caught the attention of Manila and Washington. President Aquino has gradually taken an increasingly harder line against the insurgents, and the Philippine foreign ministry asked all government agencies to be on the lookout for any Soviet activities.[59] The United States also has expanded its intelligence operations.[60] While Washington ignored Soviet inroads in the Philippines, the insurgency strengthened itself until by late 1988 it constituted a very serious threat to both the Aquino government and continued U.S. access to Philippine military facilities. A tougher U.S. policy toward Soviet meddling in the Philippines was long overdue.

THE SOUTH PACIFIC: FISHING IN TROUBLED WATERS

Moscow has carried its political offensive in Asia and the Pacific southward to Australia and New Zealand and to the newly independent South Pacific islands. A U.S. observer of the USSR has written that "the Pacific is now an arena for Soviet military-political intrusion and subversion [with] the whole bundle of island ministates . . . up for grabs."[61]

Australia and New Zealand have traditionally harbored vocal pro-Soviet minorities in communist and other leftist (notably labor) organizations. However, the June 1984 announcement by New Zealand Prime Minster David Lange, head of one of the country's leading political parties, that U.S. nuclear-armed and nuclear-powered ships would be banned from New Zealand's ports, offered the Soviet Union an opportunity it wasted no time in exploiting.[62] A Soviet media blitz lauded New Zealand's newfound nuclear allergy and urged other Pacific nations to follow suit by banning U.S. nuclear arms in their waters or airspace, dismantling existing U.S. military installations on their territory, and preventing the establishment of new installations. Moscow, however, has not been averse to expanding its own naval presence in the South Pacific through such innocent-sounding proposals as treaties on fishing rights.

The Soviets evidently regard New Zealand's antinuclear policy as the opening wedge in the undermining of the Australia-New Zealand-United States (ANZUS) treaty. Soviet spokesmen are pressing for a nuclear-free zone in the Pacific—a topic on which they can draw support from a mélange of nations that otherwise have little affinity for the USSR. The Soviet campaign is being waged not only in the media but also through various Soviet-dominated front groups. Perhaps the oldest of these groups is the Pacific Conference of Churches, founded in the 1960s and subsidized by the World Council of Churches. It propagandizes against U.S. military installations and exercises in the Asian-Pacific region and sponsors programs of "peace education." Another important front group is the Committee for International Trade Union Unity (CITUU), spawned in Sydney, Australia, by delegates to the 9th Congress of the World Federation of Trade Unions (WFTU) that took place in Czechoslovakia in 1978. According to a report in the *Washington Times*:

> CITUU has been organizing conferences and study programs in the Indian Ocean, Southeast Asia, and the Pacific regions. Pacific islanders have been sent to the Soviet Union, while Soviet and Vietnamese Communist officials have been the leading speakers at various area conferences.[63]

In 1980, three members of the Communist Party of Australia attended the "Third Nuclear-Free Pacific Conference" in Hawaii, which brought together trade unionists from a number of Pacific nations and created an organization called the Pacific Trade Union Forum (PTUF). In 1981, the CITUU and PTUF held a joint conference in Noumea at which peace and disarmament were the main issues. The Soviets and their new friends in the Pacific area have announced support for the NPA-led "liberation movement" in the Philippines and the anti-French Kanak Socialist National Liberation Front in New Caledonia. For good measure, the

Soviets have also recommended that Hawaii be returned to its "indigenous" peoples.[64]

Moscow's "peace offensive" in the Pacific can claim at least partial credit for New Zealand's action against U.S. naval vessels, for a similar ban by Vanuatu and the Solomon Islands on U.S. nuclear-armed and nuclear-powered ships, for Papua New Guinea's rejection of a U.S. request to permit Philippine-based B-52s to overfly the country, and for a movement by politicians in Palau to deny the United States a military base. The "peace offensive" is occurring against a backdrop of growing Soviet military power in the Pacific, large portions of which used to be a U.S. lake.

In September 1984, Moscow began to offer to negotiate fishing access agreements (that include hard currency payments) with Fiji, Kiribati, Papua New Guinea, Tuvalu, and Vanuatu. Moscow concluded an agreement with Kiribati in August 1985 that allowed Soviet fishing in its economic zone for an initial annual licensing fee of $1.7 million.[65] This agreement shook U.S. complacency about the South Pacific, because it allows the Soviets access to a wide area of the mid-Pacific adjacent to the U.S. missile testing range at Kwajalein.[66]

So far, Kiribati's fishing agreement has not created a domino effect in the South Pacific. The Soviet agreement with Kiribati expired October 1986 after Kiribati tried to raise the price. But it also appears that Moscow chose not to renew the pact with Kiribati when it found a better deal and more fertile soil in Vanuatu. The Soviet agreement with Vanuatu in early 1987 provides for Vanuatu to license eight Soviet fishing vessels to operate in Vanuatu's two hundred-mile exclusive economic zone (EEZ), using only approved methods to fish for tuna and tuna-like species.[67] The Soviet Union paid a licensing fee of $1.5 million for the fishing privilege. But unlike the Soviet-Kiribati deal, the Soviet fishing agreement with Vanuatu gives Soviet boats the right to make port calls for repairs and replenishment. Needless to say, Washington is concerned about these Soviet efforts aimed at expanding its presence and influence in the Pacific.

CONCLUSIONS

Soviet concerns about a threat from the United States and potential challenges from China and Japan notwithstanding, it is our opinion that the emerging security environment in the Asian-Pacific region contains a host of opportunities for the USSR. Furthermore, the accession of Mikhail Gorbachev, a relatively fresh, young leader with an aura of dynamism, puts Moscow in its best position in many years to exploit those opportunities. The replacement of veteran Soviet Foreign Minister Andrei Gromyko with Eduard Shevardnadze, who had little experience in international affairs but quickly established respect for his abilities, not only suggests Gorbachev's desire to take the lead in this realm but also symbolizes a penchant for fresh initiatives abroad. China is clearly a primary target of Gorbachev's new Eastern policies.

Vietnam, for its part, evidently hoped to head off a Sino-Soviet rapprochement at its expense by proposing high-level discussions with the United States on the unresolved issue of U.S. soldiers missing in action during the Vietnam War. Hanoi's cautious overtures for the establishment of diplomatic relations with Washington have been spurned with the admonition that such a move is impossible before the withdrawal of Vietnamese troops from Cambodia. However, the greater the possibility of a Sino-Soviet reconciliation appears to the Vietnamese leaders, the more likely they are to persist in their campaign to bring all of Indochina under their control—even if Moscow withdraws military assistance for the Cambodian war. To allow Cambodia to drift into the Soviet or Chinese orbit would be an unacceptable threat to Vietnam's security interests.

Regardless of the outcome of the Cambodian conflict, Moscow's position at Cam Ranh Bay appears secure for at least the short-term future. Thus, Moscow may well be able to have its cake and eat it too by diminishing the threat from China through political and economic gestures while retaining Soviet military investment in Southeast Asia by means of its Vietnamese bases.

Gorbachev seems only slightly more predisposed than his predecessors to making real concessions aimed at improving Soviet relations with Japan. Firmness will probably prevail over any major changes in Moscow's policy toward Tokyo. However, a more independent Japanese foreign policy has clearly emerged in the 1980s, including more independence from the United States. Thus, the Soviet's strategic nightmare of a Sino-U.S.-Japanese triangle is unlikely to materialize. Moreover, Moscow probably can take comfort in the thought that Prime Minister Nakasone's commitment to a substantial bolstering of Japanese military prowess may be eroded by Takeshita and his successors.

Elsewhere in Asia, the Soviets may worry about regional arms races, but they display no reluctance to participate. It was Soviet deployment of TU-16 Badger aircraft and MiG-23 fighter-bombers in Vietnam that contributed to a U.S. decision to sell an upgraded version of the F-16 war plane to Thailand and Singapore.[68] Other ASEAN members may seek similar purchases. On the Korean Peninsula, tension may mount as Moscow yields to Pyongyang's repeated requests for offensive weaponry. The Soviets attempt to justify such deliveries by citing South Korea's acquisition of F-16s. And yet, there are also more peaceful, countervailing trends on the peninsula and in Soviet-South Korean relations.

In surveying the overall military balance in the Asian-Pacific region, it is clear that the USSR and its allies possess an overwhelming superiority in manpower. The Soviets deploy more than 500,000 troops on the Sino-Soviet border alone and have the capability to transfer forces relatively quickly from other theaters in any emergency situation short of an East-West war in Europe. Vietnam's armed forces, totaling some 1.2 million, are larger than those of the six ASEAN countries combined. North Korea, like Vietnam, has one of the world's largest military establishments. And if Sino-Soviet relations take a dramatic turn for the better, China's massive armed forces would be effectively neutralized from threatening Soviet security in Asia.

Much as the Kremlin would like to acquire reliable allies in Asia, it must continue to rely upon its own strength and dexterity for expanding Soviet influence there. In view of the unattractiveness of communist ideology and of the Soviet economic model, the overwhelming thrust of the Kremlin's policy in Asia has been military.[69] However, under Gorbachev, the Kremlin's tactics will be far more sophisticated. In order to beguile the West, the Soviet Union will conceal its support of Communist insurgents and other warriors for "national liberation movements." Soviet support increasingly will be funneled through surrogates and a maze of religious groups, human rights organizations, trade unions, solidarity organizations, peace groups, and nonruling communist parties. Overall the Soviet Union under Gorbachev will be judged innocent of most wrongdoing as "smoking guns" will not be permitted to surface. As a Japanese observer has written:

> Gorbachev's policy toward the Asia-Pacific region is marked by a combination of change in economic policy and continuity in military and security policies. Though the Soviet Union has begun to demonstrate an unusual degree of flexibility in economic affairs, it has maintained its traditional policy of incessantly strengthening its military power.[70]

IMPLICATIONS FOR THE UNITED STATES

Mikhail Gorbachev took power in March 1985 with a new strategic vision of how to advance Soviet interests around the world. Gone is the crude Brezhnev approach, with its lopsided reliance on the military instrument of strategy. In its place is a far more sophisticated strategy that ultimately poses a more fundamental challenge to the West. To be sure, the Kremlin still seeks to alter the existing international system and establish global hegemony. However, Gorbachev intends to bring about this shift gradually, with an initial strategy of denial rather than military intimidation. Moscow seeks to isolate the United States and reverse the U.S. forward strategy by fanning peace movements, nuclear-free zones, neutralism, and nonalignment in countries and regions where the United States used to have steadfast anti-Soviet friends and allies. Gorbachev's strategy already is reaping fruit, if only because the approach of his predecessors was so counterproductive:

> His predecessors did so badly in the region—pushing, threatening, sneering, and spying, while being unable to offer tangible economic

benefits—that Gorbachev may make immediate headway by simply behaving normally. Beyond that, if successful domestic economic reforms generate Soviet trade with the region and if Gorbachev is able to prevail over forces that resist making substantive diplomatic concessions, further penetration into the region will become possible.[71]

NOTES

Opinions, conclusions, and recommendations expressed or implied in this chapter are solely those of the authors and do not necessarily represent the views of the U.S. government.

1. For an excellent early discussion of Gorbachev's Vladivostok speech, see "Moscow's New Tack," in the *Far Eastern Economic Review*, 14 August 1986, pp. 30–40. Also see Gorbachev's Krasnoyarsk speech on 16 September 1988, as printed in FBIS SOV 88181 19 September 1988.

2. See Peggy L. Falkenheim, "Japan, the Soviet Union, and the Northern Territories: Prospects for Accommodation," in Lawrence E. Grinter and Young W. Kihl, eds., *East Asian Conflict Zones*, (St. Martin's Press, New York, 1987).

3. For a detailed discussion of Soviet-Vietnamese relations, see Leif Rosenberger, "The Soviet-Vietnamese Alliance and Kampuchea, in *Survey*, Spring 1985.

4. *Far Eastern Economic Review*, 8 November 1984.

5. John J. Stephan, "Asia in the Soviet Conception," in Donald S. Zagoria, ed., *Soviet Policy in East Asia* (New Haven: Yale University Press, 1982), p. 31.

6. Paul F. Langer, "Soviet Military Power in Asia," in *Soviet Policy in East Asia*, p. 272.

7. *Far Eastern Economic Review*, 8 November 1984.

8. George Perkovich, "Moscow Turns East," *The Atlantic Monthly*, December 1987, p. 30.

9. Langer, "Soviet Military Power," p. 266.

10. Tetsuya Kataoka, "Japan's Northern Threat," *Problems of Communism*, March–April 1984, p. 6.

11. Langer, "Soviet Military Power," p. 259.

12. *Krasnaya Avezda*, 31 December 1983.

13. See, for example, the article by I. Alekseyev and F. Nikolayev in *International Affairs* (Moscow, April 1984).

14. Tass, 3 May 1984.

15. These exchanges actually were kicked off by the visit of U.S. Secretary of Defense Caspar Weinberger in the autumn of 1983.

16. See Thomas P. Bernstein, "China in 1984," *Asian Survey*, January 1985, p. 45.

17. According to an interview that Chinese Communist Party Chief Hu Yaobang gave to the Italian Communist newspaper *L'Unita*, this assurance

was passed by a high Chinese official to Rumanian President Nicolae Ceausescu, who was asked to pass it on to Moscow. See Bernstein, *Ibid.*, p. 47.

18. *Far Eastern Economic Review*, 1 January 1987, p. 47.

19. *Far Eastern Economic Review*, 13 November 1986, pp. 32–33.

20. *New York Times*, 12 January 1988.

21. *Ibid.*

22. Quoted in Langer, "Soviet Military Power," p. 264.

23. *Ibid.*, p. 261.

24. Tass, 19 January 1983.

25. Tass, 5 April 1983.

26. *Asiaweek*, 29 April 1983, p. 17.

27. *Le Monde*, 11 March 1983.

28. Marian Leighton, "De-Coupling the Allies: Soviet Strategy Toward Northern Europe and Japan," *Survey*, Autumn–Winter 1983, p. 134.

29. Bovin cited in *Mainichi Shimbum*, 21 April 1984.

30. Hiroshi Kimura, "Soviet Focus on the Pacific," *Problems of Communism*, May–June 1987, p. 7.

31. *Ibid.*, p. 9.

32. See Young Whan Kihl, "The Two Koreas: Security Diplomacy and Peace," in Young Whan Kihl and Lawrence E. Grinter, eds., *Asian-Pacific Security: Emerging Challenges and Responses* (Boulder, CO: Lynne Reinner Publishers, 1986) pp. 152–153, and Lawrence E. Grinter and Young Whan Kihl, eds., *East Asian Conflict Zones: Prospects for Regional Stability and Deescalation* (New York, St. Martin's Press, 1987) pp. 101, 111, 120.

33. *Far Eastern Economic Review*, 13 November 1986, p. 39.

34. Kihl; Grinter and Kihl.

35. Quoted in *Far Eastern Economic Review*, 13 November 1986, p. 39.

36. See *Far Eastern Economic Review*, 6 June 1985, p. 13; and *Washington Post*, 18 July 1985.

37. *Ibid.*

38. *Wall Street Journal*, 25 April 1985.

39. As cited in Leif Rosenberger, "The Soviet-Vietnamese Alliance and Kampuchea," *Survey*, Autumn–Winter, 1983 p. 230.

40. *Far Eastern Economic Review, 1984 Asia Yearbook*, p. 285.

41. *Far Eastern Economic Review*, 8 November 1984.

42. *Philippine Daily Globe*, 25 April 1984, p. 4.

43. For additional discussion regarding this important issue, see Leif Rosenberger's interview with Sinfah Tunsarawuth, "US Analyst Warns of Soviet-brokered Kampuchean Peace," in the *Nation*, 9 February 1988, p. 5.

44. Past Soviet-Vietnamese friction over economic assistance is no longer a major issue, since the new Vietnamese Secretary General, Nguyen Van Lihh, appears to be "another Gorbachev" in terms of his interest in a more rational Vietnamese economy.

45. For a detailed early study on this topic, see Leif Rosenberger, "Philippine Communism and the Soviet Union," *Survey*, Spring 1985.

46. For a more recent discussion, see Leif Rosenberger, "Philippine

Communism: The Continuing Threat and the Aquino Challenge," in Grinter and Kihl, *East Asian Conflict Zones.*

47. This material draws from Leif Rosenberger, "The Soviets' Hidden Hand," *Asian Wall Street Journal,* 1 July 1987.

48. See Ross Munro, "The New Khmer Rouge," *Commentary,* December 1985.

49. *Yomiuri Shimbun,* 15 January 1987, p. 4.

50. *News Weekly,* 5 March 1986, p. 3.

51. B.A. Santamaria, "Communist Cloud Over Aquino Victory," *Australian,* 4 March 1986, p. 13.

52. Tom Breen, "Philippine Communists Buying Arms From Hanoi," *Washington Times,* 10 October 1986, p. 6.

53. Tom Breen, "Soviets Seek to Halt Filipino Rebel Move Toward Ceasefire," *Washington Times,* 9 March 1987, pp. 1A and 10A.

54. See *Manila Bulletin,* 20 March 1987 and Manila *Times,* 20 January 1987.

55. Tom Breen, "U.S. Monitoring Soviet Role in Philippine Insurgency," *Washington Times,* 24 March 1987, pp. 1A and 6A.

56. *Philippine Star,* 14 March 1987, p. 6.

57. Foreign Broadcasting Information Service, Asia and Pacific, 21 June 1987, p. P15.

58. Tom Breen, "U.S. Monitoring Soviet Role in Philippine Insurgency," *Washington Times,* 24 March 1987, pp. 1A, 6A.

59. See Richard Fisher, "Cory's Real Enemies," *Asian Wall Street Journal,* 8 may 1987.

60. Tom Breen, pp. 1A, 6A.

61. Arnold Beichman, "Trouble in Paradise," *Washington Times,* 19 June 1985.

62. *Washington Post,* 1 February 1985.

63. Beichman.

64. *Ibid.*

65. See Testimony of Edward Baker, in the U.S. Congress, House of Representatives, Committee of Foreign Affairs, Subcommittee on Asian and Pacific Affairs, *Development in the South Pacific Region,* Hearings, 99th Congress, 2nd Session (Washington, D.C.: U.S. Government Printing Office, 1987).

66. *Ibid.,* pp. 88–97.

67. *The Washington Pose,* 3 February 1987.

68. Reuters, 8 July 1985. The previous U.S. policy had been to sell only the export versions of the F-16.

69. See Thomas W. Robinson, "On Soviet Asian Policy: A Commentary," in Robert H. Donaldson, eds., *The Soviet Union in the Third World: Success and Failures* (Boulder, CO: Westview Press, 1980), pp. 298–299.

70. Kimura, p. 13.

71. *Far Eastern Economic Review,* 13 November 1986, p. 33.

4

Pacific Rim Reactions to U.S. Military Strategy

SHELDON W. SIMON

It is generally agreed that the father of the U.S. navy's "Maritime Strategy" of the 1980s, Admiral Thomas B. Hayward, was heavily influenced by his experience as Commander-in-Chief, Pacific (CINCPAC) in the post-Vietnam period. Searching for an approach to naval warfare which would reverse the decline of U.S. maritime strength in the 1970s, Admiral Hayward focused on power projection through aircraft carrier battle groups. These forces would capitalize on the Soviet Union's geostrategic vulnerabilities by bottling up their surface ships and submarines in Soviet home waters before they were able to transit straits and other choke points to the open ocean.[1]

Because, in Asia, maritime strategy seems to require a concentration of forward-deployed U.S. naval forces in the Northwest Pacific and the Sea of Japan, naval strategists have also emphasized the important role America's Pacific allies should play in implementing the strategy. That role would be twofold: (1) the provision of bases for American naval and air forces and (2) direct cooperation through the utilization of their own air and naval assets to monitor regions adjacent to their territories and, if need be, escort and fight alongside U.S. forces.

Therein lurks one of the unresolved issues of the maritime strategy: although it requires allied cooperation to be fully effective in both deterrent and war-fighting modes, it is essentially unilateralist. Decisions ranging from probing Soviet defenses in the Seas of Japan and Okhotsk to entering actual hostilities would be made by the United States. Allies would be expected to fall in line behind these decisions regardless of their own foreign and security policies. Exacerbating the prospect of differing policy interests for Washington's Asian allies was former Secretary of the Navy John Lehman's concept of "horizontal escalation." Because the Maritime Strategy is directed primarily to the central European front, Asia is seen as a secondary battlefield that would be opened to force the Soviets to contemplate a two-front war.[2]

81

U.S. allies presumably would provide bases and logistic centers in exchange for protection by the United States and the maintenance of the sea-lanes of communication (SLOC).

According to U.S. strategic thinking, horizontal escalation would not be as threatening to the Pacific allies as it initially appears. Because the Soviet navy would be primarily concerned with protecting its ballistic missile-firing submarines (SSBNs), the bulk of its air and naval forces would be concentrated around Vladivostok and Petropavlovsk. A prompt deployment of U.S. antisubmarine warfare (ASW) forces would also precipitate a Soviet submarine retreat to home waters to protect the SSBNs. This would leave only residual Soviet forces in Southeast Asia, the eastern Indian Ocean, and the South Pacific that could be neutralized at choke points, such as the Strait of Malacca, by American and allied forces.[3] Besides, the navy argues, the enhanced threat of a two-front war strengthens deterrence and therefore reduces the probability of war in the first place.[4]

As Admiral James D. Watkins, current Chief of Naval Operations, has stated: "The idea is to counter the launch platform. To shoot the archer before he releases the arrows is very important because that cuts down on the magnitude of the defensive problem."[5] Where Admiral Watkins foresees the importance of a preemptive strike in a Soviet-American confrontation, Vice Admiral James A. Lyons, the current Commander-in-Chief of the U.S. Pacific Fleet, sees the role of U.S. Pacific Forces as sea control: to ensure that Soviet forces in Asia cannot be shifted to Europe.[6] Each of these strategies portends different roles for Asian allies—the former as passive supporter and provider of bases, the latter as active contributor to a conventional armada whose task is to constrain a Soviet breakout from its home bases or an attack on the U.S. fleet.

AMERICA'S ASIA STRATEGY AND CAPACITY

The importance of U.S. air and sea power to Asian-Pacific security has been acknowledged since the end of World War II. Initially, they formed the basis for an island *cordon sanitaire* approach to protect the chain of islands from Japan through the Philippines against continental-based Sino-Soviet power.[7] Advocates of this strategy opposed efforts to fight on the mainland, where U.S. manpower would be at a great disadvantage against Asia's huge populations. The Vietnam War's outcome strengthened the argument behind the *cordon sanitaire*. It was reflected in the 1969 Guam Doctrine under which U.S. allies were expected to take primary responsibility for their own defense, but, if attacked, could expect assistance from the United States through its air and sea power.

While the U.S. Seventh and Third Fleets combined deploy about 220 combat ships and auxiliaries, and the U.S. Pacific Air Force has approximately 500 bombers and fighters, they are all part of a global strategy, tasked with monitoring developments all the way from the Persian Gulf across the Indian Ocean and Western Pacific to the Eastern Pacific. This wide dispersal means that in any given conflict situation, the United States must depend on the capabilities of allied and friendly states to augment American force projection.

Former Secretary of Defense Caspar Weinberger articulated the Reagan administration's approach to Pacific security in 1982 when he distinguished between the U.S. roles in the Northwest Pacific and the Southwest Pacific and Indian Ocean. For the former, the United States would provide the nuclear umbrella, offensive force projection, and aid for the defense of South Korea and Japan. For the latter, there would be the nuclear umbrella, projection forces, and sea-lane protection.[8] Missing, of course, was sea-lane protection for the Northwest Pacific, a task the United States urged Japan to accept so that U.S. forces could be moved further south and west without exposing the sea-lanes from Hawaii to Japan.

The need for allied ships and planes is further underscored by examining the kinds of ships the U.S. Navy is building to augment its surface and air-strike missions. Shipbuilding plans through the remainder of this decade to safeguard the projected twelve to fifteen carrier groups include very expensive Los Angeles-class attack submarines, 38 high-cost cruisers, and 14 destroyers.[9] The high price of these ships means that they will not be produced in sufficient numbers to replace their predecessors unit for unit. The far-flung SLOCs will either be less frequently patrolled, or the United States will have to increasingly rely on other navies.

THE NEED FOR BURDEN-SHARING

High-technology warfare has driven the costs of modern navies and air forces so high that alliances between major powers and smaller allies are being reassessed. The military guarantees of twenty years ago are no longer seen as absolute. They are perceived as having become limited and conditional, reflecting the economic and political burdens they entail. As Robert Scalapino has noted, it is more appropriate in the 1980s to speak of alignments rather than alliances. The former are more complex and the reciprocal benefits are more fluid and open to regular renegotiation. "It requires a capacity for compromise, an acceptance of difference, and, above all, a willingness to consult and to develop genuinely collective policies."[10] This means a shift away from unilateralism in the determination of alliance policies.

Critics of U.S. defense burdens inherent in alliance arrangements point to this country's unprecedented global indebtedness which, by 1990, is expected to be half a trillion dollars. They note that by that time,

Washington will be paying tens of billions to foreign creditors merely in servicing costs. Because some of these creditors are also U.S. allies (Japan and South Korea, for example), the following questions arise:

1. Can the United States continue to lead allies to which it owes a huge debt?
2. If the United States tries to control the debt through protectionism, will the allies continue to rely on the United States for security when Washington is challenging the economic behavior on which their prosperity is based? And finally,
3. Will U.S. public opinion support paying for the defense of countries richer than the United States?[11]

Regarding the last question, Chicago Council on Foreign Relations polls of over 2,500 national respondents in 1978 and 1982 reveal diminishing support for expanded military spending even among those who were classified as military "hard-liners" (from 47 to 34 percent).[12]

The United States could afford the commitments it entered into along the Pacific Rim in the 1950s and 1960s when domestic social programs absorbed a smaller percentage of U.S. national product and the U.S. economy dominated the globe (producing over 40 percent of the world's goods and services). That era has passed. If deterrence is to remain viable, then the United States needs the assistance of allies and friends not only through passive provision of bases but also through positive cooperation in force deployments. Such cooperation, in turn, depends on a change in U.S. attitudes toward its Pacific partners from unilateralism to joint planning. If American protection is simply viewed by the allies as payment for services rendered rather than as a product of common interests, then the longevity and reliability of such arrangements are questionable.[13] (This is one part of the problem in negotiating a new base agreement with the Philippines.)

What roles can allies with limited navies perform in the pacific? Are joint operations feasible? Have they been conducted in the past? Can they be improved in the future? The remainder of this chapter addresses these questions and, equally important, the compatibility of security interests in whose absence cooperation would be chimeric.

Allies with even modest naval and air forces could engage in defensive sea control. Indeed, with the declaration of two hundred-mile Exclusive Economic Zones (EEZs) in the 1982 Law of the Sea Treaty, most littoral states have begun to acquire ships for the purpose of enforcing their jurisdictions. These include attack submarines, land-based patrol aircraft, fast-attack craft, destroyers, and frigates. These systems can engage in straits control, convoying, and ASW operations.[14] The question arises, Will states that are developing capabilities to defend their territorial waters and economic zones view cooperation with the U.S. Navy as a means of enhancing their own security? Or conversely and ominously for U.S. (and Soviet) naval strategies, will those states signing the Law of the Sea Treaty increasingly oppose the deployment of *all* foreign warships as incompatible with the "peaceful purposes" language of the treaty? While the latter interpretation need not inhibit U.S. deployments, it could still obstruct the kind of allied cooperation necessary for a truly effective U.S. naval strategy.[15]

JAPAN: AMERICA'S MAJOR PACIFIC ALLY

Japan's strategic situation can only be understood in light of its close proximity to the Eurasian land mass. A series of islands enclosing the Sea of Japan, Japan is only a short distance from the coasts of China, Korea, and the Soviet Union. The latter's major Pacific naval base, Vladivostok, lies only 640 miles from Tokyo. Access to and from the Sea of Japan is controlled by three straits: *Tsushima* (separating the Korean Peninsula from Honshu), *Tsugaru* (separating the Japanese islands of Honshu and Hokkaido), and *Soya* (separating Hokkaido from the heavily fortified Soviet island of Sakhalin). The Soviets also occupy the Kurile Islands, which stretch from the northern tip of Hokkaido to the Kamchatka Peninsula, forming a barrier between the Sea of Okhotsk and the Pacific Ocean. Ships traveling to and from Vladivostok must transit straits potentially controllable by U.S. allies: the ROK and Japan.

While the Japanese archipelago is a natural barrier constraining Soviet Pacific Fleet operations, Japan's cooperation is essential in controlling the apertures in that barrier in the event of a confrontation. Japanese military planners display a certain reticence, however, over the prospect of closing the straits. The Soviet belief that Japan is about to blockade or mine them could trigger a preemptive strike against Japanese bases and the occupation of northern Hokkaido. Indeed, until the 1979 Soviet invasion of Afghanistan, Japanese officials did not develop scenarios in which a military conflict would occur around their home islands. The 1976 National Defense Program Outline foresaw a low probability for Soviet-American conflict and a low probability for East Asian hostilities, expressing confidence in the deterrent value of U.S.-Japan security arrangements.[16] Nevertheless, Japanese planners realize that in a global or major East Asian confrontation, Japan's involvement could not be avoided. The Japanese straits would be either blockaded by the Americans and Japanese or controlled by the Soviets. Thus, recent joint exercises have focused on repelling a Soviet attack on Hokkaido. *Keen Edge 87-1* was the largest American-Japanese exercise held to date with 10,000 personnel from all three services. Interestingly, *Keen Edge* included U.S. aircraft stationed in South Korea for the first time, implying Japanese acceptance of a security link among the three countries (further discussed below).[17]

Soviet intransigence over negotiations for return of the northern islands is related to its naval strategy. The archipelago immediately north of Hokkaido (Habomai, Kunashiri, Shidotan, and Etorofu) commands the most readily usable exits to the Pacific Ocean which, unlike the straits, could not be easily obstructed. By fortifying the two Kurile Islands closest to Japan—Kunashiri and Etorofu—Moscow hopes to turn the Sea of Okhotsk into a Soviet lake for the protection of its SSBNs. Moreover, the Soviets have a division deployed on the southernmost Kuriles, equipped with long-range artillery, as well as MiG-24 helicopters and some 40 MiG-23 fighters—a significant concentration of force in case of a move to seize northern Hokkaido.[18]

Japan's 1987 Defense White paper for the first time stressed "air defense on the mainland," a reference to preparation for the defense of northern Hokkaido from a Soviet invasion effort to secure the southern side of the Soya Strait. Sea-land defense is seen as an integral part of this new concentration on northern Japan since the Maritime Self-Defense Force (MSDF) would be tasked with securing a route for U.S. forces to come to Japan's aid. The White Paper does not, however, outline any arrangement for a readiness system under which U.S. forces would jointly assist in Japan's defense. Nor has the United States prepositioned supplies to Hokkaido to repel an invasion force. Indeed, neither logistics, labor, land, nor transportation are currently available to the U.S. military in Hokkaido in the event of an emergency requiring a rapid buildup.[19]

Washington's military aims for Japan include: (1) the development of a capability to control the sea lanes 1,000 miles from Honshu, in particular the area south to the Bashi channel north of Taiwan and east of Guam. This would require that the Maritime Self-Defense Force develop capabilities against Soviet surface vessels and submarines as well as long-range patrol aircraft; (2) Mining and blockading the straits discussed above; and (3) The establishment of an air-defense screen around the home islands that could inflict heavy losses on Soviet bombers and fighters and therefore facilitate sea control.[20]

Japan possesses most of the systems necessary to implement these tasks, though it needs more of each (F-15 fighters, E-2C AWACs, and P3-C ASW aircraft). It currently lacks airborne refueling capacity (KC-135s), however, because the Diet has viewed these as potentially providing an offensive as distinct from defensive capability according to Article 9 of Japan's Constitution. This policy must change if Japan is to sustain air combat and patrol over time and space. U.S. Assistant Secretary of Defense Richard Armitage has praised the JSDF (Japan's Self-Defense Forces) Midterm Defense Plan, which by the early 1990s will yield 60 destroyers—two with *Aegis* defense systems, 100 P-3Cs deployed in Hokkaido, 100 F-4s, and 100 F-15s. These systems far outnumber their counterparts in the U.S. Seventh Fleet and Fifth and Seventh Air Forces.[21] The United States has also pressed Japan to set up Over the Horizon Radar (OTH), which would provide early warning of aircraft flying from Siberian bases toward the Pacific. Washington would link a Japanese system into a planned chain of OTH sites stretching from Alaska to the Philippines.[22]

The hope of the United States, then, is not that Japan becomes an independent regional military power—anathema to such neighbors as China, Korea, and the Philippines—but that Tokyo will develop the capacity to fulfill its pledge to defend the surrounding sea-lanes "for three hundred miles to the frigid north [and] to the south for over one thousand miles."[23] Japan would not "stand in" for the United States in this region. Rather, its forces would augment the Seventh Fleet by subjecting Soviet naval and air movements to close surveillance. The concept of Japanese forces being additive to U.S. forces implies, of course, that the United states has abandoned its "swing strategy" to Europe in the event of a crisis. Reassuring the Pacific allies of the United States, including Japan, that the ASDF (Air Self-Defense Force) and MSDF (Maritime Self-Defense Force) will not be primarily responsible for western Pacific defense is essential if an expanded role for these forces is to be politically acceptable in Asia.

U.S.-Japan joint exercises are increasing in scope and number with the biannual Rim of the Pacific (RIMPAC) exercises, which also involve the Australian, Canadian, and British navies. Nevertheless, unlike NATO, the United States still has no joint command structure with Japan. Current plans state that in the event of an imminent attack on Japan, the two governments will conduct closer liaison, but *no* joint command is planned—even for air defense where rapid task coordination would be essential. The reason for this anomaly is that Article IX of the Japanese constitution prohibits *collective* self-defense. Thus, joint defense beyond territorial waters and airspace is problematical. Within Japanese air and sea space, however, the LDP (Liberal Democratic Party) government interprets the constitution in a manner that permits Japan to respond to an attack on U.S. forces, arguing that such a response falls within *individual* or national self-defense. Thus, Japanese ships can protect U.S. ships within Japanese waters, though the chain of command would be through the MSDF and not the U.S. fleet.[24]

Basically, while desiring full participation with U.S. forces in Japan, JSDF hope to avoid having to justify that participation in the Diet. Hence the ambiguity surrounding the Japanese commitment to defend U.S. forces and the insistence that Japanese and U.S. forces are not integrated. The JSDF has been more concerned with defusing joint defense as an issue in domestic politics than with devising more effective security arrangements.

Obstacles to sea-lane defense for Japan include the deployment of some 80 TU-22N Backfire bombers in the Soviet Far East. With a combat radius of over 2,000 miles unrefueled, these supersonic aircraft are believed to be tasked with attacking the Seventh Fleet. Backfires, Bears, and Badgers all regularly fly over the Sea of Japan testing ASDF defense systems. Neither the MSDF nor the ASDF possess the capability to oppose the Backfires.

Combined operations with the United States would be the only effective defense. Yet, at Japan's current rate of procurement, MSDF capability to mount an effective SLOC (sea-lanes of communication) defense will probably not be realized until the mid-1990s. At that time, Japan's new FSX fighter—an upscale version of the F-16—will be deployed. Capable of flying to the Kuriles and Vladivostok with state-of-the-art avionics, the FSX will give the ASDF a strike capability against the Soviet mainland.[25]

THE JAPAN-KOREA NEXUS

Because both South Korea and Japan have security treaties with the United States and each patrols its respective side of the Tsushima Straits, it is at least theoretically possible that three-way defense cooperation could emerge. The U.S. Fifth Air Force and Seventh Fleet treat South Korea and Japan as one region although the U.S. Seventh Air Force has responsibility for the Korean Peninsula. Recent exercises in Japan included the deployment of U.S. F-16s from Korea. As long ago as 1980, a JSDF official even offered an opinion in the Diet that joint exercises with ROK forces would be legal. This idea was reinforced by Under Secretary of Defense Fred Ikle in 1983 when he urged tripartite exercises among Japan, South Korea, and the United States to control the Tsushima Straits.[26] Analysts, such as Edward Olsen of the U.S. Naval Postgraduate School, have been pointing out the logic of trilateral burden-sharing for years.[27]

Nevertheless, the ROK has displayed ambivalence toward Japan's military growth and has thus far rejected the idea of direct military cooperation with Japan. On the one hand, Seoul has requested as much as $6 billion in aid from Japan on the grounds that ROK defense on the peninsula contributes to Japan's safety. Yet, at the same time, South Koreans fear that too extensive a Japanese naval and air buildup will lead to a reduction of U.S. forces in the vicinity as well as a reactive Soviet buildup of North Korea. To a certain extent, these concerns appear justified. The Soviets accelerated arms transfers to the DPRK in 1986, including MiG-23s, though these were provided only after the United States finally sold F-16s to the ROK. More ominously, Soviet Pacific Fleet vessels are now calling at both Nampo on the west coast of the DPRK and Nanjin on the east coast. Though neither of these ports could remotely be termed a Soviet "base," such as Cam Ranh Bay, allied blockade of the Tsushima Straits would be more difficult if the Soviets deploy ships there permanently.

The ROK has certainly developed the economic capacity to play a greater role in the maritime and air defense of its vicinity. It already provides offset payments of $1.2 billion annually to help defray the maintenance costs of 42,000 U.S. forces on the peninsula. Given Seoul's rapid economic growth rate and some $8 billion in foreign exchange reserves, Seoul could significantly increase its defense role without harming its economy.[28] Additional frigates and minelaying capacity could make the ROK navy a formidable ally in defending and/or blockading its side of the Tsushima Straits while Japan's MSDF performs the same role to the east. The U.S. Seventh Fleet could coordinate these efforts while maintaining the political and legal fiction that Seoul and Tokyo do not exercise together.

Overt defense cooperation may still be a decade away,[29] though its occurrence seems inevitable, especially given the continued upgrading of North Korea's armed forces and the prospect that the Soviet Union may use DPRK harbors. Seoul already acknowledges the vital importance of U.S. bases in Japan for the ROK's defense. At the same time, Japan should encourage North Korean economic and political reforms that emulate those of the PRC. A more economically outward-looking Pyongyang could well move the foreign policy of a successor regime in a more moderate direction. This, in turn, could lead to tension reduction around the peninsula and ROK's greater willingness to see Soviet military growth in East Asia as a primary concern. Unless the North Korean threat is reduced, however, problems of threat-perception compatibility between Tokyo and Seoul will persist. Japan does not see Pyongyang as a threat as much an economic opportunity that Seoul continues to obstruct. Over the long run, both countries depend on maritime freedom, and their security concerns are similar. At present, however, Seoul's fear of and concentration on the North precludes a broader regional view.

SOUTHEAST ASIA: THE PHILIPPINE BASES AND ASEAN

Beginning well before World War II, U.S. naval presence in the South China Sea and Indian Ocean has depended on the base at Subic Bay in the Philippines. Unlike Japan and Korea, whose armed forces provide active contributions to the U.S. maritime presence, the Philippines poses a politically more difficult situation. It is a passive provider of strategic location. Neither its small coastal defense navy nor minimal air force possesses the capacity for sustained sea-lane patrol. The bulk of the Philippines's military budget, moreover, is committed to ground forces fighting (offshore) Southeast Asia's only significant communist and Moslem insurgencies. Because the Philippines is not actively involved in regional defense and the U.S. bases there are so important for both U.S. conventional and nuclear support, the bases have become a focus of controversy for the Aquino government and a rallying cry for those groups who see the bases as an affront to Philippine autonomy.

U.S. officials have traditionally argued that the bases in the Philippines are crucial for operations in three regions: the Indian Ocean, Southeast Asia, and Northeast Asia. They demonstrate America's commitment to regional deterrence, particularly in light of Soviet deployments at Cam Ranh Bay, which, by 1987, totaled some twenty-five to thirty ships at seven docks, increasing the capacity the U.S. had built during the Vietnam War. All other U.S. Pacific allies, the ASEAN states, and even China have indicated to U.S. authorities and in selected discussions with Philippine officials that they prefer to see the Seventh Fleet and Thirteenth Air Force remain in the Philippines, though none has offered to provide substitute facilities should the United States be asked to leave.

The capabilities of Clark Air Base and Subic Bay are comprehensively detailed elsewhere in this volume.[30] Suffice it to say that Subic performs 65 percent of the Seventh Fleet's repairs and that the nearest alternative facility is 1,400 miles east in Guam. Clark is the only regional staging point from which C-5As can fly nonstop to Diego Garcia, the U.S. Central Command's primary staging point for the Middle East.

The Aquino administration is "keeping its options open" with respect to the renewal of the bases agreement in 1991. It has the problem of not wanting to give the anti-bases opposition too much political grist during the review, which began in April 1988. Nevertheless, most observers believe a new agreement will be reached because the economic benefits are so great. The bases employ about 68,000 Filipinos and may contribute up to 5 percent of the country's GNP. This total is further enhanced by the spending conducted by 60,000 U.S. military and civilian personnel and their 25,000 dependents.[31]

A new treaty will undoubtedly cost the United States considerably more than the current $900 million pledge (over five years) and will be subject to more stringent criteria of use to demonstrate that the bases are more than just nominally owned by Manila. In all probability, a new treaty will be submitted to a popular referendum, the approval of which will serve to solidify U.S.-Philippine security ties. At the same time, the United States must be prepared to see the bases become targets for guerrilla attacks after 1991 if the Communist New Peoples Army can rally nationalist sentiment against this continued "imperialist encroachment."[32]

The bases have also become an issue in ASEAN diplomacy. In 1987, Philippine Foreign Minister Raul Manglapus attempted to solicit a formal statement of regional support for the bases (evidently in hopes of defusing their renewal) as an issue in Philippine domestic politics. Affirmation of the bases' importance for regional security could be used to appeal to the Philippine electorate that their renegotiation was not simply a manifestation of the country's subordination to U.S. strategic interests.[33] However, Manglapus' appeal to ASEAN members was not accepted in public. Rather than relieving the Philippines of sole political responsibility for the bases, ASEAN members insisted in public that the bases' renewal was a bilateral issue between Manila and Washington. To endorse their continuation would be a particular affront to Indonesia and the logic of the Zone of Peace,

Freedom and Neutrality (ZOPFAN), even though, privately, ASEAN members are eager to see U.S. forces remain in the region.

Even if the bases are renewed, problems concerning the presence of nuclear weapons could arise. As the Seventh Fleet deploys more vessels with such dual-capable missile systems as the Tomahawk, antinuclear concerns in the Philippines have become a political issue. The new constitution, for example, declares the Philippines a nuclear-free territory "consistent with the national interest." This latter phrase could provide a loophole for the government if it decided the presence of nuclear weapons was necessary for the country's security.[34] A public statement to that effect would be unlikely, however.

Indonesia's desire for a more prominent role in Southeast Asian affairs was demonstrated during the 1987 Manila Summit. The ASEAN statement urged efforts toward the early establishment of a Southeast Asian Nuclear Weapons Free Zone (SEANFZ). Modeled after the Treaty of Roratonga for the Southwest Pacific, Indonesia has argued that SEANFZ is a logical expansion of ZOPFAN. Its purpose, from Indonesia's perspective, would be to reduce regional dependence on external powers. As with the ZOPFAN declaration, however, ASEAN members realize that SEANFZ is also nonself-implementing. So long as Soviet and U.S. navies continue to ply the waters of the South China Sea and Indian Ocean, neither ZOPFAN nor SEANFZ will go beyond a rhetorical challenge. In contrast to the United States, though, the Soviet Union has endorsed SEANFZ. Foreign Minister Eduard Shevardnadze suggested to Indonesian Foreign Minister Mochtar that the USSR might be willing to open Cam Ranh Bay for inspection as an assurance that no nuclear weapons are deployed there.[35] A Soviet offer of this nature could provide the antibases and antinuclear movements in the Philippines with political ammunition unless the United States was willing to reciprocate. For Washington to do so seems improbable, however, since opening the bases for inspection would violate the long-standing U.S. policy of neither confirming nor denying the presence of nuclear weapons at locations outside the United States.

Soviet concern about the Philippine bases is regularly expressed. General Secretary Gorbachev, in his wide-ranging July 1986 Vladivostok address, hinted at the possibility of reducing the size of the Soviet Pacific Fleet in exchange for an American military exit from the Philippines. Soviet diplomats have reiterated that offer during the current bases review. High-level Soviet visitors to the Philippines warn that the bases put the country at risk and could involve it in war.[36]

On balance, cautious optimism over the future of the Philippine bases appears warranted. Their continued importance for monitoring and protecting the sea-lanes through the straits of Southeast Asia makes the facilities a net asset for regional security. That asset could be further enhanced, in the author's view, if the United States and the Philippines expanded the multilateral use of such facilities as the Crow Valley Gunnery Range for ASEAN navies and air forces. Joint use would facilitate the development of common doctrine among friendly armed services and help dissipate the negative image of the bases as being exclusively in U.S. strategic interests.[37]

ASEAN AND THE MARITIME STRATEGY

Although ASEAN is not allied to the United States, two of its members have security treaties (Thailand and the Philippines) with the United States, and three others (Malaysia, Singapore, and Brunei) are linked to other U.S. allies (Britain and Australia). ASEAN defense activities could contribute to the maintenance of SLOC freedom in Southeast Asia and the eastern Indian Ocean.

ASEAN security cooperation with the United States is problematic, however. First and foremost, open collaboration would violate ASEAN's primary foreign policy goal: the creation of ZOPFAN. The zone concept serves several political purposes: (1) it sustains ASEAN's credibility within the Nonaligned Movement despite the fact that most of its members have ties to Western powers; (2) it posits a long-term goal for Southeast Asia free of all great power encroachments, including those by the United States, Soviet Union, and, potentially, China; and (3) it provides a politically acceptable way of satisfying Indonesia's desire to be the security policy leader for ASEAN without requiring other Western-aligned members to sacrifice their security links to outsiders. ZOPFAN, then, is a vague and wide umbrella under which many different national security policies find shelter. They range from Indonesia's desire to establish an exclusionary zone to Singapore's belief that security lies in a balance of power, including a strong U.S. presence, as well as a Japanese one. In fact, the Singaporean view most closely represents the prevailing situation (with the exception of Japan), while the Indonesian preference would require evolution toward a future setting in which the major powers would mutually agree to withdraw their forces from the region. Given the current trends of both Soviet and U.S. military activities, Indonesia's version of ZOPFAN seems further away from realization than ever.

In general, U.S. naval and air presence in Southeast Asia is welcomed by ASEAN. Not only does it counter the Soviet buildup in Vietnam, but it also ensures that Japanese rearmament will proceed slowly and in conjunction with U.S. plans. A continuing U.S. military presence could also ensure against any future Chinese designs for the region. Moreover, if Japan were to add its ships to those of the Seventh Fleet in Southeast Asia, some ASEAN officials fear the exacerbation of a Soviet-Western naval arms race in their vicinity.[38]

In fact, most ASEAN armed services currently engage in various kinds of cooperation with their U.S. counterparts. They also buy major American weapons systems.[39] Singapore and Thailand provide access for U.S. ships and planes to ports and air bases in their countries. The Seventh Fleet conducts passing exercises with the ships of ASEAN states. Officers from ASEAN states comprise about 15 percent of all foreign military students at U.S. service colleges; the CINCPAC organizes annual maritime and logistics conferences attended by defense officials from ASEAN. Combined naval amphibious and air exercises between individual ASEAN states and the Seventh Fleet were initiated in the early 1980s. Only Indonesia and Brunei have not participated. U.S. Navy P3 Orions periodically stop at U Tapao and Don Muong airports in Thailand on their way from the Philippines to Diego Garcia.

ASEAN states, however, are less concerned about the Soviet presence in Southeast Asia than is the United States. They foresee no direct threat to themselves from the USSR. Rather, the Soviet presence is seen as: (1) part of the global superpower confrontation; (2) the exertion of its role as an Asian power; (3) necessary both to support and exert leverage on Vietnam; (4) an effort to surround China; and (5) the deployment of sufficient capability to protect its own SLOCs to and from Vladivostok.

The United States should encourage the ASEAN states to develop greater security cooperation, particularly the ability to monitor and control their coastal seas. Some ASEAN military analysts have suggested a division of labor that emphasizes each member's strengths. Thus, Singapore could stress air surveillance, the Malaysian navy could concentrate on mine countermeasures to keep the Strait of Malacca open, and Thailand would build up its armor and ground forces along the Indochina border. While such specialization may seem cost-effective, it is, so far, politically unacceptable. No ASEAN state is yet prepared to rely on its neighbors for important components of its own defense. Moreover, an ASEAN formal military pact would violate the Association's hope that Southeast Asia will not be further divided into two hostile blocs (ASEAN versus Indochina). An ASEAN military pact, it is feared, would only encourage closer ties between Vietnam and the USSR.[40]

However, ASEAN could take a number of steps toward defense cooperation without entering a formal pact. Presently, all states (are willing to exercise with each other, with the exception of the Philippines and Malaysia, due to the Sabah dispute). These exercises could work toward the creation of standard C3 procedures. Singapore's purchase of E-2C AEW aircraft could be tied into ground radar systems in Malaysia, Thailand, and Indonesia, thus providing all with a significant regional surveillance capability.

The ASEAN states are now responsible for their respective two hundred mile EEZs. Joint patrol of these zones could be highly cost-effective, especially considering their overlapping jurisdictions, the presence of hundreds of offshore drilling sites, and the fact that the ASEAN maritime region encompasses some of the most vital SLOCs in the world. Because of Vietnam's occupation of Cambodia, the Thai naval air wing, for example, is currently conducting intensive surveillance for Vietnamese naval craft along the Thai-Cambodian coast and into the Gulf of Thailand.

AUSTRALIAN AND U.S. PACIFIC SECURITY

A vast country with armed services of less that 100,000 personnel and 12,000 miles of nautical coastline, Australia's debate regarding defense has persisted since the early 1970s. Australians have long asked themselves whether a continuation of the U.S.-oriented forward defense policy of the Korea and Vietnam War periods was either practical or affordable. The Dibb Report, tabled as an advisory to the Labor Government in 1986, suggested that the answer should be a qualified "no." That is, vital American defense ties should be maintained, but Australia should create a force structure designed not to fight alongside U.S. forces thousands of miles away from the continent, but rather to defend against contingencies in its own vicinity.[41] Premised on land-based air defense, the strategy would be activated by an imminent invasion threat (an admittedly improbable contingency) and would apparently pose no deterrent to other challenges, such as threats to SLOCs or attacks on allies. Strikes against a potential adversary's bases also seemed ruled out in favor of a strategy of attrition against enemy forces en route to Australia. Sharing intelligence with friendly Southeast Asian states, such as Singapore and Malaysia, would provide Canberra with sufficient early warning of enemy moves. Along with over-the-horizon radar to be expanded in the north, Australia's F-111s and 75 newly acquired F/A18s would provide a formidable defense against surface vessels by the early 1990s.

While much of the Dibb Report's emphasis on air power was incorporated in the Labor Government's 1987 Defense White paper, Dibb's "fortress Australia" emphasis was reduced. Defense Minister Kim Beazly chose to underline the importance of Australia's contribution to U.S. strategic strength.[42] The White Paper also stressed the country's responsibilities for strengthening common interests in its regional environment—Southeast Asia and the Southwest Pacific. For the latter, Canberra will increase air and naval deployments. For Southeast Asia, Australis will rotate F/A18 and F-111 aircraft to Butterworth, hear Revang, as well as operate P3 surveillance flights over the eastern Indian Ocean and South China Sea.

From the perspective of U.S. naval strategy, the White Paper's plan to expand the Australian navy is particularly welcome. To a current complement of twelve major surface combatants and aging submarines, Australia will add a fleet of seventeen surface vessels (guided-missile destroyers, guided-missile frigates, and destroyer escorts) and six new Australian-built submarines. Most

Table 4.1   ASEAN Maritime Aircraft Inventory

	Boeing-737	C130H/MP	F-27M	F-27M-2	Nomad
Indonesia[a]	3	1	—	—	17 (11 B; 6L)
Malaysia	—	1[b]	—	—	—
Thailand	—	—	3	1(+2)	8
Philippines	—	—	3	—	—
Singapore	(non-dedicated types, incl. 2 E-2C and C-130B/H)				
Brunei	(non-dedicated types, incl. Bell 206/212 helos)				

Source: *Pacific Defence Reporter*, June 1987.

[a]Indonesia ordered six IPTN CN-235 MPAs in mid-1986.
[b]Some sources indicate three (IISS); however, two are thought to be C-130H transport versions and not specialized C-130H/MP modified aircraft.

interesting of all, for the first time in its history, the navy will be split. Half will be based in New South Wales and half in Western Australia at Cockburn Sound to provide a Southeast Asia/Indian Ocean capability in addition to the traditional Southwest Pacific orientation. By 1990, two submarines and four destroyers would form the nucleus of the western fleet. The new frigates will have an operational range of 3,000 nautical miles, extending surface patrols well into the Indian Ocean and insular Southeast Asia.

The White Paper reaffirmed the importance of the joint communications facilities at the northwest Cape and Nurrangar for mutual security. To ensure Australian knowledge concerning the use of the facilities in communicating with American SSBNs, new links are being built between the joint facilities and Canberra.[43] These links should help diffuse some of the arguments against the facilities which are said to exist exclusively for U.S. strategic needs.

Australia also plans to contribute to Southwest Pacific maritime security through a multimillion-dollar defense assistance program to the South Pacific islands. In addition to providing coastal patrol craft to Papua New Guinea, Fiji, the Solomons, Vanuatu, Western Samoa, and the Cook Islands, Canberra will increase Australian ship visits in the region and deploy long-range patrol aircraft. In fact, the Australian government has chosen to emphasize its South Pacific role over its contribution to Southeast Asian defense, since the ASEAN states have now sufficiently matured to meet their own needs.[44]

Nevertheless, in some respects, Australian defense activities in Southeast Asia will actually be enhanced. A Royal Australian Navy (RAN) submarine will deploy from Malaysia for continuous patrol of Southeast Asian Waters. Combined exercises will now be held with Thailand as well as with Malaysia and Singapore, although defense cooperation with Indonesia has been on the decline for over a decade in part because of Australian press criticism of the Suharto regime.[45]

With the break in U.S.-New Zealand defense ties over the Lange government's refusal to permit nuclear ship visits, Australia has stepped in to provide some supplementary assistance to partly compensate for the material and intelligence losses that are being suffered by Wellington. Australia will design and build frigates that will be used by the navies of both countries, providing a greater range and endurance than New Zealand currently possesses.[46] Australia has also increased binational naval exercises with New Zealand, although these cannot substitute for the training previously provided in the RIMPAC (Rim of the Pacific) naval exercises, which created a more realistic and therefore more expensive combat environment.[47]

One cloud on the U.S.-Australian naval security horizon is the Treaty of Raratonga, which took effect in December 1986. This treaty, supported by both Canberra and Wellington, has declared a South Pacific Nuclear-Free Zone. Although Australis negotiated within the South Pacific Forum to ensure that the treaty would not affect the movement of U.S. ships and planes that might be nuclear-armed through the region, the United States has rejected it on the grounds that it only benefits Soviet global strategy.[48] Unfortunately, the United States was caught in the backwash of a treaty that was directed primarily at France for its continued nuclear-testing program around New Caledonia. The Soviet Union and China have both signed the document.

CONCLUSION

At the beginning of this chapter, a distinction was made between *active* and *passive* allied contributions to U.S. naval missions in the Pacific. Generally, it has been the latter which have created greater political difficulties in countries that are sensitive to nationalist strains and whose leaders do not want to be seen as subordinates to U.S. command. Complaints about U.S. use of bases in the Philippines and Korea fit this interpretation, as does New Zealand's rejection of U.S. port calls.

The Soviets have attempted to play upon this combination of nationalist and antinuclear opinion. Both General Secretary Gorbachev's major address on Asia in July 1986 and his lengthy interview with the Indonesian newspaper *Merdeka* in July 1987 emphasized the need to denuclearize armed forces in the region. In his *Merdeka* interview, Gorbachev sought to explicitly counter the Maritime Strategy by calling for a navigational limit on ships with nuclear weapons so that "they could not approach the coast of any side to within the range of operation of their on-board nuclear systems."[49] This, of course, would remove the U.S. fleet from the northern Sea of Japan. In fact, it appears that the active cooperation of U.S. and Japanese forces in the Sea of Japan where exercises emphasize choke-point control may be keeping the Soviet Pacific Fleet closer to home. The U.S. Defense Department has noted a decline of Soviet deployments into the Indian Ocean.[50]

Similarly, Japan's active 1,000-mile sea-lane defense plans have not disturbed ASEAN leaders. Philippine and Indonesian officials, who had earlier expressed concern about the movement of Japanese forces away from the home islands, now seem to accept Japan's need for limited SLOC protection.[51]

Problems attendant upon the lease renewals for the Philippine bases are partly a product of a Filipino indifference to the American argument that the bases are important for *regional* security. If the leases are renewed, the argument that will sell in Manila is the economic importance of the bases for the country's reconstruction. Even former Philippine Defense Secretary Rafael Ileto argues for the bases' continuation on the grounds that the Philippine armed forces could not afford to maintain the facilities and spend more for external defense if the United States left.[52]

As an Asian-Pacific naval power, the United States relies more on its fleet to project power and cover vast ocean stretches than does the USSR, which still essentially follows a continental strategy. Because the Soviet need for overseas bases is limited in the Asian-Pacific, Gorbachev can play to the nationalist predilections of the countries in which the United States maintains base facilities. The Soviets can also support nuclear-free zone declarations since the forward deployment of U.S. nuclear-capable ships is an integral part of the U.S. strategy, while the Soviets retain most of their SSBNs in the Sea of Okhotsk.

Frictions with allied and friendly countries along the Asian-Pacific Rim will undoubtedly persist for Washington. Optimists, however, believe that the necessity for allied passive and active maritime cooperation with the United States against growing Soviet, North Korean, and possibly Vietnamese, navies will outweigh both antinuclear dispositions and the belief that cooperation with a superpower means dependency upon it. The evidence suggests, however, that active cooperation leads to a more stable alliance relationship than the mere passive provision of facilities. An active relationship entails mutuality and joint planning. The United States should encourage a shift from passive to active cooperation where feasible if Asian-Pacific security is to be enhanced.

NOTES

An earlier version of this paper was presented at the Naval Postgraduate School Conference, "The Navy in the Pacific," Monterey, California, August 13–14, 1987. Research for this study was supported by a grant from the Earhart Foundation, Ann Arbor, Michigan.

1. A useful panel discussion on the Maritime Strategy was held at the April 1987 meeting of the International Studies Association (ISA), Omni-Shoreham Hotel, Washington, D.C. Papers from that panel may be obtained from ISA headquarters at the University of South Carolina, Columbus.

2. Richard H. Soloman, "The Pacific Basin Dilemmas and Choices for American Security," *Naval War College Review* (40, 1), Winter 1987, p. 38.

3. David Winterford, "The Soviet Naval Buildup in Southeast Asia: Implications for China and ASEAN Defense." Paper prepared for the Lingnan College Center for Pacific Studies' *ASEAN-China Hong Kong Forum*, 1987, 3–5 June 1987, pp. 2–4.

4. Jack Beatty, "In Harm's Way," *The Atlantic*, May 1987, pp. 38, 42.

5. Statement by Admiral James D. Watkins to the Seapower and Strategic and Critical Materials Subcommittee, Committee on Armed Services, *The 600-Ship Navy and the Maritime Strategy* (Washington, D.C., 99th Congress, First Session, 24 June, 5, 6, and 10 September 1985), p. 46. (Hereafter referred to as *Hearings*.)

6. *Hearings*, p. 133.

7. The naval and air strategies for Pacific security ar assessed by Robert Scalapino, *Major Power Relations in Northeast Asia* (Lanham, MD: University Press of America for The Asia Society, 1987), pp. 61–62.

8. Cited in Ensign Thomas B. Modly (USN), "The Rhetoric and Realities of Japan's 1000-Mile Sea-Lane Defense Policy," *Naval War College Review* (38, 1), January–February 1985, p. 27. Also see Edward A. Olsen, "Determinants of Strategic Burdensharing in East Asia," *Naval War College Review* (39, 3), May–June 1986.

9. Robert J. Hanks (Rear Admiral, USN, Ret.), *American Sea-Power and Global Strategy* (New York: Pergamon-Brassey's, 1985); pp. 34, 51, 80.

10. Scalapino, *Major Power Relations in Northeast Asia*, p. 24.

11. These questions are raised by C. Fred Bergsten, "Economic Imbalances and World Politics," *Foreign Affairs* (65, 4), Spring 1987; pp. 770–771.

12. Eugene R. Wittkopf, "Elites and Masses: Another Look at Attitudes Toward America's World Role," *International Studies Quarterly* (31, 2), June 1987, p. 147.

13. Terry C. Deibel, "Hidden Commitments," *Foreign Policy* (67), Summer 1987, p. 59.

14. John J. Mearsheimer, "A Strategic Misstep: The Maritime Strategy in Europe," *International Security* (11, 2), Fall 1986, pp. 12, 13. Also see the statement by Rear Admiral Eugene J. Carroll, Jr. (USN, Ret.) in *Hearings*, p. 263.

15. Ken Booth, *Law, Force and Diplomacy at Sea* (London: George Allen & Unwin, 1985) Chapter Six; "EEZs and Naval Diplomacy," pp, 137–169.

16. The NDPO is discussed by Edward Ok Su Andrews, *Japan's Emerging Role as an Asian-Pacific Power*. Master's thesis, Naval Postgraduate School, Monterey, California, June 1986, p. 43.

17. Daniel Sneider, "US and Japan Join in Military Maneuvers," *Far Eastern Economic Review*, November 13, 1986, p. 36. See also Edward Olsen,

"Security in the Sea of Japan," *Journal of Northeast Asian Studies* (5, 4), Winter 1986.

18. Denis Warner, "It is Always Hotter Closer to the Fire," *Pacific Defence Reporter*, June 1986; p. 21.

19. *Asahi*, 28 August 1987, and *Sankei*, 29 August 1987.

20. Paul Keal, "Japan's Role in U.S. Strategy in the Pacific," *The Strategic and Defence Studies Center* (Canberra: The Research School of Pacific Studies, Australian National University, Working paper No. 106, October 1986), pp. 5–9. Also see Sheldon W. Simon, "Is There a Japanese Regional Security Role?" *Journal of Northeast Asian Studies* (5, 2), Summer 1986, pp. 30–52.

21. Paul Keal, "Japan's role in U.S. Strategy in the Pacific," p. 9.

22. Address by Assistant Secretary of Defense Richard Armitage to the National Defense University Pacific Symposium, Washington, D.C., 25 February, 1988: "The U.S. Security Role in East Asia," p. 6.

23. Address by Assistant Secretary of Defense Richard Armitage to the Pacific and Asian Affairs Council, Honolulu, 17 January, 1986, p. 3.

24. Research Institute for Peace and Security (Tokyo) *Asian Security, 1986* (London: Brassey's Defence Publishers, 1986), pp. 179–181. See also Frank Langdon, "The Security Debate in Japan," *Pacific Affairs* (58, 3), Fall 1985, pp. 397–410.

25. Tsuneo Akaha, "Japan's Response to Threats of Shipping Disruptions in Southeast Asia and the Middle East," *Pacific Affairs* (59, 2), Summer 1986, pp. 272–273. Also see *Asahi Evening News*, 9 November 1987.

26. Yatsuhiro Nakagawa, "Japan's New Role in East Asia/Pacific Collective Security, *Asian Survey* (24, 8), August 1984, pp. 832–835.

27. See, for example, Edward A. Olsen, "Security in Northeast Asia: A Trilateral Alternative," Naval War College Review, January–February 1985, and "Stability and Instability in the Sea of Japan" in Lawrence E. Grinter and Young W. Kihl, eds., *East Asian Conflict Zones: Prospects for Regional Stability and Deescalation* (New York; St. Martins Press, 1987), pp. 82–85, 90–94.

28. Selig Harrison, "A Divided Seoul," *Foreign Policy* (67), Summer 1987, pp. 172ff.

29. Edward A. Olsen, "A U.S. Perspective on Northeast Asian Security." Paper presented to the annual meeting of the International Studies Association, Washington, D.C., April 1987); pp. 35–45.

30. Sheldon W. Simon, "ASEAN's Strategic Situation," *Pacific Affairs*, Spring 1987, v. 60, no. 1 (Spring 1987); F.A. Mediansky, "The U.S. Military Facilities in the Philippines," *Contemporary Southeast Asia* (8, 4), March 1987; William R. Feeney, "The United States and the Philippines: The Bases Dilemma," *Asian Affairs* (10, 4), Winter 1984; and Lawrence E. Grinter, *The Philippine Bases: Continuing Utility in a Changing Strategic Context* (Washington, National Defense University, February 1980).

31. Feeney, *Ibid.*, p. 71 and *Background on the Bases*, Second Edition, United States Information Service, 1987, Manila.

32. See the excellent discussion in William R. Feeney, "Countdown to 1991: The Philippine Insurgency and the U.S. Bases." Paper presented to the

Strategic Studies Institute, U.S. Army War College, Carlisle Barracks, 29–30 April, 1987.

33. A good discussion of the Manglapus initiative is found in Donald Weatherbee, "Looking Through the ASEAN End of the Telescope." Paper presented to the National Defense University Symposium on Pacific Basin Security, Washington, D.C., 25–26 February 1988, pp. 15–16.

34. William Feeney, "Countdown to 1991," pp. 5–8.

35. *Ibid.*, p. 16.

36. Sophie Quinn-Judge, "A Bear Hug for ASEAN," *Far Eastern Economic Review*, 3 March, 1988; pp. 16–17.

37. This argument is expanded in Sheldon W. Simon, *The Future of Asian-Pacific Security Collaboration* (Lexington, MA: Lexington Books, 1988). Also see Grinter and Kihl, *East Asian Conflict Zones*, p. 219.

38. Charles E. Morrison, *Japan, the United States, and a Changing Southeast Asia* (Lanham, MD: The University Press of America for The Asia Society, 1985), pp. 58–59.

39. See the discussion in J.N. Mak, *Directions for Greater Defence Co-Operation* (Kuala Lumpur: Institute for Strategic and International Studies, 1986), p. 5. Also see Donald E. Weatherbee, "ASEAN: Patterns of National and Regional Resilience," in Young Whan Kihl and Lawrence E. Grinter, eds., *Asian-Pacific Security: Emerging Challenges and Responses* (Boulder, CO: Lynne Reinner Publishers, 1986).

40. G. Jacobs, "ASEAN Needs to Improve Maritime Surveillance," *Pacific Defence Reporter* (13, 12), June 1987; pp. 7–12. Also see Sheldon W. Simon, "Issues and Regional Security" in William Dowdy and Rusell Trood, eds., *The Indian Ocean: Perspectives on a Strategic Region* (Durham, NC: Duke University Press, 1985), pp. 377–393.

41. A balanced assessment of the Dibb Report may be found in Andrew Mack, "Defence versus Offence: the Debate Over Australia's Defence Policy." Paper presented to the annual meeting of the International Studies Association, 15–18 April 1987, Washington, D.C.

42. A good review of the Defence White Paper is written by Ian Hamilton in the *Pacific Defence Reporter* (13, 10), April 1987, pp. 19–26.

43. Frank C. Langdon, "Challenges to the Old Order in the South Pacific," *Pacific Affairs*, 1988. Forthcoming.

44. Melbourne Overseas Service, 20 February 1987, in FBIS *Daily Report, Asia-Pacific*, 25 February, 1987, M3–M4.

45. Hamish McDonald, "Have Gun, Will Travel," *Far Eastern Economic Review*, 10 march, 1988; pp. 33 and 35.

46. Melbourne Overseas Service, 19 March, 1987 in Foreign Broadcasting Information Service, *Daily Report, Asia-Pacific* 20 March, 1987, pp. M3–M4.

47. Thomas Durell-Young, "Australia Can't Fill U.S. Shoes," *Pacific Defence Reporter* (13, 12), June 1987, pp. 49, 50, 55.

48. *Asian Security*, 1986, pp. 140–141.

49. *Pravda*, 23 July, 1987, in FBIS, *Daily Report-Soviet Union*, 23 July, 1987, p. CC5.

50. Hamish McDonald, "The Cam Ranh Bugbear," *Far Eastern Economic*

Review, 18 June, 1987, pp. 34–35.

51. Edward Ok Su Andrews, *Japan's Emerging Role as an Asian-Pacific Power*, p. 88.

52. James Clad, "The Bases are Loaded," *Far Eastern Economic Review*, 8 August 1987, p. 16.

Part 2
Northeast Asia

5

China: Coping with the Evolving Strategic Environment

ROBERT SUTTER

There is no consensus among specialists as to which factors—internal or international—are more important at any given time in determining the course of Chinese foreign and security policy. Thus, there is no agreement as to whether Chinese policy tends to be more reactive to outside events or tends to evolve as a result of forces inside China. Some analysts have tried to bridge the gap between those specialists who stress foreign determinants and those who stress domestic ones in Chinese foreign and security policy. Some point to "policy packages" of mutually reinforcing and compatible foreign and domestic policies advocated by a particular group of leaders, and note how these leaders fare in promoting their approaches in the face of opposition from other leaders with competing foreign-domestic policy arrangements. Others have tried to isolate those aspects of Chinese foreign and security policy (e.g., certain aspects of security policy) that are more likely to be reactive to international pressures from those foreign policy concerns (opening Chinese society to Western economic contact) that are more likely to be affected by Chinese domestic determinants.[1]

The record of Chinese foreign and security policy since the late 1960s has shown a fairly consistent Chinese effort to deal with often difficult changes in the strategic environment surrounding China. It depicts China emerging from a period of serious dislocation and ideological excess during the violent stage of the Cultural Revolution and its attendant Red Guard "diplomacy." Faced with dangerous international circumstances, Beijing felt compelled to begin a more conventional and rational balance-of-power approach to foreign affairs that would shore up its national security and foreign-policy interests, and ensure a more favorable environment for restoring disrupted political order inside China and pursuing the development of national wealth and power. Key aspects of this balance-of-power approach involved the perceived power and policies of the Soviet Union and the United States.[2]

Moscow's persisting military buildup and search for greater political influence around China's periphery have represented the strategic center of gravity for Chinese foreign and defense policy since the late 1960s. Despite their background or ideological inclinations, top-level Chinese leaders were forced by Soviet actions to focus their foreign policy on how to deal effectively with Soviet military threat and political intimidation without compromising Chinese security and sovereignty or mortgaging Chinese aspirations for independence and development. Initially, Chinese leaders came up with strikingly different approaches, leading in the late 1960s to the most serious leadership dispute over foreign and security policy in the history of the People's Republic of China (PRC).[3]

The death of Defense Minister Lin Biao and the purge of a large segment of the Chinese military high command in 1971 markedly reduced the political importance of Chinese leadership differences over how to handle the Soviet Union. From that time on, China developed a fairly consistent strategy, at first under the leadership of Premier Zhou Enlai and Chairman Mao Zedong, and later under Deng Xiaoping. It attempted to use East-West differences pragmatically to China's advantage. Chinese leaders recognized that China— only at tremendous cost and great risk—could confront the Soviet Union on its own. It relied heavily on international counterweights to Soviet power, provided mainly by the United States and its allies and associates. As the United States reevaluated its former containment policy directed against China and no longer posed a serious military threat to Chinese security, Beijing maintained a collaborative relationship with the United States and the West as a key link in Chinese security policy against the USSR.

Meanwhile, Chinese internal policy increasingly focused on economic development and modernization. Chinese leaders, especially in the post-Mao period, saw that these goals would be best achieved through closer economic relations with the West. The United States, Japan, and other noncommunist developed states had the markets, technology, managerial expertise, and financial resources that were seen as crucial in speeding up and streamlining China's heretofore troubled modernization efforts so as to increase material benefit to the Chinese people and thereby sustain their political loyalty and support.

This simple outline of a framework for recent Chinese foreign and defense policy clearly portrays China as often reactive to the actions of foreign powers, especially the Soviet Union and the United States. It shows that Chinese leaders were well aware of China's internal weaknesses and wished to remedy those flaws through a prolonged effort at economic modernization. In the meantime, these leaders recognized that China needs to secure its international environment in order to focus energies internally. They also recognized that although China influences the situation around it in the Asian-Pacific region to some degree, the USSR, the United States, and their friends and allies exert far greater influence there. As a result, China was forced repeatedly to adjust to perceived changes in the surrounding international situation.

Indeed, the record shows that many of the changes in Chinese policy during this period were caused chiefly by Chinese reactions to perceived shifts in the international balance of forces and influence affecting Chinese security and development. Salient examples include:[4]

1. *August 1968.* The Soviet invasion of Czechoslovakia and Moscow's subsequent announcement of the so-called Brezhnev doctrine of limited sovereignty caused China to view the recently expanded Soviet military presence along the Sino-Soviet border in a more ominous light. It prompted at least some Chinese leaders to advocate a more activist, conventional Chinese approach to foreign affairs in order to enhance Chinese international leverage in the face of Soviet power.

2. *August 1969.* Six months of Sino-Soviet military conflict along the frontier reached a climax as the largest Sino-Soviet border clash on record resulted in a serious Chinese military defeat and was followed by Soviet warnings of possible military "preventive strikes" against China. This pressure tipped the scales in the ongoing policy debate in Beijing against those, led by Lin Biao, who held out for uncompromising opposition to the Soviet Union. China eventually favored a tactically more flexible posture advocated by Premier Zhou. The fruits of Zhou's efforts were seen in the use of Sino-Soviet talks and Chinese diplomatic maneuvers, along with Chinese defense preparations, to deal with Soviet pressure. Zhou's strategy included the start of Sino-U.S. diplomatic contacts focused on the two sides' common opposition to Soviet attempts at dominance in Asia—contacts that led directly to President Nixon's landmark visit to China.

3. *1975.* The rapid collapse of U.S.-supported governments in Indochina prompted China to adopt a much more active approach throughout East Asia in order to shore up a united front against the perceived danger of Soviet expansion around China's periphery as the United States withdrew.

   Concurrent signs of U.S. weakness seen in the face of growing Soviet military power and in breakthroughs by both countries in negotiating East-West accords over arms control and European security caused China to raise vocal opposition to U.S.-Soviet détente to unprecedented heights. In the process, China underlined its keen suspicion that Western accommodation with Moscow would allow the Soviets a free hand to deal with China.

4. *1978.* Soviet gains in the Third World, especially the areas of direct importance to China (i.e., Vietnam), enhanced Chinese interest in fostering a common front with the United States, Japan, and other

Western states against the USSR. Prospects for such cooperation increased as opinion in the U.S. government gradually shifted from the view that gave priority to U.S.-Soviet arms control (advocated by Secretary of State Cyrus Vance) to the view that advocated confronting Soviet expansion in sensitive Third World areas (favored by National Security Adviser Zbigniew Brzezinski).

5. *April 1979.* China's efforts to confront Soviet expansion focused on Vietnam and led to direct Chinese military intervention; that intervention produced mixed results for Chinese interests and left Beijing dangerously exposed in the face of increasing Soviet military pressure. Chinese leaders were compelled to change tactics, moderate their anti-Soviet stance, and open a political dialogue with Moscow in order to manage the danger of Soviet military power.

6. *January 1980.* The Soviet invasion of Afghanistan and stiffened Western resolve to Soviet expansion prompted China to change direction again: China reverted to a firmly anti-Soviet posture and suspended talks with the USSR.

7. *1981 to 1982.* A Chinese perceived shift in the international balance of power against the Soviet Union, and a revival of U.S. power and determination against the USSR under the Reagan administration gave China more freedom to maneuver. These changes allowed China to distance itself from the Reagan administration over Taiwan and Third World and other issues, reopen talks with the Soviet Union, and adopt an ostensibly more independent posture in foreign affairs.

8. *1983 to 1984.* Beijing's growing concern over a projected long-term downturn in Sino-U.S. relations at a time of increasing Soviet pressure on China prompted China's leaders to compromise for a time. They modified their hard line on sensitive bilateral disputes with the United States in order to solidify relations with the Reagan administration in preparation for a period of difficult relations with the USSR.

9. *1984 to 1985.* Following consolidation of relations with the United States, Beijing was in a good position to respond in a forthcoming way to the rise of power of the Gorbachev leadership in the USSR, thereby attempting to encourage Moscow to curb its military buildup in Asia and its pressure against China.

Despite such repeated examples of reactive Chinese foreign and security policy, especially with regard to perceived changes in the international balance of power affecting Chinese interests in Asia, there are instances that vividly demonstrate that wellsprings of particular Chinese policies also lie within China. For one thing, Chinese views of their surroundings and the international balance of power are filtered through lenses colored by Chinese history, culture, and ideology. The strength and unity of China's political leadership has had a profound effect as to whether or not China can take the initiative in international security affairs or merely respond to international circumstances. Domestic demands for economic development, military modernization, and political control often have had a vital impact on the course of such Chinese decisionmaking. Meanwhile, Chinese leaders have demonstrated a desire to manipulate international events and to maneuver more freely among competing outside pressures in order to enhance their particular interests within China, especially their leadership standing.

Key examples of such domestic determinants influencing the course of Chinese foreign policy since the late 1960s include:[5]

1. *February to August 1969.* Intense competition for political power in China led to the debate over competing approaches to international developments, especially concerning relations with the United States and the Soviet Union. Lin Biao and others advocating a tough line toward both powers were able to reverse the opening to the United States initiated by Zhou Enlai and other leaders a few months earlier calling for revived political discussions with the United States. They succeeded in following their hard line posture for seven months.

2. *1973 to 1974.* Leadership conflict over internal political and development questions rose during the intense political campaign against Confucius and Lin Biao. The campaign spilled over into foreign policy, resulting in an across-the-board toughening of China's approach to the Soviet Union, the United States, and their allies and associates, and a cutback in China's interest in greater economic and cultural contacts with the West.

3. *1976 to 1977.* Beijing's preoccupation with post-Mao leadership transition and major economic problems resulted in a much less active Chinese approach to most foreign issues, even those having a direct bearing on China's security, such as increasing Soviet-Vietnamese collaboration.

4. *1979.* Some Chinese leaders questioned China's previous emphasis on establishing close ties with the West in order to better confront the USSR. They stressed China's need for "breathing space" in competition with the USSR, emphasized that defense modernization would have to be prolonged for the sake of speeding higher priority economic modernization, and wished to reestablish China's flagging ties with the developing countries and the international communist movement. For a time, they were successful in advocating an easing of Chinese confrontation with the USSR and a cutback in China's developing strategic alignment with the United States and the West.[6]

5. *1981 to 1982.* These same leadership concerns helped push China to reassert its policy independence of the United States, adopting in the process a more balanced stance between the superpowers and

adhering more closely to Chinese nationalistic principles on such sensitive issues as Taiwan.

DETERMINANTS OF RECENT
CHINESE FOREIGN AND SECURITY POLICY

In assessing the relative importance of the strategic environment and domestic developments in the recent Chinese approach to international security affairs, the scales appear to tip decidedly in favor of strategic factors. In effect, the two sets of factors appear to interact in the following manner.

The objectives of Chinese foreign and security policy have been determined by a small group of top-level Chinese leaders who have reflected the broad interests of the Chinese state as well as their own parochial concerns. In the past, Mao Zedong, Zhou Enlai, and other senior leaders exerted overriding control over foreign policy. In recent years, there has been an increase in the number of officials involved in advising about Chinese foreign policy, but key decisions remain the preserve of a small group of leaders, especially Deng Xiaoping.[7]

The primary concerns of these leaders have been to guarantee Chinese national security, maintain internal order, and pursue economic development. The top priority of Chinese leaders, especially since the death of Mao in 1976, has been to promote successful economic modernization. This development represents the linchpin determining the success or failure of their leadership. Thus, Chinese officials have geared China's foreign and security policy to help the modernization effort.[8]

In order to accomplish economic modernization as well as to maintain national security and internal order, Chinese leaders recognize the fundamental prerequisite of establishing a relatively stable strategic environment, especially around China's periphery in Asia. The alternative would be a highly disruptive situation requiring much greater Chinese expenditure on national defense and posing greater danger to Chinese domestic order and tranquility. Unfortunately for China, it does not control this environment. Despite some Chinese influence, the environment remains controlled more by others, especially the superpowers and their allies and associates. As a result, China's leaders have been required repeatedly to assess their surroundings for changes that could affect Chinese security and development interests. They have been compelled repeatedly to adjust Chinese policy to take account of such changes.

At the same time, Chinese leaders also have nationalistic and ideological objectives regarding irredentist claims (e.g., Taiwan). They have a desire to stand independently as a leading force among "progressive" nations of the Third World. These goals have struck a responsive chord politically inside China. Occasional leadership discussion and debate over these and other questions regarding foreign and defense policy have sometimes had an effect on the course of Chinese policy. Since the early 1970s, the debates have become progressively less serious, and the policy differences raised in these debates have become more moderate and less of a challenge to the recent dominant objective of national development and security.

Thus, China's top foreign and defense policy priority has remained the pragmatic quest for a stable environment needed for effective modernization and development. Since 1969, Chinese leaders have seen the main source of negative change in the surrounding environment as the Soviet Union. At first, China saw Soviet power as an immediate threat to its national security. Over time, it came to see the USSR progressively as more of a long-term threat, determined to use its growing military power and other sources of influence to encircle and pressure China into accepting a balance of influence in Asia dominated by the USSR and contrary to PRC interests.[9]

China's strategy against the Soviet danger has been both bilateral and global. Bilaterally, China has used a mix of military preparations, political discussions, economic and cultural exchanges, and other interaction to keep the Soviets from pressuring China while gaining whatever material or technological advantage it can from its neighbor to the north. China also uses such interchange to encourage the USSR to moderate its military-backed expansion around China's periphery in Asia. Globally, China's strategy has focused on developing—either implicitly or explicitly—an international united front designed to halt Soviet expansion and prevent the consolidation of Soviet dominance abroad. During the 1970s, China focused explicitly on developing such a front. In recent years, the perceived immediate threat from the USSR has lessened, and Chinese leaders are satisfied with an implicit anti-Soviet arrangement focused on areas of Asia of greatest concern to China, notably Cambodia.

As the most important international counterweight to Soviet power, the United States has loomed large in Chinese calculations. Under terms of the Nixon Doctrine announced in 1969, the United States seemed determined to withdraw from its past policy of containing China in Asia, and thereby ended a perceived U.S. threat to China's national security. In response, the PRC was prepared to start the process of Sino-U.S. normalization. The process has been complemented in recent years by China's enhanced interest in pragmatic economic modernization, which has emphasized the importance of technical and financial help from abroad and access to foreign markets.

Thus, China views the United States as economically important, not only for its own sake; it also sees the United States influencing Japan, West European countries, noncommunist countries in East Asia, and international financial institutions to provide the economic aid, markets, and technical assistance needed to promote Chinese economic modernization. In recent years, China also has broadened its economic interchange with the Soviet bloc, and Sino-Soviet trade has grown more rapidly (from a much lower base) than Sino-U.S. trade. But no leader in China has suggested that contacts with the Soviet bloc could rival the importance to China of economic interchange with the noncommunist, technically advanced nations led by the United States.

Closer Chinese ties with the United States have continued to be complicated by Chinese nationalistic and ideological concerns over Taiwan, policy in the Third World, and other questions, as well as by fundamental differences between the social-political and economic systems of the United States and the PRC. Most notably, U.S. support for Taiwan is seen as a continued affront to China's national sovereignty. But Chinese leaders have differentiated between substantive threats to their security, posed by continued enhancement of Soviet military power and military-backed influence around China's periphery in Asia, and threats to their sense of national sovereignty, posed by U.S. support for Taiwan.[10]

In short, China has worked hard, and continues to do so, to ensure that its strategic environment, endangered mainly by Soviet power, remains stable so that it can focus on economic modernization. The USSR is seen as having a strategy of expansion that uses military power and other means in order to achieve political influence and dominance throughout its periphery. China has long held that the focus of Soviet attention is in Europe but that NATO's strength requires Moscow to work in other areas, notably the Middle East, Southwest Asia, Africa, and East Asia, in order to outflank the Western defenses. China is seen as relatively low on Moscow's list of military priorities, although Chinese leaders clearly appreciate the dire consequences for the PRC should the USSR be able to consolidate its position elsewhere and then focus its strength to intimidate China.[11]

The ascendancy of the new Gorbachev leadership in the USSR has prompted some Chinese commentators to note the possibility of a major change in Soviet policy in Asia. Of course, a substantial shift in the Soviet pressure on China would have a corresponding impact on calculations that have governed Chinese policy since the late 1960s. Thus far, however, the Soviets have only begun to address the so-called "three obstacles" that Beijing says lie at the heart of its security concerns vis-à-vis the USSR. These involve Soviet support for Vietnam's occupation of Cambodia, Soviet military occupation of Afghanistan, and the buildup of Soviet forces along the Sino-Soviet and Sino-Mongolian borders. In particular, Moscow carried out a token withdrawal from Afghanistan, withdrew one of its several divisions in Mongolia, and promised to remove SS-20 missiles from Asia as part of the Intermediate Nuclear Forces (INF) agreement with the United States signed in December 1987.

As a result, China's strategy of deterrence and defense continues to depend on international opposition to Soviet expansion, and raises the possibility of the Soviet Union facing a multifront conflict in the event it attempts to pressure or intimidate China. Chinese leaders see their nation's cooperation with the United States as especially important in strengthening deterrence of the Soviet Union and in aggravating Soviet strategic vulnerabilities. Beijing also encourages anti-Soviet efforts by so-called Second World, developed countries—most of which are formal allies of the United States—and by Third World developing countries. the intensity of such Chinese efforts has varied, with more intense efforts accompanying Chinese perception of more immediate danger from the USSR. At the same time, Beijing uses a mix of political talks, bilateral exchanges, and other forms of dialogue to help manage the danger posed by the much more powerful USSR.

Within this overall strategy to establish a stable environment in Asia, Chinese leaders have employed a varying mix of tactics to secure their interests. These depend on such international variables as the perceived strength and intentions of the superpowers, and Chinese domestic variables, such as leadership cohesion or disarray. For example, when Chinese leaders have judged that their strategic surroundings are at least temporarily stable, they have seen less immediate need for close ties with the United States; they have felt more free to adopt strident policies on Taiwan and other nationalistic issues that appeal to domestic constituencies but offend the United States. (This type of logic was in part responsible for China's tougher approach to the United States over Taiwan and other issues between 1981 and 1983.) But when the Chinese leaders have judged that such tactics could seriously alienate the United States and thereby endanger the stability of China's environment, they have put them aside in the interest of preserving peaceful surroundings. (Such reasoning is seen by some as having undergirded much of China's moderation in its approach to the United States in 1983 and 1984).[12]

In short, therefore, Beijing's first priority in foreign and security affairs is to secure a stable environment in Asia that will allow internal reform and modernization to proceed smoothly. The recent record shows that other factors influencing Chinese policy (domestic politics, ideology, and nationalistic goals, for example) have not been allowed to upset seriously China's continued efforts to deal pragmatically with the Asian balance, especially the superpowers' influence in Asia, from what is clearly seen as a position of relative weakness. The result is a Chinese policy in Asia that is quite responsive to and dependent upon Soviet and U.S. actions in the region.

CHINA'S CHANGING CALCULUS
IN THE GREAT POWER TRIANGLE IN ASIA

China's changing response to the great power relations was amply illustrated by the adjustments in China's "independent" stance in foreign affairs in 1983 and 1984.[13] At that time, Beijing moved to halt the decline in Sino-U.S.

relations and attempted to consolidate relations with the Reagan administration on an anti-Soviet basis.

The changes in Chinese policy were based largely on perceptions of shifts in the international balance of power affecting China. Chinese leaders became increasingly concerned about the stability of the nation's surroundings at a time of unrelenting buildup of Soviet military and political pressure along China's periphery. They also were concerned about what they considered a serious and perhaps prolonged decline in relations with the United States. Chinese leaders decided that the foreign policy tactics of the previous two years, designed to distance China from the policies of the United States and to moderate and improve relations with the Soviet Union, were less likely to safeguard the important Chinese security and development concerns affected by the stability of the Asian environment. They recognized in particular that Beijing would have to stop its pullback from the United States for fear of jeopardizing the maintenance of China's security and development interests in the face of persistent Soviet pressure in Asia. Thus, in 1983, Beijing began to retreat from some of the previous tactical changes made under the rubric of an independent approach to international and security affairs. The result was a substantial reduction in Chinese pressure on the United States concerning Taiwan and other issues; increased Chinese interest and flexibility in dealing with the Reagan administration and other Western countries across a broad range of economic, political, and security issues; and heightened Sino-Soviet antipathy.

By employing such foreign policy tactics effectively, Beijing was able to secure its concerns without substantially disrupting efforts to modernize internally. Thus, economic reforms continued to receive high priority as military modernization received relatively low priority. Plans to streamline and reduce the size of the Chinese army could move ahead; these plans held out the hope that overall defense spending could be held down and that selective modernization of military equipment and organization could be funded by savings generated by a cutback in personnel and other related expenses.[14]

The key element in China's decision to move toward the United States was an altered Chinese view of the likely course of Sino-U.S.-Soviet relations over the next several years. When China began its more independent approach to international events and its concurrent harder line toward the United States in 1981 and 1982, it had hoped to elicit a more forthcoming U.S. attitude toward issues sensitive to Chinese interests, notably Taiwan. Beijing almost certainly knew that there were serious risks to be incurred by alienating the United States, which had provided an implicit but vital counterweight against the USSR for more than a decade and had assisted more recent Chinese economic development concerns. But the Chinese seemed to have assessed that their room for maneuver had increased because the United States had reasserted a balance of East-West relations likely to lead to a continued major check on possible Soviet expansion. In addition, the Soviet ability to pressure China had appeared to be at least temporarily blocked by U.S. power as well as by Soviet domestic and international problems. At least some important U.S. leaders continued to place a high strategic value on preserving good U.S. relations with China as an important element in U.S. efforts to confront and contain Soviet expansion.

By mid-1983, China saw these calculations upset. In particular, the United States adopted a new posture that publicly downgraded China's strategic importance to the United States.[15] U.S. planners now appeared to consider improved relations with China less important than in the recent past because:

1. China seemed unlikely to cooperate further with the United States (through military sales, security consultations, etc.) against the Soviet Union at a time when the PRC had publicly distanced itself from the United States and had reopened talks on normalization of relations with the USSR.

2. At the same time, China's continued preoccupation with pragmatic economic modernization and internal development made it appear unlikely that the PRC would revert to a highly disruptive position in East Asia that would adversely affect U.S. interests in the stability of the region.

3. China's demands regarding Taiwan and other bilateral disputes and Beijing's accompanying threats to downgrade U.S.-China relations if its demands were not met appeared open-ended and excessive.

4. U.S. ability to deal militarily and politically with the USSR had improved, particularly as a result of the large-scale Reagan administration military budget increases and perceived serious internal and international difficulties of the USSR.

5. For the first time in years, U.S. allies were working more closely with Washington to deal with the Soviet military threat. This was particularly true in Asia where Japan's Prime Minister Nakasone took positions and initiatives underlining common Japanese-U.S. concerns against the Soviet danger.

6. Japan and U.S. allies and friends in Southeast Asia—unlike China—appeared more immediately important to the United States in protecting against what was seen as the primary U.S. strategic concern in the region: safeguarding air and sea access to East Asia, the Indian Ocean, and the Persian Gulf from Soviet attack. By contrast, China did not appear as important in dealing with this perceived Soviet danger.

In effect, the U.S. shift meant that Chinese ability to exploit U.S. interest in strategic relations with China, in order to compel the United States to meet Chinese demands on Taiwan and other questions, had been sharply reduced. Underlining this trend for China was the continued unwillingness of the United States throughout this period to accommodate high-level PRC pressure over Taiwan, the case of Hu Na, the tennis player who sought political asylum while on tour in the United States, the Chinese representation issue in the Asian Development Bank, and other questions.

Moreover, Beijing perceived its political leverage in the United States to be small. Chinese press reports noted the strong revival in the U.S. economy in 1983 and the positive political implications this had for President Reagan's reelection campaign.[16] China also had to be aware through contacts with leading Democrats, notably Speaker of the House Tip O'Neill, that Beijing could expect little change in U.S. policy toward Taiwan under a Democratic administration.[17]

Meanwhile, although Sino-Soviet trade, cultural, and technical contacts were increasing, Beijing saw little sign of Soviet willingness to compromise basic political and security issues during the vice foreign ministerial talks begun in October 1982. The Soviet military buildup in Asia—including the deployment of highly accurate SS-20 intermediate-range missiles—continued unabated.

In short, Beijing faced the prospect of a period of prolonged decline in Sino-U.S. relations which could last until the end of Reagan's second presidential term if it continued to follow the hard line of 1986-1988. This decline ran the risk of cutting off the implicit but vitally important Chinese strategic understanding with the United States in the face of a prolonged danger posed by the USSR.

China's incentive to accommodate the United States was reinforced by Beijing's somber view of Sino-Soviet relations. Disappointed with China's inability to elicit substantial Soviet concessions—or even a slackening in the pace of Soviet military expansion in Asia—during the Andropov administration, Beijing saw the Chernenko government as even more rigid and uncompromising. In response, China hardened its line and highlighted public complaints against Soviet pressure and intimidation—an approach that had the added benefit of broadening common ground between China and the West, especially the Reagan administration.

The Sino-Soviet vice foreign ministerial talks,[18] revived in October 1982, met semiannually, alternating between Beijing and Moscow. Although some progress was made on secondary issues, these talks were unable to bridge a major gap between the positions of the two sides concerning basic security and political issues. Thus, Beijing stuck to its preconditions for improved Sino-Soviet relations: withdrawal of Soviet forces from the Sino-Soviet border and Mongolia (later China added specific reference to Soviet SS-20 missiles targeted against China), end of Soviet support for Vietnam's occupation of Cambodia, and withdrawal of Soviet forces from Afghanistan. Beijing sometimes said that Soviet movement on only one of these questions would substantially open the way to improved Sino-Soviet relations, but Moscow remained unwilling to compromise, stating that the USSR would not discuss matters affecting third countries.

In part to get around this roadblock, a second channel of vice foreign ministerial discussions began in September 1983. Progress in both sets of talks came only in secondary areas of trade, technical transfers, and educational cultural exchanges. Both sides attempted to give added impetus to progress in these areas coincident with the exchange of high-level Sino-U.S. visits in early 1984. In particular, Moscow proposed, and Beijing accepted, a visit to China by Soviet First Deputy Prime Minister Arkhipov, reportedly to discuss longer term economic and technical assistance to China.[19]

Nevertheless, both sides proved willing to disrupt these contacts when more important strategic and political issues were at stake. Beijing in particular was disappointed with the new Chernenko regime. China had sent its ranking vice premier, Wan Li, as its representative to the funeral of Andropov in February 1984—marking a substantial upgrading from Beijing's dispatch of Foreign Minister Huang Hua to Brezhnev's funeral in 1982. But Wan received only a cool welcome in Moscow. Moreover, the Soviets then appeared to go out of their way to publicize strong support for Mongolia and Vietnam against China, and they underlined Soviet unwillingness to make compromises with China at the expense of third countries.

Beijing also saw Moscow resorting to stronger military means in both Europe and Asia in order to assert Soviet power and determination at a time of leadership transition in the Kremlin. Chinese media portrayed Moscow as on the defensive regarding a range of international issues, particularly its failure to halt the deployment of U.S. Pershing and cruise missiles in Western Europe or to exploit the peace movement in Europe as a way to disrupt the Western alliance over the deployments and other issues. They now saw Moscow—faced with ever-growing Western military power and greater solidarity in the face of the Soviet threat—as lashing out with new demonstrations of Soviet military power.[20] In Asia, this perceived Soviet approach directly affected Chinese security and ultimately appeared designed to bring China to heel. Thus, in February and March 1983, the Soviet Union deployed two of its three aircraft carriers to the Western Pacific; one transited near China in late February on its way to Vladivostok.[21] In March, the USSR used an aircraft carrier task force to support its first joint amphibious exercise with Vietnam, which was conducted fairly close to China and near the Vietnamese port city of Haiphong. This followed the reported stationing of several Soviet medium bombers at Cam Ranh Bay in Vietnam in late 1983—the first time such Soviet forces were reported stationed outside areas contiguous with the USSR.[22]

Meanwhile, the Chinese escalated their military pressure against the Vietnamese—taking their strongest action precisely at the time of President Reagan's visit to China in late April and early May 1984. The result was the most serious downturn in Sino-Soviet relations since the Soviet invasion of Afghanistan in late 1979. Both Moscow and Beijing revived polemical exchanges, trading particular charges over issues involving sensitive security issues in Asia, East-West arms control in Europe, and the international communist movement. Their bilateral diplomatic dialogue was disrupted for a time, as the USSR—presumably concerned and irritated by China's closer relations with the United States and tougher posture toward Vietnam—postponed for an indefinite time the visit of First Deputy Prime Minister Arkhipov to China. Sino-Vietnamese military confrontation along their common border continued into the summer of 1984, well beyond the usual period of fighting coincident with the annual Vietnamese dry-season campaign against Chinese-supported resistance forces in Cambodia. Sino-Soviet political competition heated up in Korea as both sides maneuvered to improve relations with Kim Il-sung and his successors. In particular, Moscow welcomed Kim Il-sung in May—the Korean leader's first visit to the USSR since 1961. At the same time, Beijing continued to move ahead in establishing closer economic and military ties with the United States despite the absence of ostensibly balancing progress in Sino-Soviet relations.

China was still anxious to manage the Soviet threat without recourse to force, however. It held out the option of resumed Sino-Soviet border talks: Hu Yaobang reportedly told visitors that a border settlement could be reached with relative ease.[23] China agreed to remark frontier lines with the Soviet satellite, Mongolia, and agreed to set up joint economic commissions to discuss economic exchanges with Moscow's close East European allies. Moscow, of course, had long proposed renewed border delineation agreements and the establishment of similar joint economic commissions with China. Beijing also said that it was willing to receive Arkhipov whenever the USSR would send him, and it was also willing to conduct foreign ministerial consultations with the Soviets during the U.N. General Assembly in September.

Moscow moved to respond to the Chinese gestures and to resume forward movement in the less-sensitive economic and technical areas. The Soviets sent Arkhipov to China in late December. He was warmly received and signed three economic agreements that would provide for a broad array of economic cooperation, including the exchange of production technology, the construction and revamping of industrial enterprises, and technical training and exchanges of experts and scientific data under the supervision of a new Sino-Soviet economic trade, scientific, and technological cooperation committee. It was announced that the two countries would sign a five-year trade agreement and that their trade level in 1985 would be 60 percent greater than their trade in 1984.

PROSPECTS AND IMPLICATIONS FOR ASIA AND THE PACIFIC

The advent of the Gorbachev administration has recently brought unprecedented flexibility to Soviet foreign policy in Asia that could have a major effect on future Chinese policy in the region. Not only is the Soviet leader offering China and other Asian countries a complex array of economic, political, and security initiatives, he has taken the first meaningful steps to address what Beijing sees as the core of its dispute with the USSR—the Soviet military ring around China's periphery. Thus, the Soviets have withdrawn one division from Mongolia, pledged to destroy their 200 SS-20 missiles in Asia, and, at the time this book went to press, were withdrawing their troops from Afghanistan.

Chinese leaders thus far have responded cautiously to Gorbachev's initiatives. They have pointedly rebuffed his more prominent initiatives, such as his call for a Sino-Soviet "summit" meeting with Deng Xiaoping, until the USSR moves to encourage Vietnam to withdraw from Cambodia. At bottom, Chinese officials, like other outside observers, are uncertain as to the future course of Soviet policy in Asia. They see it as potentially volatile in large measure because it reflects a serious contradiction. On one hand, Soviet leaders do not want to give up the gains the USSR has made as a result of its military-backed expansion in Asia over the past twenty years. Thus, the USSR continues to modernize its land, sea, and air forces along China's northern border and in the Western Pacific, to support Vietnam's occupation of Cambodia, and to deploy forces out of Cam Ranh Bay. In addition, Soviet leaders continue to be willing to use military power to exploit targets of opportunity that emerge from time to time. Thus, Moscow has used military aid to obtain overflight rights in North Korea and to improve its position, relative to the PRC, in Pyongyang.[24]

On the other hand, Soviet leaders are increasingly aware that these military actions are of great concern to the PRC, Japan, and other Asian countries; increase anti-Soviet feeling to a point where these states are very reluctant to respond positively to Soviet overtures for improved relations unless Moscow takes some actions to reduce its perceived military threat; and prompt these Asian states to work more closely with the United States in order to offset the perceived danger posed by the USSR.

To break out of their relatively isolated position in Asia, Soviet leaders have issued a series of political, economic, and military initiatives designed to reassure and improve relations with East Asian countries, but without giving up recent Soviet military gains. Soviet leader Gorbachev has appeared particularly adroit in using political, economic, and military initiatives in an effort to improve Moscow's diplomatic position. He has focused these efforts on the PRC. Beijing has responded positively to Soviet offers of increased trade, technical assistance, and cultural exchanges. Beijing balances this by continuing to confront Soviet and Soviet-backed forces around China's periphery and by developing closer political, economic, and military ties with the United States and its allies and friends.

Looking to the longer-term future, it appears that Moscow does have the option to promote a major change in PRC policy toward East Asia. The

Soviets could do this by reducing the perceived Soviet threat to China. But in the process, it would appear that Moscow would have to meet at least some of the PRC demands regarding the three obstacles. Yet, significant Soviet movement on the three obstacles could jeopardize important Soviet interests in Indochina, South Asia, and elsewhere. Thus, the key question for Soviet leaders will remain: Would the likely benefit of improved relations with the PRC justify the likely risks associated with movement on the three obstacles?

Meanwhile, China is likely to remain preoccupied internally with major leadership and economic changes into the 1990s. These proposed changes have been set forth in recent Chinese pronouncements promising shifts in the urban economy, party ranks, and the military. It seems logical that under these circumstances, China would not be inclined to upset the prevailing acceptable balance in Asia or otherwise exacerbate tensions along its periphery in ways that would upset the modernization and reform process. China would probably prefer, if possible, to encourage Soviet moderation in Asia and a curb in Moscow's military buildup there.

China's incentive to continue this balanced, relatively moderate approach to security policy issues in Asia will likely be underlined by the continuation of military reforms, including the major cutback in the size of the Chinese armed forces. The resulting savings presumably will be used to modernize Chinese military equipment and thereby make the Chinese armed forces more streamlined and effective over the longer run. But the short-term effect of such changes will likely be a reduction in Beijing's inclination to confront its adversaries militarily and a strengthening of China's reliance on effective diplomacy to meet national-security problems.

Beijing, of course, retains the option of attempting to reach on its own a substantial accommodation with Soviet power in Asia. This path could help China's modernization and reform by reducing the need for extensive defense expenditures to deter Soviet power, thus allowing greater Chinese resources to be applied to economic development. But the Chinese leadership is doubtless aware that any serious Chinese effort to accommodate the USSR in Asia would cause the United States and Japan and their allies and friends in Asia to reassess their policies toward China and would run the risk of leaving China isolated as it dealt with the USSR. Under these circumstances, China almost certainly would risk mortgaging its long-term development and independence to the dictates of Soviet power and influence.

China therefore is unlikely to pursue such a risky course unless it perceives that Soviet leaders are no longer interested in using military power to exert dominating influence over China. The proof of such intent would be seen in Soviet efforts to curb military power in the region. Whether or not the Gorbachev administration will adopt such policies is doubtless a key determinant in the future course of Sino-Soviet relations and China's response to its perceived security threat in the Asian-Pacific region.

IMPLICATIONS AND OPTIONS FOR THE UNITED STATES

The overall result of China's efforts to deal with its strategic environment in the Asian-Pacific area and its concern with domestic political and economic reform is that Chinese foreign and defense policy is likely to remain aligned with the interests of the United States, at least during the next few years. In fact, it seems fair to say that Chinese policy will continue in a direction favorable to U.S. interests.

China probably will continue to work cooperatively and parallel with the United States and its allies and friends in the Asian-Pacific region to keep in check Soviet power and influence in the region. As it has in the past, Beijing will play an important role along the Sino-Soviet and Sino-Vietnamese borders and an indirect role in Indochina (as well as a lesser degree in Afghanistan). At the same time, China will probably continue to use bilateral political, economic and other contacts with the USSR—in part to ensure that Sino-Soviet tensions remain low and do not endanger the stability of the region. Although there remains a concern that the recent Sino-Soviet contacts may develop to a point where they could undermine China's utility as an anti-Soviet counterweight in Asia, the likelihood of that happening appears remote so long as the USSR continues to use strong military power to assert its influence in Asia.

China also appears likely to sustain a moderate approach toward its noncommunist Asian neighbors and to seek closer economic and political ties with them. Many of these states are allies or close associates of the United States that in the past required direct U.S. military support against the "China threat"—notable examples are Thailand and South Korea. In particular, Beijing seems determined to complement its avowed peaceful approach toward Taiwan with recent unprecedented efforts to work with the United States to ease tensions between North and South Korea, something that until recently China had been loathe to do for fear of alienating North Korea.

In general, China can be expected to follow a path toward becoming a greater source of stability in Asia and an important source of economic expansion there. Thus, Chinese economic growth and rapidly expanding foreign economic exchanges have promoted opportunities for U.S. entrepreneurs and those of its friends in Asia and elsewhere to invest and trade with the PRC.

U.S. policymakers may be inclined under these circumstances to follow policies more in accord with Chinese interests. They could:

1. Reduce arms sales and sensitive political contacts with Taiwan in order to help ease this long-standing source of irritation in Sino-U.S. relations;

2. Be more forthcoming with military supplies and economic and technical assistance and supplies. This could include increased

willingness to train Chinese in the United States (there are over 19,000 such students at present), and follow the example of path-breaking U.S. management schools in China (e.g., the Dalien Institute) with additional such institutions;

3. Avoid policies toward the USSR that could be seen by China as endangering the balance of power in Asia so essential to China's ability to focus on internal economic modernization; and

4. Encourage a more forthcoming attitude on the part of other capitalist powers and international financial organizations regarding economic interchange with China. This would involve avoiding restrictions on Chinese imports.

Each of these options, however, has important, potentially negative trade-offs for U.S. interests. Thus, for example, a sharp reduction in arms sales and contacts with Taiwan could be seen as contrary to the Taiwan Relations Act, upsetting to the stability of Taiwan, and damaging to the U.S. reputation as a reliable supporter of allies and friends. U.S. military exchanges with China could unnerve Taiwan and other noncommunist friends in Asia, and might complicate U.S. efforts to reach understandings with the USSR on arms control. More extensive economic exchanges with China could come at the expense of U.S. manufacturers or economic support elsewhere in the developing world. U.S. encouragement of greater Western and U.N. involvement with China might require greater outlay of U.S. aid funds for such endeavors, a potentially unpopular trend at a time of U.S. budget constraint.

As a result, unless the United States sees a greater need to accommodate Chinese interests than it has recently, it is unlikely to make rapid policy changes more favorable to Beijing. A more evolutionary approach, consistent with recent policy, appears more likely as the administration and the U.S. Congress continue to value good relations with China but do not place the heavy emphasis on the importance of those ties, as was done in the late 1970s and early 1980s.

NOTES

The views expressed in this chapter ar the author and not necessarily those of the Congressional Research Service, Library of Congress.

1. This chapter relies heavily on the research conducted by the author for his book entitled *Chinese Foreign Policy Developments After Mao* (New York: Praeger, 1985). Concerning the concept of "policy packages," see Carol Hamrin, "Emergence of an 'Independent' Chinese Foreign Policy and Shifts in Sino-U.S. Relations," in James Hsiung, ed., *U.S.-Asia Relations* (New York: Praeger, 1983). On differentiating between aspects of Chinese foreign and security policy, see Michael Yahuda, *Towards the End of Isolationism: Chine's Foreign Policy After Mao* (New York: St. Martin's Press, 1983).

2. For a full discussion of events in the period, see Sutter, *Chinese Foreign Policy*. For a different perspective regarding Chinese foreign policy at this time, see Harry Harding, ed., *Chinese Foreign Relations in the 1980s* (New Haven: Yale University Press, 1984).

3. For background, see Thomas Gottlieb, *Chinese Foreign Policy Factionalism and the Origins of the Strategic Triangle* (Santa Monica, CA: Rand Corporation, 1977).

4. Assessments particularly useful in charting these instances in Chinese foreign and security policy are: A. Doak Barnett, *China and the Major Powers in East Asia* (Washington, D.C.: Brookings Institute, 1977); Joseph Cammilleri, *Chinese Foreign Policy: The Maoist Era and Its Aftermath* (Seattle, WA: University of Washington Press, 1980); Harry Gelman, *The Soviet Far East Buildup and Soviet Risk-Taking Against China* (Santa Monica, CA: Rand Corporation, 1982); and Richard Solomon, ed., *Asian Security in the 1980s* (Santa Monica, CA: Rand Corporation, 1982). See also Robert Sutter, *Chinese Foreign Policy After the Cultural Revolution* (Boulder, CO: Westview Press, 1978) and Robert Sutter, "Realities of International Power and China's 'Independence' in Foreign Affairs, 1981–1984," *Journal of Northeast Asian Studies*, Winter 1984.

5. For background, see sources cited in Notes 3 and 4, as well as Jonathan Pollack, *The Sino-Soviet Rivalry and Chinese Security Debate* (Santa Monica., CA: Rand Corporation, 1982).

6. See Hamrin, "Emergence." See also Kenneth Lieberthal's article in Harding, *Chinese Foreign Relations*.

7. See, in particular, A. Doak Barnett, *The Making of Foreign Policy in China* (Boulder, CO: Westview Press, 1985).

8. For background on this change in priorities, see U.S. Central Intelligence Agency, *China: The Continuing Search for a Modernization Strategy* (Washington, D.C.: CIA, Report No. ER-80-10248, April 1980).

9. For a clear articulation of this view, see Banning Garrett and Bonnie Glaser, *War and Peace: The Views from Moscow and Beijing* (Berkeley: University of California Press, 1984).

10. For background, see Jonathan Pollack, *The Lessons of Coalition Politics: Sino-American Security Relations* (Santa Monica, CA: Rand Corporation, 1984).

11. These themes have occurred repeatedly in the author's conversations with Chinese officials over the past ten years.

12. See Sutter, *Chinese Foreign Policy*. See also Sutter, "Realities of International Power."

13. For background on this period, see Sutter, *Chinese Foreign Policy*, Chapter 9. See also Jonathan Pollack, *The Lessons of Coalition Politics*.

14. This calculus was clearly evident in statements by Deng Xiaoping and other Chinese leaders leading up to the Chinese Communist Party conference of September 1985.

15. For background, See Robert Manning, "Reagan's Chance Hit," *Foreign Policy*, Winter 1984; and Richard Nations, "President Ronald Reagan Charts a New Course in Asia," *Far Eastern Economic Review*, 21 April 1983.

16. See Chinese coverage of U.S. developments replayed in the U.S. Foreign Broadcast Information Service *Daily Report, China,* April–June 1983.

17. See Speaker O'Neill's official report in the U.S. Congress, House of Representatives, *The United States and China* (Washington, D.C.: Government Printing Office, 1983).

18. For background, see article by Chi Su in Samuel Kin, ed., *Chinese Foreign Policy in the 1980s* (Boulder, CO: Westview Press, 1984).

19. See Note 18; also see Chi Su, "China and the Soviet Union," *Current History*, September 1984.

20. These themes were common in Chinese media coverage during March–May 1984.

21. These ship movements were disclosed in the Japanese press and replayed in U.S. Foreign Broadcast Information Service, *Daily Report, Asia and the pacific,* March 1984.

22. Beijing published U.S. and Japanese references to these Soviet activities in March, April, and May 1984.

23. *Washington Post,* 22 June 1985.

24. On the latter subject, see *Sankei Shimbun,* 28 June 1985.

6

The Evolution of Japan's Security Policy Options

EDWARD A. OLSEN

Japanese security policy is a multifaceted subject. It can be approached in the relatively narrow terms of "defense" policy, focusing on hardware and armed capabilities. It can also be approached in the broad terms embodied by the notions inherent in what Tokyo calls its "Comprehensive Security Doctrine." Each approach has merit. Many analysts in Japan, the United States, and elsewhere have dwelled on the narrower aspects of Japan's security. This chapter will briefly cover those facets, but—in keeping with this book's orientation toward the prospects for security in Asia—the emphasis is on security, broadly defined.

Before assessing where Japan's security policy may go, one must understand where it came from and where it is in the late 1980s. Therefore, it is worthwhile surveying the history and current status of Japan's security policy.[1]

CHANGING SECURITY PERCEPTIONS IN JAPAN: PAST AND PRESENT

Origins of Japan's Security Policy

To truly understand why Japan's post-World War II security evolved as it did, one must take a look at the early and mid-1940s. Between 1940 and 1945, the Japanese people witnessed the ecstasies of victory and agonies of defeat because of their government's military policies. Military successes proved ephemeral and inordinately costly to the Japanese. Devastated by conventional and nuclear weapons, Japan was prostrate by the war's end. The willingness of some military fanatics to fight to the bitter end in the face of such overwhelming destruction reinforced for many Japanese the foolishness of militarism and the futility of war. The great majority of Japanese faced the dawning postwar era with a profound hatred of those elements in domestic and international politics that caused Japan to follow policies leading to what it called the "Great Pacific War" (*Dai Heiyo Senso*). In short, World War II in the Pacific produced a major transformation in Japanese attitudes toward security. Virtually overnight, many Japanese abandoned militarism and adopted pacifism of various sorts.

The explanation for this shift can be traced to several roots. In part, it was simply a pragmatic response to new circumstances. In these terms, the Japanese were doing what their emperor told them to do, namely "bearing the unbearable." In all likelihood, the pragmatism of necessity initially motivated most Japanese. After all, they had been defeated and considered themselves dishonored by their loss. Japanese values predisposed most Japanese to follow the orders of their new bosses. It was no accident that General Douglas MacArthur, as the Supreme Commander of Allied Powers (SCAP), wielded power in a manner that made him seem to Japanese observers like their new "shogun." It would not have surprised the defeated Japanese had they been ruled harshly by the American victors. As history shows, this did not occur. The Japanese initially were surprised, but later pleased, that the U.S. occupation authorities proved to be benefactors in many ways.[2] U.S. policies aimed at the reform and renaissance of a peaceful and prosperous Japan were a godsend to the Japanese. The motives behind their pragmatism toward U.S. occupation directives changed from unavoidable acceptance to an enthusiastic embrace.

This change of perspective was most dramatic with regard to the anti-war clause, Article Nine, of Japan's postwar Peace Constitution, which the Japanese people have adopted and espoused as though it were of their own design, and not a U.S.-imposed law.[3] For many postwar Japanese, Article Nine embodies what they want their country to stand for—a nonaggressive state engaged in peaceful pursuits. For some Japanese, this approach also represents an intellectual and commercial continuum with one of Japan's prewar options that a combination of domestic and international events conspired to block.[4] If the world had been ready to accord Japan the equality and fair treatment Japanese liberals sought in the post-World War I years, it would not have driven Japan into an economic and strategic corner where military fascists were able to seize control.

Be that as it may, most Japanese were not inclined to be historical revisionists. Instead, they were anxious to put the past behind them and get on with their lives in a new and improved international environment. This reaction on the part of the early postwar Japanese went beyond mere pragmatism. It represents yet another example of the Japanese societal tendency to engage in *henka*[5]—a sudden shift toward a position radically opposed to one formerly held. Individual Japanese do *henka* in their lives when they shift from one position to a radically different one—such as strident student radicals who overnight don suits and become loyal "salary men." In Japanese society as a whole, shifts of the *henka* variety are necessarily slower, but they have occurred. An excellent example was the apparent flip-flop of the Meiji state's founding fathers who quickly changed from conservative obstructionists, who fought Tokyo over concessions to Western interlopers, into progressive advocates of Western-style modernization.

The key to understanding *henka* is to recognize that beneath the apparent shifts remains a crucial constant: loyalty to the common good that is vital to Japan's national interests. Changed circumstances and altered contexts may compel the Japanese to adapt by jettisoning old ways in favor of new means, but essentially the loyalties remain intact. In this context, one can best understand the postwar transformation of the Japanese into a "peace-loving" people.

A Changed Security Environment

In a sense, the Japanese had the best of all possible worlds—they were relieved of the onerous responsibilities and risks of providing for their own security because their newfound U.S. benefactor simultaneously protected Japan and facilitated its access to Western markets. The Cold War and the war in Korea caused that situation to change. The outside world once more intruded on Japan's aspirations. Under the guidance of SCAP and the strong encouragement of postoccupation American officials, Japan reluctantly created new armed forces. There was little enthusiasm for these forces among the Japanese people. During the 1950s, these forces remained fledgling, eventually devising their current name—the Self-Defense Forces (SDF). This was, and is, a euphemism because they functioned as Japan's postwar army, navy, and air force. Legally, however, they always have been something short of true "armed force" as that phrase is construed in nearly all other countries. Despite many changes in the SDF since the 1950s, they remain in legal limbo.

Had the Japanese not been pressured by the United States to strengthen the national defense capabilities of the SDF, it is doubtful that they would have moved beyond the ill-conceived paramilitary entity of the 1950s. The growth of the SDF cannot be considered a solely Japanese process, however, because American officials motivated Tokyo. There was little evidence in the formative stages of postwar Japanese national-security policy that Tokyo was stimulated by concerns about external dangers to Japan. Actually, U.S. protection of Japan was so complete that the Japanese had nothing to fear except the possibility that Americans would fail in their "duty" to Japan. Without the U.S. defense shield, Japan was completely at the mercy of an aggressor. Consequently, it was entirely in Japan's interests to take the token self-defense measures it was initially called upon to take by the United States. Japan's indigenous postwar security policy thus began as a form of appeasement by a client state to satisfy the demands of its benefactor. The pragmatic responses of postwar Japanese pacifism, though no less pragmatic than previous iterations, were being reshaped by altered circumstances. The Japanese were en route to becoming an ally of the United States, but an inordinately reluctant ally.

During the 1960s, circumstances again conspired against Japan to compel it to become a militarily stronger state and an even more reluctant "ally." The economic renaissance of Japan had reached significant proportions, making it possible for Tokyo to assume more responsibility for its own defenses. This caused a slight increase in U.S. pressures on Japan to accelerate its self-defense efforts, partially corresponding to the changes in Japan. In light of subsequent U.S.-Japan economic and security controversies, one can legitimately question why the United States did not press for much larger (and more expensive) defense increases by Japan during the 1960s. Had that occurred and succeeded, Japan today probably would be a more capable and cooperative ally, and less of an economic challenger for the United States. In any event, Washington did not push Japan forcefully.

U.S. caution was partially due to the slow momentum of the 1950s policy and to superpower hubris on the part of the United States, because it did not visualize the ways in which its caution might contribute to altering the ratio of economic power between itself and Japan. Few during the 1960s or early 1970s thought seriously about Japan as a prospective major power that might again challenge the United States.[6] U.S. caution also was stimulated by its concerns that troubles in Sino-Soviet affairs, the deterioration of the Indochina war, and uncertainties in Korea were a double-edged sword. While those concerns bolstered U.S. arguments about the need for enhanced Japanese self-defense in a more dangerous world, they also induced U.S. reluctance to push Japan so hard that U.S.-Japan ties might be jeopardized in dangerous times. Out of this mix grew a nascent level of awareness in Japan that Tokyo now had some leverage. By the later 1960s, Japanese leaders were beginning to think of Japan as a latent world power again, but they did so in an ultracautious manner. Particularly because the Vietnam War was being fought by its benefactor, many Japanese remained extremely reluctant to consider Japan an ally of the United States.

NATIONAL SECURITY AMBIGUITY

Thus, Japan entered the 1970s on a note of ambiguity. Its leaders were increasingly proud of their economic achievement. In short, they were "feeling their oats" and anxious to assert Japan's presence in international affairs. Tokyo was, however, uncertain how best to go about it. The feelings of the Japanese public, expressed routinely in opinion polls, was that Tokyo should proceed cautiously, and that sentiment constrained the actions of Japan's leaders. Moreover, before they had begun seriously considering

Japan's alternatives, the outside world once more intervened—this time in the form of the 1973 oil *shokku* and spillover from the Vietnam

Because it starkly exposed Japan's resource feet of clay,[7] the oil crisis rocked the budding confidence of Japan's leaders. Tokyo's immediate reaction was to cling with renewed fervor to the security blanket provided by its U.S. benefactor. The United States reassured Japan of continuity in their military and economic security. These reassurances might have been as convincing as previous U.S. measures had it not been for Japanese uncertainties about the ability of the United States to keep its word. The Nixon administration suffered from a mixed image in Japan. The infamous "Nixon shocks" (relating to manipulation of soybean sales and to a secretive China policy) won the administration few friends in Japan. Furthermore, reports of National Security Adviser Henry Kissinger's negative attitude toward the Japanese circulated widely in Japan. The Nixon-Kissinger word lacked credibility among many Japanese. The slow unraveling of their policy in Indochina, followed by profuse reassurances to the rest of the U.S. Asian allies, did not bolster Japanese confidence in the United States. Consequently, by the mid-1970s, Japan confronted a more uncertain international milieu. Though primarily concerned about its economic security, Tokyo was also concerned about the stability and durability of the U.S.-led system it had relied upon for years.

Japan's reaction to this collection of events was an ambiguous form of pragmatism. After Japan survived the first oil shock, it established an improved network of economic ties that created a form of security based on diversifying both suppliers and consumers. In turn, Japan sought acknowledgment from its trade partners that their economic interdependence was truly mutual so that none of them would want to pull the rug out from under Japan. While the rhetoric of *seikei bunri* (Separating economics from politics) remained alive, the reality of Japan's security policy was shifting toward what later become known as "comprehensive security." Japan was *actively* seeking to integrate the economic and political facets of its national policy into the defense portion, treating the former as major supplements to the latter. Its reasons for this shift were partially economic, but largely political—it no longer had sufficient confidence in the United States to put all its eggs in the U.S.-held basket. Japanese doubts about the United States were reinforced by the fall of Saigon, the gradual growth of the Soviet armed presence in Asia during the 1970s, and the controversy over President Carter's efforts to cut back the numbers of U.S. forces in Korea.

Perversely, American efforts to reassure Japan—while fairly persuasive—also caused more worry in Japan because the Japanese were uneasy about U.S. needs to reassure allies. Though many U.S. officials fretted over these developments, on balance, they proved salutary because they precipitated Japan's first serious postwar national debate over its security policy. During the late 1970s and early 1980s, Japan finally started to engage in a serious domestic discussion over the pros and cons of its security options. This exchange of views was widely covered in the media and generally lauded for breaking important new ground. Coupled with the guarded apprehension caused in Japan by the election of Ronald Reagan as president (he was initially expected to push Japan much harder for defense burden sharing), Tokyo seemed on the verge of momentous decisions. Most of this great commotion, however, proved illusory in an important sense.

SECURITY POLICY: IMAGE AND REALITY

To be sure, the Suzuki and Nakasone administrations preached an improved line. They spoke of Japan's desires to participate as a security partner of the United States and pay for a fair share of the costs of defenses. Also, to be sure, both administrations committed Japan to larger defense missions (such as defending one thousand miles of "SLOCs"), to being an "unsinkable aircraft carrier," to being an "ally," and to spending more for U.S. and Japanese forces. Furthermore, Japan generally fulfilled these commitments. Why, then, refer to the results as "illusory?" Most U.S.specialists in U.S.-Japanese security affairs go out of their way to praise Japan for its statements and actions. The prevailing attitude among these specialists is: Be thankful for small favors and patient with Tokyo's gradualist approach. Compared to the relatively empty "glass" that once symbolized Japanese security policy, most U.S. analysts of Japanese affairs now view Tokyo's efforts as proof that the glass is half full. Optimism prevails because the achievements of the 1970s and 1980s appear enormous in contrast to the dismal accomplishments in the early years. Without undue pessimism, however, it also is fair to say that the Japanese security glass remains half empty. While Japan's defensive accomplishments are significant in absolute terms (measured in missions, hardware, and personnel), they have not truly kept pace with its rapidly accelerating potentials. This is the sense in which its gains are illusory.

Despite all the improvements in recent years, Japan remains an overwhelmingly reluctant ally, engaged in a minimalist defense policy. As of 1988, Japan's security policy is the product of an evolutionary process of pragmatic pacifism. The means Tokyo has used to meet its goals have changed dramatically, but Japan's security policy is still aimed at minimizing its responsibilities, costs, and risks that Tokyo and the Japanese people consciously refuse to accept. Japan does what it believes is minimally necessary to keep the United States committed in terms of cost-sharing, military burden-sharing, and refocusing its appropriate burdens on economic and political endeavors. However, it assiduously avoids giving the United States the impression (and hope) that Japan might become a full-fledged security partner.

If one examines the important notions guiding Tokyo's contemporary defense policy, one is struck by their negative nature. Its foundation is the "Comprehensive Security Doctrine,"[8] whose ostensible purpose is to stress Japan's desires to contribute to economic and political stability as Tokyo's way of helping to preserve security in Asia. Implicit in this self-serving doctrine is a rationale as to why Japan should be considered above the nastiness, danger, and great expense of providing military security. Japan's renowned three non-nuclear principles,[9] its prolonged self-imposed budgetary limitations, and emphasis on Article Nine of the Constitution are comparable examples of Tokyo fostering or perpetuating constraints that limit its ability to be a fully cooperative ally. From a U.S. perspective, Japan's approach leaves much to be desired. However, from a Japanese perspective, it is a wise and modest approach to security policy.

It makes little sense for Japan to spend more than it can avoid spending. Similarly, there is no reason for the Japanese to voluntarily go in harm's way, jeopardizing their security, economy, and domestic tranquility—as long as another nation is willing and able to protect Japan's interests. Consequently, there is no sign that Japan's contemporary security policy will be altered because of Japanese initiatives. If nothing disrupts it, there is every reason to expect Tokyo to try to perpetuate a very beneficial arrangement.

DETERMINANTS OF JAPAN'S SECURITY RELATIONS

By definition, the future is uncertain. Consequently, when projecting future Japanese security policy, one can visualize options ranging from unilaterally disarmed, unarmed neutrality to an armed-to-the-teeth, militaristic, expansionist, and reckless Japan—reminiscent of Imperial Japan. The spectrum in between these extremese is diverse and complicated. In order to ascertain what Japan might actually do, one must examine the circumstances in which Tokyo will pick and choose its options. Here, too, the variables are immense. One cannot hope to outline their full array, but the most likely ones are presented so that some judgments can be offered.

Japan-U.S. Factors

The key relationship for Japan's security is almost certain to be the U.S.-Japan tie. If the United States remains tolerant of Japan's contemporary security policies indefinitely, there is little reason for Tokyo to change them. All the attention to ascendant nationalism in contemporary Japan notwithstanding,[10] Tokyo is not likely to jettison such a low-risk, cost-effective approach to preserving its security. Continued U.S. tolerance of Japan's approach may occur for a combination of two reasons. Many people in the United States remain uncertain about Japan's trustworthiness and fear a heavily rearmed Japan could once more become a danger to peace and stability in the Pacific. This possibility—however remote—inhibits U.S. pressures on Japan to share defense burdens because it instills ambiguity in U.S. decisionmaking. In addition, the interdependent trade and financial relationships between Japan and the United States have attained proportions that allow Tokyo to exert major influence over Washington's readiness to pressure Japan to help bolster the alliance militarily. A normally unspoken element in Japan's comprehensive security approach is the degree to which Japanese technology and Japanese subvention of the U.S. budget deficit shore up the United States' own defense effort. Tokyo's ability to reduce this support is valuable leverage that causes Washington to treat Japan gently.

Countervailing domestic and international pressures on the United States promise to overpower any U.S. reluctance to nudge Japan into a more responsible security relationship. Relative to the early days of its superpowerdom, the United States is overextended militarily, less powerful economically, less certain about its political purposes, and confronted by a markedly different international milieu. Many allies, adversaries, and neutrals are more capable of handling their own security affairs. Consequently, there is less need for the United States to do so much for its allies and more reason to expect them to help each other and the United States. These conditions prevail worldwide and will influence the United States' security relations with other states in Asia, too. This, in turn, promises to have an impact on Japan's security perspective throughout the region.[11]

Japan-Soviet Factors

Another key relationship in determining Japan's security policy will be the position of the Soviet Union. Japan-Soviet relations often have been difficult. The legacy of the Russo-Japanese War, Soviet treatment of Japan during and after World War II, and heavy-handed Soviet policies in the depths of the Cold War have caused considerable Japanese rancor toward the USSR. While neither Tokyo nor the Japanese people have normally perceived the Soviet Union as an armed threat to Japan in the ways the United States frequently does, it is widely seen as a source of trouble for other Japanese interests. Fortunately for Japan, the United States has fended off the Soviet Union for Japan, so far obviating the need for Tokyo to be confrontational toward Moscow. Should reduced U.S.-USSR tensions prevail as the Gorbachev era continues, the U.S. role in Asian security might be modified in ways that would compel Tokyo to address its own security interests versus the Soviet Union in a more forthright and creative manner. Should U.S.-USSR tensions not be ameliorated, Japan also will have to deal more directly with its role in a more equal superpower balance. In either case, Japan's bilateral issues with the Soviet Union are unlikely to be so readily deflected by the U.S.-USSR relationship in the future as they have been in the postwar era. Both the United States and the USSR now recognize Japan as a formidable economic challenger, as well as a useful partner for the United States. Depending upon what path the contemporary superpower relationship takes, Japan will have to adjust many of its policies, including its security policy.

Sooner or later, Tokyo will have to come to grips with its own strategic interests in regard to the Soviet Union, the military role of the Northern Territories as seen from Tokyo, and how the Japanese "navy" (Maritime Self-Defense Force) may best cope with a growing Soviet naval presence in the Western Pacific. It also must deal with the possibility of the U.S. departure from its Philippine bases while the Soviets remain in Vietnam and the prospects for improved Sino-Soviet ties. In short, Tokyo must address virtually the same array of issues confronting Washington, but in an era when the United States probably will not be so omnipresent as Japan's strategic backstop. Furthermore, Tokyo will need to deal with Soviet perceptions of Japan's ambition to be another superpower. Depending on the character of the regime in power in Moscow at that point, this problem could be a particularly troublesome one because Russian leaders have shown no sign of being as tolerant of Japan's ambivalent ambitions as have U.S. leaders. Tokyo cannot be confident that Moscow would be as accepting of a future Japan that professes claims to be an autonomous factor in Asian security. Neither can Tokyo contemplate with equanimity the prospect of Japan shifting its allegiance from the United States to the USSR in the event of a hypothetical catastrophic rupture in U.S.-Japan relations. The United States probably could not passively acquiesce in such a major realignment in the global power balance. Surely Tokyo would understand the U.S. position in such a hypothetical scenario. As important, Tokyo presumably would not relish the constraints Moscow would place on Japan should Tokyo ever pursue such a presently farfetched option.

Japan-China Factors

Turning to more realistic prospects regarding Japan's relations with the world's other major power, China, Tokyo again confronts considerable uncertainty. It faces a China that may pose a variety of problems for Japan. The question of how much Chinese success is in Japan's interest is as difficult for the Japanese as is the nature of U.S. hopes regarding Gorbachev's reforms. In both cases, it is possible to visualize there occurring too much success. Japan is not anxious for China to replicate Japan's successes. It does not need the economic competition such a China might pose. Nor does it want to see an economically stronger China move toward becoming a truly powerful nation militarily. Neither, however, does Japan want to see China fall on its face and risk new instability in Asia. All these concerns closely echo U.S. fears about the Soviet Union. In both cases, the preferred course of events seems to be progress, slow and steady—but especially *slow*. Also, in both cases, the ambiguity of Tokyo and Washington is sensed in Beijing and Moscow. In neither the PRC nor the USSR are the mixed feelings of the Japanese welcomed, any more than they respond well to U.S. ambiguity.

This feeling is particularly acute in China where there is a deep-seated strain of envy, resentment, and hatred regarding the Japanese people's ability to outdo the Chinese. For all their Marxist ideology and high-flown rhetoric, the Chinese remain fixated upon their place as the "Middle Kingdom." They have great difficulty accepting the Japanese as modern Asia's most successful society. More grating still, Japan has succeeded *twice* within a century, while China stumbled from failure to failure. Should China manage to get on the same fast track economically that Japan has been on for years, it will do its best to catch up with, and surpass, its upstart neighbor. What makes this entire contest especially delicate is Japan's awareness of China's profound feelings, its abundant confidence that Japan will prevail, and its renewed willingness to display Japanese national pride in a way that strikes many Chinese as arrogant.

Given this mixture of tensions between Japan and China, it is difficult to take seriously those analysts who project close cooperation between them in the future in diverse fields, including security.[12] China and Japan may never become battlefield enemies again, though that is not impossible to visualize, but neither are they likely to become allies anytime soon. Their national interests are too disparate and their animosities too powerful for that to be feasible. Short of devising a dual leadership system in which Chinese and Japanese would share power in a symmetrical manner, neither would sanguinely accept the other's leadership. Crucial here, the concept of co-equality in these essentially Confucian societies (in which hierarchical "equality" is virtually unknown) is oxymoronic. Consequently, no one need worry unduly about the prospect of some sort of Sino-Japanese hegemony. Such thoughts—redolent of yesteryear's "yellow peril" notions—do circulate in the West and in the Soviet Union, but they are unwarranted.

Japan-Korea Factors

Japan's security interests in neighboring Korea are much more tangible and less esoteric than its potential concerns about the Soviet Union and China. Because U.S.-South Korean relations are subject to strains similar to those afflicting U.S.-Japan ties, there are real possibilities for disruptions in the long-standing U.S.-ROK security and political and economic bonds.[13] Since Japan depends on the U.S. commitment to South Korea for its security interests in Korea, the fate of U.S.-ROK relations is crucial to Tokyo. Should the relationship between its main ally and its closest neighbor sour for any reason, Japan might be placed in a double bind. It would have to cope with potential instability on the Korean Peninsula without the United States, and it would have to absorb the impact of U.S. strategic reverses in Korea upon U.S.-Japanese security ties. Clearly, this is something Tokyo will do its utmost to avoid. Japan can be expected to be as supportive as it must be to preserve the U.S.-ROK bond. Japan's need to bolster that bond cannot be overstated and gives Washington and Seoul potentially useful leverage in their separate, and joint, relations with Tokyo.

Were Japan's best efforts to prove incapable of preventing a rupture in U.S.-ROK security relations, Tokyo would face very difficult choices. It might try to fill some, or all, of the U.S. vacuum. Under such trying circumstances, that option seems untenable. Tokyo might also try to ameliorate the tension in Korea, but the bitter historical legacy of Japan's involvement in Korea does not augur well for that prospect. Most likely, Japan would adapt to the new circumstances that would evolve in Korea. The essential alternatives are the perpetuation of the divided nation by the actions of each Korea or unification by their actions. The latter could be peaceful, but also could be the result of another war. In any of these events, Japan would face Koreans with arms who have reason to dislike Japan, but who would not be constrained by the presence of U.S. forces. Either a divided Korea or a unified one (regardless of how it might be achieved) could readily be a more dangerous place from Japan's perspective if there is no U.S. buffer to distance Japan from the events there. Many Japanese businessmen also are concerned about the potential of Korea (divided or unified) to pose an economic challenge to Japan that increases the "threat" to Japan's economic security. Consequently, the potential for serious disruptions in Japan's security may be most plausible in the Korean context.

Broader Factors

Japan's long-term security concerns in Southeast Asia are predicated on the future durability of U.S. bases in the Philippines that are vital for the defense of Japan's economic lifelines. The SLOCs to Middle East Oil, to Australian and Oceanic markets, and to markets throughout South and Southeast Asia are crucial to Japanese economic well-being. Loss of those bases might force Japan to make difficult strategic choices and certainly would compel Tokyo to spend more money and take more risks. Here, too, Japan will do its utmost to perpetuate the status-quo security situation. Should those arrangements collapse, Tokyo might opt to cut a deal with the USSR or PRC which would help assure its regional security interests, but this is unlikely for the reasons already cited in regard to Japan's relations with the Soviet Union and China. More likely, Japan would have to cut other sorts of security deals with a retrenched United States and with diverse regional powers. All of these options are far less palatable to Tokyo than its contemporary arrangements. Consequently, Tokyo has little choice other than to support the status quo.

FUTURE SECURITY OPTIONS

To sum up this look at Japan's options as they pertain to its changing security environment, one must note the concept raised by Prime Minister

Nakasone about Japan's "common destiny" (*unmei kyodotai*) with its neighbors. While Tokyo has not yet spelled out what Japan intends to do to work with its neighbors around the Pacific en route to this common destiny, recognition of a sense of commonality is a major step forward. For most of the postwar period, the Japanese have avoided any acceptance of foreign conflicts as central to their security. Instead, they prefer to view such events as happenings that may be important to others, but have no direct bearing on Japan. To describe them, the Japanese use the expression *kaigan no kasai* (conflagrations on distant shores), implying a remoteness from Japanese abilities to effect the outcome. This denotes an attitude of aloofness from foreign problems and a desire to abstain from getting involved.

Traditional Japanese feelings of insularity have been reinforced by the postwar beneficence of the United States as Japan's protector. For centuries, the Japanese had little reason to fear foreign aggression against their island redoubt in world affairs, buffered by the seas. One writer correctly likened the Japanese nation's attitude toward security to its attitude toward water—it is all around, ever-present, free, and does not have to be earned.[14] Changes in Japan's security and economic environment appear to be chipping away at this predilection for noninterventionism that verges on isolationism. The world is already impinging on Japan's desires to avoid involvement. Recognition of a sense of common destiny represents an admission that Japan can no longer avoid responsibilities for circumstances that may determine its well-being. The Japanese no longer can leave arduous tasks to others.

It is uncertain what Japan may actually do as it addresses its security agenda. It has a broad array of strategic options that include various forms of neutralism—from unarmed utopianism to heavily armed neutralism based on the Swiss or Swedish models. At the other extreme, Japan may contemplate several Gaullist options, in which a lightly or heavily armed Japan would go it alone as an autonomous actor in world affairs. The Gaullist model might also involve acquisition of nuclear weapons, an acquisition which is entirely within the realm of possibility for a state possessing Japan's advanced technological levels. The existence of Japan's renowned "nuclear allergy" is no guarantee that Tokyo will not consider nuclear arms in the future. Japan's middle options revolve around variations on the contemporary U.S.-Japan defense relationship. This could entail expanded military roles for Japan, or altered politico-economic roles. The latter presently is Tokyo's preference. Japan's middle option might also involve transferring its allegiance to a new protective power—though this is highly unlikely for reasons already stated.

As Japan addresses these options, it also must confront its choices as an economic actor in defense affairs. Will Japan become a major arms producer and exporter? Japanese leaders routinely say "no" to that question, denying any such intention. Will Japan be compelled to enter this field in a major way in order to keep up with its competition? Will it be compelled to produce and sell weapons so that it can maintain the economies of scale necessary for the efficient creation of large armed forces? These questions are less easily turned aside by Tokyo. How will Japan's security partner(s) deal with it as it acquires arms-production power? Similarly, how will they deal with Japan as it plays a crucial role in the high technology weaponry certain to be at the frontiers of future defenses? Even more tricky, how should Japan's evolving role in dual-use technologies be handled by Tokyo and Japan's security partner(s)? These are questions that demand answers now, but are not being adequately addressed.

Out of this mix will come Japans' future security posture. Two outcomes seem most likely. To preface the following judgment, it must be noted that either outcome is entirely in keeping with Japan's Meiji-era drive for *fukoku kyohei* (rich country, strong forces). However, Japan would achieve the outcomes through different means. It is likely that Japan will try to hedge its security bets by pursuing a continued noninterventionist security policy, but will keep its armed Gaullist/armed neutralist options discreetly viable. Japan's clear preference is to perpetuate the cheapest, least risky security options open to it. Japan also is predisposed to making its latest form of pragmatic pacifism work. Tokyo knows the Japanese people march to the beat of a different drummer and hopes earnestly that the rest of the world will get into step with Japan. However, it does not seem to seriously expect anything of that sort to occur. On the contrary, it seems prepared to persist in its ideosyncratic ways, to let the super-powers engage in a wasteful arms race that harms their economies, and to be around to pick up the pieces after the superpowers dissipate themselves.

En route to that end, Japan seems prepared to tag along on the strategic coattails of the United States. In the process, of course, it also anticipates being forced to chip in a larger share of the funding and assume somewhat more responsibility. The most likely venues for this enhanced cooperation militarily are its air and naval power, not ground power. It also anticipates having to play a larger politico-economic role. Both of these means toward increased cooperation with the United States will also facilitate its hedging of its bet, because they will allow Tokyo to create capabilities that could be transformed into armed Gaullist or neutralist stances. At that hypothetical future point, Japan would be ready to create major forces for its autonomous self-defense or for other purposes, using funds it had not had to use for decades. Either way, Japan stands to benefit from what is now a prudent, cost-effective, and flexible approach to its national security that leaves its options remarkably open.

NOTES

The views expressed are solely those of the author and do not necessarily reflect those of his employer.

1. For further, in-depth, analyses of that history, see Martin Weinstein, *Japan's Postwar Defense Policy, 1947–1968* (New York: Columbia University press, 1971); James H. Buck, ed., *The Modern Japanese Military System* (Beverly Hills, CA: Sage Publications, 1975); Richard L. Sneider, *U.S.-Japanese Security Relations: A Historical Perspective* (New York: Columbia University, East Asian Institute, 1982); Edward A. Olsen, *U.S.-Japan Strategic Reciprocity; A Neo-Internationalist View* (Stanford, CT: The Hoover Institution Press, 1985); and Okazaki Hisahiko, *A Grand Strategy For Japanese Defense* (Lanham, MD: University Press of America/Abt Books, 1986).

2. Perhaps the most insightful assessment of that era remains Kawai Kazuo, *Japan's American Interlude* (Chicago: University of Chicago Press, 1960).

3. For a sympathetic analysis of Article Nine's importance to postwar Japanese, see the writings of Professor Theodore McNelly, especially his *Politics and Government in Japan*, Third Edition (Lanham, MD: University Press of America, 1984) and its excellent suggested readings.

4. This view finds its fullest expression among those contemporary conservatives in Japan who contend Japan was forced into World War II by the actions of Western imperialist states that impeded Japan's peaceful ambitions. The controversies surrounding Japanese textbook revisions that so aroused other Asians, and the ham-handed statements in April 1988 by Okuno Seisuke, Director General of Japan's National Land Agency, about others misunderstanding Japan's wartime motives, exemplify these views.

5. Doing *henka* is a well-understood concept among the Japanese.

6. For an insightful example of one who did, see Warren Hunsberger; *Japan: New Industrial Giant* (New York: American-Asia Educational Exchange/National Strategy Information Center, 1972).

7. The author examined Japan's potentially dire resource vulnerabilities in *Japan: Economic Growth, Resource Scarcity, and Environmental Constraints* (Boulder, CO: Westview Press, 1978).

8. For a sympathetic evaluation of this approach, see Robert W. Barnett, *Beyond War: Japan's Concept of Comprehensive Security* (Washington: Pergamon-Brassey's, 1984).

9. For background on these principles, see Weinstein, *Japan's Postwar Defense Policy*; and Sneider, *U.S.-Japanese Security Relations*.

10. For an excellent example, see Abe Motoo, "Nakasone-ryu Gomennasai Gaiko" (Nakasone-style Apologetic Foreign Policy), *Bungei Shunju*, November 1987, pp. 146–152.

11. Support for this interpretation is evident across the U.S. political spectrum. For prominent academic examples of such thinking from very different ideological perspectives, see conservative Melvyn Krauss, *How NATO Weakens The West* (New York: Simon and Schuster, 1986) and liberal Paul Kennedy, *The Rise and Fall of the Great Powers*, (New York: Random House, 1987).

12. See, for example, Robert Taylor, *The Sino-Japanese Axis: A New Force in Asia?* (New York: St. Martin's Press, 1985).

13. The author addressed this in detail in *U.S. Policy and The Two Koreas* (Boulder, CO: Westview Press/San Francisco: The World Affairs Council of Northern California, 1988).

14. Isaiah Ben Dassan. *The Japanese and the Jews* (New York: Weatherhill, 1983).

7

The Korean Peninsula
and Security Dilemma
in the Late 1980s

YOUNG WHAN KIHL

The arms race between North and South Korea has reached the point of no return—the Korean Peninsula in the late 1980s has turned into a heavily fortified armed camp. As a result of each Korean state pursuing a policy of enhanced security measures, including the receipt of sophisticated weapons from their respective allies, the inter-Korean arms race has intensified in the 1980s and with it the danger that Korea's powder keg may explode with only slight provocation. The Korean security dilemma is how to defuse the Korean time bomb, thereby moving the glacier that is divided Korea toward the warmer diplomatic climate, while each regime maintains defense against the perceived external threat adequate to assure independence and autonomy.[1]

Peace in the Korean Peninsula in the late 1980s depends to a large extent on the military deterrence existing between North and South Korea in terms of their defense preparedness. Other variables include both internal and external factors associated with each country's political forces and movements (i.e., domestic political stability as well as foreign allied support), which each Korean regime is capable of generating vis-à-vis its opponent.[2]

This chapter will first discuss the strategic environment surrounding the Korean Peninsula, with a view to the major powers' security interest and calculus toward Korea. This will be followed by an overall comparative assessment of the Korean military balance in terms of the force capabilities and deployment of the two Koreas. The chapter will conclude with a discussion of Korea's security dilemma and implications of the economic race between the two halves of the divided nation on the future of the Korean Peninsula in the late 1980s and beyond.

THE EVOLVING SECURITY ENVIRONMENT AND
THE KOREAN PENINSULA

The shifting major power relations in the region have had a great impact on the Korean Peninsula, especially on the diplomatic alignment of the respective Korean states. As the child of the Cold War era, the political character of the two Korean regimes was stamped, from the very outset, by the ideological rivalry between the United States and the Soviet Union in the post World War II era. The subsequent diplomatic activities of the Koreas have also been largely affected by the ebb and flow of the U.S.-Soviet competition and cooperation in world politics.

Geopolitically, the Korean Peninsula is the strategic fulcrum of East Asia, where the interests of four major powers—the Soviet Union, China, Japan, and the United States—converge and crisscross.[3] It is not surprising, therefore, that between 1888 and 1988 three major international wars have been waged over the control of the Korean Peninsula: the Sino-Japanese War of 1894 and 1895, the Russo-Japanese War of 1904 and 1905, and the Korean War of 1950 to 1953, the latter involving the United States and China, among others, as major belligerents.

As a peninsula, Korea is not only vulnerable to attack by sea, but it is also deeply affected by the latest developments in naval warfare since support form any ally not on the Asian mainland must arrive by sea or air.[4] Because the Korean Peninsula is poor in natural resources, its economic well-being also depends on world trade; its import and export activities depending on the supply line from the sea. The fact that South Korea controls one side of the important Strait of Korea (Tsushima), one of the four main choke points for entrance into the Sea of Japan from the Pacific, also enhances strategic value.[5]

In the 1980s, the strategic environment surrounding the Korean Peninsula has drastically changed. Following the Soviet invasion of Afghanistan in December 1979, the security environment in the Asian-Pacific remained rather conflictual and tension-ridden. Increased Soviet military activities in the region led to the renewal of the "cold war" in U.S.-Soviet relations, the continued persistence of the Sino-Soviet conflict, and the improvement in U.S.-Sino and Sino-Japanese relations. However, the signing of the INF reduction treaty in December 1987 and its subsequent ratification timed with the Reagan-Gorbachev summit in Moscow in May 1988 provided a turning point in U.S.-Soviet relations, promising to bring about a ripple effect on the northeastern corner of the global and regional political arena.

Korea and the Strategic Calculus of the Superpowers

Both North and South Korea are considered strategic assets by the superpowers and countries that border the two Koreas. Should a major war arise, both Korean states could provide excellent naval support facilities and air bases to outside powers.

The Soviet Strategy. The Soviet interest in Korea is closely tied with its overall global strategic designs.[6] Although the Soviet force deployment in the region—both conventional and nuclear—is aimed primarily at the rival countries surrounding the Soviet Union, such as China and Japan, it has also extended beyond its traditional line of defense to include other countries like Korea and Vietnam.

The Soviet military buildup and force deployment in the Asian theater is quite extensive in spite of the Soviets' recently announced scheduled force reduction as part of the terms of the 1988 U.S.-Soviet INF reduction treaty. Intermediate-range nuclear delivery systems maintained by the Soviet Union in Asia, for instance, include the SS-20, a mobile missile with a range of about 5,000 kilometers, and the Tu-22M Backfire, a high-performance bomber capable of penetrating airspace at low altitudes and high speeds. Of the 351 SS-20s (each carrying three MIRVed warheads) deployed since 1977, about 144 are deployed in the Far East, and 80 of the more than 200 Backfire bombers are in Asia, according to a Japanese source.[7] All of these 144 SS-20s in the region will be removed if and when the U.S.-Soviet INF treaty is complied with.

The Soviet Union has also deployed considerable conventional forces in the region east of Lake Baikal, with approximately 370,000 troops, 820 vessels displacing over 1.6 million tons, and 2,100 aircraft. The main components of the Soviet weaponry include MiG-23s, long-range 130mm cannons, and MI-24 Hind ground-attack gunship helicopters.[8]

The Soviet Union presently maintains no naval support facilities, ground forces, or air bases in North Korea. However, it has acquired an important concession and privilege from North Korea in exchange for the latest weaponry system. The Soviet Pacific Fleet headquartered in Vladivostok (across from the Soviet-North Korean border) is seeking the right to berth its naval vessels in North Korea's ports. It could easily use several of North Korea's excellent port facilities in the Sea of Japan, such as Chongjin, Unggi, and Najin, which could very well serve as subsidiary loading points for the cargo destined for the Soviet Maritime Province.

The border treaty between North Korea and the Soviet Union, signed in 1984 and put into effect in 1985, may give both countries better access to one another's territory, both economically and militarily. Both countries share the border along the Tumen River in the northeastern corner of the Korean Peninsula, with several crossing points acting as vital connecting transportation links for both railways and highways. With the Soviet technical support, the port facilities of Najin have been expanded and modernized. An oil refinery was also built in Unggi, halfway between Najin and the Soviet border.[9]

Soviet test-flight across the narrow neck of North Korea's east-west corridor took place in 1985 along the DMZ, a flight that may have political as well as strategic significance. This may have been one of the results of Kim Il-sung's 1984 Moscow visit and the subsequent border treaty negotiated in 1984. Politically, North Korea has now agreed to support Soviet access to North Korea, as it did with China in 1983 (which it subsequently suspended). In that instance, North Korea made the port city of Chongjin available for cargo transshipment for Japan-China trade in order to serve the interior of China's Northeast Province.[10]

Strategically, Soviet access to North Korea's airspace is important because it provides the Soviets with an alternative route and channel for the transair link between the Soviet Far East and Soviet stations in the Cam Ranh air base in Vietnam. Prior to this access, the Soviet air route had been over the narrow strait of Tsushima between the Sea of Japan and the South China Sea. Now with the cooperation of North Korea, the Soviet Air Force can proceed from the Sea of Japan to the Yellow Sea via North Korea, thereby bypassing and avoiding the dangerous corridor between Japan and South Korea.

The United States Strategy. The United States maintains ground troops in South Korea as part of the overall global strategy vis-à-vis the Soviet Union. It maintains no naval support facilities in South Korea, perhaps because the United States has access to Japan's nearby naval facilities in Sasebo and Yokosuka. However, the United States has extensive use of air bases in South Korea in four locations: Kunsan, Osan, Suwon and Taegu. Together with other air bases in Japan and Okinawa (such as Iwakuni, Atsugi, Yokota, Misawa, Futenma, and Kadena), U.S. planes on Korean air bases provide tactical support not only to U.S. ground forces in Yongsan and along the DMZ in Camp Casey, but also to the Republic of Korea (ROK) defense forces.

Total U.S. forces in Korea currently number about 40,462. Of these, about 29,232 are assigned to the Eighth U.S. Army, which includes the Second Infantry Division, the 19th support command, supporting aviation and engineer groups, and various smaller support units. The other component of U.S. forces is the 314th air division, with tactical fighter wings and squadrons located in the four separate air bases already mentioned.[11]

The U.S. deployment of forces in the region is considerably fewer in number than that of the Soviets. The mainstay of the U.S. force in East Asia are U.S. combat forces in Korea, with approximately 100 aircraft, and the U.S. Seventh Fleet, with 230 aircraft and 65 vessels amounting to some 670,000 tonnages. Also, about 33,000 U.S. Marines are on Okinawa assigned to the Seventh Fleet. In addition, the United States can rely on Japan Self-Defense Forces (SDF) consisting of 156,000 troops, 350 aircraft, and 166 vessels, amounting to some 232,000 tonnages.[12]

The United States can also rely on Taiwan and possibly China for support against the Soviet threat in the region. Whereas Taiwan maintains sizable military forces consisting of 330,000 troops, 547 aircraft, and 170 vessels, amounting to a tonnage of 86,000, China is Asia's largest military power with 4,000,000 regular troops, 6,100 combat aircraft, and 2,650 vessels, amounting to a tonnage of 665,000.[13]

With the renegotiation of U.S. base rights in the Philippines now under way, South Korea has been mentioned openly as a possible alternative to U.S. naval and air bases in the Philippines. This scenario is interesting but premature to press on at this time. Establishing major U.S. naval bases in South Korea will not be received favorably by those elements in South Korea that exploit the anti-U.S. sentiment to counter the U.S. pressure on trade with South Korea. Without first winning broad public support or neutralizing the escalated anti-U.S. sentiment, no effective security policy is likely to emerge.

Although no known deployment of nuclear warheads exists in North Korea, in the South the United States reportedly maintains a tactical nuclear weapons system, consisting of more than 1,000 warheads. Establishing a nuclear-free zone for the Korean Peninsula, proposed so far by various peace movement groups, may be a viable option in the future, but now it is an ideal plan rather than a practical alternative.

Major Powers Policies and Changing Attitudes Toward Korea

The major powers surrounding the Korean Peninsula generally maintain an active interest in the overall situation and specific developments in each Korean state, and they actively pursue a publicly stated policy of promoting peace and stability on the peninsula. Security ties that both North and South Korea maintain with their respective allies are an indication of the strategic values and importance that the major powers attach to the Korean Peninsula.

North Korea is the only communist country, for instance, that is allied with both the Soviet Union and China by virtue of a Treaty of Friendship, Co-operation and Mutual Assistance signed with each country in 1961. Likewise, South Korea is an important U.S. ally in East Asia, with the Mutual Security Treaty signed in 1954. The Combined Forces Command and the annual US-ROK Security Consultative Meetings are institutional manifestations of the close security ties established between the two countries.[14] Neither North Korea nor South Korea, however, is party to multilateral defense agreements, such as the North Atlantic Treaty Organization (NATO) or the Warsaw Treaty Organization (WTO).

The United States. U.S. policy toward Korea focuses on maintaining a stable strategic and political environment through the prevention of armed conflict between the two hostile Korean states and the avoidance of hegemony on the peninsula by any outside power. Renewal of armed conflict in Korea would pose a potentially grave threat to the security of Japan, to regional stability, and to U.S. interests.[15] The presence of U.S. combat forces in South Korea is thus an important means of preserving stability on the Korean Peninsula.

In the wake of rapid change in the Asian strategic environment following Sino-American rapprochement in the early 1970s, the United States has not always followed a consistent policy toward Korea, as the reversal of the ill-fated Carter administration policy on ground troops withdrawal from Korea illustrates.[16] Nevertheless, the basic U.S. policy goal of maintaining a security alliance with South Korea will remain consistent. In spite of anti-U.S. sentiment expressed by some radical students in 1988, the new U.S. administration in 1989 is expected to reaffirm the continuing importance of close U.S.-ROK cooperation for regional stability and for bilateral trade.[17]

Japan. Japan shares a common interest with the United States in preserving regional stability and reducing tension on the Korean Peninsula in order to promote Japanese security and economic interests. Because of its constitutional restrictions and the absence of defense arrangements with the Republic of Korea, however, Japan depends heavily upon the United States to preserve security and stability on the Korean Peninsula. In fact, the Japanese leadership was quite reluctant to see the withdrawal of U.S. ground forces from South Korea under President Carter.[18]

For reasons of trade promotion and neighborly concern, Japan wishes to improve relations with North Korea and maintain what the Japanese call a policy of equidistance toward Seoul and Pyongyang. Now that President Roh Tae Woo's government proclaimed a new policy toward North Korea on July 7, 1988, thereby removing restrictions on contacts with North Korea, Tokyo-Pyongyang relations are expected to improve and normalize in due course.

The Soviet Union. Soviet policy regarding the Korean Peninsula was governed less by its bilateral relationship with North Korea than by its concern about Sino-Soviet conflict and Soviet rivalry with the United States and Japan.[19] The USSR's military buildup and proclamation as an Asia-Pacific power, however, seem to have contributed toward reversing its past policy toward the Korean Peninsula.

Gorbachev's Korea policy has led to a shift, since Kim Il-Sung's Moscow visits in May 1984 and October 1986, from one of limited logistic and military support to a more active and aggressive military assistance to North Korea. As a result of this changed policy, the Soviet Union has supplied North Korea with its latest weaponry system, including MiG-23 fighters, SA-3 missiles with a range of 300 kilometers, SA-5 antiair missiles, and SU-25 high-performance planes that are about to be delivered.[20]

Given the Soviet preoccupation with *perestroika* at home, however, the Gorbachev regime is unlikely to endorse Kim Il-sung's adventurism and recklessness. The fact that the Soviet Union and East European countries are sending athletes to the 1988 Seoul Summer Olympics, in spite of Pyongyang's strenuous objection, is an indication of Moscow's desire to promote peace and stability on the Korean Peninsula. North Korea will be compelled to adjust its behavior and abandon its bellicose stance toward the South in the face of possibly improved cultural and economic ties between Seoul and Moscow and between Seoul and Pyongyang's allies in Eastern Europe in the post-Seoul Olympic era.

China. The People's Republic of China (PRC) appears momentarily satisfied with the status quo and stability on the Korean Peninsula. It does not wish to see the Korean Peninsula peace upset as a result of Pyongyang's reckless and belligerent behavior. However, as China sees it, North Korea serves as an important buffer between itself and outside forces, including the Soviet Union, and the U.S. forces in South Korea may also help to counter Soviet expansionism.

Military confrontation in Korea would place China in the strategic dilemma of either supporting the Democratic People's Republic of Korea (DPRK), thereby jeopardizing U.S.-PRC relations, or abandoning North Korea totally to Soviet influence. Beijing, therefore, has consistently discouraged Pyongyang's belligerence.[21] China is therefore sensitive to the evolving closer military tie between Pyongyang and Moscow, lest it would be used against Beijing. Maintaining friendly relations with North Korea, nonetheless, has been China's continuous policy objective.

Since the mid-1980s, China has maintained a nonpolitical and trade relationship with South Korea, its bilateral indirect trade via Hong Kong amounting to $1.9 billion in 1987. China's new policy of developing its coastal regions, announced in January 1988, will involve South Korea in the promotion of trade and investment in China's coastal regions, including the Shandung Province. So long as China pursues its open door policy and the policy of attaining four modernization goals by the year 2000, it will be in China's interest to preserve peace and stability on the Korean Peninsula. This attitude underlies the Chinese decisions to participate in the 1986 Asia Games in Seoul and the 1988 Seoul Summer Olympics, in spite of the North Korean objection and boycott.

THE KOREAN MILITARY BALANCE AND SECURITY POSTURES

Since peace on the Korean Peninsula largely depends on military balance and deterrence, defense preparedness undertaken by North and South Korea must be examined. This section will present comparative assessments of the security postures of the two Korean States, followed by a discussion of security options and implications in the late 1980s and beyond.

Force Capabilities and Deployment

The military balance between communist North Korea and noncommunist South Korea, according to many analysts, favors the North in the 1980s.[22] However, the military capabilities of the South continue to improve with the successful completion of a series of five-year programs of armament, including the Force Improvement Plan (FIP) I (1976 to 1981) and FIP II (1982 to 1987). In due course, therefore, a situation will eventually arise wherein the South will come to surpass the North militarily.[23] Until 1990, however, the military balance between the two Koreas may be described as relatively evenly matched.[24]

Both Korean regimes have maintained a huge military establishment, the result being that the Korean Peninsula has become a heavily armed camp and fortress. The image of the peninsula as a powder keg, ready to explode with slight provocation, seems to be an apt description of the tense security posture of the Koreas in the 1980s.[25]

The heavy defense expenditure is undoubtedly beyond the individual capabilities and means of support of each Korean state. Valuable finite resources, which otherwise would have been wisely invested in economic development projects, are obviously wasted; military spending can be channeled into the more positive purposes of production rather than of consumption.

Growing Military Expenditures. The DPRK and the ROK typically spend a large sum of money on the military, thereby fueling an arms race on the Korean Peninsula. As the following tables show, some 15 to 23 percent of the GNP on the average is believed to be spent on defense by North Korea, while about 5 to 6 percent of the GNP goes toward defense in the South.[26]

In the late 1980s, North Korea is said to possess a substantial advantage over the South in overall quantity of military equipment. This is the result of intensive defense buildup during the 1970s.

The ROK's recent military expansion since the mid-1970s, under FIP (Force Improvement Plan) I and II, represents a delayed response to the DPRK's earlier initiative in military buildup. The military budgets of North and South Korea, as Table 7.1 shows, have been increased steadily, measurably, and substantially.

The North was judged by military analysts to hold a clear military advantage, with quantitatively superior amounts of weapons and equipment. Its offensive capabilities are also fashioned precisely to the battlefield's tactical contours.[27] North Korea also maintains a variety of special forces, including the Eighth Special Corps of commando troops (approximately

Table 7.1   Comparison of North and South Korean Military
Expenditures, 1968–1987 (in millions of U.S. dollars)

Year	North Korea	South Korea	Ratio South/North
1968	1,398	1,195	.85
1969	1,366	1,289	.94
1970	1,655	1,358	.82
1971	1,952	1,499	.77
1972	2,266	1,537	.68
1973	1,980	1,596	.81
1974	2,341	1,827	.78
1975	2,079	1,978	.95
1976	2,236	2,409	1.08
1977	2,489	2,727	1.10
1978	2,251	3,184	1.26
1979	2,405	3,154	1.31
1980	2,655	3,431	1.25
1981	2,676	3,276	1.22
1982	2,523	3,399	1.35
1983	2,598	3,612	1.39
1984			
1985	n.a.	4,550[a]	1.32
1986	3,870[a]	5,110[a]	1.32
1987	4,450[a]	n.a.	
Cumulative			
1968–1983	35,150	37,381	1.06
1976–1983	20,113	25,102	1.25

Sources: Charles Wolf, Jr., et al., *The Changing Balance: South and North Korean Capabilities for Long-Term Military Competition* (Santa Monica, CA: Rand, December 1985), p. 43.

[a]*The Military Balance, 1987–1988*, pp. 162–163.

100,000 men), whose primary mission is to create a second front deep in South Korea in the nonconflict zone.

South Korea's armed force, said to be well trained, might retain a qualitative advantage in military equipment, including aircraft and ground weapons. According to military analysts, these are not sufficient, however, to offset quantitative disadvantages.

The existing military imbalance and arms race between the two Korean states will therefore continue as each Korean regime outspends the opponent in defense. Each Korean regime has also acquired the latest advanced equipment from its respective ally. For the South, such equipment includes 20 F-16s and 1,000 M55-1 light tanks from the United States, while the North acquired 40 Soviet MiG-23s and an unspecified number of Soviet T-72 tanks.[28]

The Military Balance and Force Distribution. Table 7.2 shows the comparison between the North and South Korean military balance in 1987, as it was estimated by the London-based International Institute for Strategic Studies.

In 1987, North Korea's military forces numbered some 838,000 personnel, with an army organized into 25 infantry divisions, 2 armored divisions, and 5 mechanized divisions, including 2,900 tanks. North Korea also has a navy of 27 submarines, 2 frigates, and 34 high-speed missile launchers; its air force has some 840 combat planes, including 150 MiG-21 and 40 MiG-23 fighter planes (the latter were added to the fleet in 1985).[29]

South Korea's military forces in 1987, on the other hand, consisted of 629,000 personnel, with an army organized into 19 infantry divisions and 2 mechanized divisions, including 1,300 tanks. South Korea has a navy of 6 frigates and 11 missile-carrying launchers, and 2 marine divisions; its air force has some 476 combat planes, including 20 F-16s, 260 F5A/B/E/F and 65 F-16 fighter planes (the latter were added in 1986).[30]

Pattern of the Korean Arms Race and Force Deployment. There is a dynamic action-reaction pattern in the arms race on the Korean Peninsula. Until 1975, North Korea's military expenditures were much higher than that of South Korea. Since about 1976, however, the ROK's military spending has outstripped that of North Korea, although the estimate for the North was subsequently upgraded in 1978, based on new U.S. intelligence reports. In 1979, U.S. intelligence data showed a rather rapid increase in North Korean military strength since 1971, indicating that the DPRK might have spent as much as 15 percent of its GNP on military expenditures during the 1970s.[31]

This pattern of military spending in the Koreas reflects the changes in defense policy orientation and the security posture of the Korean regimes. North Korea has continued its policy of military buildup since 1962 under the so-called "Four Great Military Policylines," adopted during the Fourth KWP (Korean Workers' Party) Congress in 1962, which contained the slogans, "arm the entire population," "fortify the entire country," "cadetify the entire units," and "modernize the entire army."[32]

South Korea has enhanced its defense capability and preparedness since 1971 by implementing the Five-Year Force Modernization Plan (1971 to 1976) and the FIP I (1976 to 1981) and II (1981 to 1986). While North Korean under Kim Il-sung sought military superiority over the South

Table 7.2 The Military Balance: Comparison of North and South
Koreas' Security Postures, 1987

	North Korea	South Korea
Population, 1987	21,153,000	42,126,000
Total Active Forces	838,000	629,000
Total Reserve Forces	540,000	4,840,000
Paramilitary Forces[a]	3,738,000	4,100,000
Military Expenditures as % of GNP		
1982 estimate	22.4	6.2
1983 estimate	22.7	6.8
1984 estimate	22.6	5.4
Army	750,000	542,000
Armored Divisions[b]	2	0
Mechanized Divisions[b]	5	2
Infantry Divisions[b]	25	19 + 2c
Tanks	2,900	1,300
Navy	35,000	29,000
Submarines	27	0
Destroyers (Frigates)	0 (2)	0 (6)
Missile Launchers	34	11
Naval Bases	9	8
Air Forces	53,000	33,000
Combat Aircraft	840	476
	incl. 40 MiG-23	incl. 20 F-16 C/D
	150 MiG-21	260 F-5A/B/E/F
	100 MiG-19/Q-5	65 F-4/D/E
	280 MiG-15/17	23 A-37B

Sources: The International Institute for Strategic Studies: *The Military Balance,
1987–1988* (London: IISS, 1986), pp. 162–164; U.S. Arms Control & Disarmament Agency, *World Military Expenditures & Arms Transfers, 1986* (Washington,
D.C.: Arms Control & Disarmament Agency, December 1988), p. 81.

aParamilitary forces include security forces, border guards, militia, etc.
bNorth Korean divisions are modeled after USSR/PRC divisions and number
about 10,000 men, about 65 percent of the strength of a South Korean division.
The latter follows U.S. division organization. Most of the manpower differences
lie, however, in combat support and logistics troops; the North Korean divisions
are roughly equivalent to the combat strength of South Korean divisions.
cRefers to Marine divisions.

throughout the 1960s and 1970s, South Korea under Park Chung Hee's rule
worked to achieve economic supremacy over the North during the same
period. Since the 1970s, the South has accelerated its efforts of military
buildup so that the military gap between the two Korean states has now been
narrowed measurably.[33]

Apart from the number of men in arms and the weapons count, the military strategy and battle plans of the respective Korean states are influenced by geography and terrain. The location of the respective capitals of North and South Korea, for instance, makes an important difference in terms of strategic vulnerability and force deployment. Whereas South Korea's capital city, Seoul, is only 50 km (31 miles) from the DMZ, North Korea's capital city, Pyongyang, is 145 km (90 miles) from the DMZ. With a population of nearly ten million (almost 25 percent of South Korea's entire population), Seoul is highly vulnerable to a possible surprise attack by the North. The defense of Seoul, therefore, is the foremost concern expressed by the ROK government leaders.[34]

For these and other reasons, North Korea would have a significant advantage in the initial days of fighting, provided it achieved a tactical and strategic surprise. North Korea has the capability to produce its own weapons, such as tanks and artillery, but it has to rely on outside supplies for such strategic items as fuel. Depending on the duration and intensity of warfare, therefore, North Korea is said to require the storage of sufficient supplies to continue fighting for approximately thirty to ninety days without being resupplied by the Soviet Union and China.

The U.S. command in Korea insists that the military posture of the North is offensive, and cites the forward deployment of troops and the discovery of three "invasion" tunnels as evidence for this offensive war preparedness.[35] North Korea in 1986 was said to have deployed 480,000 troops (57 percent of its estimated 838,000 armed forces) in the forward position near the DMZ, thereby reducing the lead time for a surprise attack to less than twelve hours.[36]

South Korea's Defense-Oriented Posture. South Korea's military posture is described by Washington as defensive, with U.S. troops playing the pivotal role of deterrence or "tripwire" for possible North Korean attack.[37] Tactical nuclear weapons deployed by U.S. troops in South Korea provide a bulwark against potential aggressive moves by the North, although the danger that the United States may become a hostage in an armed conflict in Korea has led some critics of the U.S. policy toward Korea to urge the removal of nuclear weapons and, eventually, U.S. troops from Korea.[38]

Until the ROK achieves self-reliance in defense and full control in command, however, the current defensive force deployment and forward strategy under U.S. supervision is unlikely to change. In view of South Korea's rapid progress in building its defense industry and its desire to obtain a nuclear capability of its own, the future military balance between North and South Korea may shift to favor the South, largely owing to the superior performance of the South Korean economy over that of the North.[39]

North Korea's Offensive Posture. North Korea's military strategy in the 1980s is noted for three characteristic features, according to a South Korean national security specialist. These are: (1) a "Combined strategy of regular and irregular wars," i.e., a Soviet-style military operation and Mao Zedong-style guerrilla warfare; (2) a "strategy of preemptive massive surprise attacks," especially against the capital city of Seoul in the so-called "three-day war" bitzkrieg-type operation; and (3) a "strategy of quick war and quick decision" by concentrating on swift initial military victory and subsequently waging propaganda campaigns to hold the territory through negotiation.[40]

The same expert believes that the DPRK's strategy is to try to avoid direct confrontation with U.S. ground forces by bypassing its position as much as possible so as to take civilians as hostages. Under such circumstances, U.S. forces could not use nuclear weapons against North Korean invading forces.[41] The possible scenario of the North Korean attack is graphically depicted, by the same observer, as follows:

> The North Korean 8th Special Army Group would make a surprise landing of AN-2 light aircraft and gliders at a point south of Seoul to create a bridgehead. An amphibious mechanized unit would come from the west coast and land on the banks of the Han River. From the midwest in front of the DMZ, light infantry would be sent through tunnels to emerge behind the front line and create confusion. Then, tanks and mechanized units would pour in from three sides to either capture or isolate Seoul. Under these new operational arts, the North Korean forces would not have to engage directly with U.S. ground force troops on the central front. In addition to this advantage, the North Korean forces would be able to take ROK civilians hostage, making it impossible for U.S. forces to use their sophisticated weaponry (probably including tactical nuclear weapons) and thus facilitating a political settlement.[42]

According to a *Japan Military Review* article, ten North Korean divisions and the Special Eighth corps, consisting of some 300,000 soldiers, are reportedly deployed along the frontline areas near the DMZ, ready to pounce on South Korea. Each of these North Korean divisions is said to command an infantry regiment, an artillery battalion, a mortar regiment, a tank battalion, an antitank battalion, and an antiaircraft regiment, while the Special Eighth corps has under its command four reconnaissance brigades, eight light infantry brigades, 23 special brigades, three amphibious brigades, and five airborne battalions.[43]

U.S. strategy in the ROK currently calls for a strike against the North in the event of a blitzkrieg type attack on the South. This strategy serves as a potent deterrence to North Korea's possible action against the South, given U.S. air superiority in the region. The capability for striking against North Korean targets has been beefed up recently, in preparation for the scheduled 1988 Seoul Summer Olympic games and the increasingly bellicose North Korean activities such as the state-sponsored terrorist acts.

SECURITY IMPLICATIONS OF THE ECONOMIC RACE

Korean Economic Competition

The economies of both North and South Korea underwent major structural changes in the 1970s. Both Koreas, for instance, advanced from a largely agricultural economy in the 1960s to a semi-industrial economy a decade later. In the South, the share of agriculture declined from 40 percent of the GNP to 20 percent between 1965 and 1976, while industry's share increased from 16 percent to 36 percent.[44] Although the details are unknown, trends in the North are believed to have followed a similar course.

In terms of per-capita distribution of the economy, the wealth of the Koreas was quite evenly matched until the early 1970s, when the South started to outdistance the North. The aggregate GNP of South Korea in 1974, for instance, was approximately twice that of North Korea, which meant that the GNP per capita was almost evenly matched between the two Korean societies in the same year. (The population ratio between South and North Koreas is approximately 2 to 1.)

Since the early 1970s, however, South Korea's economy started to grow at a much faster rate than that of North Korea so that the 1980 GNP ratio for the two nations was estimated to be almost 3 to 1; in 1987, it was more than 5 to 1 in favor of the South.[45] Whereas the GNP per capita in the North grew at an average annual rate of 5.2 percent between 1960 and 1976 and at a much slower rate thereafter up until 1987, South Korea averaged a rate of 7.3 percent between 1960 and 1976, and 7.6 percent between 1961 and 1984. In South Korea, the GNP per capita increased from U.S. $590 in 1975 to $810 in 1977, $1,500 in 1981 and $2,813 in 1987; in North Korea, it changed from U.S. $620 in 1975 to $700 in 1977, $950 in 1981, and just over $1,000 in 1985.[46]

South Korea generally enjoys far more advanced economic and industrial capabilities than the North.[47] The total volume of the South's foreign trade was also more than ten times that of the North in 1975; by 1987, the ratio could very well be almost twenty to one.[48] South Korean technology is far superior to that of the North in almost every category.

In the early 1980s, both Korean economies suffered from economic difficulties in the wake of worldwide economic recession. South Korean economic growth and stability were adversely affected by high inflation, worldwide oil shocks, and uncertain supplies of other key raw materials. South Korea's export of manufactured products also encountered the rising pressures of protectionism in world trade. North Korea's economic problems in the early 1980s appeared even more serious as a result of heavy defense expenditures, increasing foreign debt (approximately U.S. $3.5 billion), and lagging technology.[49]

Soviet and Chinese economic aid to North Korea is not sufficient to enable the North to catch up with South Korea's economic and industrial advances. Under such circumstances, the North seems to have no alternative but to turn outward economically, patterning itself after China's successful program of "four modernizations" and economic reform measures. The new joint venture law enacted on 8 September 1984, together with "the trade development resolution" adopted by the Third Session of the Seventh Supreme Peoples Assembly on 26 January 1984, is an expression of North Korea's altered economic development strategy.[50] Its implementation has not been encouraging or successful, however.

Consequences of the South Outperforming the North. The differential pattern and rates of economic growth will have far-reaching consequences and policy implications for inter-Korean relations. In this regard, it will be helpful to examine some of the probable causes for the ROK's outperformance of the DPRK economically.

Many reasons are given as to why the GNP grew much faster in South Korea than in the North in the 1970s. According to a U.S. government study, three factors were responsible for the South's outperforming the North in the decade prior to 1976.[51] First, the South spent proportionately much less on defense than did the North; second, the South, by importing more efficient technology, had a much higher rate of return on industrial investment; and third, the South developed a dynamic, export-oriented economy that generated the foreign exchange necessary to finance rising levels of capital imports.[52]

The study also noted the structural contrast between the two Koreas. North Korea is "a tightly closed society with a planned economy with many elements of the bureaucratic Soviet model of the 1940s and 1950s," and "its educational system spends about as much time imparting the ideology of Kim Il-sung as instilling more practical knowledge."[53] The technical competence of North Korea's labor force and bureaucracy suffers as a result, and North Korea remains inferior to the South.

The economic planners and top businessmen in South Korea are not only well educated, many with advanced degrees from foreign universities, but they are providing extensive training facilities for upgrading the technical skills of a diligent labor force. In the early 1980s, firms with more than 200 employees in South Korea were required to provide training for 15 percent of their employees.[54] In the communication field, especially, the South has been way ahead of the North. The number of vehicles, radio stations, and television stations is much greater in South Korea, for instance, than it is in the North.

Political Significance of the South Overtaking the North Economically. The principal strengths of North Korea, according to one study, are its tight and absolutely controlled political structure, its potent military establishment, and Kim Il-sung's absolute control of the economic and social structure.[55] These characteristics may be weaknesses as well under varied circumstances. Thus, the North Korean vulnerabilities, according to the same study, are fourfold: its economic weakness relative to the South, its potential for political instability during succession, its declining international position relative to the South, and the limited support received from its allies, the Soviet Union and the PRC.[56] The widening gap of the economy between North and South Korea will accentuate the vulnerabilities of the North vis-à-vis the South.

The immediate consequence of the ROK's outperforming the DPRK in the economic race is obviously the question of how to institutionalize the peace process on the Korean Peninsula, as Seoul sees it, and how to help North Korea to overcome its status of isolation which is largely self-imposed. South Korea will benefit in the long run if North Korea acquires a capability to see the world as it actually is and become more realistically and pragmatically oriented. North Korea in the post-Kim Il-sung era may by necessity adopt the posture of pragmatism and an open-door policy in line with the model of China under Deng Xiaoping. North Korea must come to accept the reality that South Korea is outperforming the North economically and thus militarily as well.

If North Korea does not reform from within, it may eventually be compelled to accept an inferior position in regard to South Korea. This will mean that the North can no longer afford to be intransigent toward the South and that the South will be able to dictate the terms of *modus operandi* vis-à-vis the North regarding matters of inter-Korean relations, especially with regard to the important question of Korean reunification and peace in the Korean Peninsula.

The challenging question, from the perspective of the Seoul government, will be how to manage smoothly the "crossover" in the military power relations between the North and the South and to capitalize on the consequence of the ROK outperforming the DPRK economically.

In the final analysis, the outcome of the current military and economic competition between the two Korean states will be determined by the quality of political leadership and institutions. The leaders of the two Koreas are expected to translate economic resources and military capabilities into workable political capital and assets. How to manage the "crossover" in power relations between the ROK and the DPRK, emanating from a major shift in economic and military power relations, remains one of the most important policy issues.[57]

The time will come for South Korea to outpace and outperform North Korea militarily. The time will also come for the United States to reassess its security role abroad and to withdraw troops form South Korea. A challenging question for South Korea's political leadership will therefore be how to cope with the evolving situation so that that nation can maximize the benefit and values for maintaining peace and stability on the Korean Peninsula without the presence of the U.S. troops on Korean soil.

While the current modernization efforts continue, the more self-sufficient ROK army could have the unintended effect of hastening the withdrawal of U.S. forces from South Korea, thereby destabilizing the region more broadly. Under the circumstances, the challenging question is, as already noted, "how to manage the crossover in power relations between North and South Korea smoothly." The related important policy question for the ROK will be how to prevent a possible U.S. force withdrawal from South Korea as a result of the South overtaking the North militarily.

CONCLUSION

Given the existing trends of growing disparity in powers between the ROK and the DPRK, it will be to the advantege of all parties concerned in the Northeast Asian security system to enable a smooth transition of the military balance of power to occur between the divided states of Korea. It will be to everyone's interest and advantage to see the powder keg of the Korean Peninsula begin to defuse its explosive potential. The time has come to put an end to the arms race on the Korean Peninsula and to take steps toward deescalating the level of lethal conflict between the two halves of embattled Korea.

Specific measures of tension reduction and confidence-building are needed, of course, as are the broad measures of deescalation of regional conflict on the Korean soil. Time will not permit us to elaborate and belabor here the details of these and other related measures.[58] Suffice it to say that any move toward institutionalizing the peace process on the Korean Peninsula will help to maintain regional stability and peace in Northeast Asia, thereby enhancing the cause of global and world peace.

In order for the Korean people to play such a constructive regional role, however, the present state of the intensified and wasteful arms race must come to an end. This will require a move toward the normalization of inter-Korean relations through mutual reconciliation and the policies of détente and rapprochement between the two hostile regimes.

Both Korean governments are obviously using the 1988 Seoul Olympics for political gain and propaganda. North Korea's demand for cohosting the Summer Olympics is not acceptable to South Korea and to the International Olympics Committee, which failed to persuade Pyongyang to accept a compromise package of holding a few games.

Finally, any progress toward military deescalation on the Korean Peninsula must be accompanied by prior political and diplomatic moves that will assist and induce North Korea to abandon its long-standing policy of self-imposed isolation. North Korea needs to keep up with changes by adopting its own version of the *glasnost* open-door policy and *perestroika* economic reform and reconstruction (similar to what China under Deng Xiaoping and the Soviet Union under Gorbachev have also initiated). South Korea and her allies will be able to exert some influence on North Korea's future behavior, however limited that influence might be, by offering an incentive for North Korea to seek peace and reconciliation instead of war and confrontation.

In this regard, the pronouncement of South Korea's Roh Tae Woo's government on 7 July 1988 toward North Korea was both positive and encouraging. The Seoul government announced its intention of reversing its traditional anti-North Korean diplomatic stance by removing restrictions on cross-contacts by its allies with North Korea. This act of positive diplomacy may ameliorate tensions on the Korean Peninsula and improve the prospect of resuming inter-Korean dialogue and negotiation regarding the future of Korea. It is hoped that the situation in the post-Seoul Olympics era will be one where "normalcy" is restored rather than one wherein the Koreas revert to heightened tension. Perhaps the miracle of turning swords into plowshares will be possible for the two Koreas.

NOTES

An earlier version of this chapter was presented at the Western Michigan University Symposium on "Asian Security Issues," Kalamazoo, Michigan, 7–9 April 1988. The author wishes to thank Professors C. I. Eugene Kim and Lawrence Ziring for their helpful comments.

1. Regarding South Korean perspectives concerning Korean security, in English, see: Sang-Woo Rhee, *Security and Unification of Korea*, (Seoul: Sogang University Press, 1984); Young Choi, "The North Korean Military Buildup and Its Impacts on North Korean Military Strategy in the 1980s," *Asian Survey* 25, No. 3 (March 1985): pp. 341–355; and Young-Ho Lee, "Military Balance and Peace in the Korean Peninsula," *Asian Survey* 21, No. 8 (August 1981), pp. 852–864.

On non-South Korean perspectives, including those of U.S. analysts, see Larry A. Niksch, "The Military Balance on the Korean Peninsula," *Korea & World Affairs*, Vol. 10, No. 2 (Summer 1986), pp. 253–277; Edward N. Luttwak and Steven L. Canby, "The Defense of Korea," in Robert L. Downen, ed., *Northeast Asia in the 1980s: Challenge and Opportunity*, Washington, D.C.: CSIS, 1983; William Scully, "The Korean Peninsula Military Balance," Backgrounder No. 2 of Asian Studies Center (11 July 1983) (Washington, D.C.: The Heritage Foundations, 1983); and Franklin B. Weinstein and Fuji Kamiya, eds., *The Security of Korea: U.S. and Japanese Perspectives on the 1980s*, (Boulder, CO: Westview Press, 1980).

2. This theme is further elaborated in Young Whan Kihl, *Politics and Policies in Divided Korea: Regimes in Contest*, (Boulder, CO: Westview Press, 1984).

3. Young Whan Kihl, "The Korean Peninsula Conflict: Equilibrium or Deescalation?" In Lawrence A. Grinter and Young Whan Kihl, eds., *East Asian Conflict Zones: Prospects for Regional Stability and Deescalation* (New York: St. Martin's Press, 1987), pp. 97–122.

4. Joseph A. Yager, "The Security Environment of the Korean Peninsula in the 1980s," *Asian Perspective* (Seoul), 8–1 (Spring–Summer 1984), pp. 85–105.

5. See, for instance, President Ronald Reagan's press conference of 13 February 1986 in reference to the Philippine situation, regarding some of these choke points to contain the Soviet expansionism.

6. Donald S. Zagoria, ed., *Soviet Policy in East Asia* (New Haven: Yale University Press, 1982). See, especially, Ralph N. Clough, "The Soviet Union and the Two Koreas," in Zagoria, *Soviet Policy*, pp. 175–200.

7. Japan Defense Agency, *Defense of Japan, 1983*, as cited in *Japan Economic Institute Report No. 8A* (Washington, D.C., JEI, 1985), p. 8.

8. *Ibid.*

9. Young Whan Kihl, "North Korea: A Reevaluation," *Current History*, Vol. 81, No. 474 (April 1982), p. 181.

10. Young Whan Kihl, "North Korea in 1983: Transforming 'The Hermit Kingdom'?" *Asian Survey*, 24–2 (January 1984), p. 105.

11. Scully, "Korean Military Balance," p. 14.

12. *Defense of Japan, 1983.*

13. Far Eastern Economic Review, *Asia 1985 Yearbook*, 20 November 1984), pp. 26–27, 30.

14. Chae-Jin Lee and Hideo Sato, *U.S. Policy Toward Japan and Korea* (New York: Praeger, 1982).

15. Nathan N. White, *U.S. Policy Toward Korea: Analysis, Alternatives, and Recommendations* (Boulder, CO: Westview Press, 1979).

16. Larry Niksch, "U.S. Troop Withdrawal from South Korea: Past Shortcomings and Future Prospects," *Asian Survey* 21, 3, (March 1981), pp. 325–241.

17. Paul D. Wolfowitz, "Recent Security Developments in Korea," U.S. Department of State Bureau of Public Affairs, Current Policy No. 731, 12 August 1985.

18. Weinstein and Kamiya, *Security of Korea*,.

19. Young Whan Kihl, "Sorenno Kanhanto Seisaku (Soviet Policy Toward the Korean Peninsula)," *Koria Hyoron* No. 270 (November–December 1984, Tokyo), pp. 3–15; Clough, *The Soviet Union*, pp. 175–176.

20. Press report of 2 May 1988 as cited in Myung-o Bae, "Prospects of Inter-Korean Military Relations," paper prepared to be presented at the International Conference on Inter-Korean Relations After the Seoul Olympics: 1–3 July 1988, Crystal Gateway Marriot Hotel, Arlington, VA, p. 15.

21. Young Whan Kihl, "North Korea in 1984: The 'Hermit Kingdom' Turns Outward!" *Asian Survey* 25–1 (January 1985), pp. 65–79.

22. For instance, see Larry A. Niksch, "The Military Balance"; William Scully, "The Korean Peninsula Military Balance"; and Sang-Woo Rhee, *Security and Unification of Korea.*

23. Charles Wolf, Jr., et. al., *The Changing Balance: South and North*

Korean Capabilities for Long-Term Military Competition (Santa Monica, CA: Rand, December 1985).

24. The London-based International Institute of Strategic Studies sources indicate that "the opposing forces in the Korean Peninsula are roughly equivalent" *The Military Balance, 1986–1987* (London: IISS, 1986), p. 118.

25. Young Whan Kihl, "The 5th Column: Korea's North-South Dialogue Rests on a Powder Keg," *Far Eastern Economic Review*, 17 October 1985, pp. 44–45.

26. U.S. Arms Control & Disarmament Agency, *World Military Expenditures and Arms Transfers, 1986* (Washington, D.C.: Arms Control & Disarmament Agency, December 1988), pp. 162–163.

27. Japan Defense Agency, *Defense of Japan, 1983* (Tokyo: JDA, 1984), as cited in *Japan Economic Institute Report*, No. 8A (Washington, D.C., JEI, 1985) .

28. *The Military Balance, 1987–88*: pp. 162–163.

29. *Ibid.*

30. *Ibid.*

31. "New Study Raises U.S. Estimate of North Korean Army Strength," *New York Times*, 4 January 1979 and Vernon Guidry, "How the Tow Koreas Stack Up Militarily," *Washington Star*, 27 May 1977, p. 3.

32. Kihl, *Politics and Policies*, p. 147.

33. Military analysts disagree as to whether the military balance between the ROK and the DPRK is evenly matched or is in favor of the North. The trend, however, seems to be toward an arms equilibrium between the two Koreas. Also see, in this regard, Charles Wold, *The Changing Balance*.

34. Kihl, *Politics and Policies*, p. 149.

35. *Ibid.*, p. 150.

36. This is a statement made by Admiral Ronald Hays, Commander-in-Chief of the U.S. Pacific Command, at a news conference in Bangkok, Thailand, in February 1986. See *The Korea Herald*, 7 March 1986.

37. U.S. Congress, Senate Committee on Foreign relations, *U.S. Troop Withdrawal from the Republic of Korea, A Report to the Committee by Senators Hubert H. Humphrey and John Glenn*, 9 January 1978, 95th Congress, 2d Session (Washington, D.C.: Government Printing Office, 1978), p. 33; and Ralph N. Clough, *Deterrence and Defense in Korea: The Role of U.S. Forces* (Washington, D.C.: Brookings Institution, 1976), as cited in Kihl, *Politics and Policies*, p. 150.

38. Kihl, *Politics and Policies*, p. 150.

39. Wolf, *The Changing Balance*.

40. Young Choi, "The North Korean Military Buildup," pp. 343–348.

41. *Ibid.*, p. 355.

42. *Ibid.*

43. *Japan Military Review* (February 1986), as reported in *The Korea Herald*, 18 February 1986.

44. *U.S. CIA, Korea: The Economic Race Between the North and The South: A Research Paper* (Washington, D.C.: National Foreign Assessment Center and the Library of Congress, 1978); and The National Unification

Board, *A Comparative Study of the South and North Korean Economies* (Seoul: The National Unification Board, 1986): pp. 34–35.

45. *A Comparative Study of the South and North Korean Economies*, p. 35.

46. *Ibid.*; Also, see: Young Whan Kihl, "The Political Economy of Development in Divided Korea," *Journal of Economics and International Relations*, Vol. 1, No. 2 (Summer 1987): pp. 125–136.

47. *Ibid.*; Kihl, The Political Economy.

48. *Ibid.*

49. *Ibid.*

50. Young Whan Kihl, "North Korea's New Pragmatism," *Current History*, Vol. 85, No. 510 (April 1986): pp. 164–167, 198.

51. *U.S.CIA, Korea, The Economic Race*, p. 2.

52. *Ibid.*, p. 6.

53. *Ibid.*

54. *Ibid.*

55. Richard L. Sneider, *The Political and Social Capabilities of North and South Korea for the Long-Term Military Competition* (Santa Monica, CA: Rand, January 1985), pp. 35–36.

56. *Ibid.*

57. On this and related issues of changing U.S. policy toward Korea, see Edward Olsen, *U.S. Policy and the Two Koreas* (Boulder, CO: Westview Press, 1988).

58. On some of the possible measures of deescalating Korean conflict, see Kihl, "The Korean Peninsula Conflict," pp. 112-118.

Part 3
Southeast Asia and Oceania

8

Vietnam's Strategy for Indochina and Security in Southeast Asia

WILLIAM S. TURLEY

As power diffuses and hegemony wanes, local actors gain ability to shape political and security arrangements for their regions. Such is the case in Southeast Asia which, like Northeast Asia, is an area where there is a strong potential for the interests of the United States, the Soviet Union, China, and Japan to conflict. Local rivalries have reemerged after a century of colonial rule and warfare, and despite an overlay of great power competition, initiative belongs to the states of the region. Vietnam in particular has responded to its own national reunification, the U.S. retreat from the mainland, and a reaasertive China by seeking to consolidate a new pattern of relations with its neighbors and extra-regional powers. This striving already has affected security in Southeast Asia and the strategic positions of the great powers in the Western Pacific. Significant long-term implications hinge on the goals, perceptions, determination, and capabilities of the Vietnamese. In this chapter, "Viet-centric" views of strategic security and regional order are examined in order to determine what some of these implications might be.

Attention necessarily focuses on the conflict that centers upon Cambodia. There, Pol Pot's Khmer Rouge broke away from Vietnamese tutelage even before the Second Indochina War ended. As Hanoi tilted toward Moscow, China supported the Khmer Rouge against the Vietnamese. Finally, in 1978, Hanoi obtained reassurance from Moscow and intervened in December to suppress a Cambodian regime it judged to be subservient to China.[1] That intervention provoked attack by China and opposition from the noncommunist Association of Southeast Asian Nations (ASEAN) supported by the United States and Japan. The ensuing conflict facilitated Soviet efforts to consolidate a closer relationship with Vietnam, and it deepened Vietnamese dependence on the Soviet Union. The conflict was entangled from the beginning in the Sino-Soviet dispute and had potential to create a deep regional cleavage subordinate to the rivalry of Beijing and Moscow.

However, the trilateral great power competition permits regional actors a greater degree of flexibility than they had during the period of U.S. hegemony. Great powers supply local contestants, thereby sustaining conflicts in the region, but they gain little leverage over them in return. Vietnam's dependency on the Soviet Union, for example, is matched by the Soviet dependency on Vietnam to extend the range of its largest fleet into waters hitherto a preserve of the United States, and for a foothold on China's southern flank. The Soviet Union has, so far, no other viable way other than cooperating with Vietnam to project power into the South China Sea and Indian Ocean competitively with the United States. In turn, Soviet dependency on Vietnam assures Hanoi of support for its own goals in Indochina. Those goals are incompatible with the Thai perception that Thailand's security is threatened by a Vietnamese military presence in the Mekong basin, while protracted conflict disturbs other ASEAN states because it provides opportunities for great powers, principally China and the Soviet Union, to gain influence in the region. For U.S. policy to respond effectively, it is necessary to understand Hanoi's goals in some detail and to gauge its commitment and ability to attain them.

THE SETTING

Without implying geopolitical determinism, certain environmental features of Southeast Asia must be given their due. Though Vietnamese communist leaders hold conceptions about security and international politics that distinguish them from other elites that have governed Vietnam, geography and history shape their views. These influences help to explain the recurrence of certain features of conflict in the region.

The dominant geopolitical feature of Southeast Asia is political fragmentation combined with the region's location on China's periphery. China historically has sought to keep regional powers weak, divided, or deferential and to exclude competitors in order to minimize threat from this quarter. Except in the ultimately unsuccessful attempt to conquer Vietnam, China pursued this strategy before the colonial period by manipulating trade privileges, mediating disputes, and maintaining tributary relations, and by implementing limited military forays. China pursued this strategy up to the late nineteenth century(even though challenged on its own territory) in an attempt to avert the unification of Indochina by France. Following the revolution, for lack of alternatives while the Western presence was still strong, Chinese tactics emphasized support of insurgencies, but the strategy was the same. Ironically, the Vietnamese were the first to benefit as China sought to terminate the French presence on its southern flank and then to prevent the United States from obtaining a second foothold on the Asian mainland. Communist China supported the Vietnamese not so much for ideological reasons as to push back Western power from China's periphery.

Over the years, China has supported insurgencies in virtually every Southeast Asian country. It has given this support sometimes to weaken regimes and sometimes to secure leverage over them (e.g., to enforce Burma's neutrality). In 1979, it suspended support of insurgencies in the ASEAN countries in exchange for improved state-to-state relations. Since then China has assisted insurgencies in Laos, Cambodia, and Vietnam in an attempt to break up an emergent bloc and to deter an alliance between that bloc and the Soviet Union. Throughout the 1980s, it was the only great power supplying direct military support to insurgencies in Southeast Asia. Only internal upheaval and external challenge have ever created breaks in China's striving for predominance within the region. Of all Southeast Asian countries, Vietnam has most often fallen within the scope of China's strategic concern—whether as beneficiary or victim.

A second important feature to consider is the process of state consolidation that has taken place in Southeast Asia over the period of two thousand years. For the Vietnamese, this process occurred in the context of repeated attempts by China to subjugate them. The consequences were to implant a deep antipathy to China and to steel the Vietnamese for southward expansion at the expense of weaker neighbors. The Thai likewise expanded southward, and with the same result. By the seventh century, Vietnam and Thailand had emerged as the leading contenders for power on the Southeast Asian mainland and commenced a rivalry for influence in the buffers between them. The root of conflict was the shared perception that the Mekong basin comprising lowland Laos and most of Cambodia was a line of unity (and not a division) that neither power could let fall to the other without a threat to its security.[2]

Sporadically over two centuries, beginning in 1623, the two countries supported rival claimants to the Cambodian throne and attempted to enforce exclusive claims to suzerainty. These interventions involved armed action inside Cambodia, the supply of arms and troops to the Khmer contestants, one outright military occupation (by Vietnam), the annexation of Cambodian territory (by both nations), and general warfare. Colonial rule suspended this rivalry, just as it removed China as a factor in Southeast Asia international politics. It also unified Indochina under a single administration for the first time in history, much to the Thais' consternation. When colonial power receded, Thailand had the advantage of having escaped direct rule, while Vietnam went through two devastating wars. Rivalry resumed as the Thais seized this opportunity to work for the fragmentation of Indochina and weaken Vietnam. Between 1959 and 1973, the Thais sent twenty-five battalions of "volunteers" into Laos and facilitated the U.S. bombardment of Vietnam from Thai territory. Vietnam simultaneously responded by aiding an ongoing insurgent movement in Thailand and placing regular troops within Laos.

Last is Vietnam's construction as a thin sliver of land on the edge of the Asian landmass. Open deltas at either end of this sliver support dense populations, but these are flat, vulnerable, and separated by over a thousand kilometers of cross-running ridges. Between these ridges lie small areas of human settlement and coastal enclaves. The terrain is hostile to internal communication and traditionally has made Vietnam difficult to govern and defend. Whereas Thailand is held together by its topography, Vietnam is divided by it; Thailand has flourished under informal state structures, while Vietnam has relied on bureaucracy to hold it together.[3] The sea can be a link, but the concentration of people along the coastline also places the bulk of resources within easy range of seaborne attack. Consequently, the Vietnamese have felt it neccessary to control the mountainous hinterland shared with Laos and Cambodia in order to have a secure rear and linkage between regions. To the Vietnamese, this requirement has seemed to grow in importance since in modern times three great powers, two of them with Thai connivance, have intervened in Laos and Cambodia to obstruct a struggle for national independence and unity in Vietnam.

These considerations encourage Vietnamese communist leaders, as they did their predecessors, to view Vietnam as the vanguard of geo-cultural values (Chinese in the past, Marxist-Leninist in the present) in Southeast Asia and the region's bulwark against China's political and military power. They also provide a basis for the Vietnamese, so long as there is no revolution in Thailand, to interpret Thai policy as a traditional pursuit of power and expansion, now aided by a hostile United States and China. These contexts also make the Vietnamese extremely sensitive to threats against their internal lines of communication, which causes the Vietnamese to insist upon unimpeded access to Laos and Cambodia. Such perceptions, however, are only a substratum compared with others that reflect the current Vietnamese leadership's experience on the road to power, strategic aims, and ideology.

INDOCHINA IN VIETNAMESE COMMUNIST STRATEGY

The most common assumption about Vietnamese strategy is that it aims to establish Hanoi's dominion over all of Indochina, perhaps in some kind of federal structure. Evidence for this perception is found in precolonial Vietnamese relations with Laos and Cambodia, the Communist party's claim to responsibility for revolution in all three countries up to 1951, and in references to an Indochina Federation in early party documents. It is reinforced by awareness that the French colonial regime relied on the Vietnamese to administer Laos and Cambodia, that the Vietnamese have tutored Lao and Khmer communists down to the present, and that Le Duc Tho boasted in secret talks with Henry Kissinger (according to Kissinger) of "his people's destiny not merely to take over South Vietnam but to dominate the whole of Indochina."[4]

The conventional view, however, rests on simplistic historicist premises. It also assumes a uniformity of experience among Vietnamese elites that did not exist. The true inheritors of the French mandate were Vietnamese employees of the French colonial administration, and these wound up in Saigon and not Hanoi, in 1954. For these reasons, the evolution of communist strategy in regard to Indochina, though familiar in broad outline, deserves close attention.

That evolution began with a dispute over the party's name at the time of its founding. In February 1930, representatives of four Vietnamese communist groups met at a "merger conference" at the behest of Ho Chi Minh to found the Vietnam Communist Party (VCP). The name reflected a wish to concentrate on achieving independence for Vietnam and low esteem for the revolutionary potential of Laos and Cambodia. Delegates from northern Vietnam also asserted that "in accordance with Leninist self-determinism they could not make the Cambodian and Lao proletariats enter the party with them."[5] The idea of assuming responsibility for revolution in all Indochina seems to have had little support. That responsibility was assumed later in order to bring VCP policy into line with the Comintern principle of matching parties in the colonial world with colonial (not ethnic) jurisdictions. Accordingly, the first Plenum of the Central Committee, held in October 1930 principally to correct the "errors" of the merger conference and without Ho present, gave considerable attention to the question of the party name. The plenum resolution stated that "instructions from the Comintern" were to "drop the name 'Vietnam Communist Party' and take the name 'Indochina Communist Party'" (ICP).[6] Although the reasons for this change were by no means obvious to the membership, the explanation given was that despite differences of custom, language, and "race," the Vietnamese, Cambodian, and Lao "proletariats" had formed a close political and economic relationship due to their joint subjugation by French colonialism. Since the colonial administration was a "unified concentrated force," it was necessary to "have a single Communist Party to concentrate the force of the proletariat in all of the countries of Indochina."[7] The Central Committee further explained that since the three countries had grown interdependent under colonial rule, each required the support of the other two to overthrow colonial rule and "if separated each would lack sufficient conditions for economic activity. Erroneous recognition of these conditions, has resulted in many dangerous interpretations of the party's ideology. The 'name' problem may seem only a matter for form, a small matter, but in reality it has importance because it can influence the thought and actions of the Party."[8]

Though this affair took place when the party had only two hundred to three hundred members, it had lasting importance because these founders, who were to lead the party down to the present, passed on views formed during this period to the membership as a whole. The incident revealed important formative elements in Vietnamese communist orientations toward

Indochina. First, the perception of Indochina as a unity did not come naturally to the majority of party members who tended to dismiss the revolutionary potential of Laos and Cambodia. The need to involve Laos and Cambodia was not evident. The requirements of ideological orthodoxy and subservience to Moscow caused a split within the party on this issue, with Ho himself at odds to the Comintern.[9] Second, in 1930, few Vietnamese Communists perceived any threat emanating from Laos and Cambodia. Obsession with their own subjugation to French rule and the decades of "protection" afforded by it weakened the perception of events in those countries as vital to Vietnam. It took time and experience to ingrain the idea that Vietnam's revolution would be jeopardized if French power remained unchallenged in Laos and Cambodia.[10] Third, ideology reshaped, if it did not completely supplant, traditional Vietnamese attitudes toward the Lao and Khmer. Although the low esteem for the revolutionary potential of these peoples resonated with an older belief in their cultural backwardness, the evidence given to support this view was that they lacked the requisite class structure to sustain a proletarian party. Such reasoning implied poor prospects for a Marxist *mission civilisatrice* and ruled against organizing proletarian revolutions in Laos and Cambodia contemporaneously with that of Vietnam. Fourth, the concept of trinational unity embodied in the name, Indochinese Community Party, grew out of general guidelines on organizing against colonial rule. These guidelines were drawn up by Comintern officials (including a few Vietnamese) and were imposed on those who attended the first plenum in October 1930. There is no evidence that the concept was camouflage for an ancient ambition of the Vietnamese to dominate all of Indochina. Last, the assertion that the three countries had become economically interdependent implied that their ties should be preserved in some form following colonial rule. With little foundation in fact, this assertion was but an echo of the Comintern principle that peoples united by colonial rule should remain federated pending establishment of a global union of socialist republics (though it was an assertion that would be resuscitated in the 1970s—see below).

For the remainder of the 1930s, the ICP did little to live up to its name. Very little effort was made to recruit members in Laos and Cambodia. Directives from the Comintern to extend organizing work among non-Vietnamese went largely ignored as members focused on people whose language and patriotic aspirations they shared. Federating Indochina after independence appeared among the goals laid down at the 1st Party Congress in 1935 and again in the resolution of the 8th Plenum in 1941, but they were otherwise disregarded. Party members were too concerned with their own survival to take interest in the practical implications of what some say was a vague expression of solidarity, not a concrete objective.[11]

The first serious attempt to broaden the revolution cross-nationally flowed from support for Lao residing in Vietnam who were swept up in the anti-French fervor of 1945. The event that did most to awaken Vietnamese Communists to the unity of Indochina was the first French attacks from bases in these countries against the Viet Minh's mountain redoubts in 1947. The Vietnamese soon saw revolutions in Laos and Cambodia as means to tie down the French from the rear. The Comintern's instructions, in retrospect, must have seemed extraordinarily prescient. The "internationalists" views in the party were vindicated. Indochina henceforward was to be considered a "single strategic unit," though principally for military reasons. As Vo Nguyen Giap put it in 1950;

> Indochina is a single strategic unit, a single battlefield, and here we have the mission of helping the movement to liberate all of Indochina. This is because militarily, Indochina is one bloc, one unit, in both the invasion and defense plans of the enemy. For this reason, and especially because of the strategic terrain, we cannot consider Vietnam to be independent so long as Cambodia and Laos are under imperialist domination, just as we cannot consider Cambodia and Laos to be independent so long as Vietnam is under imperialist rule.
>
> The colonialists used Cambodia to attack Vietnam. Laos and Cambodia temporarily have become the secure rear areas of the enemy and simultaneously their most vulnerable area in the entire Indochina theater. Therefore, we need to open the Laos-Cambodia battlefield resolutely and energetically.[12]

It was against this background that the ICP decided to push revolutions in Laos and Cambodia. In February 1951, the party invited Lao and Cambodian leaders to attend its 2nd Congress, which proclaimed the formation of the Vietnam Worker's Party to replace the ICP. The Congress resolution noted that "the people of Viet-Nam are wiling to enter into long-term cooperation with the peoples of Laos and Cambodia, with a view to bringing about an independent, free, strong and prosperous federation of states in Vietnam, Laos and Cambodia, if the three peoples so desire."[13]

A month later, a Joint Conference attended by representatives of the three national united fronts for Vietnam, Laos, and Cambodia established an "alliance . . . on the basis of free choice, equality, mutual assistance, and mutual respect of national sovereignty" and elected a Joint Committee "with a view to strengthen friendly relations and realize mutual assistance between the three peoples."[14] References to an Indochina Federation then disappeared form party texts, and separate Lao and Cambodian communist parties were established. The purpose was to capitalize on patriotic sentiment in all three countries and mobilize joint struggle against French colonialism and U.S. interventionism.[15]

By the end of the war, as the Viet Minh strove to link up their far-flung base areas, they also noted that the central highlands were of "extreme strategic importance." "Only by developing into the Central Highlands," observed the political bureau's military committee in November 1953, "is it possible to obtain the most important strategic position in the South. If the enemy controls that strategic zone, it will be very difficult to improve the situation in the South."[16]

The validity of perceiving Indochina as having unity imposed on it by the strategies of others seemed, to the Vietnamese, confirmed by subsequent events. Even before the Second Indochina War began, the United States, with Thai connivance, took advantage of instability in Laos to secure a foothold in the same lowland from which the French had attacked the Viet Minh. The United States and Thailand undermined Laotian neutrality and equipped the Royal Lao Army and hill tribes to attack the Ho Chi Minh Trail. The United States also capitalized on Sihanouk's overthrow in 1970 to attack Vietnamese sanctuaries in Cambodia. Although the Vietnamese were hardly innocent of provocation, the implications for Vietnam's security and unity seemed clear. By 1977, as relations between Beijing and Hanoi deteriorated, the Vietnamese could not but view Chinese support for the Khmer Rouge as the third attempt by a great power in modern times to encircle and attack Vietnam from the west. The Vietnamese thus were satisfied in their own minds that their responses were first defensive and then, in December 1978, preemptive.

Hanoi's Indochina strategy grows principally out of the perception that the three countries remain security interdependent. This perception has been expressed both privately and publicly by Hanoi officials as a "law" since adversaries must gain a foothold in at least one of the states in order to attack another and the three states must be joined in alliance to guarantee the peace and independence of each. In the words of the commander of Vietnamese forces in Cambodia, "Experience over more than half a century on the Indochinese peninsula shows that the aggressive plots of the Japanese fascists, French colonialists, and U.S. imperialists as well as the Chinese expansionists and hegemonists down to the present have always treated Indochina as a target of aggression and a unified battleground. . . . In their plots to annex Indochina and expand into Southeast Asia, the Beijing reactionaries cannot help but follow this law."[17]

Vietnamese leaders who have come to maturity over the course of the three wars with major powers cannot accept the reconstitution of Laos and Cambodia as "neutral buffers" if that means having governments in Vientiane and Phnom Penh that are divided or vulnerable to penetration by powers besides Vietnam. Since proposals for coalition governments like those put forth by ASEAN for Cambodia could have this result, they are thus far unacceptable—so would any other forms of *real* power-sharing, recent signals to the contrary notwithstanding.[18] This has become so basic in Vietnamese thinking that leaders in Hanoi up to now have been unable to distinguish between consolidating friendly regimes in Laos and Cambodia and defending their own country.

Hanoi's ties with Moscow are almost certainly subordinate to its aims in

Indochina. Relations with the Soviet Union are, of course, enormously important as a vital source of economic and military assistance and as a counterweight to the Chinese. But it is quite unrealistic to expect Moscow to force a Cambodian settlement on Vietnam that fundamentally dilutes Hanoi's influence in Phnom Penh, except in the unlikely event that the Soviet Union sacrificed important interests in Vietnam.

IDEOLOGICAL PERCEPTIONS

Though, in general, it may be true that realism prevails over ideology, it would be an error to overlook the influence of ideology in regard to Vietnamese perceptions and strategy.[19] The Vietnamese are in the early stages of consolidating their revolution, whose success in attaining power they attribute to the correct application of doctrine. Though economic problems already have pushed them toward revisionism regarding "socialist construction," leaders who have so recently applied doctrine to achieve national independence and unity still place great faith in its utility to analyze and manage external threats.

The Vietnamese rely heavily on ideological concepts, particularly in assessing long-term trends and attempting to predict internal shifts in countries of concern to them. Since the late 1960s, they have joined the Soviets in maintaining that the "central contradiction" in the present era places "three revolutionary currents" in opposition to capitalism and imperialism. These currents are the socialist camp headed by the Soviet Union, the national liberation movement in the Third World, and the workers' movement in capitalist countries. As these currents gain strength, so will the nations that coordinate their policies with them, the theory predicts.

This theory, combined with a doctrine of historical inevitability, reduces diplomacy and strategy to matters of adjustment to the winning trends. As a deputy foreign minister put it: "In assessing the situation for purposes of making policy decisions, it is necessary above all else to look at the trends. Certain trends are inevitable. Those who see these trends and follow them succeed, those who oppose them fail. . . . Vietnam has been successful because it is on the side of the growing number of countries that have won their independence. Though these countries have economic problems, they are developing while peace is being consolidated."[20] It follows that if statesmen have assessed the trends correctly and devised policies that conform to the winning trends, the nation will benefit from change over the long run, regardless of trials in the short-term. To the nostrum that patience assures success, ideology adds confidence that the trends have been assessed correctly.

Marxism-Leninism also directs attention to internal structures of class and power when assessing the cohesion, capabilities, and external behavior of other societies. The application of these ideas by the Vietnamese is based on an interpretation of their own experience, however. Convinced that they achieved power by manipulating inequalities in their own society, and confident that equality is the foundation of their national solidarity and strength, Vietnamese strategists are not much impressed by the aggregate wealth of their neighbors. What captures their attention is the unequal wealth distributions in these countries, distributions which they regard as a cause of grave weakness. Moreover, ideology predicts that these inequalities will grow worse under capitalist-driven, export-oriented development strategies. While they do not expect revolutions identical to their own to occur, they are confident that rising social tensions will preoccupy ASEAN elites in the future, making them eager to remove sources of friction from the region.[21] These expectations have been confirmed by the sharpening of communal tensions in Malaysia, the continuing insurgency and political instability in Malaysia, the first stirrings of opposition in Indonesia, and the growing political assertiveness of Thai business interests—all occurring in the period when ASEAN's unity on the Cambodia question began to show signs of strain.

One of the practical effects of ideology is to sustain confidence despite setbacks. Indeed, ideology defines setbacks as temporary aberrations in the historical trend that require only tactical adjustment. Setbacks, in this view, cannot be cumulative. The hope that Hanoi will see the direness of its straits *as others see it* founders on this confidence. Second, ideology encourages the Vietnamese to anticipate the emergence of anti-imperialist, anticapitalist forces in the ASEAN countries that will divide those countries internally and provide an incentive for the VCP to settle differences with the socialist bloc (and Vietnam). This expectation reduces concern about ASEAN's support for Thailand over the long-term. But this does not imply that Hanoi wishes to divide ASEAN itself to the point of collapse. For who but China would pick up the pieces? Moreover, the Vietnamese are ideologically predisposed to viewing the ASEAN nations as part of the Third World, striving to perfect their independence and thereby potentially within the "current" on whose ascendancy the Vietnamese count for their own safety.

As for global strategy, the Vietnamese analyze their own struggles alternately as central or peripheral to those of a socialist camp headed by the Soviet Union.[22] In this conception, it is the "internationalist duty" of communist states to support the camp member that at a given time finds itself the focal point of conflict between socialism and imperialism. The Vietnamese accept Soviet leadership not only for historical reasons and capability, but also because the only plausible alternate, China, broke from the camp at the very moment Vietnam most needed the support of a united bloc in its war with the United States. Thus, an ideological interpretation of alliance obligations influenced Hanoi's decision to align with Moscow in the Sino-Soviet dispute. Obviously, the Vietnamese interpretation has been partly self-serving, as all interpretations of alliance obligations tend to be, but the ideological context encourages the Vietnamese, so long as they are actively engaged in conflict with bloc enemies, to expect support as a moral right.

These ideological perceptions should leave a deep imprint on Vietnamese policy as long as generations that came to maturity before 1975 remain in power, working against radical shifts of doctrine for a decade or more to come. Ideological perceptions are not the only source of policy, however.

REALIST PERCEPTIONS

In addition to ideology, the influence of realpolitik is readily apparent. Forced to choose between competitive patrons in the Second Indochina War, Hanoi leaned toward the one that had the most to give, particularly for aerial defense of the North and equipping main force divisions, and away from the one that was turbulent and inward-looking. While the Soviet Union was a reliable supplier of crucial military hardware, China during the same period refused to coordinate with the Soviets against the United States, was distracted by the Cultural Revolution, and mounted a challenge to Soviet leadership of the bloc. To the Vietnamese, China also seemed more willing than the Soviets to improve relations with the United States at Vietnam's expense as the war neared its end.[23] Since the war, the Soviet Union has been viewed as the only possible counterweight to a hostile China. Ideology was certainly the last thing on the mind of the Hanoi diplomat who told me: "In all of history, we have been secure from China in only two conditions. One is when China has been weak and internally divided. The other is when she has been threatened by barbarians from the north. In the present era, the Russians are our barbarians."[24]

Ideological analysis of trends and enemy vulnerabilities shapes responses, but experience has imparted to the Vietnamese a fine appreciation for the realities of power, which is their principal basis for assessing present threats and planning strategic security. Thus, the Vietnamese regard the United States as imperialist, an enemy by definition, but they no longer consider the United States a significant direct threat. This is because U.S. leaders must contend with the "lesson" of Vietnam and domestic opposition to interventionism. The Indochina Foreign Ministers' meeting in January 1985 urged the United States to "assume a responsible role in contributing to long-term peace and stability in Southeast Asia," which barely disguised the hope that U.S. aversion to Pol Pot would develop into support for the supression of the Khmer Rouge and restraint in supporting the non-communist Khmer resistance.[25] Moreover, the Vietnamese vastly prefer U.S. to Chinese influence in Thailand because they believe U.S. aims are limited and U.S. power is declining in Southeast Asia compared to that of China.

Japan is more problematic. On the one hand, Japan is a natural market for Vietnam's raw materials and is potentially its major source of hard currency earnings and noncommunist investment and assistance. The Vietnamese have realistic expectations of gaining significantly from future economic ties with Japan. Despite the suspension of Japanese government credits since 1979, two-way trade between the two countries recovered and in 1987 surpassed the 1978 peak of $270 million. Japan, Vietnam's largest nonoil creditor, held 60 percent of Vietnam's total outstanding debt to private creditors in 1985.[26] Japanese business also was poised to take advantage of Vietnam's new liberal foreign investment code issued in late 1987.

On the other hand, Japan is the most important forward base of American power in the Pacific, a direct threat to the sea link with Vladivostok on which Vietnam (through the USSR) depends. Japan's location gives it and its allies the potential to cut off Soviet assistance to Vietnam in the event of hostilities. Sea-lanes that ASEAN, American, Japanese, and Chinese strategists see bristling with Soviet ships look like extremely vulnerable supply lines to the Vietnamese.[27] The inescapable conclusion for Hanoi is that Japan's defense cooperation with the United States or China, or Japan's rearmament, poses a theat to Vietnam. Japan's support of ASEAN on the Cambodian question is said by a Hanoi spokesman to disguise a cynical attempt to strengthen its economic position among the ASEAN states and, in cooperation with the United States, to play the role of "regional gendarme" in Southeast Asia.[28] Any tendency on the part of Japan to rearm, defend its sea-lanes, or join with the United States, China, and South Korea in containing the Soviet Union is viewed with deep misgivings in Hanoi. The newspaper, *Quan doi nhan dan* (People's Army), for example, described the moves by Japan's Premier Yasuhiro Nakasone in 1983 to bolster Japan's contribution in the Western Pacific as a "new phase in Japan's service to American global strategy."[29] The Vietnamese regard Japan as the only country besides China capable of expanding in the region. Thus, one SRV foreign ministry official speculated that China's "four modernizations" and pursuit of a hegemonistic foreign policy might produce a defensive reaction in Japan in the form of a military buildup and resurgent militarism; such activities would present Vietnam with a dual threat from the north that it could offset only by cooperating still more closely with the Soviet Union. Increased Soviet access to naval and air facilities, he indicated, could not be ruled out in that event.[30]

Hanoi is similarly ambivalent in regard to ASEAN for a number of reasons that include power calculations. The organization was founded by the region's anticommunist regimes partly in reaction to instability in Indochina, and two of its members, Thailand and the Philippines, assisted U.S. efforts to destroy the communist revolution in Vietnam. Following the end of the Second Indochina War in 1975, Hanoi expressed hostility toward ASEAN as an instrument of U.S. imperialism, an emergent successor to SEATO, and a group of nations whose independence was still in thrall to Western capital. In Vietnamese eyes, ASEAN elites were a mixed bag of militarists, feudalists, and stooges of a neocolonial world order. The ASEAN concept of a Zone of Peace, Freedom and Neutrality (ZOPFAN) was found wanting for not including "independence," meaning an end to military ties with the United States and dependency on Western capital.

But Hanoi softened these views in 1978 as it sought to preempt opposition to its planned move into Cambodia. It has continued to speak in tones of relative moderation. Though the Soviets may have nudged Hanoi to strike a less-strident note, the Vietnamese recognized it was in their own interests to adopt a rhetorically conciliatory posture and to draw the ASEAN states into dialogue.[31] Without yielding anything in Cambodia, Hanoi needed to placate fears that had united ASEAN behind Thailand and that could facilitate China's further penetration of the region. It also wished to capitalize on the fact that ASEAN's natural leader, Indonesia, shared the Vietnamese view of China as the principal long-term threat.

Thus, Vietnam's strategic security concerns overrode its ideological distaste. The objectives were to obtain acceptance of Vietnam's position in Cambodia and to preempt tendencies in ASEAN to seek reassurance from the great powers hostile to Vietnam. These objectives required Vietnam to improve relations with ASEAN states, preferably on a bilateral basis, but on a multilateral one as well. Hanoi therefore has subscribed to the Malaysian proposal "to turn Southeast Asia into a nuclear-free zone and to materialize the ZOPFAN concept [without insisting on inclusion of "independence"] pending a solution to the Cambodian problem."[32] The manifest hope of these moves, aside from offering bait for ASEAN to move toward a Cambodian settlement on Vietnam's terms, was to encourage those in ASEAN wishing to minimize great power involvement in the region and to discourage ASEAN's transformation into a military alliance.[33] A victory for the New People's Army or for anti-Marcos politicians responsive to the demand for closing U.S. military facilities in the Philippines would be highly favorable to Vietnam. Ideally, in Hanoi's view, these developments could lay foundations for a Southeast Asian united front against China in tacit cooperation with the Soviet Union. But such a front, suitably neutral and providing links to the developed capitalist world economy, also could serve as a long-term alternative for Vietnam to the Soviet guarantee.

Nevertheless, for the present and foreseeable future, Vietnamese leaders perceive their country, in their words, as "surrounded by enemies." This perception, combined with trust only in their own determination and ability to defend themselves, has caused Hanoi throughout the 1980s to maintain the world's fourth largest military establishment. Of the total regular armed forces numbering 1,155,000 in 1986, the People's Army numbered one million. That actually represented a slight decline from the peak of 1,227,000 in 1984 as the army began a delayed move toward a more compact force structure. In almost continuous combat since its founding in 1944, and with some tactical as well as strategic victories over three great powers to its credit, the People's Army is the most experienced, battle-hardened armed force in Asia today. With 61 divisions averaging 7,500 men each, for a total of 457,500 troops, plus 20 brigades of armor and marines and 10 regiments of artillery, infantry is predominant. A 15,000-man air force, a 40,000-man navy (including marines), and a 100,000-man air-defense force round out the figure for standing regulars. Paramilitary forces, quick reinforcement reserves, and strategic reserves consist of 60,000 Border Defense Force troops, 500,000 Peoples' Regional Force troops, and one million militia of the People's Self-Defense Force.[34]

The overwhelming emphasis given to ground combat forces and popular territorial defense is the legacy of two long revolutionary wars against technologically superior fores. It is also a response to the post-1975 threat environment. At the end of the last war, professional elements in the military proposed to streamline this structure in exchange for technical modernization, but this argument was overridden by a need to use the military in economic construction. The People's Army therefore maintained a high force level and created, for a time, a special command for units engaged in economic work. (In 1986, the army included 10 to 16 economic construction "divisions" and 14 independent engineering brigades of about 3,000 men each.[35] The looming conflict with Cambodia and China also provided a reason not to demobilize. Since 1979, when the Chinese attack on the northern border was met primarily by local militia, regional forces, and a trainee division, the People's Army has deployed from 20 to 25 divisions of infantry (roughly one-half of all assets, including support units) north of Hanoi.

Obviously, China is the direction from which the major threat is seen to come. To Hanoi, threats in Laos and Cambodia appear to be abating. During the spring of 1988, Hanoi halved, to between 20,000 and 25,000 the number of troops it had stationed continuously in Laos since 1975. And on 26 May, Hanoi formally announced it would withdraw 50,000 troops from Cambodia by year's end. If executed, which seemed unlikely by late 1988, that withdrawal would have brought down the number of troops stationed there to about 70,000, according to Western estimates.[36] Hanoi would not make these withdrawals if it believed such action placed Vietnam's national security in jeopardy.

The officer corps long has wished to modernize and diversify its force structure, but cost, limited technical capability, and Soviet aid priorities have been major constraints. The small navy's six frigates and assorted large patrol craft are just adequate for coastal patrol and surveillance. Though conflicting claims to territories in the South China Sea among all the littoral states, especially between Vietnam and China over the Spratly archipelago, provide strong incentive for Vietnam to strengthen its navy, Vietnam cannot match the growing Chinese naval forces in this area. The air force, with 293 combat aircraft spearheaded by MiG-21s, overshadows its neighbors in aerial interception, but it is inexperienced in support of ground combat and weak in transport. The squadron of MiG-23s at Da Nang airfield is under Soviet command, and Soviet fulfillment of Vietnamese officers' known wish for this aircraft probably is contingent upon deployment of the F-16A in Thailand. On the other hand, Vietnam has acquired late-model helicopters useful in counterinsurgency.

Although these forces give the Vietnamese confidence that they can cope with any threat on the horizon, including a "second lesson" from China, the cost is dear. Military expenditures have been estimated at 35 to 50 percent of the national budget:[37] as a proportion of the gross national product (GNP), they must rank among the highest in the world. In some ways even more damaging, the army takes a large proportion of technical-school graduates and absorbs much precious human capital. Such costs, combined with the inability to manufacture any but the simplest equipment and ammunition, force Vietnam to obtain between half a billion and one billion dollars annually in foreign military assistance, overwhelmingly from the Soviet Union. Though Vietnamese military spokesmen flatly deny that any integration with Soviet strategic planning has taken place,[38] Soviet military support of Vietnam is a relatively cheap way for Moscow to have over a quarter of a million troops hostile to China stationed on the latter's southern border and to secure Vietnam's participation in surveillance of the south China Sea. It also assures that Vietnam will have the means not only to defend its northern border, but to pursue its goals in other parts of Indochina.

SECURITY RESPONSES:
CONSOLIDATING INDOCHINESE UNITY

Meanwhile, the Vietnamese believe their security requires them to strengthen solidarity among the three Indochinese countries, or at least to maintain predominant influence in the governments of Laos and Cambodia at almost any price. How does Hanoi intend to do this? For the present, it can shore up the two client regimes with its own army and advisory assistance, which is not difficult in Laos where the government was born after decades of revolutionary warfare under Vietnamese tutelage. But this is costly in Cambodia, where the Vietnamese have had to construct a government from scratch in the teeth of domestic and international opposition. The idea of federation was abandoned long ago, and the Vietnamese seem genuinely aware that such a move now would only play into the hands of their adversaries. It also would be opposed by the Soviet Union, which insists upon its right of direct, unfettered relations with Laos and Cambodia. Periodic summits, semiannual foreign ministers' meetings, exchanges of technical teams, and a Vietnamese advisory presence are satisfactory means to coordinate policies of the three countries. If the Vietnamese have a model, it could be the Soviet role in Eastern Europe; although they do not themselves draw this parallel, they do not object when it is made.

But the Vietnamese do intend to promote "economic integration," in the words of a senior foreign ministry official. It is in this regard that Vietnamese policy shows the most continuity with the Comintern legacy; namely, in the perception that colonial rule created economic ties between the three countries that did not exist before and which now can be exploited for mutual benefit. National committees for cultural and economic cooperation were formed in early 1983 and held their first joint meeting in July of that year. The appointment of fairly powerful central committee members to head each national committee indicates the importance attached to this goal. But the committees have only consultative powers, and the goal is a very distant one. It could hardly be otherwise, given the extremely low level of economic development in each country and the fact that while they have "cooperated" in military matters for years, as the Vietnam committee's deputy director put it, economic cooperation is "a new problem for us."[39] "Cooperation," in fact, consists almost entirely of Vietnamese assistance to the other two countries, and priority is given to development of food self-sufficiency. No proposals for complementary development or for industrial coproduction were on the agenda as of the summer of 1988. Nor had linking intra-Indochina cooperation with CMEA activities been mentioned in any of the committees' joint meetings. Cooperation on truly major projects, such as Mekong basin development, has been ruled out for lack of capital. The main physical links built as of late 1988 are improvements to portions of the Ho Chi Minh Trail complex astride the Annamite Cordillera, a 286-km petroleum pipeline from Vinh in Vietnam's Nghe Tinh province to Route 13 in Laos that each country separately manages on its respective territory,[40] and the extension of Route 9 to connect Savannakhet with Da Nang[41] that the Vietnamese acknowledge will never provide Laos access to the sea as cost-efficient as the rail link across Thailand.[42] Transnational institutions, not to mention economic integration in the accepted sense of the term, hardly seem likely to emerge in the foreseeable future.

More interesting for what it reveals of the Vietnamese orientation toward "cooperation" is the spirit in which Hanoi gives assistance. In the past, Vietnamese communists admired the relative egalitarianism of their neighbors' traditional societies, and "cooperation" is conducted among putative equals. For decades, the party has attempted to indoctrinate its cadres to respect ethnic minorities and the other peoples of Indochina since the cooperation of these groups has been crucial to the attainment of party objectives. The Vietnamese, however, take naturally to the role of senior partner and patronize other groups. Historian Alexander Woodside has suggested that this attitude resonates with Confucian "cultural evangelism" and "hierarchical vision of inter-state relations," reinforced by a "psychologically defensive imitation" of the way Vietnam was treated by Western colonial powers.[43]

Whatever the source, a tone of benign paternalism ("maternalism" might be a better word—see below) is certainly present, particularly with regard to Cambodia. This is illustrated in a collection of poems, one of which is entitled "Orphaned Younger Sister," written by Le Duc Tho during a visit to Cambodia.[44] In the spring of 1984, Foreign Minister Nguyen Co Thach described the Phnom Penh regime to this writer as a "child" that Vietnam had to put on its feet and encourage to walk alone.[45] Though Thach's purpose was to emphasize Hanoi's determination not to let Phnom Penh become permanently dependent on Vietnam's defensive shield, the language was strikingly similar to that of Emperor Gia Long (1802-1819), who said: "Cambodia is a small country. . . . And we should maintain it as a child. We will be its mother, its father will be Siam. When a child has trouble with its father, it can get rid of suffering by embracing its mother. When the child is unhappy with its mother, it can run to its father for support."[46] Given that the genocidal Khmer Rouge could not survive without Thai connivance in China's support, the Vietnamese might well see the child as unhappy with its father, therefore running to its mother. Nevertheless, the Vietnamese communists draw tremendous pride from protecting and developing other societies. In fulfillment of their "internationalist duty," the Vietnamese find confirmation of Vietnam's full sovereignty and membership in the modern world community. This is a tremendously important psychological satisfaction that is felt all the more intensely because of the considerable sacrifice at which assistance is given.[47]

A last option for consolidating Vietnamese hegemony over Indochina could be "Vietnamization" in the form of settlement and eventual absorption of Laos and Cambodia. This specter was raised in the mid-1980s, principally by Khmer resistance groups and their ASEAN supporters, who charged that Vietnamese by the hundreds of thousands already had settled in Cambodia with Hanoi's encouragement and assistance. But evidence of settlement of this magnitude is, as it was then, thin. Hanoi's principal concerns regarding settlement were to curb the movement of smugglers, black marketeers, draft dodgers, and political dissidents seeking refuge or opportunity in Cambodia's post-1979 disarray, yet to permit some settlement that might help economic recovery. It is doubtful that the aim was assimilation. Policy documents that came to light suggested an aim of regulating an ongoing movement so as to guarantee that Vietnamese in Cambodia would contribute to the economy, not to turbulence.[48] The Vietnam-Cambodia border is closely patrolled to stop unauthorized crossings,[49] and a plan to screen settlers in Cambodia was discussed in the spring of 1984.[50] As for numbers, they are undoubtedly higher than the 56,000 Vietnamese (and over 60,000 Sino-Khmer) cited by Phnom Penh in mid-1983, the last time an official estimate was given.[51] While admitting the difficulty of measurement, foreign observers in 1987 leaned toward an estimate of 150,000, debunking the figure of 700,000 commonly cited by Beijing and Khmer resistance sources.[52] Foreign Minister Nguyen Co Thach told this writer in 1984 that migration had tapered off due to tighter controls and, on the part of law-abiding Vietnamese, the memory of earlier treatment at the hands of the Khmer.[53] Hanoi foreign ministry analysts further argued, quite logically, that an officially sponsored program of massive settlement of the kind alleged would provoke Cambodian, ASEAN, and world opposition and would be self-defeating.[54] However, Hanoi sources refer to the 500,000 Vietnamese who lived in Cambodia until 1970 as precedent for a sizable community that might be tolerated again, which reveals striking obtuseness given the reasons that this community subsequently was reduced nearly to zero.[55] It is possible that opinion in Hanoi was divided on this issue, with some officials willing to consider the implantation of Vietnamese communities in certain areas for security reasons (similar to the Jewish settlement of the West Bank) if other means were seen to fail or as support for Phnom Penh when the People's Army withdraws.

Hanoi does not seem to have perceived any significant failures in its strategy toward Cambodia thus far, however. Though building a new Cambodian party, state, and army has proven more difficult than the Vietnamese initially anticipated, the difficulty can be explained by the fact that few educated Khmer survived the Pol Pot years. Khmer resistance forces made minor gains rather than fading away between 1983 and 1984, but Hanoi could attribute this to external support and diplomatic constraints on the use of force along the Thai border. The Khmer Rouge subsequently shifted to a more political strategy aimed at laying a base for renewed warfare after Vietnamese forces withdraw, but Hanoi seemed confident that this would create little more than a nuisance for the increasingly strong Phnom Penh government. The Khmer People's National Liberation Front, the once stronger of the two noncommunist elements in the resistance coalition, partially disintegrated due to factional infighting. China persists in applying pressure on Vietnam's northern border, but no "second lesson" has materialized. And Beijing's search for balance between Moscow and Washington, the Vietnamese believe, constrains Chinese action against Hanoi.

The main fear of the Vietnamese has been that the Phnom Penh government and the Khmer people would become dependent on the People's Army for protection and grow apathetic about the Khmer Rouge threat. Two "traps" appeared to them: one was Khmer dependency leading to an interminable military involvement, while the other was the premature withdrawal that would permit the Khmer Rouge—and behind them the Chinese—to return.[56] The unprecedented attacks on all major border encampments of the resistance in the 1984 to 1985 dry season were part of an attempt to avoid both of these traps through more vigorous military action. The immediate objectives were to disprove claims that the resistance forces had grown stronger and to roll back their progress, which the attacks did. But the strategy was justified only if it helped to shift the burden to Phnom Penh.

In the respite, therefore, the most urgent objective was to consolidate the Phnom Penh apparatus at all levels in the densely populated basin around the Great Lake. It was calculated that if Phnom Penh could mobilize the resources of this, the "inland front," it would be able to handle the skirmishing at the "border front" with reduced Vietnamese assistance. The Vietnamese also formed joint command structures for Vietnamese and Cambodian units in the field to stiffen the latter while nonessential Vietnamese troops were withdrawn.[57] Though attention focused on the presumed purpose of annual withdrawals to appease foreign opinion, the withdrawals also were consistent with Hanoi's desire to put the Khmer on notice that they soon would have to defend themselves. By 1988, many parts of Cambodia were still judged too insecure to permit travel by foreign corespondents. However, with a regular army of 30,000 troops, a militia of 40,000, an administration extending down to the village level, and a Hanoi-aligned Communist party of 16,000 to 20,000 (up from almost nil in 1979), the Phnom Penh government looked considerably more permanent than its rivals.[58] Though the Vietnamese undoubtedly would like to have left Cambodia long ago, completely secure and with an international recognized government, they were not unjustified to bill their readiness to withdraw in 1990 as a measure of success, and not failure.

Given that strategy, the effect of continuing support for the Khmer resistance is to let the Cambodian conflict develop (assuming the resistance remains viable and the Vietnamese do withdraw) into a civil war between externally supported Khmer parties. Although Thai military leaders have suggested that the partition of Cambodian territory might be an acceptable outcome of such a conflict,[59] the Vietnamese categorically rule this out.

THE CHALLENGE AND THE RESPONSES

Vietnam has the means and determination to persist in its present course, albeit at great cost to itself. The People's Army is better equipped and more combat-ready than Chinese units stationed across the border, Hanoi perceives no geostrategic alternative to its own predominance in Laos and Cambodia, and the Soviet Union cannot withhold support without jeopardizing its most valuable strategic relationship outside the Warsaw Pact. Serious as Vietnam's economic situation may be, domestic reforms and a very gradual broadening of contacts with the free-market area sustain Hanoi's hope that present difficulties will be overcome without major adjustment of the objectives it has pursued since 1978.

Success for Vietnamese strategy implies the consolidation of an Indochina bloc, with Hanoi as chief partner, easy access for Vietnamese armed forces to the Mekong basin, protracted tension between Vietnam and China, and the maintenance of strong security ties between Vietnam and the Soviet Union. While Sino-Soviet rapprochement could modify these outcomes somewhat, they still would imply a redistribution of power on the mainland to Thailand's disadvantage and further entrenchment of the Soviet military presence in Vietnam.

These are prospects that the noncommunist states of the Association for Southeast Asian Nations, but especially Thailand, have contemplated most gravely. In response, Thailand has sought reassurance from China and the United States while diverting capital from economic to military development. These trends in Thai policy have tended to divide ASEAN, as members not directly threatened by Vietnam have grown impatient to end a confrontation that invites intrusion by the great powers. That confrontation is especially troubling to ASEAN members (like Indonesia) that still fear China more than the Soviet Union. However, impatience to end the conflict has been offset by fear that an open split in ASEAN could drive Thailand to go it alone in alliance with China, the United States, or both. Alternatively, a split in ASEAN could prompt Thailand to adopt a posture of accommodation and neutrality, leading toward the "Burmanization" of mainland Southeast Asia, to the satisfaction of Vietnam. Since both alternatives are unsavory in all ASEAN capitals, the organization has maintained a facade of unity behind Thailand. But the longer the conflict goes on, the sharper the contradiction grows between Thailand's interests in Indochina and the collective desire to turn the region into a Zone of Peace, Freedom, and Neutrality (ZOPFAN) and a Nuclear-Weapons Free Zone (NWFZ)—goals the third ASEAN summit in December 1987 declared the organization would intensify efforts to achieve. Meanwhile, pressures have emerged in the Bangkok business community for permission to participate in the growing trade between the ASEAN countries and Vietnam. These are exactly the kind of phenomena that Vietnamese statesmen interpret as signs of "movement" that will leave their accomplishment in Cambodia intact, whether in the form of a negotiated settlement or tacit acquiescence.

No fundamental shift in Vietnamese policy, or of alignment and power between Vietnam, its allies, and adversaries seems likely in the near future. In Cambodia, Vietnam may succeed in imposing an outcome based exclusively on its own security, but only at extreme cost to its future welfare and by prolonging frictions with its neighbors. Perhaps more obviously, Thailand, ASEAN, and their supporters will be unable to impose their preferred outcome by pressuring Vietnam as they have up to now. However, ASEAN has a powerful incentive to continue backing Thailand—if Thailand lost ASEAN's support, Bangkok might feel constrained to adopt an even less-pleasant option than the one it has pursued since the conflict's beginning. The one aim shared by the regional contestants—a balanced relationship between Southeast Asian countries and the great powers to minimize opportunities for the latter to interfere in national and regional affairs—thus far has been held hostage by both Vietnam and ASEAN to demands for concessions over Cambodia. As long as Vietnamese troops remain in Cambodia, diplomatic deadlock, low-intensity conflict, and accelerated military modernization by all the major players seem likely to continue.

This prospect poses much the same problems for the United States as it has since 1978. Washington must seek a resolution of the Cambodian question in such a manner as to reduce Soviet opportunities for expanded influence while maintaining ASEAN unity and sound U.S.-ASEAN and U.S.-China relations. At first, the United States did this by maintaining its diplomatic isolation and economic embargo of Hanoi in coordination with China's strategy of "bleeding" Vietnam and supplying the Khmer Rouge. Washington also helped to sustain ASEAN resolve to extract concessions from Hanoi. Although these policies were useful in demonstrating solidarity with China and Thailand, they did nothing to evict Vietnamese troops from Cambodia, added incentives for Hanoi to expand Soviet military access to Vietnamese facilities, and associated American policy with efforts by others to support the Khmer Rouge. They also abdicated influence to China. American policy thus helped to confirm the belief in Hanoi that Vietnam could rely only upon itself to extinguish the threat posed by a China-backed Khmer Rouge and on close ties with the Soviet Union to offset Chinese pressure. It was after several years of what Hanoi considered diplomatic patience that in 1984 it ordered its army to attack in major force on the border of Thailand. Vietnamese forces in regimental strength crossed that border several times. With the Khmer resistance camps removed as a buffer, the scene was set for a confrontation that could have forced the United States to choose between a politically unpalatable involvement or abandonment of a treaty ally had the fighting spread.

It is in the interest of the United States to avoid having to face such choices. This can be done in Indochina by facilitating efforts to liquidate the Khmer Rouge, which may require a larger security commitment to Thailand to reassure Bangkok for the loss of this "buffer" and the repercussions in relations with China. Sustaining the noncommunist Khmer resistance with "humanitarian assistance" was useful once as a show of solidarity with ASEAN, but it can no longer be given with any expectations of obtaining a share of power for noncommunists in the Phnom Penh government. And since there is little the United States realistically can do to modify Vietnam's relations with the Soviet Union, it is in the interest of the United States to support ASEAN efforts to find common ground with Hanoi on regional order over the long-term. The order desired by ASEAN, shared in large measure by Hanoi, is more compatible with U.S. interests than the regional polarization and encroachment of Chinese and Soviet influence, which the policies of all the great powers, including those of the United States, thus far have exacerbated.

Moreover, the United States may have to accept an accommodation between ASEAN and Vietnam if Hanoi fulfills its pledge, contingent upon the security of the Phnom Penh government, to withdraw the People's Army from Cambodia by 1990. Unlike the Soviet pullout from Afghanistan, the Vietnamese will leave when their Khmer allies are able to defend themselves and the conflict is winding down. Then the task of realizing a nuclear-free ZOPFAN is sure to rise in ASEAN priorities, forcing even Thailand to reduce its aims in Cambodia in order to preserve the cushion of solidarity with noncommunist neighbors. The main locus of regional tension will then shift to the South China Sea. There, Vietnam must be as concerned as it was in Cambodia to secure, with Soviet assistance, the defense of a two thousand kilometer coastline that borders one of the world's most contested marine territories and vital sea-lanes of communication between the Western Pacific, the Indian Ocean, and the Middle East.

NOTES

Research for this chapter, including two trips to Hanoi, was conducted while I was a visiting professor in American Studies, Chulalongkorn University, Bangkok, Thailand, under the auspices of the Fulbright-Hayes Program and the John F. Kennedy Foundation of Thailand. I also wish to acknowledge the support given to me by the International Relations Institute, Hanoi, during my visit to Vietnam in 1984.

1. For background and analysis, see David W.P. Elliott, ed., *The Third Indochina Conflict* (Boulder, CO: Westview Press, 1981) and William S. Turley and Jeffrey Race, "The Third Indochina War," *Foreign Policy*, no. 38 (Spring 1980), pp. 92–116.

2. See Sukhumbhand Paribatra, "Strategic Implications of the Indochina Conflict: Thai Perspectives," *Asian Affairs: An American Review*, vol. 11, no. 3 (Fall 1984), pp. 30–35.

3. For further comparison, see R.V. Smith, "Thailand and Vietnam: Some thoughts toward a comparative historical analysis," *The Journal of the Siam Society*, vol. 60, part 2 (July 1972), pp. 1–21.

4. Henry A. Kissinger, *White House Years* (Boston: Little, Brown and Company, 1979), p. 433.

5. Tho cua Trung uong gui cho cac cap Dang bo," 3 December 1930, in *Dang Cong San Viet Nam, Ban chanh hanh Trung uong, Van Kien Dang, 1930–1945* [Party Documents, 1930–1945] (Hanoi: Central Committee Commission for the Study of Party History, 1972), p. 190. This volume, marked Luu hanh noi bo" (for internal distribution), is an unexpurgated documentary record.

6. "An nghi quyet cua Trung uong toan the hoi nghi noi ve tinh hinh hien tai o Dong duong va nhiem vu can kip cua Dang (10–1930)," *Van Kien Dang*, p. 87.

7. "Truyen don giai thich viec doi ten Dang," *Van Kien Dang*, n.d., p. 188.

8. "Tho cua Trung uong gui cho cac cap Dang bo," 3 December 1930, p. 191.

9. For a detailed analysis of this split, see Huynh Kim Khanh, *Vietnamese Communism 1925–1945* (Ithaca, NY: Cornell University Press, 1982), pp. 99–119.

10. Which is not to say the idea was not current. The party newspaper, *Cong Nong Binh* (Worker, Peasant and Soldier), 6 February 1931, explained that "if the Vietnamese revolution succeeds but French imperialism is lurking in Laos and Cambodia, the revolutionary power in Vietnam will be shaky." Quoted in Gareth Porter, "Vietnamese Communist Policy Toward Kampuchea, 1930–1970," in *Revolution and Its Aftermath in Kampuchea: Eight Essays*, David P. Chandler and Ben Kiernan, eds., (New Haven: Yale University Southeast Asia Studies, Monograph Series, No. 25, 1983), p. 60. Porter implies that Vietnamese party leaders fully appreciated Indochina's strategic unity from the beginning and differed mainly over the methods, feasibility, and timing of the revolution in Laos and Cambodia. It is my impression that few of them, if any, had thought very hard about this question until jogged by the Comintern directive.

11. For further discussion of these points, see Porter, "Vietnamese Communist Policy Toward Kampuchea," pp. 61–64.

12. Vo Nguyen Giap, "Nhiem vu guan su truoc mat chuyen sang Tong phan cong" [The Military Mission in Transition to the General Offensive and Uprising] (Ha Dong Committee for Resistance and Administration, 1950), p. 14, in the Library of Congress, Orientalia/South Asia 4 microfilm collection, *Vietnamese Communist Publications*, P.T. Chau, ed., item 40.

13. In Allen W. Cameron, ed., *Viet-Nam Crisis: A Documentary History*, vol. 1: 1940–1956 (Ithaca, NY: Cornell University Press, 1971), p. 174.

14. *Ibid.*, p. 183.

15. Joseph J. Zasloff, *The Pathet Lao: Leadership and Organization* (Lexington, MA: D.C. Heath & Company, 1973), p. 13.

16. Circular dated 27 November 1953, quoted in *War Experiences Recapitulation Committee, Vietnam: The Anti-U.S. Resistance for National Salvation 1954–1975: Military Events* (Hanoi: People's Army Publishing House, 1980), trans. Joint Publications Research Service No. 80968 (Washington, D.C., 3 June 1982), p. 62.

17. Gen. Le Duc Anh, "Quan doi nhan dan va nhiem vu quoc te cao ca tren dat ban Cam-Pu-Chia" (The People's Army and its Lofty Internationalist Mission in Friendly Kampuchea), *Tap chi Quan doi nhan dan* (People's Army Journal), December 1984, p. 32.

18. For a long time, Phnom Penh spokesmen ruled out any dilution of the power monopoly held by the Communist party. For example, see comment that "internationally supervised elections" must be in accord with the PRK constitution by PRK Foreign Minister Hun Sen on Phnom Penh Radio, 11 December 1984, in Foreign Broadcast Information Service, *Daily Report: Asia & Pacific* (hereinafter FBIS-APA), 14 December 1984, and Hun Sen's statement that "the leading role of the KPRP cannot be questioned" in an interview on Budapest Radio, 30 May 1985, FBIS-APA, 31 May 1985. This line appeared to soften when Hun Sen, now Premier, held informal talks in December 1987 and

January 1988 with Prince Norodom Sihanouk. Sen indicated that a pluralist democracy with Sihanouk acting as something more than just a figurehead president might be acceptable. However, the offer almost certainly was intended to draw Sihanouk into a diplomatic offensive against his coalition partners, not a commitment to share real power. See James Pringle, "Pressures for Peace," *Far Eastern Economic Review* (25 February 1988), p. 33, Michael Field, "Sihanok - Act II," *Far Eastern Economic Review* (4 February 1988), p. 31, and Elaine Sciolino, "Talks Among Cambodia Factions Seem to Unravel Over Basic Issues," *New York Times* 28 July 1988 p. A1, A9.

19. For an analysis that emphasizes ideological influences in Vietnamese views, see Gareth Porter, "Hanoi's Strategic Perspective and the Sino-Vietnamese Conflict," *Pacific Affairs*, vol. 57, no. 1 (Spring 1984), pp. 7–25.

20. Vo Dong Giang, interview with the author, Hanoi, 31 March 1983. Giang subsequently became Minister of State for Foreign Affairs.

21. Such views were expressed to the author by several sources in Hanoi's Ministry of Foreign Affairs.

22. See Gareth Porter, "Vietnam and the Socialist Camp," in *Vietnamese Communism in Comparative Perspective*, William S. Turley, ed., (Boulder, CO: Westview Press, 1980), pp. 225–264.

23. The Vietnamese retrospect on this break is the Ministry of Foreign Affairs "white book," *The Truth about Vietnam-China Relations over the Last Thirty Years* (Hanoi, 1979).

24. In private conversation with the author.

25. Communiqué of the 10th Indochina Foreign Ministers' Conference, Radio Hanoi, 18 January 1985, FBIS-APA 23 January 1985.

26. International Monetary Fund, "Viet-Nam—Recent economic Developments," 15 May 1987, p. 34.

27. A map in *Quan doi nhan dan* (People's Army), 1 October 1983, emphasizes the U.S. emplacement in the Western Pacific as virtually encircling Vietnam and threatening sea communications to the north.

28. *Quan doi nhan dan*, 1 July 1983.

29. *Quan doi nhan dan*, 26 January 1983; also *Quan doi nhan dan*, 7 March, 4 and 24 April, and 25 and 28 September 1983.

30. Pham Binh, Director of the International Relations Institute, Ministry of Foreign Affairs, interview with the author, Hanoi, 21 April 1984. Also see Bihn's paper, "Prospects for Solutions to Problems Related to Peace and Stability in Southeast Asia," presented at the CSIS-IRS meeting in Hanoi, February 1984 and *The Indonesian Quarterly*, vol. xii, no. 2 (1984), pp. 221–222.

31. One foreign ministry official told this writer in 1983 that Hanoi had dropped its insistence on the inclusion of "independence" in the ZOPFAN concept upon discovering it was "offensive" to ASEAN countries, particularly Indonesia, though the ASEAN countries, he went on, "still depend on others and need to complete their independence in the sense of reducing this degree of dependence."

32. Communiqué, Radio Hanoi, 18 January 1985.

33. Vietnam News Agency, Hanoi, 2 February 1985, FBIS-APA, 4 February 1985.

34. The International Institute for Strategic Studies, *The Military Balance 1986–1987* (London, 1986), p. 172.

35. *Ibid.*

36. Barbara Crossette, *New York Times*, 27 May 1988, p. 4. According to another estimate, Vietnamese troop strength in Cambodia in early 1988 was 100,000, which would imply a reduction to 50,000 by year's end if the withdrawal is carried out. Pringle, "Pressures for Peace," p. 31. Hanoi announced its intention in 1987 to withdraw the bulk of its troops from Cambodia by 1990. But late 1988 reports indicated Hanoi was slowing its pullout from Cambodia. See, for example, Keith B. Richburg, *The Washington Post*, 17 September 1988, p. A15, A18.

37. "Background Notes—Vietnam," United States Department of State, Bureau of Public Affairs, July 1986.

38. Col. Nghiem Tuc, deputy editor of *Quan doi nhan dan*, interview with the author, Hanoi, 23 April 1984.

39. Pham Bao, interview with the author, Hanoi, 24 April 1984.

40. Vientiane radio, 9 March 1985; FBIS-APA, 3 April 1985.

41. Vientiane KPL, 5 December 1984, FBIS-APA, 7 December 1984.

42. Pham Bao interview.

43. Alexander Woodside, "Vietnam and Laos: The Continuing Crisis." paper presented at the meeting of the American Historical Association, Washington, D.C., December 1969.

44. *Nhan dan* (The People), 18 January 1984.

45. Nguyen Co Thach, interview with the author, Hanoi, 25 April 1984.

46. Manuscript chronicle quoted in David P. Chandler, *A History of Cambodia* (Boulder, CO: Westview Press, 1983), p. 116.

47. Pham Bao, in the interview cited above, said: "Vietnam despite its own difficulties has given Cambodia an average of $30 million worth of assistance every year since 1978. This was mostly food at first, but now it includes consumer goods and capital goods. The Soviets give more—over $50 million worth annually—and additional aid is received from international organizations. Vietnam's $30 million is large in relation to its capacity."

48. Circular No. 38, PRK Council of Ministers, 9 October 1982 and Circular No. 240, People's Revolutionary Party of Kampuchea Central Committee, 13 September 1982. For discussion, see William S. Turley, "Is Hanoi Trying to Vietnamize Kampuchea?" *Asian Wall Street Journal*, 20–21 May 1983.

49. This was affirmed to the author by "land people" refugees, including recently arrived draft-age males, in Dongrak camp on the Thai-Cambodian border, 25 March 1984.

50. PRK Deputy Foreign Minister Kong Korm, interview with the author, Phnom Penh, 3 April 1984.

51. Press Department, Ministry of Foreign Affairs, "Policy of the People's Republic of Kampuchea with Regard to Vietnamese Residents" (Phnom Penh, September 1983), pp, 7, 8.

52. See Martin Stuart-Fox, *Sudest Asie*, No. 50 (1987), translated in Joint Publications Research Service, *South east Asia*, no. 88–018 (28 March 1988), p. 15.

53. Thach interview. Following the overthrow of Prince Sihanouk in 1970, the military government instigated or tolerated attacks on Vietnamese civilian residents in Cambodia. Thousands died, while other sought refuge in Vietnam. Under Pol Pot, the remainder either fled or were killed.

54. These points were made by members of the International Relations Institute in a group discussion with the author, Hanoi, 24 March 1983. Also see Turley, "Is Hanoi Trying to Vietnamize Kampuchea?" See also Stuart-Fox, who points out that "the few Western scholars who speak the Khmer language and who have traveled a great deal in Kampuchea agree on the fact that an officially sponsored massive migration of Vietnamese to Kampuchea never took place."

55. Half a million is widely accepted as a reasonably accurate estimate. A senior official, interviewed 31 March 1983, made the unattributable comment that "it is normal for Vietnamese to live in Cambodia, but treatment of them has not always been good." Lengthy commentary in *Quan doi nhan dan*, 27 September 1983, portrayed the half million Vietnamese who lived in Cambodia before 1970 as mostly working folk who shared the Khmers' suffering under colonial rule. In rare comments on the subject, Khmer antipathy to the Vietnamese under Lon Nol and Pol Pot is either glossed over or ascribed to instigation by U.S. and Chinese anti-Vietnam policies.

56. This was the point of Thach's reference above to Cambodia as a "child" needing to stand alone to stimulate further growth.

57. Le Duc Anh, *Quan doi nhan dan va nhiem vu quoc te* . . .

58. Pringle, "Pressures for Peace,' pp. 31, 33.

59. The idea has circulated among Royal Thai Army officers for some time. Gen. Pichit Kullawanich, commander of the First Army Region, is a powerful proponent: "Maintaining that the nationalists would not be able to drive out the Vietnamese from Kampuchea, Lt. Gen. Pichit said the future of Kampuchea is that the country will be divided in zones controlled by the Vietnamese and the resistance." *Bangkok Post*, 24 April 1985, FBIS-APA, 26 April 1985.

9

ASEAN Defense Programs: Military Patterns of National and Regional Resilience

DONALD E. WEATHERBEE

In December 1978, a unified Vietnam, led by a skilled, cohesive communist elite that disposed of the largest and most battle-tested military force in the Southeast Asian region, sent its military machine into action across its international boundary with Kampuchea. Hanoi's invasion and occupation of Kampuchea, followed by persistent Khmer low-intensity warfare against the Vietnamese, has turned the border regions of the Association of Southeast Asian Nations (ASEAN) into zones of conflict for a decade. In effect, the Thai-Kampuchean border has become ASEAN's strategic frontier with Vietnam-dominated Indochina. The westward military thrust into Kampuchea by the Vietnamese gave concrete expression to the foreboding and looming menaces that had informed the ASEAN security managers since the communist victories in Indochina in 1975. No matter how complex the factors may have been in Hanoi's decision to invade, it was a dramatic demonstration to a worried ASEAN of the willingness of its potential adversary to use force in pursuit of its external political objectives. The perception was that the first Southeast Asian "domino" had fallen to aggressive Vietnamese expansionism.

THREAT PERCEPTIONS AND DEFENSE POLICY IN ASEAN

ASEAN's confrontation with Vietnam initially occurred in a wider regional strategic environment that had since 1975 been made more dangerous for ASEAN by the seeming withdrawal of the U.S. power presence and the apparent detachment of the United States from local security interests. The relative diminution of U.S. great power in the region was accompanied by a rising profile of the USSR. In virtual alliance with Vietnam and providing the support necessary for Hanoi to carry out its policy in Kampuchea, the

Soviet Union obtained military access to the former U.S. bases at Da Nang and Cam Ranh Bay. Post-Mao Chinese strategic policy was also intruding in the region in direct support first of the ruling Democratic Kampuchea and then the Khmer Rouge forces of the Kampuchean resistance to the Vietnamese fait accompli.

The changed regional distribution of power in Southeast Asia directly impacted on security planning in the ASEAN states (Brunei, Indonesia, Malaysia, the Philippines, Singapore, and Thailand). While they could not militarily influence the great power balance, they felt an acute need to redress the local balance of regional military power in order to deter and, if necessary, repel any Vietnamese incursions across ASEAN strategic frontiers. These frontiers include not only the bleeding Thai-Kampuchean border, but also the potential conflict zone in the South China Sea where unresolved conflicts over territorial and maritime jurisdictions pit five of ASEAN's six members against Vietnam and the PRC.

In a semi-ideological sense, ASEAN's efforts to increase its indigenous security capabilities have been encapsulated in an originally Indonesian concept of "national resilience." In the abstract, national resilience means the total mobilization and utilization of all the tangible and intangible resources of a nation in defense of its interests against all forms of threat.[1] Instrumentally, in the face of a manifest Vietnamese threat, national resilience became a euphemism for beefed-up military establishments. As Indonesia's President Suharto warned his countrymen in his 1981 Independence Day address: "In this turmoil filled world, whoever wishes to preserve his independence must be ready to take up arms to defend it."[2]

The intensity of the perceived Vietnamese threat was shaped by a People's Army of Vietnam (PAVN) order of battle that in 1979 was quantitatively and qualitatively superior to any combination of ASEAN states.[3] As Goh Keng Swee, then Singapore Defense Minister, said in mid-1979: "The dominant feature in the relationship between the Indochinese and ASEAN states is the superiority of the armed forces of the DRV over those of ASEAN singly or collectively . . . in any military contest between the two sides—assuming there is not third power intervention—the outcome would be quick and decisive."[4] The realistic view in ASEAN security circles held that as long as major power asymmetries marked ASEAN-Vietnamese relations, Vietnam's putative hegemonic ambitions might remain unchecked. The possibility was, as one analyst put it in the early 1980s, that the continued military "imbalance" between Vietnam and ASEAN "will give rise to the continued probability of further conflict in the region."[5]

The ASEAN policy response was an unparalleled militarization. A close examination of the ASEAN states' actual defense planning and ways in which scarce human and budgetary resources were deployed is perhaps a better guide to security concerns than the nuanced and diplomatic rhetoric of ASEAN conference halls. Furthermore, official public discussions of ASEAN security policy tend to be muted by the self-conscious requirement of a generalized lower-common-denominator consensual posture. The term regional resilience was coined to describe euphemistically what was in fact a region-wide military buildup in the early 1980s.

Preparing for defense is expensive. Faced with the changed security environment, the ASEAN states made a significant indication of what their new priorities were in the allocation of state resources. Between 1979 and 1982 there was a sharp upwards jump in ASEAN defense expenditures. This is shown in Table 9.1. ASEAN's rising defense budgets were meant to finance increases in military personnel, infrastructure development, acquisition of high-technology modern weapons systems, and training. The rate of increase leveled off and declined in some cases. After a 1982 peak as a result of global recession-forced budget cuts, with the exception of the Philippines, the planning momentum has been maintained. Historically, defense planning, force structure, and tactics in ASEAN countries have responded to threats originating from internal insurgencies. The ASEAN militaries were built around counterinsurgency (COIN) warfare. The post-1978 militarization programs in most of the ASEAN region have been directed toward the creation of a conventional warfare capability, particularly the strengthening of naval and air arms, COIN's poor relations. If defense policy is to be rational so as to maximize investment, priorities must reflect an appreciation of the capabilities of potential enemies. It is obvious that the new conventional warfare capabilities of the ASEAN states are not geared to nuclear threats or great power interventions, but to threat assessments at levels of response in which the self-defense capabilities provide a measure of security in deterring or repelling regional enemies. Realistically—if not diplomatically—the threats controlling ASEAN's military policy in the wake of the invasion of Kampuchea seem to have been based on estimates linking Vietnam's possible intentions to its real capabilities.

The value of defense planning in regard to security policy and threat perception is particularly relevant when we realize that planning for enhanced military capabilities in the face of threat requires mental projection of the threat beyond an immediate crisis. The way in which investment in military development is made may be a more objective, longer term measure of threat perceptions that the verbalizations of the moment since "the need to acquire arms and increase military spending is closely related to the country's perceptions of its security situation."[6] Given the fact that there is a long lead time between decisionmaking about acquiring new capabilities and their becoming operational, it is obvious that the military upgrading of conventional warfare capabilities of the ASEAN states was directed to future security goals beyond just the demands of the immediate crisis over Kampuchea.

The fear of both Vietnam's military might and Vietnamese political ambition has abated considerably over the years. There are a number of reasons

Table 9.1   ASEAN Defense Expenditures in Millions of U.S. 1980 Dollars

	1978	1982	1985
Brunei	172	195	205
Indonesia	2,036	2,926	2,610
Malaysia	71	2,077	1,604
Philippines	794	878	463
Singapore	444	852	1,042
Thailand	79	1,436	1,583

Source: International Institute of Strategic Studies, *The Military Balance, 1987–1988.*

for a more sanguine outlook on Vietnamese capabilities and perhaps even intentions, not the least of which is the confidence inspired in ASEAN by the dreary record of domestic economic failure in Vietnam. Rather than adding to Vietnamese power potential, Vietnam's Kampuchean military expedition sapped it. Furthermore, Vietnam's vaunted military invincibility proved a myth. In Kampuchea, the PAVN has not been able to eliminate a border-crossing, foreign-supplied, numerically inferior Khmer resistance. Even frontline Thailand no longer sees an immediate threat from Vietnam. Thai Army Commander-in-Chief General Chaovalit has stated that "in view of the external threat, when considering capabilities against intention, there is no danger of full scale aggression against Thailand at least within the next five years."[7]

Not only has ASEAN's appreciation of the Vietnamese "threat" changed, but so too has the broader security environment. Since 1980, a reinvigorated American political/military presence has been generally welcomed by the ASEAN nations. The new emphasis of Soviet regional policy under Gorbachev is to project the image of legitimate great power interests into the whole range of international relations, not just its military face. In Vietnam, a new, reformist leadership is in office, promising a pragmatic restructuring of the economy. A possible break in the ASEAN-Vietnam diplomatic stalemate over the terms of a political settlement in Kampuchea now seems underway as a vigorous Indonesian "dual track" political approach to Hanoi coincides with the approaching self-imposed 1990 deadline for Vietnamese troop withdrawal from Kampuchea. While the Thais may officially argue that "accepting a solution to the Kampuchean problem on Vietnam's terms will not only deny the region a guarantee of security, but also accelerate the threat from Vietnam,"[8] that threat becomes increasingly remote. This fact seems to be reflected in practice since at the end of 1987, the Thai army chief-of-staff was charged with drawing up a comprehensive strength reduction and redeployment plan to thin out Thai military forces along the Thai-Kampuchean border.[9]

Despite probable qualitative changes in ASEAN's security perceptions and threat assessments as they move into the 1990s,[10] the military programs of the 1980s have created new defense capabilities in the region that serve as deterrents and meet local threats from whatever source. At the same time, in some cases, the military component of national and regional resilience has raised serious policy questions with respect to the costs of expensive defense programs, the political quality of civil-military relations, and the creation of new intra-ASEAN threat perceptions.

MILITARY PROGRAMS OF THE ASEAN STATES

Thailand

With the Vietnamese invasion of Kampuchea, Thailand became ASEAN's frontline state. Given the historical Thai perception of the crucial strategic importance of the trans-Mekong area, Thai security was seen as acutely menaced by this new projection of Vietnamese power.[11] The threat posed by the large, hostile Vietnamese armed presence was exaggerated by the support given to Vietnam by the USSR, which itself was seen as a potential threat. As one Thai military planner put it, "In the event of a Vietnamese invasion of Thailand, the Soviet Union may compensate Vietnam's handicap in its naval power by staging a blockade of the Gulf of Thailand or offer sea protection of the Vietnamese in support of their invasion."[12] No matter how unlikely such a scenario might now seem, it was this kind of perception that allowed the mobilizing of budgetary support for sustaining and modernizing the Thai armed forces. The continuing intensity of the buildup and "frontline" status is suggested by the fact that Thailand seems to have more equipment and weapons on order than the rest of ASEAN combined.[13]

The Thai-U.S. connection has been a major factor in enhancing Thai military readiness. Both the Carter and Reagan administrations publicly reiterated the U.S. commitment to Thailand and under the Manila Treaty, with pledges of support in the event of external aggression. The U.S. accelerated delivery of military hardware in the pipeline while substantially upping its level of military assistance to the frontline state. During Prime Minister Prem's 1984 visit to Washington, President Reagan expressed his "full support" for the modernization of Thailand's defense forces.[14] In the 1986 annual U.S.-Thai joint/combined "Cobra Gold" military exercises, more than 15,000 U.S. and Thai military personnel participated in "Cobra Gold 86," which was highlighted by a predawn amphibious assault by a thousand U.S. and Thai marines.[15] In January 1987, Thailand and the United States signed an agreement to set up a joint war-reserve stockpile in Thailand. The stockpile will be sited in Korat in northeast Thailand, and the war material will begin to arrive in fiscal year 1989. The stockpile can be drawn on by Thailand in a "nation-threatening situation."[16]

The Royal Thai Army (RTA) has been reoriented away from the internal war against the armed guerrillas of the Communist Party of Thailand, now essentially defeated, to conventional war scenarios involving possible Vietnamese border incursions and lodgments. While contemporary military doctrine reflects these kinds of threat perceptions, it also seems designed to justify the army's preeminent position in the national political system. Defense expenditures in fiscal year 1988 were set at nearly $1.6 billion, or 17 percent of the budget. To this it is necessary to add the services' "secret funds."[17] While in some parliamentary circles there may be criticism of the drain on scarce resources due to military spending, the institutional dominance of the military, buttressed by the bleeding border, has allowed the government to beat back efforts to cut defense spending.

The force improvement program of the 15-division, 160,000-strong Royal Thai Army was originally concentrated on creating a more credible deterrent to conventional threats.[18] With the September 1, 1986 appointment of General Chaovalit Yongchaiyut as RTA commander, new emphasis has been given to modernization and operational readiness.[19] In Chaovalit's program, a modernized force structure was the main objective, with a stress on armor and mechanized infantry.[20] Two infantry divisions are to be mechanized, and two cavalry divisions are to be reequipped. The force level is to be trimmed down, with conscription being phased out and more effective ready reserve divisions being developed. General Chaovalit has stressed the financial burden of force modernization; a reduction in size of the standing army, perhaps by as much as 15 percent when the force restructuring is complete, would mean a substantial cut in personnel costs.[21]

Procurement policies also have been controversial. For example, an aura of corruption surrounded the September 1987 decision to buy 106 Stingray light tanks, thus starting up the U.S. manufacturer's production line against a background of charges of overpricing and "commission" payments.[22] Thailand's ASEAN partners and the United States have been jarred by a new dimension in the developing Thai-Chinese strategic relationship. In 1987, Thailand made a major buy of military equipment from China, which included 400 armored personnel carriers (APCs), 50 T69 battle tanks and 27-mm antiaircraft guns. China had already been a supplier of 30 103-mm artillery pieces and 20,000 to 30,000 rounds of ammunition.[23] The first delivery was ceremonially welcomed by General Chaovalit in September 1987. According to the RTA's deputy chief-of-staff, the equipment was being sold at a "friendship price," to be paid in installments and with a "generous grace period,"[24] new evidence of the closeness of Thai-Chinese military ties.

The Thai navy and air force procurement programs have not had similar political surprises. The Thai navy has acquired modern missile capabilities. It has in commission the Exocet SSM as well as the Gabriel SSM systems. It will be adding Exocet coastal defense missiles to its inventory. Larger ships include seven older frigates. Although Thailand has an Indian Ocean coast, the fleet operates basically in the Gulf of Thailand. The Soviet naval presence in Vietnam has given impetus to naval modernization. In September 1987, a contract was signed to build two antisubmarine frigates by Italthai with a third frigate to be built by the RTN from Italthai plans and material and with Italthai technical assistance. The cost ($76 million) will be financed between 1988 and 1991.[25] A major deficiency has been the absence of sophisticated airborne radar systems. This will be alleviated with the delivery of additional F-27 maritime patrol aircraft. Although no order has been placed, there has been talk of adding at least two submarines to the fleet. There could be a possible future Chinese connection, since China has offered to sell submarines.

It is the Thai air force that has most dramatically, and in weapons systems most expensively, made the transition from a counterinsurgency mission to a technologically modern tactical defense force.[26] The critical choice was made with the decision to purchase two squadrons of F-16As to develop a counterstrike air capability in a future MiG-23 environment that could not be met by its two air-defense squadrons of F-5Es and attack squadron of F-5As. The F-5Es had been the most advanced combat aircraft in ASEAN air forces. When Thailand opted for the F-16A in 1983, 84 F-Es were in the ASEAN inventory (Thailand, 34; Singapore, 25; Malaysia, 14; and Indonesia, 11) to balance the 180 MiG-21s that are the combat backbone of Vietnam's air force.[27] While the United States was willing to provide an export replacement for the F-5Es, it had been reluctant to provide an export license for the top-of-the-line General Dynamics F-16A, preferring to promote either the lesser powered F-16/79 or the Northrup F-20. Thailand, however, made the issue a political test of the strength of the U.S. commitment. The question was high on Prime Minister Prem's agenda for his April 1984 meeting with President Reagan. In the wake of the 1984 and 1985 Vietnamese dry-season offensive along the Thai-Kampuchean border, the U.S. government approved the F-16 sale.

Nevertheless, there were strong arguments made against the sale, not the least of which was the question of cost. The proposed sale of two squadrons (14 F-16A/4 F-16Bs), with delivery in the fall of 1988, would cost half a billion dollars. In September 1987, the Thai cabinet suddenly approved the purchase of six additional F-16s. One plane and its logistic tail costs about as much as raising and equipping an army division.[28] It was suggested that the introduction of this most-advanced combat aircraft into a Southeast Asian air force would be escalatory, guaranteeing the Soviet transfers of MiG-23s to Vietnam and forcing budget-straining F-16A purchases on other ASEAN countries.

For the Thais, the acquisition of the F-16 was seen as enabling the RTAF to keep abreast of modern weapons technology and maintenance, thereby preventing any lag from developing. To complement the F-16 purchase, an expensive upgrading of the F-5E's weapons systems, avionics, and radar has been undertaken. The air force is also embarked upon an expensive modernization of its air-defense and warning system at a cost of $207 million.[29] This program, begun in 1984, is financed by foreign military sales credits and is designed to "strengthen Thai air defenses and thereby reduce the possibility of armed aggression against Thailand."[30]

How far the Thai military still has to go to its defense goals was bloodily demonstrated in 1987 and 1988 in the battles of Chong Bok and Ban Romklao. In the former, Thai troops had a five-month struggle to dislodge a PAVN battalion that had dug in at Chong Bok Pass where the borders of Thailand, Laos, and Kampuchea intersect. Estimates of the casualties on the Thai side run into the hundreds as infantry, artillery, and air strikes in operations begun in January 1987 sought to force the entrenched Vietnamese to withdraw.[31] RTA leaders refused to provide parliament with details, despite opposition demands for an explanation as to why Thai causalities had been so "staggering."[32] Again, late in the year, the RTA was engaged in a raging battle with Lao troops in a disputed border area on the border of Pittsanulok and Sayaboury provinces in the vicinity of the village of Ban Romklao. In fighting that did not end until 17 February 1988, 147 Thai soldiers and more than 400 Lao troops were killed and hundreds wounded, at a financial cost to Thailand of more than $100 million.[33] In the after-action postmortems, serious questions arose regarding Thai command capabilities and logistical planning. The RTA's performance against an inferior force in these two limited actions threw into doubt the cost effectiveness of the huge defense outlays.[34] This is particularly apropos when the Chong Bok and Ban Romklao incidents are viewed against the earlier shortcomings displayed in the RTA's performance during the March 1985 engagements with the Vietnamese at Tatum and again in May 1985 in Trat.

Part of the problem of professionalizing the Thai military is rooted in its continued institutional involvement in politics and business. Prime Ministerial Directives 66/2523 (1980) and 65/2325 (1982) provide a sophisticated doctrinal base for military participation in eliminating injustice in the economic, social, and political spheres of national life, not just security narrowly defined. The ideas embodied in these directives, which were associated with General Chaovalit, seemed reflected in his 1987 efforts to spur *patiwat*, or "peaceful revolution," in the pursuit of "grass roots" democracy that would put an end to the corruption of the competitive political party system.[35] Popular Bangkok Governor Chamlong Simuang, unhappy with the Ban Romklao cease-fire that former Prime Minister Khukrit had termed a "defeat" for Thailand, was quoted as saying privately that "the Army should detach themselves from non-military affairs in order to concentrate more on their duty."[36]

Perhaps a more immediate negative impact on Thailand's defense capabilities is to be found in the internal politics of the military itself. The making of senior military appointments is a highly charged task that often leads to internal dispute and resistance. For example, in September 1987, hundreds of senior air force officers protested against the naming of the new RTAF chief and disrespectfully demonstrated against the prime minister.[37] Furthermore, the politics of the military seems at times to produce an allocation of resources designed to protect the institutional balance of interests on a roughly 2:1:1 (army:navy:air force) ratio rather than in terms of real defense needs given realistic threat scenarios.[38] The F-16 purchase or the proposed submarine buy may be examples of this. It may be that the loss of military prestige attached to the Chong Bok and Ban Romklao battles will prompt a reassessment of the future needs of ASEAN's frontline state. Certainly it has provoked debate over the military's role.

Malaysia

Although Thailand is ASEAN's "frontline" state, nowhere in the region has the shift from COIN to conventional preparedness been more dramatic than in Malaysia. The Malaysian Armed Forces (MAF) have been turned around at great financial cost to face a potential external threat. Between 1979 and 1982, the total defense and security budget increased by nearly 200 percent. The Fourth Malaysia Plan (1981 to 1985) had a military expansion program built into it that had as its goal the acquisition of the means to deter or repel any attack by a regional aggressor. In the language of the plan: "A substantial programme for national defence will be carried out to increase the capability and effectiveness of the armed forces to meet any *external contingency*" [emphasis added].[39] More directly, the external contingency was stated by the MAF Chief of Staff to be "external threats posed by developments in Indochina."[40] Deputy Prime Minister Musa Hitam put it more bluntly: "If you dare attack us, we will give you a bloody nose. Then we will bleed you to death."[41] The MAF's new mission was represented in tactical and strategic planning and exercises in which the "opposing" forces had the command structure, deployments, and tactics of the PAVN.

However, the Malaysian defense budget was severely impacted negatively by the strained economic circumstances after 1982. From the $2.08 billion in 1982, the defense budget plummeted to 1987's $850 million. A number of major infrastructure projects fell by the wayside.

Even though the current economic slowdown has halted a number of defense developmental projects, the goals of the Special Expansion Plan of the Armed Forces (*Perkembangan Istimewa Angkatan Tentera*, or *Perista*) still remain in place. The timing, however, has been stretched out in a current twelve-year plan to the year 2000.[42] *Perista* is intended to develop the following capabilities:[43]

- Contain and defeat the communist insurgency in all its phases without external assistance;
- Develop a nucleus conventional capability to deter and repel limited external aggression. In the event of major aggression, the Malaysian armed forces should be able to "hold" for a specified period until external assistance is forthcoming;
- Be able to operate simultaneously in peninsular Malaysia and Sabah/Sarawak; and
- Secure the lines of communications between peninsular Malaysia and Sabah/Sarawak and to protect Malaysia's offshore interests.

The pause imposed on the MAF's expansion by the budget cuts is not wholly undesirable from a managerial point of view. The slowdown also allows time for a reassessment of strategic requirements. In the Fifth Malaysia Plan (1986 to 1990), attention is given to consolidation and absorption and is further rationalized in the twelve-year program from 1988 to 2000, the accomplishment of which depends upon Malaysia's economic recovery.[44] Currently, the plans call for the Malaysian Army to reach 100,000 men and have its 36 infantry battalions at full strength by 1990. Since the delivery of 25 new British Stormer ATPCs and 26 new Scorpion AC90 light tanks for its newly created Cavalry Corps, other major weapons purchases—new armor and 155-mm artillery—have been shelved. The more restricted goal, according to the army chief, is for a "small and mobile army but one with enough punch."[45] It is still essentially a light-infantry force deficient in artillery, antitank weapons, and air defense. To give it more conventional "punch," three battalions have been converted into special units: a parachute battalion, a mechanized battalion, and a support battalion. By the year 2000, the army is to have three each of these units in the force structure.

The long-term combat development program for the Malaysian Air Force was designed to give it a new image and role in the country's defense strategy. Historically, it operated in support of COIN. The new emphasis is on the RMAF's acquiring modern conventional war capabilities.[46] For the time being, at least, the RMAF will remain a small air force having to content itself with its two squadrons (40 planes) of reconditioned A-4 Skyhawks from the 88 mothballed Skyhawks purchased by Malaysia in 1982, and its single squadron (16 planes) of F-5E/F Tiger armed with AIM-9P Sidewinders and two RF-5E reconnaissance aircraft delivered at the end of 1983. Depending on budget availability, future plans call for more combat aircraft, airborne radar, and SAM defense systems. Indicative of the direction the RMAF would like to move is the air force chief's statement that Malaysia needed to update its inventory to make it comparable with neighboring countries, pointedly referring to Thailand's and Singapore's F-16 purchases.[47]

The expansion and modernization of Malaysia's navy has also been a priority effort. It has recently put in commission two German-built corvettes armed with Exocet missiles. At the end of 1985, it took delivery of two-1,800 ton Korean-built patrol craft for coverage of the EEZ. It has also accepted four Italian-built Lerici class mine hunters. A naval air wing is planned, beginning with the commissioning on 1 July 1988 of six British Wasp ASW helicopters. Since 1984, Malaysian naval officers have been sent to England, France, West Germany, and Sweden to receive training in conventional submarines. The decision has been made in principle to purchase at least one training submarine as the pioneer for a proposed submarine fleet.[48]

Realistically, in terms of Malaysia's maritime interests and defense responsibilities, the capabilities of the navy and air force must be addressed in terms of joint operations or coalition warfare with other friendly navies in the region. Kuala Lumpur's geostrategic problems were considerably complicated when it became a claimant in the South China Sea scramble for territory in the Spratly Islands. It occupied the Terumbu Layang-Layang atoll in the summer of 1983, bringing it into jurisdictional conflict with Vietnam and the People's Republic of China. Malaysia also claims Amboyna Key, which has been occupied by Vietnam since 1978. Malaysia's injection of its power presence into the disputed South China Sea area has given new strategic importance to the island of Labuan off the Borneo coast where Malaysia's military presence is being strengthened.[49] The flare-up of armed conflict between China and Vietnam in the Spratly Islands in the spring of 1988 was a reminder to Malaysia of the volatility of the area, prompting it to reaffirm its sovereign claims.[50] In announcing plans in February 1988 to intensify patrols in its South China Sea EEZ, Malaysian Admiral Ramachandran called attention to the strategic implications of recent developments there.[51]

Singapore

Singapore's defense policy is based on the premise that "if you want peace you should prepare for war." As Second Minister for Defense Brigadier General (Reserves) Lee Hsien Loong (son of Prime Minister Lee Kuan Yew) stated: "You do not know what South-east Asia will be like in the year 2000 or more. If you did not make provision for defence now, my descendents will be going to curse me."[52] But how does a small island nation of only 2.6 million people, sea- and air-locked by larger neighbors, defend itself? The answer is expensively. Defense expenditures as a percentage of GNDP are the highest in ASEAN, as is the per-capita cost of defense.

The Singapore strategy is that of the poison shrimp or porcupine—small but dangerous to predators. That means, according to General Lee, conventional forces that are "better equipped and better organized than their opponents, which means exploiting technology and human talent to the full."[53] Starting from scratch after separation from Malaysia in 1965, and with the Israeli model in mind, Singapore has built a small (55,000) conscript-based military force that is probably the best equipped and trained in the region.[54] Unlike other ASEAN armed forces, a significant part of its weaponry is locally produced by the region's most extensive indigenous defense industries.[55] The SAF is more than just a "poison shrimp." Like Israel, it has both convincingly credible deterrent capabilities as well as preemptive strike potential.[56]

A concentration of capital resources on air defense has maximized Singapore's modern technological base with the ability to operate and maintain sophisticated weaponry. Singapore's air force is the most advanced in the region. It has an inventory of more than 180 combat aircraft, with a squadron of 29 F-5Es and three squadrons of reengined A-4 Skyhawks. The A-4s will eventually be armed with Maverick AGMs. Singapore has on order 8 F-16s (4A/4B), with delivery beginning in 1988 and an option for twelve more. Missile defense is based on four SAM squadrons. The newest system is the Rapier/Blindfire. The air defenses will be augmented by the purchase of four Grumman E2C Hawkeyes with sophisticated airborne radar surveillance systems. The Hawkeyes cost $450 million. The first was delivered in March 1987. In justifying the deal, Minister of Defense Goh Chok Tong stated that "We must continually maintain our air defense capability to ensure Singapore's security in a world of constant turmoil"[57] In 1984, the air force chose Aerospatiale's Super Puma transport helicopter over Sikorsky's UH–60 and British Westland's Sea King. The buy was for 22, with options for 12 more. At least 17 to 19 of them will be assembled by Samaero in Singapore, a joint venture between Aerospatiale and Singapore Aerospace Maintenance Company. The Super Puma is a weapons platform as well as a transport. In the regional geostrategic context, we would note that the aircraft can be outfitted for antisubmarine warfare as well as being equipped with antiship missiles.

The Singapore navy's role is geostrategically limited. The government made the decision not to make a major investment in high-cost naval systems, preferring to build up the air force. The pride of the combat fleet will be six new Lursson TNC-62-type missile corvettes armed with Harpoon SSMs. The first ship of what Singapore calls the Victory class was due from the builder's Bremen yard at the end of 1988. The other five will be built in Singapore by Singapore Shipbuilding and Engineering, Ltd., at a cost of $50 million each. The last is due by mid-1990.[58] Singapore's 6 Lursson TNC-45 missile gunboats currently armed with Gabriel II SSMs will likely also be rearmed with Harpoons. These twelve missile-equipped ships, together with a variety of patrol craft, are deemed sufficient for the navy's limited mission.

The army, now at full planned strength, has a regular cadre of 15,000 and a conscript force of 30,000, with a twenty-four-month service obligation. There is a regularly exercised combat reserve of 150,000. Its combat strength consists of three infantry brigades and an armored brigade. The SAF is equipped with 300 AMX–13 light tanks that are being locally reengined and given automatic transmissions. Additional strike mobility is given by over 700 M113 APCs. Singapore's Ordinance Development and Engineering Company produces its own 155mm towed howitzer of domestic design. The army has been described as a "well-organized, reasonably equipped, and cohesive force capable of home defense and some power projection abroad in a coalition context."[59]

One military analyst has written that the preponderance of armor and artillery assets in the Singapore army has given it an ability to "strike deep," which confers the SAF "with superior combat power relative to that of neighboring land forces."[60] Singapore's political leaders have gone out of their way to place its defense buildup in a regional perspective, seeking to allay any fears its neighbors might have. On his first official visit to Singapore in late 1981, Malaysia's Prime Minister Mahathir remarked: "I cannot see why Singapore has to bolster its defense except to complement the defense capability and greater resilience of this region against any external threat to the security of the area.[61] This was rhetorically interpreted by Singapore's Lee Kuan Yew to mean that the SAF "should be there to augment Malaysia's armed forces to meet any threat of external aggression."[62] Singapore's political strategy is to prove to its neighbors that Singapore would be a useful ally in any collective effort to maintain regional peace and security. For example, given its capabilities, the E2C Hawkeye missions can be placed in a regional air-defense framework. Nevertheless, given the SAF's relatively superior capabilities with respect to Malaysia, and in a bilateral political context full of religious and racial irritation, Singapore's leaders still find it necessary to reassure Kuala Lumpur about their intentions. Foreign Minister Dhanabalan has stressed that Singapore will not do anything that will threaten Malaysia's security.[63]

Brunei

When U.S. Commander-in-Chief Pacific Admiral William Crowe made the first official CINCPAC visit to ASEAN's newest member state in October 1984, he remarked that he was "extremely encouraged by the Royal Brunei Armed Forces rapid development."[64] Given a population of only 238,000 and the relative magnitude of its defense expenditures (more than 40 percent of its public expenditure), Brunei may be proportionately the "garrison state" of the region. Fueled by its huge oil and natural gas revenues, from 1978 to independence on 1 January 1984, substantially more than one billion dollars was spent on weapons acquisitions for the 4,000-man force. These included 3 Exocet-armed fast-attack craft, 6 Bolkow 105 helicopter gun ships, 16 Scorpion light tanks, and a Rapier air-defense battery.[65] As one analyst noted, "The equipment level of the Royal Brunei Malay Regiment would be the envy of any armed force."[66] It is constantly being upgraded. For example, Blindfire radar is being added to the Rapier SAM system. Fixed-wing strike and surveillance aircraft and shoulder-fired antiarmor weapons are also planned for the future.

The RBAF (Royal Brunei Air Force) has essentially two missions. The first is internal security in a rapidly changing political and social environment historically dominated by the impact of the rebellion of 1962. The sultan himself holds the defense portfolio in the cabinet. The second is protection of Brunei's sources of wealth, the on- and offshore oil and natural-gas fields. In this respect, Brunei's military capabilities are linked to the continuing presence of the British Gurkha battalion based at Seria. Since the battalion's presence is a function of British decisionmaking, Brunei has long planned to expand its own armed forces by raising a third infantry battalion. The constraint on this plan is not budgetary, but one of manpower. The 1987 decision to create a military reserve force may also be related to the manpower shortage.

Although Brunei's capital, Bandar Seri Begawan, is the ASEAN capital nearest to Vietnam, the sultanate's external environment is strategically dominated by Malaysia. Malaysia's military buildup at Labuan, which controls the mouth of Brunei Bay, makes more pressing common security understandings between Malaysia and Brunei with respect to their bilateral overlapping maritime jurisdictions and their common problems of Vietnamese and PRC claims in the South China Sea ASEAN EEZs. Brunei also has close military ties with Singapore. Since 1983, SAF has occupied a permanent camp complex for jungle training in Brunei's Temburong District, which is located north of Brunei Bay.

Indonesia

Since 1979, Indonesia's military program reflects a geostrategic appreciation that the most vulnerable borders of the nations are in its maritime zones, and the Indonesian Armed Forces (*Angkatan Bersenjata Republik Indonesia* or ABRI) must therefore be prepared to meet the enemy there. Although still conscious in East Timor and Irian Jaya (West New Guinea) of its doctrine of territorial warfare, Jakarta has given new priorities to the creation of capabilities to meet conventional threat and assuming responsibilities for surveillance over its archipelagic maritime jurisdictions and EEZ. The magnitude of this latter task is suggested by its extent of some two-and-a-half million square miles. The Second and Third Strategic Development Plans (*Rencana Strategis* or RENSTRA), 1979 to 1983 and 1984 to 1988, provided the general framework for rebuilding and reorienting ABRI.[67]

The military weaknesses of ABRI were demonstrated in the mid-1970s in the East Timor campaign. ABRI was shown to be ill-trained, ill-equipped, and understrength for the changing regional security needs. Building up national resilience in ASEAN's southern flank required a substantial investment of new resources. The defense and security development budget jumped 500 percent between 1978 and 1983. This was a period of military expansion under General Mohammad Andi Jusuf financed by oil revenues. General Jusuf's successor was General Benny Murdani. His program for ABRI was one of consolidation and rationalization in a budgetary framework of relative austerity corresponding to the sharp drop in oil revenues. In addition to upgrading equipment and training, under General Murdani a major reorganization of ABRI's command structure was carried out.[68] General Murdani was succeeded as ABRI chief by General Try Sutrisno in February 1988. The military expansion program was paralleled by a major investment in the development of a domestic defense industrial complex to reduce dependence on external sources of weapons and logistical support.[69]

ABRI's active force level is about 280,000 men, 210,000 of whom are in the army. It was claimed that in RENSTRA II the army was expanded to 100 combat battalions. If so, they were considerably under authorized strength. General Murdani admitted that "from the very beginning we have counted that of the 100 battalions only about 20 battalions are really the combat troops."[70] The army's conventional warfare capabilities are centered on the 20,000-man Strategic Reserve Command (KOSTRAD), which is made up of two infantry divisions with armor and artillery battalions, as well as three infantry brigades (nine battalions). Two of the infantry brigades are airborne. There is also a separate 4,000-man special paracommando elite strike force (KOPASSUS) under the direct command of the ABRI chief. Under current deployments and with existing lift capacity, KOSTRAD units can be quickly placed anywhere in the archipelago. It is also from KOSTRAD that any forward strategic projection could be made. The KOSTRAD units have been the first to receive new weapons. The armored batallions have adopted the AMX–13 light tank as the main armor, of which there are about 100 in the inventory. A heavy vehicle repair center in Bandung keeps a mixed inventory of other armored vehicles and APCs—Saladins, Saracens, and Ferrets—operational.

Although still relatively modest in size, the Indonesian Navy (ALRI) is becoming a more technologically advanced force, having some interdiction capability. The first major additions to its fleet rebuilding were the three Exocet-armed, Dutch-built corvettes of the Fahatillah class. Plans for two additional ones were shelved after budgetary shortfalls. At the end of 1986, two ex-Dutch frigates of the van Speijk class were added to the three ex-British Tribal class, four ex-U.S. Jones class, and two ex-Soviet Riga class frigates in commission. Two additional van Speijk class frigates, to be delivered at the close of this decade, are armed with eight of the latest version Harpoon SSMs. In the opinion of one naval expert, "With their more advanced version of the Harpoon, the new Indonesian ships have the advantage over the RAN's (Royal Australian Navy) DDGs, anything in the Vietnamese Navy or anything else in the region except, perhaps, India."[71] Four Korean-built, Exocet-armed fast-attack craft are included in the arsenal. To these primary combatant surface ships we can add numerous other attack, patrol, and auxiliary vessels. On order from the Netherlands are two Tripartite mine hunters, among the most modern mine-hunting vessels in the world, and two others may be purchased. Four of them were deployed to the Persian Gulf in 1987.[72] Two German built-type 209 submarines are in commission, with another on order. If budgetarily possible, a submarine fleet of six to ten vessels is planned.

A developing naval air arm is enhancing ALRI's antisubmarine warfare capability. It is built around ten ship-based ex-Dutch Wasp ASW helicopters. There are two Exocet-armed Super Puma ASW helicopters being flown off converted Korean-built landing support transports. Two dozen or more Super Pumas are being built under license from Aerospatiale by Indonesia's government-owned IPTN Nusantara aircraft industry. Armed with Exocet antisubmarine missiles, these helicopters are formidable weapons platforms. The transport version will also give greater mobility to the army. The acquisition by Indonesia's air force of three Boeing 737s fitted with sidelooking radar with 100-mile coverage on each side permit the monitoring of the full width of Indonesia's EEZ on a mission range of three thousand miles. IPTN Nusantara also produces a variety of other rotary and fixed-wing aircraft that have marine-patrol capability.

Orphaned in the post-1965 ABRI has been the Indonesian Air Force (AURI), which inherited not only the taint of complicity in the leftist-adventurist aborted coup, but also an inventory of obsolescent and unserviceable Russian aircraft. Rebuilding AURI has focused on creating a reaction force capable of supporting ground and naval operations. It has been a target for reorganization, being, in General Murdani's opinion, overmanned and resource-wasteful (the ABRI commander unfavorably compared AURI's 27,000 men and 100 aircraft to Singapore's 7,000 men and 150 to 160 aircraft).[73] There is a combat force consisting of a squadron of F–5Es, two squadrons of ex-Israeli A–4 Skyhawks, and a COIN squadron of OV–10F Broncos. As the regional combat aircraft environment has changed, Indonesia, despite the heavy costs, committed itself to purchase a squadron of F–16As (12 planes) at a total cost of $337 million. The manufacturer, General Dynamics, agreed to the local production and assembly of some components by IPTN Nusantara. The first delivery is scheduled for 1989.

Indonesia has shown great concern for its air-defense capabilities. AURI accepted delivery of the first two French Thomson radar units in September 1983, which were to be used to control F–5 intercepts. Since 1982, Swedish Bofors RBS–70 Giraffe surface-to-air missiles have been deployed. On his visit to Vietnam in February 1984, General Murdani was very impressed by that country's air-defense system. It may have been coincidental, but within days of his return, he told the Indonesian parliament that an advanced SAM system was necessary for Indonesia.[74] After looking at a number of possibilities, including the American Chapparal and Vulcan systems, Indonesia placed a 100-million-pound order in December 1984 with

British Aerospace for the Rapier system. This order has been followed by two additional contracts for the Rapier in deals that include technology transfer.

Indonesia's investment in upgrading ABRI's capabilities as a deterrent and defense military force has been marked by new strategic orientations as well. Indonesia has made significant efforts at infrastructure creation to support its ability to project its power into its South China Sea territorial and maritime zones. From the former eight naval area commands, the navy has been reorganized into two fleets, an eastern one based at Surabaya and a new Western base at Teluk Ratai in West Sumatra. Originally budgeted at U.S. $5 billion, the Teluk Ratai facility will be the keystone of Indonesia's intention to defend conventionally the northern approaches to the archipelago. Special attention has been given to the establishment of a forward base on Natuna Besar. In 1981, a new runway was opened at the Ranai Air Force Base that could take any aircraft in AURI's inventory. It is known that other ASEAN air forces have operated through Ranai in training. The special Marine unit formed in 1982 and dedicated to the protection from seizure of offshore platforms in zones disputed with Vietnam can jump off from Natuna Besar. Regular and more frequent naval deployments are made into the South China Sea zone as well as routine combat air patrols.

Although Indonesia has not really been "muscle flexing," its new military acquisitions and the purchases in the pipeline have prompted some concern about its long-term regional ambitions. The memories of Sukarno's confrontation with Malaysia, the integration of Timor, and continuing border security problems with Papua New Guinea stimulate questions concerning possible future Indonesian "threat" to its neighbors. Jakarta has found it necessary to explicitly disavow any link between rebuilding its military and Indonesian aggressive intentions. For example, General Murdani gave assurances that Indonesia's naval buildup—giving it the largest regional fleet—was purely for defensive purposes and did not pose a threat to any neighboring country: "We hope that this [the fleet's development] will not be misinterpreted."[75] In meeting a number of regional leaders since 1986, President Suharto has pledged a noninterventionary Indonesian policy.[76] But the issue and latent suspicion are there. Like the escalatory impact of Thailand's F–16 buy, Indonesia's fleet's development shows that the response to one set of threat perceptions can have unintended political consequences.

There has been some question as to whether another potential political consequence of ABRI's technical upgrading and increasing "professionalization" might not be a diminished role for the military in Indonesian politics. This does not appear to be likely. ABRI's "dual function" as a security and social/political institution has been given a strong statutory base. In the spring of 1988, transfer of command from General Murdani to General Try, President Suharto reminded the new ABRI chief of the military's commitment to it as "dual function," and General Try, the first member of the post-independence struggle generation of officers to become armed forces commander, vowed that the military would remain a social/political force as well as a defense force.[77]

The Philippines

Of the ASEAN states, the Philippines has been the least affected as to its defense planning by perceptions of new or future external threats. While its ASEAN partners have made substantial investments in reorienting their armed forces to externally based conventional threat, the Armed Forces of the Philippines (AFP) have been continuously preoccupied with ethnic and communist insurgencies.[78] Moreover, the AFP's security capabilities and performance role have been degraded in the course of political involvement in the support of the Marcos regime and the factionalism of the army in the Aquino government. The rapidly expanded intake, training, and deployment of officers and men in the 1970s to the bitter war against the Moro Islamic insurgency in the south had a corrosive effect on traditional military values and a breakdown in civil-military relations exacerbated by martial law and the counterinsurgent war against the growing forces of the Communist New People's Army.

Professionalization and upgrading of the AFP has become a priority of the Aquino government, but all evidence points to the fact that there is a long way to go before the *New* AFP restores discipline and morale and becomes an effective combat force insulated from politics.[79] In addition to political factionalism, continuing budgetary constraints have impeded a sustained effort to modernize forces and equipment. After threats by the military, personnel costs were dramatically increased by the implementation of a 60 percent across-the-board pay hike in 1987. Even with the U.S. "best effort" to provide the military aid promised in the base agreement package, "the financially strapped AFP appears always to be in a state of crisis."[80]

The atmosphere of uncertainty in regard to the continuity of the U.S.-Philippines military relations in the framework of the Military Bases Agreement raises serious questions about the AFP's future development. In 1985, for example, the United States supplied $40 million dollars in military assistance, 92 percent of which was allocated for AFP maintenance programs.[81] Perhaps more important than the direct assistance to the AFP is that U.S. military forces based in the Philippines and under terms of the Mutual Security Agreement have provided the Philippines with the high-technology, conventional-warfare capabilities for the defense of Philippine air and maritime frontiers. This U.S. role has allowed the Philippines to maintain a relatively low defense budget by ASEAN standards. On a per-capita GNP basis, it is the lowest in ASEAN. U.S. calculations indicate that by providing for the external defense of the Philippines, the bases save that country an estimated 2.1 percent of its GNP.[82] The Philippines is an archipelagic state with an extensive maritime zone. Its navy, however, is essentially a coast guard with no SSM capability; the air force has a ground-support mission and no high-performance combat aircraft. It is the U.S. forces in the Philippines that face any possible strategic challenge; in their absence in the event of a nonrenewal of the Military Bases Agreement, the Philippines would have to pay very heavy opportunity costs to create new capabilities or be willing to accept new vulnerabilities. These realities have been pointed out to Manila by U.S. authorities.

ASEAN DEFENSE COOPERATION

The concept of national resilience is complemented by the notion of regional resilience. In defense terms, this means that as each ASEAN member state increases its capabilities to defend itself, the region as a whole becomes more capable in regard to its defense. The question of defense cooperation, however, is that of militarily relating the efforts of the individual states to one another in a tactical or strategic fashion that will in fact enhance regional security. At the foreign policy level, a coordinated response to external challenge has been possible.

In a major address before a Pacific Armies Management Seminar in November 1986, Thai Army Commander-in-Chief Chaovalit elaborated on the fact that "considering the increasing threats from the communist's expansionist policy, no nation will be able to defend their country with only their own individual efforts."[83] This point underlies what he termed the "principle" of collective defense; in other words, nations must unite their political, economic, and military efforts to resist the common enemy. Chaovalit singled out NATO as "an excellent example of this cooperative spirit among friendly nations," adding that "ASEAN is another." He pointed out that "although ASEAN has been organized without any aim at military cooperation, the association provides effective deterrence against any act of aggression."

Malaysia's defense minister has stressed that although ASEAN is not a military pact and each member is responsible for its own defense, cooperation on defense matters is vital in order to build an effective defense against a common enemy if the need should arise.[84] This attitude is echoed throughout the region.

Defense cooperation can take many forms. There is intelligence-sharing among and between the ASEAN states. There is a regular procession of defense and security official visitations with constant contact between military and civilian defense officials and their ASEAN-wide counterparts. ASEAN officers train in each other's military schools. There is some mutual use of facilities: for example, Singapore jungle training in Brunei, Brunei's navy use of Malaysia's Lumut naval base, or Malaysian Air Force stagings through Indonesia's Ranai Air Base on Natuna Besar. Perhaps the most visible element of growing defense cooperation has been the pattern of

ASEAN joint military exercising on a bilateral basis. The emphasis has been on naval and air exercises. The annual *Elang* (Hawk) series of air exercises that Indonesia holds with Singapore (*Elang Indopura*), Thailand (*Elang Thainesia*) and Malaysia (*Elang Malindo*) are examples. These exercises are aimed at familiarizing air-force personnel with the procedures of joint air-force operations and the planning of joint air-strike strategy. Indonesia also holds annual naval exercises with ASEAN partners: *Malindo Jaya* with Malaysia, *Sea Garuda* with Thailand, and *Englek* with Singapore. Other series of bilateral military exercising includes Singapore-Thailand naval (*Sing-Siam*), Thailand-Malaysia air (*Air Thamal*), Malaysia-Singapore naval (*Malapura*), and Singapore-Brunei naval (*Pelican*). Only Malaysia and Indonesia have developed a regular pattern of bilateral army field exercises in the Kekar Malindo series.

At the core of regional resilience is the implicit strategic alliance that has developed between Indonesia and Malaysia. Indonesia's General Murdani has described Indonesian-Malaysian military ties as "the best" compared with those of other countries.[85] Malaysia is Indonesia's strategic frontline as well as a buffer. For Malaysia, Indonesia is a reliable geostrategic partner in the geographic lock they hold on the vital sea and air lanes of communication in the Straits region. There is full mutual appreciation of their common security interests in the South China Sea zones. By treaty in 1982, Malaysian rights of access between East and West Malaysia through Indonesia's archipelagic seas were defined. The accord preserves Malaysia's communications as well as acknowledging security interests. The two countries jointly exercise their navies and air forces in Indonesia's jurisdictional space north of the Natuna Islands. At the end of the September 1984 Elang Malindo IX, the Malaysian air force chief stated that the two partners would present a united front against challenges or threats from other countries.[86] For his part, General Murdani has said that Indonesia is prepared to help Malaysia defend its territorial claims in the disputed Spratlys.[87]

The basic instrument linking the two is the Malaysian-Indonesian Border Agreement, which, after twelve years, was revised in 1984 and broadened to extend military cooperation to all borders—including maritime borders—and covered the joint use of naval and air forces. This border agreement is the most comprehensive security arrangement existing between two ASEAN partners. Its scope was further enlarged in 1987.[88]

It is obvious that Singapore also occupies a strategic position in the Straits region. If placed in a regional maritime and air-defense system, its capabilities, together with those of Brunei, would add substantially to deterrence or interdiction. The number of SSM-capable vessels operated by the four navies is not insignificant, nor is their air power at the F–5E level to be augmented by F–16s to be dismissed as long as we are talking about potential regional adversaries. The political problem is how to enhance what is a *de facto* Malaysia-Indonesia alliance with greater cooperation with Singapore in order to create an effectively integrated defense system. Singapore still seeks a regional role for the Singapore armed forces that is acceptable to its neighbors. Singapore officials have most insistently spoken out in favor of expanding the pattern of ASEAN military cooperation beyond just bilaterally based activity.[89]

So far, Singapore's call has fallen on deaf Malaysian ears and Malaysia-sensitive Indonesian ears. This can be largely attributed to continuing political irritants in the relations between Singapore and Malaysia that spill over into security considerations. Highly charged ethnic issues are disruptive. For example, there was a storm of controversy in Malaysia over Israeli President Chaim Herzog's official visit to Singapore. This was followed in February 1987 by Lee Hsien Loong's comments that explained the lack of intake of Singapore Malays into the SAF in terms of avoiding possible divided loyalties on their part. For Malaysia, this raised the issue of what potential enemy Singapore was preparing to defend against—possibly Malaysia or even Indonesia.[90] Nevertheless, in the aftermath of the Herzog and Lee Hsien Loong affairs, both Jakarta and Kuala Lumpur have made overtures for greater bilateral defense cooperation with Singapore, recognizing that security for the three is interdependent.[91]

One area that has often been mentioned as ripe for greater ASEAN cooperation is in standardizing weapons systems and the joint purchase of components.[92] Proposals for procurement cooperation and ASEAN defense-industrial complementarity stumble, however, on the desire for as much self-sufficiency as possible and on the fact that Singapore's existing defense technological and industrial base would threaten the infant defense industries of other ASEAN countries. Singapore's defense industries are world-class in terms of competitiveness. For example, for a number of years, Singapore manufactured its own assault rifle, the SAR 80, which has been improved in its SAR–88 version. It is priced between $400 and $450 (compared to the M16's price tag of $600 to $900). Malaysia, which talks of standardization, plans to manufacture its own assault rifle on a European joint-venture basis. Indonesia is replacing the M16 as its standard infantry weapon with the Belgian FNC 5.56mm rifle manufactured under license by PT Pindad in Bandung. On every count, there is great reluctance in Malaysia and Indonesia to become defense-dependent on Singapore. Indonesia's General Murdani put it bluntly: Under no circumstances will Indonesia buy armaments from Singapore.[93] But just as high-technology weapons systems and platforms may drive an integrating defense strategy in the region, so, too, will budgetary and efficiency rationality of common service facilities and depots (be they for F–16s or Exocets) move ASEAN toward greater cooperation, particularly the more removed the activity is from linkages with domestic industries.

ASEAN DEFENSE COOPERATION WITH EXTERNAL PARTNERS

For the ASEAN member states, regional resilience is enhanced by the continued military presence in the region of friendly states. While even more "non-ASEAN" in any alliance fashion than the network of interlocking bilateral activities characteristic of intra-ASEAN cooperation, ASEAN's cooperative ties with the military establishments of the United States, Australia, New Zealand, and other countries is part of any deterrent capability that might exist in the region. All of the ASEAN states except Indonesia have some kind of formal mutual security tie to Western partners.

The U.S. security presence in particular is substantial. We have already noted the role of the United States in bolstering Thai defense and its part in the strategic defense of the Philippines. From the Philippine bases that rest on bilateral American-Philippine agreements, an umbrella of U.S. power shelters the ASEAN region. Under this generalized shield, a variety of other U.S. military interactions with ASEAN takes place. The United States is a major security assistance supplier to ASEAN. Although the absolute amount of direct assistance is declining, it is still substantial, as well as being a symbolic representation of U.S. interest in the security of the ASEAN states. Security assistance categories include Foreign Military Sales (FMS), which finance sales with direct credits; Military Assistance Programs (MAP), which provides grant funding; International Military Training (IMET), which provides military training on a grant basis; and Economic Support Funds (ESF), which help pay for the opportunity costs of defense spending. The priorities in terms of where the proposals are concentrated represent U.S. appreciation of the level of threat in the region: a strong communist insurgency in the Philippines and Vietnamese forces on the Thai border. In the case of the latter, Assistant Secretary of State Sigur termed U.S. support "crucial" not only because of our interest in Thailand per se but "because of the stake we have in the independence, integrity, and prosperity of the nations of the Association of Southeast Asian Nations (ASEAN)".[94]

The United States carries out training and operational exercises with ASEAN armed forces (we have already noted the U.S.-Thai "Cobra Gold" series). From Clark Air Force Base, the "Cope Thunder" series of exercises provides realistic combat air force training in a simulated combat environment. In addition to the Philippines air force, Thai and Singapore air force planes have participated. Indonesia and Malaysia have observer status, though Indonesia is considering participation. Certainly, if Indonesia's combat pilots are to attain the same level of F-16 proficiency as those in other ASEAN air forces, they will need this kind of exercise. Further U.S.-ASEAN exercising includes the "Commando West" series, which has involved bilaterally Royal Thai Air Force and U.S. aircraft from Clark and Misawa, and Malaysia and the United States, which in 1987 moved to Malaysia's Butterworth base. In addition to port calls, elements of the U.S.

Table 9.2   Cumulative Total of U.S. Assistance to ASEAN States to 1985
(in $ millions)

	Total (Loans & Grants)	Military Loans	Military Grants
Indonesia	3,941.6	329.2	290.7
Malaysia	282.3	180.9	9.2
Philippines	4,022.5	359.1	941.7
Singapore	22.1	17.2	2.1
Thailand	2,412.1	563.2	1,537.0

Source: United States Information Agency, *U.S. Defense Posture in the Pacific*
(September 1987).

Table 9.3   Fiscal Year 1988 Security Assitance Request for ASEAN
(in $ millions)

	FMS	MAP	IMET	ESF	Total
Indonesia	20		2.		22.
Malaysia	4		1.		5.
Philippines		110	2.6	124	236.6
Singapore			.05		.05
Thailand	10	50	2.2	5	67.2
ASEAN total	34	160	7.85	129	330.85

Source: *Department of State Bulletin*, May 1987, pp. 30–35.

Seventh Fleet regularly maneuver or have passing-exercises with the friendly navies of the Straits region as they move to and from the area in their deployments. The U.S. commander of the Seventh Fleet and the U.S. CINCPAC often tour the region.

While certainly not as powerful a deterrent, the Commonwealth military presence in the region has been almost as visible as that of the United States. Malaysia and Singapore are linked to Great Britain, Australia, and New Zealand in the Five Power Defence Arrangement (FPDA), while a bilateral agreement with London keeps the Hong Kong-based Ghurka battalion in Brunei. Brunei has also developed close bilateral ties with Australia. With the future of the Ghurkas in doubt after Hong Kong's coming retrocession to China, Brunei is seriously exploring accession to the FPDA. Historically, the FPDA has been given "symbolic" teeth as a result of the basing of first two (and then one) Australian Mirage squadrons in Malaysia at Butterworth and a New Zealand infantry unit in Singapore. It also has provided the framework for intensive bilateral training exercises involving all services, in Southeast Asia and in Australia and New Zealand.

Australian participation is a key element in the maintenance of the Integrated Air Defence System (IADS) for Malaysia and Singapore. This is exercised regularly through ADEX or air-defense exercises in which Australian air units operate with Malaysia and Singapore. In June 1984, ADEX 84-3 saw a political breakthrough when, for the first time, Malaysian fighter planes flew from a Singapore base. Even though there will be no permanent Australian basing in Southeast Asia with the withdrawal of the second of the two Mirage squadrons from Malaysia in April 1988, Australia will continue to be an active military partner. Australia has promised to rotate through Butterworth its new F-18A Hornets for a minimum of sixteen weeks a year. Australian P-3 surveillance flights will continue to operate from Butterworth, and RAAF ground support personnel will stay in place along with an army rifle company. Furthermore, according to Australian Defense Minister Beazley, the Hornet deployments will be "supplemented" by F-111 long-range strike aircraft deployments, as well as of continuous rotational deployments of combatant Royal Australian Navy units to Southeast Asian waters which is to begin at the end of 1988.[95] This will include an RAN submarine deploying from the Malaysian naval base at Lumut.

In December 1986, New Zealand announced it was withdrawing its 740-man infantry- and air-support unit based in Singapore by 1989. Like Australia, the New Zealand government has sought to reassure its FPDA partners of its continuing commitment to the region's security. Together with Australia, New Zealand will continue to participate in joint exercises and provide training facilities. It also claims to be developing a full-scale overseas military deployment capability that, according to Defense Minister Tizard, will be sent on regular exercises in Singapore and Malaysia to maintain preparations for civil emergencies and external aggression.[96]

Deteriorating Indonesian-Australian political relations have led to an erosion of long-established military cooperation between the two states under their Defense Cooperation Agreement. The tension that has characterized the relationship from 1986 exists at two levels. The refocusing of Australian strategy to northern defense has raised the question in Jakarta of who Canberra considers a potential enemy. At the same time, Indonesian officials have reacted angrily to criticism of Indonesian domestic affairs by Australian politicians and media. There was a tremendous row when, in April 1986, the *Sydney Morning herald* published an article suggesting corruption in President Suharto's family. ABRI Commander Murdani threatened at that time to scrap all defense cooperation with Australia. Since then, in fact, military cooperation has been carried out, to use General Murdani's words, "on a very selective basis."[97] For example, Jakarta rejects training places in Australian military schools for its officers. While Australia presses for closer ties, Indonesia sees no need for a higher level of activity. We would point out that to Australian difficulties with Indonesia's domestic arrangements, we now have to add questions deriving from the increase of open authoritarian politics in Singapore and Malaysia and the abuse of civil and political liberties through the application of draconian internal security acts.

Although Indonesia is not a member of the FPDA, its pattern of defense cooperation with the FPDA partners, including Australia, has enhanced the functional operation of the military grouping. Its geostrategic location between Malaysia and Singapore and their commonwealth partners is a planning factor for all. This fact becomes more significant as the shape and capabilities of the future ABRI become clear. In the words of one Australian military analysts; "The combination of a rapidly expandable force of F–16s, submarines and naval ships equipped with the most advanced tactical SSGW available in the Western world would make passage through the Indonesian archipelago very difficult for any but the forces of the U.S. or the Soviet Union."[98] FPDA's vulnerability to the Indonesian lack of cooperation was demonstrated in September 1986 when Indonesia suddenly withdrew refueling rights to RAAF planes on their way to or from Butterworth. While only a temporary interruption, it did get attention, with Australian Foreign Minister Hayden warning it could disrupt Australian cooperation with Malaysia.[99] General Murdani, for ABRI's part, said that Jakarta treated Australia just like any other country when it came to military ties. As far as Indonesia was concerned, Australia did not enjoy any "special privileges," concerning landing facilities.[100]

A final aspect of ASEAN's external defense cooperation should be mentioned. As the above discussion of the military programs of the ASEAN states shows, they are closely tied in terms of weapons purchases to U.S. and Western European manufacturers. The only major exception has been the Thai purchase of Chinese tanks and APCs, although Malaysia toyed with a Russian helicopter purchase (the Mi-26 Halo heavy lift model). The sales efforts have been heavily competitive, leading to better terms for the buyers. For example, General Dynamics had to sweeten the offset and coproduction kitty for Indonesia in order to clinch the F-16 sale in its competition with the French-built Mirage 2000.[101] Greater interoperability among ASEAN's high-technology weapons is being achieved and joint maintenance programs are being established for F-16s, Exocets, and other systems. As buyers increasingly demand terms, including coproduction, the integration of the indigenous defense industries with the defense industries in the United States and Europe will tie them even more closely to their external security partners, and, ironically, perhaps increase rather than decrease dependence.

THE FUTURE POLICY HORIZON

While the concept of "national and regional" resilience has provided ASEAN a unifying theme, embracing their individual policy responses to threat perceptions, it has not provided for a common security strategy except at the most minimum level of self-defense against direct aggression. As the threat of a Vietnamese blitzkrieg has receded, singularly different long-term threat perceptions in the ASEAN region have become manifest. Indonesia and Malaysia feel that the years of confrontation with Vietnam over Kampuchea have made the region vulnerable to Chinese political ambition and strategic design. There is concern that a *de facto* Thai-Chinese alliance could have an ultimately destabilizing impact. In this respect, while the continued U.S. political-military presence in the region is welcomed as a necessary ingredient in the great power regional balance, especially given the Soviet-Vietnamese link, it does not require Jakarta or Kuala Lumpur to mortgage their future options vis-à-vis playing out Sino-Soviet relations to U.S. global security concerns. This has become especially noteworthy in the aftermath of Gorbachev's July 1986 Vladivostok speech and the ensuing Soviet peace offensive in Southeast Asia.[102]

The decisions that led to the kinds of military programs of the ASEAN states analyzed above were based on perceptions of trends emerging from a prolonged crisis over Kampuchea, leading to a permanent hard division of Southeast Asia into two military conflicting blocs facing each other across the Thai front lines and in the South China Sea. In a scenario of conflict, the opportunity costs, economic and political, were acceptable. However, questions can be raised as to whether a final balance sheet would show the investment of more than five years in attempting to redress the local imbalance of power did contribute to "resilience" broadly conceived.

ASEAN now, however, looks to a different future scenario—a post-Kampuchean conflict scenario, in which the pattern of external-security connections in particular are different. We refer specifically to the movement for a declaratory Southeast Asian Nuclear Weapons Free Zone as the first step toward the realization of a Southeast Asian Zone of Peace, Freedom, and Neutrality. To the kinds of policy questions raised by efforts to implement a nuclear-weapons free ZOPFAN, we have to consider the future of U.S. bases in the Philippines. Although ASEAN insists that this is a bilateral U.S.-Philippines issue, at the same time they recognize the troublesome regional strategic implications of a U.S. redeployment from Clark and Subic. They have not been able to forge a consensual ASEAN position on the issue.[103] The U.S. has made the potential consequences of such a forced move crystal clear.[104] In that event, one wonders whether the defense components of policies of "National and regional resilience" designed to meet the threats of the 1980s will be relevant to a dynamically changing security environment in the 1990s.

NOTES

1. See, for example, Laksmana Pertama [Admiral] Soewarso, *Saran Pertimbangan Parameter Kethanan Nasional* in his collected works, *Wawasan Nusanatara, Ketahanan Nasional, Keamanan Nasional* (Jakarta: 1980).

2. Suharto, 17 August 1981, text as reported by Foreign Broadcast Information Service, *Daily Report: Asia and the Pacific*, 21 August 1981, p. N–7 (hereafter cited as *FBIS-AP*. Since 1987, it has been retitled *East Asia* and will be cited as *FBIS-EAS*).

3. The standard source for order of battle comparisons is *The Military Balance*, published annually by the International Institute of Strategic Studies, London; see also G. Jacobs, "Vietnam's threat potential to ASEAN," *Asian Defence Journal*, May 1982, pp. 16–27 and Douglas Pike, "Vietnam, a modern Sparta," *Pacific Defence Reporter*, April 1983, pp. 33–39.

4. Goh Keng Swee, "Vietnam and Bi-Polar Rivalry," in Richard Soloman, ed., *Asian Security in the 1980's: Problems and Policies for a Time of Transition* (Santa Monica, CA: Rand Corporation R-2402-ISA, November 1980), p. 113.

5. Jacobs, p. 27.

6. Khaw Guat Hoon, "Weapons Proliferation and Security in Southeast Asia," in Robert O'Neill, ed., *Insecurity: The Spread of Weapons in the Indian and Pacific Oceans* (Canberra: Australian National University Press, 1978), p. 153.

7. General Chaovalit Yongchaiyut's speech on the "Modernisation of the Royal Thai Army," 11th Pacific Armies Management Seminar, Bangkok, 27 November 1986 (text as reported in the *Bangkok Post*, 28 November 1986).

8. Lieutenant General Panya Singsakda, "Thailand and Indochina." Paper presented at a seminar entitled "Thailand's Strategy and Stability of Southeast Asia in the Next Decade," Institute of Security and International Studies, Chulalongkorn University, Bangkok, 22 May 1987 (text as reported in the *Nation*, 23 May 1987).

9. *Straits Times*, 2 December 1987, from *Agence France Presse*.

10. See, for example, Sheldon Simon, "ASEAN's Strategic Situation in the 1990s," *Pacific Affairs*, 60:1 (Spring 1987), pp. 73–95.

11. Sukhumbhand Paribatra, "Strategic Implications of the Indochina Conflict: Thai Perspectives," *Asian Affairs*, 11:3 (Fall 1984), p. 32; Kanala Sukhabanij-Khantaprab, "The Strategic Thinking of Thai Military Leaders on Regional Security and Modernization of the Royal Thai Army." Paper presented at the National Defense University's 1988 Pacific Symposium.

12. Lieutenant General Panya.

13. Tim Huxley and Amitav Acharya, "Security Perspectives in South-East Asia," *International Defence Review*, December 1987, p. 1603.

14. "Take-off for F-16s," *Far Eastern Economic Review*, 26 April 1984, p. 17.

15. "Cobra Gold 1986," *Asia Pacific Defense Forum*, Spring, 1987, pp. 14–19.

16. "U.S. and Thailand to sign war stores pact," *Straits Times*, 7 January 1987.

17. "Thai Parliament reverses plan to cut army fund," *Straits Times*, 1 December 1986.

18. Hans Indorf, "Thailand: A case of multiple uncertainties," *Pacific Defense Reporter*, September 1983, pp. 23–35.

19. Jacques Bekaert, "The Royal Thai Army—Its Role in National Unity," *Asian Defense Journal*, March 1987, pp. 4–18.

20. Chaovalit.

21. Paisal Sricharatchanya, "A 'lean, mean machine,'" *Far Eastern Economic Review*, 19 February 1987, pp. 26–27.

22. Paisal Sricharatchanya, "The military merchants," *Far Eastern Economic Review*, 3 December 1987, p. 28, and the *Bangkok Post* report on the purchase of 106 new tanks, 6 December 1987, in *FBIS-EAS*, 8 December 1987, p. 56.

23. "Troop carriers, tanks to be purchased from PRC," *The Nation*, 22 March 1987, as reported in *FBIS-AP*, 24 March 1987, p. J–2.

24. *Ibid.*

25. "Contract Signed for Antisubmarine Frigates," *The Nation*, 25 September 1987, as reported in *FBIS-EAS*, 29 September 1987, p. 30.

26. Major Randall J. Larsen, USAF, "The Modernization of the Royal Thai Air Force," *Asian Defence Journal*, May 1987, pp. 4–15.

27. This is as given in *The Military Balance 1984*.

28. "F-16 counter-attacked," *Far Eastern Economic Review*, 25 October 1984, p. 50.

29. Shuhud Saaid, "Automating the RTAF's Air Defence and Warning System," *Asian Defence Journal*, May 1987, p. 13.

30. *Straits Times*, 18 march 1985.

31. Rodney Tasker, "The battle of Chong Bok," *Far Eastern Economic Review*, 18 June 1987, p. 19.

32. Samak Sundaravej as quoted by Albert Ramalingam, "'no' to House," *Straits Times*, 1 June 1987.

33. See the reportage of Gen. Chaovalit's analysis of the human and material costs of the Ban Romklao battle in *FBIS-EAS*, 8 and 9 March 1988, p. 47 and p. 34, respectively.

34. Banyat Thasaniyawet, "Never Victorious; Never Defeated," *The Nation*, 27 February 1988, as reported in *FBIS-EAS*, 29 February 1988, pp. 51–52.

35. "Thai Army chief calls for sweeping democratic reforms," *Straits Time*, 5 November 1987.

36. Banyat, p. 51.

37. "Thai air force upset over choice of its new chief," *Straits Times*, 21 September 1987.

38. M.R. Sukhumbhand Paribatra, "New defence priorities to counter aggression needed," *The Nation*, 30 July 1986.

39. *Fourth Malaysia Plan, 1981–1985*, (Kuala Lumpur: National Printing Office, 1981), p. 185.

40. General Tan Sri Sany Jaffar as quoted in the *Straits Times*, 12 March 1979.

41. Deputy Prime Minister Musa Hitam, "Malaysia's Doctrine of Comprehensive Security," *Foreign Affairs Malaysia*, 17:1 (March 1984), p. 97.

42. "Armed forces chief on 12-year plan to boost military," *Straits Times*, 2 July 1987.

43. "A Conversation with Malaysia's Chief of Defence Forces," *Asian Defence Journal*, September 1987, p. 35.

44. "Armed forces chief on 12-year plan to boost military," *Straits Times*, 2 July 1987.

45. "Army to get more punch with three special units," *Straits Times*, 11 December 1986, and "Towards a smaller, more effective army," *Malaysian Digest*, 31 December 1985.

46. *Straits Times*, 4 January 1983.

47. "Malaysia needs to update fighter planes: Air chief," *Straits Times*, 25 April 1987.

48. "Submarine core unit plan for navy," *Malaysian Digest*, April 1986, and "Malaysia may buy subs from Europe," *Straits Times*, 30 November 1987.

49. For a more detailed discussion of the Malaysian claims, see Donald E. Weatherbee, "The South China Sea: From Zone of Conflict to Zone of Peace?" in Lawrence E. Grinter and Young Whan Kihl, eds. *East Asian Conflict Zones* (New York: St. Martin's Press, 1987), pp. 129–130.

50. Malaysian Foreign Ministry statement as reported by *Bernama* as given in *FBIS-EAS*, 25 February 1988, p. 24.

51. "Malaysian navy to set up patrols," *Straits Times*, 2 February 1988.

52. "No reasons for Singapore to be offensive to Kuala Lumpur—Brig. Gen. Lee," *Straits Times*, 10 February 1988.

53. Brigadier General Lee Hsien Loong, "Security Options for Small States." Speech to the Singapore Institute of International Affairs, 16 October 1984.

54. In addition to the *Military Balance*, for the buildup of Singapore's armed forces, see Kirpa Wong bin Rahim, "The Singapore Armed Forces," *Pacific Defense Reporter*, November 1980, pp. 56–58; Patrick Smith and Philip Bowering, "The citizen soldier," *Far Eastern Economic Review*, 13 January 1983, pp. 26–32; S. Bilver, "Threat Containment in Singapore," *Asian Defence Journal*, January 1987, pp. 34–38; and Shuhud Saaid, "The Singapore Army," *Asian Defence Journal* June 1987, pp. 4–18.

55. For Singapore's defense industry, see Michael Richardson, "Singapore's defence industry," *Pacific Defence Reporter*, May 1983, pp. 69–75.

56. Huxley and Acharya, p. 1604.

57. *Straits Times*, 1 January 1984.

58. "Singapore navy to get six Corvette warships," *Straits Times*, 9 January 1988.

59. Special correspondent, "Singapore: The reserves provide the teeth," *Pacific Defense Reporter*, October 1983, p. 20.

60. Saaid, "The Singapore Army," p. 13.

61. *Straits Times*, 18 December 1981.

62. *Straits Times*, 19 December 1981.

63. "Singapore won't threaten KL's security—Dhana," *Straits Times*, 2 February 1988.

64. *Straits Times*, 12 October 1984.

65. In addition to *The Military Balance*, in general for Brunei's force structure see Hans Indorf, "Brunei—The vulnerabilities of a mini-state," *Pacific Defence reporter*, September 1984, pp. 46–49, and Shuhud Saaid, "The royal Brunei Armed Forces: Money Cannot Buy Men," *Asian Defence Journal*, January 1988, pp. 12–23.

66. Michael Leigh, "Brunei Darussalam: The Fruits of Independence?" *Ilmu Masyarakat*, 9 (April to September 1985), p. 68.

67. In addition to *The Military Balance*, in general for Indonesia's force structure, see Donald E. Weatherbee, "Indonesia: A Waking Giant," in Rodney W. Jones and Steven A. Hildreth, eds., *Emerging Powers: Defense and Security in the Third World* (New York: Praeger, 1986), pp. 124–171, and A.W. Grazebrook, "Indonesia builds for its needs," *Pacific Defence Reporter*, October 1986, pp. 15–17.

68. A detailed survey of the reorganization is given in "Indonesia's ABRI: Consolidation, Command and Control," *Asian Defence Journal*, May 1986, pp. 4–15.

69. An extensive treatment of Indonesia's defense-related industries can be found in Donald E. Weatherbee, "Indonesia: Its Defense-Industrial Complex," in James Everett Katz, ed., *The Implications of Third World Military Industrialization: Sowing the Serpents' Teeth* (Lexington, MA: Lexington Books, 1987), pp. 165–186.

70. Interview in *Tempo*, 15 October 1983.

71. Grazebrook, p. 16.

72. "Holland sells two mine-hunters to Indonesian navy," *Straits Times*, 15 January 1988.

73. Interview in *Tempo*, 15 October 1983.

74. *Straits Times*, 21 February 1984.

75. "Fleet is for our own protection: Murdani," *Straits Times*, 16 February 1987; see also, "Border co-operation vital, says Murdani: Jakarta military chief also assures neighbors on naval build-up," *Straits Times*, 19 February 1987.

76. See for example, "Suharto: Indonesia has no military ambitions, Assurance given to Lange during private talks," *Straits Times* 19 March 1986, and "We have no plan to annex territory, says Suharto," *Straits Time*, 19 June 1986.

77. "Gen Try told to keep military's dual role," *Straits Times*, 1 March 1988.

78. In addition to *The Military Balance*, in general for the order of battle of the Armed Forces of the Philippines, see Shuhud Saaid, "The NAFP:

Opland Mamamayan and the Unfinished Revolution," *Asian Defence Journal*, January 1987, pp. 4–32.

79. "New Marching Order," *Asiaweek*, 12 February 1988, pp. 12–19, and James Clad, "Philippines Military: Forces for change," *Far Eastern Economic Review*, 26 November 1987, pp. 36–37.

80. John Peterman, "Unsuitably equipped," *Far Eastern Economic Review*, 26 November 1987, p. 39.

81. United States Information Service, *Background on the Bases: American Military Facilities in the Philippines* (1986), p. 23.

82. James Clad, "Sovereignty and security," *Far Eastern Economic Review*, 21 April 1988, p. 23.

83. Gen Chaovalit, *op. cit.*

84. "Malaysian Defense Minister stresses ASEAN defense coop.," *Indonesian Times*, 6 August 1986.

85. "Jakarta-KL army ties 'the best'," *Daily Express* [Kota Kinabalu], 19 July 1986.

86. *Antara*, 29 September 1984.

87. *Straits Times*, 4 December 1984.

88. *Bernama*, 7 December 1987, as reported in *FBIS-EAS*, 8 December 1987, p. 30.

89. "A new call for unity," *Asiaweek*, 2 October 1982, p. 24.

90. See, for example, "Which countries are a threat to Singapore?" *Berita Minggu Malaysia*, reprinted in the *Straits Times*, 3 March 1987.

91. "Murdani on closer ties between armed forces," *Straits Times*, 3 July 1987, and "Malaysia hopes to step up military ties with Singapore," *Straits Tims* 5 November 1987.

92. Zakaria Haji Ahmad, "ASEAN countries should jointly produce weapons," *Far Eastern Economic Review*, 20 February 1986, pp. 26–27.

93. *Straits Times*, 21 February 1984.

94. "FY 1988 Assistance Requests for East Asia and the Pacific," *Department of State Bulletin*, May 1987, p. 31.

95. "Farewell Ceremony for Australian Air Squadron," *Bername*, 16 April 1988, as reported in *FBIS-EAS*, 18 April, 30; "Aussies to step up naval presence in region," *Straits Times*, 13 February 1988, and Hamish McDonald, "Have gun will travel, Australian aircraft leave Malaysia," *Far Eastern Economic Review*, 10 March 1988, pp. 33–34.

96. "S'pore and KL get NZ defence pledge," *Straits Times*, 2 February 1988, and David Barber, "Phasing out the force New Zealand to withdraw troops from Singapore," *Far Eastern Economic Review*, 8 January 1987, pp. 15–16.

97. Australia not a threat says Murdani," *Straits Times*, 20 February 1988.

98. Grazebrook, p. 17.

99. "Defence training may be hit by ban—Hayden," *Straits Times*, 6 September 1986.

100. "No special treatment for Australia—Murdani," *Straits Times*, 11 September 1986.

101. Nayan Chanda, "F16 wins sales dogfight, Indonesia opts for US aircraft over Mirage 2000," *Far Eastern Economic Review*, 25 September 1986, pp. 29–30.

102. For a discussion of Soviet policy, see Stephen M. Young, "Gorbachev's Asian Policy," *Asian Survey*, XXVIII:3 (March 1988), pp. 317–339.

103. For a discussion of the linkage between the base issue and the nuclear weapons free zone, see Donald E. Weatherbee, "Looking Through the ASEAN End of the Telescope," in the Proceedings of the National Defense University Symposium Patterns of Cooperation and Pacific Basin Security, 25–26 February 1988.

104. Ambassador Paul Wolfowitz, address to International Herald Tribune Centennial Conference, (text as printed in the *Straits Times*, 16 September 1987).

10

Divergence in Australia-New Zealand Security Relations

MICHAEL McKINLEY

Death is the cessation of heart, lung, and brain functions, but in the international political sphere, dysfunction frequently results in the continuance of many activities despite the fact that they are essentially purposeless. Since 1985, the activities undertaken in the name of the defense and security relationship between Australia and New Zealand have increasingly come to enjoy (if that is the word) this status. Since New Zealand's adoption of a "non-nuclear" defense policy, its multifarious nature no longer reflects the traditional ANZAC mythology so badly stated in the 1983 New Zealand Defence White Paper that held that it was "inconceivable" that Australia and New Zealand would set radically divergent courses in defense and strategic policy, and that ANZUS was "fundamental" to their joint and separate defense interests. Instead, in a world in which the trilateral treaty has been rendered "inoperative" in terms of New Zealand, thereby becoming bilateral, they are to be seen more as an expression of persistence in the face of utterly changed circumstances (and perhaps of disbelief) that were once so apparently vital having now passed into history. To this extent they are commemorative acts, pointing to the fact that ANZUS, like Count Dracula's Transylvania, is much troubled by the undead. Whereas this character was given to forms of mysterious and macabre return, both Australia and New Zealand are set on courses that are not only radically divergent, but also unlikely to admit any significant degree of reversion to the *status quo ante*. To argue this case, this chapter has been divided into two substantive parts. While both are concerned with the *prospects* for a close defense relationship between Australia and New Zealand, the second is related solely to Australia's interests and obligations in the Indian Ocean/Northern Australia area.

It is, of course, a matter of historical fact that the security relationship between Australia and New Zealand has been very close—so close in fact that the authors of the 1983 New Zealand White Paper entitled *Defence Review*

1983 chose to describe the two countries as constituting a "single strategic entity."[1] In the fields of shared alliances, consultative machinery, supply and logistic cooperation, major joint procurement programs, technical cooperation, training, secondments and exchanges, joint exercises, naval visits, and intelligence sharing, over one hundred agreements and memoranda of understanding were supportive of this conclusion.[2] Consequently, between 1984 and 1985, when ANZUS as a tripartite alliance began to unravel as a result of the Lange Labour government's non-nuclear policy, the expectation emerged in various New Zealand government statements that an even closer nexus might be established. This was, however, incompatible with the *nature* of the policy reforms that were underway in New Zealand. Effectively, the Labour government had embarked on a defense policy revolution that rendered traditional modes of thinking on central strategic issues inappropriate, even as regards Australia—a country with which New Zealand never intended to alter its relations. Nevertheless, by 1987, this development had not only come to pass but was, in fact, formalized with the publication of the government White Paper, *The Defence of New Zealand*.[3] It was, moreover, heralded as the most significant security policy document a New Zealand government had brought down since 1945.

Foremost among the principles proclaimed in the White Paper was the New Zealand government's rejection of nuclear deterrence, a concept to which, in the absence of general and complete nuclear disarmament, Australia subscribes. Furthermore, Australia does so both in a declaratory sense by statements in support of deterrence (enhancing measures undertaken by the United States) and in an operational sense (hosting the so-called U.S.-Australian joint facilities, particularly those at Nurrungar, North-west Cape, and Pine Gap; between them, they provide essential arms control, early-warning, and communications functions).[4] In addition, though New Zealand expressed a preference for maintaining the pre-1985 levels of bilateral cooperation and operating, as circumstances required, with Australia, it was really only interested if the latter took place within its area of circumscribed strategic interest, the South Pacific. Thus, the emphasis placed on the traditional Australia-New Zealand relationship in the White Paper was testimony to the strength of an almost involuntary reflex and, at the same time, discounted by the imperatives of regional focus, the credibility of origin of threats, and the perceived need to pursue more independent, less alliance-derived modes of strategic thought.

To the extent that the New Zealand government has the rights to determine how best its national interest might be served, Canberra has had no option but to accept the non-nuclear *demarche*. Equally, to the extent that Wellington induced anxiety into the ANZUS relationships, Canberra has also been unsympathetic to the overall thrust of New Zealand policy. As New Zealand moved to codify its non-nuclear policy in legislation, which it did in the form of the *New Zealand Nuclear Free Zone, Disarmament and Arms*

Control Act (June 1987), antipathies developed between the trans-Tasman partners. These in turn degenerated from time to time into the trading of insults. In November 1985, New Zealand Prime Minister David Lange denied that Australia had any role in the ANZUS impasse as an "honest broker" between the United States and his country—on the grounds that the Australians "were neither honest nor broker."[5] As the cost of the contradictions and confusions in New Zealand's policy became apparent throughout 1985 and early 1986, and as Canberra's anxiety over the future of ANZUS increased as a concomitant result, Australian Minister for Foreign Affairs Bill Hayden cracked that "[a]t times, New Zealand is like the cross-eyed javelin thrower who doesn't win any medals but keeps the crowd on its toes."[6] By late 1986, the flippancy that disguised the fundamental difference between the two countries had departed: Hayden, visiting Wellington for ministerial talks, was not only critical of New Zealand's stand, but contradictory of previous statements by Lange and Minister for Defence Frank O'Flynn that there would be no problems in the switch to a security relationship with Australia instead of the United States.[7] Hayden emphasized, therefore, both the "marked additional expense" for Australia that accommodating New Zealand had already involved and that there would be no further expansion of defense ties. Curiously, even disingenuously, Lange then denied that New Zealand ever considered Australia a substitute for the United States, adding that such a view was "alarmingly bizarre."[8] By early 1987, the New Zealand Defence White Paper, while expressing the sentiments noted earlier, had incorporated this position as policy.[9]

Subsequently, a return to more cordial relations was effected by Australian Prime Minister Bob Hawke's first visit (in over four-and-one-half years in office) to New Zealand in November 1987. But it was a tribute to the significance of vital common, but nondefense issues, especially those relating to economic relations, rather than the neutralizing of the differences. Indeed, although it is now the case that the 1983 Closer Economic Relations (CER) agreement between Australia and New Zealand is facilitating greater commercial and industrial competitiveness faster than was originally envisaged, and although the communality of general interests is thought to be so extensive that the cover story of Australia's main weekly current affairs magazine, the *Bulletin*, proposed in April 1988 that the two countries should unite, it is also the case that security policy differences are now excepted in the interests of achieving other equally important objectives.[10] They still retain, however, their own significance and the potential for discord in the bilateral relationship. Without wishing to be unduly repetitive, it is in this context that the Lange-Hayden "exchange" must be placed. The differences are now entrenched and passing beyond learned behavior into instinct, carrying with them a high risk of mutual misunderstanding, different usages accorded to common terms, and the deleterious effects each could induce. When an expansion of trans-Tasman security ties was first bruited by New Zealand, it was largely unspecified. In Australia, it was initially left unanswered but, if an impression might be ventured, was understood in terms consistent with Hayden's interpretation. In other words, the assumptions each country brings to security policy are not *explicitly* different; so much so, indeed, that the historical differences that were concealed in the general ANZUS consensus existing prior to July 1984 are to be seen as an affirmation of Weber's notion of routinization (of differences).[11] In the late 1980s, though, the energizing power of anxiety over a monolithic communist threat is absent, or at least not shared equally or accorded the same priority. Accordingly, there is a change from the centripetal to the centrifugal in the determinants of policy and the redefinition of interests and obligations in terms lesser than those that previously existed.

In practical terms, the defense relationship still includes the cluster of cooperative endeavors mentioned earlier but on a scale revised downward as determined by the overriding requirements of the United States in certain areas (intelligence sharing, for example) or the more pressing needs perceived by Australia to promote its security objective outside traditional avenues that included New Zealand.

New Zealand's decision to reequip the army with the Australian-designed, Australia-made Steyr rifle is, therefore, not exceptional, nor is the Lange government's decision to proceed with Australia to the second (documentation development) phase for a new light patrol frigate that is to become operational in the early to mid-1990s.[12] But these are basically lowest-common-denominator ventures. If any significant level of defense cooperation at all is to be ongoing, the very least that is required is compatibility of basic equipment.[13] The CER agreement probably demands something of the type also since Hayden (as but one exemplar) was at pains to point out to New Zealand the disproportionate advantages it enjoys from access to the very much larger Australian market.[14] In this regard, it is noteworthy that despite progress through the first stage of the light frigate project, there remains considerable skepticism in the relevant Department of Defence offices in Canberra that New Zealand will actually commit itself to the procurement of four vessels as provided for in the project agreement.[15] But this only reflects the long record of noncooperation in the procurement of major defense items including, as recently as February 1985, when New Zealand's relations with ANZUS were deteriorating rapidly, Lange's peremptory withdrawal from further participation in the Australian replacement submarine project.[16] Beyond the levels of cooperation outlined, however, there are five what might be called structural and political factors of an Australian character that militate against a closer defense relationship with New Zealand, many of which would be extremely difficult to counter even if the political will to develop such a relationship existed. In approximate order, these are public opinion, strategic doctrine, bureaucratic resistance, development in the Pacific, and budgetary and resource constraints. Overlaying all of these, and therefore entitled to separate consideration, is the newly-found preoccupation with the defense interface between developments in the Indian Ocean and the security of northern Australia.

FACTORS EXACERBATING THE DIVERGENCE

Structural Factors

The extent to which public opinion, broadly defined, is perceived as influential in establishing the parameters of Australian security policy is well documented and widely referred to in current analyses.[17] Recent papers, moreover, note the increased level of support for ANZUS in the period since it was threatened in 1985 and the marked lack of support for the New Zealand case.[18] Interestingly, even when New Zealand was operational within ANZUS (November to December 1984), the attitudes of Australian "key subgroups—those who are likely to be influential in shaping or administering public policies" tended to be "significantly more critical or dismissive of New Zealand and its concerns than the remainder of the population."[19] In other words, despite the country's fine standing with the Australian public in general, it still has a serious image problem: "Its image is weakest precisely where it counts most."[20]

The level of support for ANZUS not only reinforces current initiatives in the defense field, but in some cases would facilitate developments more radical than any Australian government has seriously entertained to date. For example, of the four polls taken concerning the (hypothetical) acquisition of nuclear weapons by the Australian armed forces, three (including the most recent) showed that 60 percent or more approved of the idea.[21] This is a finding consistent with a late 1987 poll which, for the third year in a row, revealed that a substantial majority of Australians believe their defense forces are inadequate and, for the second year running, that Indonesia, immediately to Australia's north, was the most likely threat (ahead, for example, of the Soviet Union).[22] An environment exists, therefore, in which tampering with the alliance, or even dealing with those who do so, is perceived as politically dangerous. And this has not been lost on the conservative political parties whose spokesman, in opposition, have consistently advocated that sterner measures, most often in trade, be taken to encourage New Zealand to abandon its non-nuclear policy.

Strategic Doctrine

It is not an exaggeration to say that Australian strategic doctrine, like that of New Zealand, is now in the process of a fundamental reorientation. With the publication of Paul Dibb's *Review of Australia's Defence Capabilities* (March 1987), there are clear indications that Australia is confronting its unique strategic circumstances and attempting to pursue a policy of maximum self-reliance in defense matters.[23] Such has been the intent and immediate effort of these papers that it is commonplace in Australia for analysts and commentators to speak of "Australia's Defence Revolution."[24] For the first time, Australia has enunciated a coherent strategy for national defense and established a sophisticated conceptual basis for appropriate force structures and capabilities. Insofar as New Zealand is concerned,both documents are at pains to emphasize the continuing relevance of the ANZAC nexus but do so, it should be noted, in the context of a clear and unmistakable disagreement with the non-nuclear policy and the reallocation of resources required by the new policy direction.

The task for Australia, it must be said, is daunting: the reviews propose a force-in-being strong enough to meet any foreseeable challenge to Australia's national interests in an area extending 7,000 kilometers from the Cocos Islands to New Zealand, and 5,000 kilometers from the archipelagos in the north to the Southern Ocean—in other words, 10 percent of the earth's surface. As both Defense Minister Kim Beazley and Ministerial Consultant Paul Dibb are given to observing, this is equivalent to defining an area of "direct military interest" that covers the same distance as those from Sweden to Afghanistan or from Finland to the Suez Canal.[25] In terms of the broader area termed the "sphere of primary strategic interest," the figures are almost imperial—extending through Southeast Asia, the Eastern Indian Ocean, and the South Pacific—to the point where Australia, with a population of 16 million, has declared for itself almost a quarter of the surface of the globe.[26]

In order to give substance to this revolution, it has become necessary for Australia to both redeploy many of its existing defense assets and to develop and deploy others. Accordingly, the remnants of the old "forward defence" strategy (whereby Australia maintained permanent forces in Southeast Asia) have been abandoned in line with the logic of the prime objective, the defense of the Australian continent, and the likelihood that any potential threats the country might face are located to the north. Thus:

> [A]n FA-18 fighter base is being constructed at Tindal south of Darwin, and bare bases capable of handling the FA-18s have, or will be, constructed at Learmonth and Derby in the North-West, and on Cape York in the North-East. There are already major Air Force bases at Darwin and Townsville. The Orion P-3C LRMP aircraft can operate from mainland airbases in the North and from the Cocos and Christmas Islands in the Indian Ocean. The 2nd Cavalry Regiment is to be relocated to Darwin with the prospect of locating a full brigade in the North later. Units of the Army's reserves with special responsibilities for surveillance will be allocated to the North. The White Paper also announced that half of the Navy would be deployed from the East coast to Western Australia—which is closer in terms of steaming time to the critical northern approaches than the Navy bases in the East.[27]

Consonant with this reorientation is the fact that the Australian Defence Forces have increased the level of "exercises with, and ship and aircraft visits to, not just the ASEAN states, but also Japan."[28] It is also well to note that within the region to the north the growth in military expenditure for more than a decade has been relatively sustained and spectacular, primarily in response to the developments in Vietnam, Laos, and Kampuchea; the growing Soviet North Pacific presence; and concerns (mainly Indonesian) about the long-term role of China in the region:

> Between 1974 and 1985, the defence budget of Indonesia increased by 145% in real terms; that of Malaysia by 120%; Brunei by 709%; Singapore by 183% and Thailand by 244%.[29]

For New Zealand, then, the northern and western geographical foci dominating the Australian defense revolution imply the relative downgrading of areas of interest closer to its own.

Bureaucratic Resistance

As Hayden's jest concerning the "cross-eyed javelin thrower" indicated, there is at the ministerial level a certain frustration evident concerning New Zealand. Within senior levels of the defense bureaucracy, the same disposition is found, although it is difficult to attach any greater significance to it other than to acknowledge its existence and, of course, its relationship to the aforementioned factor of elite public opinion. Whereas that factor was treated on the basis of New Zealand's initiatives after Labour came to office in July 1984, there is evidence indicating Australian bureaucratic dissatisfaction prior to that time. For example, the early 1984 *Strategic Basis of Australian Defence Policy* paper, a confidential (but leaked) document supposed to be the cornerstone of government thinking on national security and foreign policy issues, noted in its two-paragraph mention of New Zealand that "it has *still* developed no policy for national defence [which] coupled with opposition in some sections of the New Zealand Labour party to ANZUS . . . indicate potential difficulties in our defence relations"[30](emphasis added). In any event, the prediction was accurate even if the deficiency mentioned was corrected.

Also of interest is the fact that one of the first public references to Australian bureaucratic resistance was made by New Zealand Minister for Defense Frank O'Flynn during the Defence Estimates debate in Parliament in December 1986.[31] Ross Babbage, at that time a senior (assistant secretary rank) bureaucrat on leave of absence form the Defence Department, confirmed O'Flynn's observation. In two papers presented between December 1986 and February 1987, he wrote of "the very serious obstacles to progress," the "numerous policy and practical difficulties for Australia in maintaining many existing forms of cooperation with New Zealand," and finally, the "irritating" nature of the costs to Australia of New Zealand's stance.[32] From any other have to result from imputation, but originating as they do from an informed and most recent "insider" whose analyses are widely respected as sound, they must be accorded relevance, and even influence.

Once again, it must also be said that the relevant New Zealand ministers have done little to help their case. To the forefront in this regard have been the statements of Prime Minister (and Minister for Foreign Affairs until late 1987) David Lange. From time to time, and indeed frequently, he appears to many observers in Australia to have adopted a somewhat cavalier and even mischievous attitude toward security matters. In December 1985, he hinted that the way might be open for selective visits by U.S. Navy vessels on the basis that his government possessed secret new technology capable of determining the presence of nuclear weapons.[33] He then went on to challenge some of the findings of the 1985-86 Defence Committee of Inquiry, a group picked (in part) on the basis of diversity, when it reported back to him *unanimously* that the public of New Zealand was more favorable to remaining in ANZUS than maintaining the non-nuclear policy.[34] Subsequently, he ordered a detachment of the elite New Zealand Army Special Air Service toward Fiji in response to a relatively low-key hijacking of an Air New Zealand jetliner at Nadi airport—the hijacking itself related to the first coup undertaken by Colonel Rabuka. In the realization that the move could achieve nothing positive, he had the mission aborted. All that time, of course, he ran the risk of precipitating in Fiji the very violent type of situation that South Pacific nations were hoping to avoid. In 1987, he chose to disavow his previous pro-ANZUS statements with the declaration that "in the long run" New Zealand was "better off" out of an operational alliance with the United States.[35] Moreover, the current Minister of Defense, Bob Tizard, on a visit to Australia in March 1988, embarrassed his host, Kim Beazley, with a news conference disclosure that the New Zealand signals intelligence facility being built at Waihopai in the north of the South Island was "compatible with" (i.e., performed the same function as) a facility Australia was establishing.[36] The embarrassment stemmed from the fact that the Australian facility, at Geraldton in Western Australia, had, until the Tizard gaffe, not been officially detailed. If such accounts are accepted as representative, and it is asserted here that they are, then in the overall context of bureaucratic perceptions New Zealand's difficulty is that of being taken seriously and perceived favorably at the same time.

Pacific Ocean Developments

Ever since the U.S. withdrawal from Vietnam, the Pacific Ocean, by which most strategic analysts mean the *North* Pacific rather than the South Pacific, has received more attention than at almost any time since 1945. Although geographic logic determines that both of these areas are related, the prime focus for Australia and New Zealand has been the latter. In this region, a shared concern for the security and stability of the island-states was an obvious imperative, providing the cause for close liaison, coordination, and cooperation. At the same time, the South Pacific's ills, such as they are (French colonialism, French nuclear testing and U.S. tuna-boat incursions) were not susceptible to ANZAC military action. Within the orbit of Australia's new policy directions, moreover, the prospects for an expanded defense relationship are limited, as Babbage notes: "the further west and north one goes, the more New Zealand's real interests decline."[37] And though the South Pacific is one area that has encouraged Australian-New Zealand cooperation, the scale of increased Australian operations to be undertaken is quite unlikely to be marched by New Zealand. The South Pacific, too, has been elevated in priority as a result of the capabilities and policy reviews. Accordingly, in 1987, ship visits to the South Pacific tripled—to seventeen deployments, visiting ports in twelve countries. Similarly, five-day sorties by RAAF P3-C Orions increased from six to ten, while the Pacific patrol boat program saw twelve Australian-built craft go to six South Pacific countries.[38] To the extent that New Zealand simply lacks the resources to cooperate or follow suit at this level, the Australian initiative can only be characterized as unilateral, and therefore once again relegates New Zealand operations to a secondary and circumscribed realm.

Budgetary/Resource Constraints

If there is a single, major area of consternation in defense circles at present, it is that occasioned by the apparent inconsistencies between the Dibb *Review* and the policy *Review*. The former was predicated on a defense outlay of around 3 percent of Ground Domestic Product (GDP) and a slightly high figure for annual real growth; the latter, on the other hand, posits that the defense program can be afforded without real growth. Both must be seen against a recent historical background in which 3 percent of GDP has seldom been obtained, a 1987–1988 budget decrease of 1 percent, a 1988–1989 increase of only 0.5 percent and a *forecast* restoration of 3 percent growth by 1990–1991. Thus the question arises whether, in the distinct possibility that Canberra will underfund its current defense program, there is any scope for financing New Zealand-related activities when over time the associated costs have come to be classified as "marked" (Hayden)[39] and "complicated, quite demanding and expensive" (Babbage).[40]

Financial resources are not the full extent to which Australia might be limited in its defense policies. In terms of manpower attrition in the Australian Defence Forces (ADF), a crisis has clearly developed: As of August 1987, official statistics revealed the highest rate of resignation for years (for 1986)—12.6 percent.[41] More significantly, the total losses of the ADF over the previous three years were 36 percent of the entire force, and over the previous four years, over 50 percent.[42] Alarmingly, at a time when Australia is investing heavily in a high-technology deterrent—in procurement of FA-18s—the RAAF is consistently sustaining pilot losses at a rate faster than they can be trained;[43] indeed, in the case of the FA-18s there is, as of August 1988, a shortage of not only line pilots but qualified instructors.[44]

In summary, this brief account of the factors that impinge directly on Australia-New Zealand defense relations points most forcefully to the conclusion that a return to the *status quo ante* 1985 is, whatever its desirability, a highly unlikely eventuality. The purpose of the foregoing was not, however, merely to make this case; it was also to establish the nature of the difference in outlook that is now pronounced in the respective security policies of Australia and New Zealand. In no aspect is this to be found more than in the manner by which Australia relates to the Indian Ocean-Northern region of its strategic environment.

THE INDIAN OCEAN AND
THE DEFENSE OF NORTHERN AUSTRALIA

The Indian Ocean and the defense of northern Australia is, without wishing to put too fine a point on it, what Ireland is to the British or what Central and Latin America is to the United States: a foreign and defense policy enigma. At one time, it is challenging, puzzling, or ambiguous. For Australia, however, it has yet to be as costly as the enigmas suffered by Britain and the United States. Nevertheless, as regards the essential attributes of the enigmatic, it is redolent with puzzlement. Why, for example, when Australia's north-west is just about its most resource-rich area, are there so few defense assets devoted to its protection; why, when its Indian Ocean coast is its most vulnerable littoral, did it take until the 1980s to establish a permanent surface combatant presence from the Royal Australian Navy there; and why, when any significant military threat to Australia could only be projected from or through the extensive archipelago to the north, has the role that Western Australia should perform in the defense of the continent been substantially neglected until relatively recently? The conclusion that might be arrived at would no doubt embody the notion that, in the higher realms of Australian security policy making, and in relation to the west and northwest of the county's strategic environment, logic was a dispensable virtue. This would, of course, be the case if the Indian Ocean region were without menace, or if the ocean itself comprised an insignificant sea-lane of communication (SLOC), or if western and northwestern Australia's strategic assets were so without value that their loss could be accepted with equanimity. If fact, though, none of these is true.[45]

To understand this claim, it is important to first grasp the essentially complex nature of the Indian Ocean basin. Within the forty-four independent nations washed by the Indian Ocean are found Arab, African, European, Indian, and Malay peoples, practicing the faiths of Buddhism, Christianity, Hinduism, and Islam. Taken together, they constitute nearly one-third of the

Hinduism, and Islam. Taken together, they constitute nearly one-third of the world's population, but this statistic by itself obscures the range of contrast—from India, with a population of more than 700 million, down to Comoros, with fewer than 500,000 residents. More importantly, the region is host to a representative sample of the major ills beseting political society, both domestic and international, in the closing years of the twentieth century. It is a pathology whose constituent parts include political and social deprivation, economic underdevelopment, colonial and post-colonial exploitation, racism, sectarianism, and dynastic differences. The politics of much of the region tend therefore to be characterized by the relative fragility and vulnerability of democratic institutions, where they exist, but transcending this, almost permanent conflict, particularly in the so-called "arc of instability" stretching from the Horn of Africa to the Indian subcontinent, including the hinterland of the littoral states. Furthermore, in the eastern recesses of the eastern Indian Ocean lies what is arguably Australia's greatest external security preoccupation in the form of border tensions between Indonesia and Papua New Guinea.

One of the serious consequences of this condition has been the frantic race for arms within the region to the point where it now includes one of the world's largest military powers (India) and at least four of the world's actual and potential nuclear proliferators (Israel, India, Pakistan, and South Africa). By virtue of this fact alone, the region has attracted various manifestations of interests by external powers, from attention, to presence, to outright interference. Overall, the Indian Ocean basin is so riven with externally induced (and internally generated) tension and conflict that it does not so much describe a region as it does the geographic setting for fissiparous forces that result in a collection of subregions.

It would, however, be a cruelly distorted analysis that claimed the regional peoples were *entirely* responsible for their own predicament. Indeed, it is perhaps their misfortune to inhabit lands which, irrespective of their intrinsic status, were bound to achieve significance in the context of the global strategic rivalries between the superpowers and their respective alliance and trading systems. The Indian Ocean is accorded fundamental strategic importance[46] because it lies at the intersection of three continents, its underwater topography is ideally suited for locating submarine strategic nuclear systems, the bulk of the noncommunist world's proven oil resources are located near it; its surface waterways carry the strategic raw materials and trade products of much of the industrialized world, and its seabed is repository for essential high-grade minerals. Because of their respective locations, a similar status has devolved upon many of the islands and territories within it such as Djibouti, Reunion Island, Socotra, and the British Indian Ocean Territory (particularly the coral atoll of Diego Garcia).

Despite Australia's past reluctance to seriously address the issue of Indian Ocean security, the SLOCs across it have been traditionally of the highes significance; they were, as T.B. Millar observes the "life-line" of the empire and of Australian trade with Britain and Western Europe."[47] With the sun now almost set on that empire, the analogy of "life-line" is still, however, appropriate, at least in terms of trade. The Indian Ocean SLOCs account for nearly 40 percent of all shipping *movements* and over 51 percent of the *tonnage* shipped to and from Australia.[48]

Additionally, Australia's Indian Ocean coastline and hinterland are among the most remote, underdeveloped, yet resource-rich regions of the country. Currently, great economic benefit, and the promise of considerably more profit, has been derived from the largest natural-resource development in Australia's history (the North West Shelf Gas Project); the diamond, alumina, iron ore, oil, and natural gas deposits of the Kimberley; and the unique importance of the port of Darwin in the context of any large-scale enemy lodgment or invasion. Their loss or lengthy interruption would constitute a disruption of serious proportions to both the domestic and overseas components of the national economy.[49] It is not surprising, then, that the minister for foreign affairs, Mr. Bill Hayden, chose to redefine the Indian Ocean's position in Australia's foreign policy with a major speech in 1984 during which he proposed that there were "unassailable reasons of national self-interest why the region should hold a consistent and sensible place in our scale of priorities."[50] Subsequently, Defense Minister Beazley described government policy as an "emphatic move away" from the old views of defense within an enterprise of "totally re-orientating the direction of security policy."[51]

In substance, this translated to the August 1984 announcement that the RAAF would be relocating its 75 Squadron with the new FA/18 tactical fighter at Tindal, near Katherine in the Northern Territory. This expensive (in excess of $A240 million over the first five years, in 1984 dollar terms) project is, however, to be seen not only in Indian Ocean terms but also in the context of the development of northern defense from Learmonth in the northwest through Derby Darwin, and Townsville in the northeast, and in conjunction with the JINDALEE over-the-horizon-radar system.

Subsequently, a 1985 statement named Cockburn Sound as the new home-port for some of the Royal Australian Navy's (RAN) fleet of six aging Oberon class submarines, thus preparing the way for the eventual west-coast basing of the current entire submarine fleet and eventually the Oberon replacements now under construction. But, more importantly, the *Review of Australia's Defence Capabilities* (undertaken by Paul Dibb) of March 1986 and the Defence White Paper tabled twelve months later provided the rationale and extent to which the Indian Ocean dimension of Australia's security was a priority concern.[52] Within a concept known as "greater defence self-reliance," policies were announced consistent with, but in scope far beyond, the decisions of 1984 and 1985.

In addition to measures already covered, a considerably increased army facility on the northwest coast and a substantial new intelligence facility at Geraldton, to be operated by Defence Signals Directorate. The most radical development, however, concerned the decision to transform the RAN into a "two-ocean navy"—or, more correctly, a navy with a two-ocean basing regime, with half of the fleet to be based at HMAS *Stirling* near Perth complementing the redeployment of the submarine force. In time-on-station alone, the move, which admittedly will be staged over ten years, will increase the effectiveness of destroyer types by 13 percent and submarines by 31 percent.

While this initiative met with widespread approval, it should be noted that it gives rise to two reservations. The first concerns whether or not splitting into two constituent parts what was effectively not substantially more than a one-ocean navy until 1987 warrants use of the term "two-ocean navy." The second, mentioned earlier, is financial; it concerns the strength of purpose of Australian governments to adequately finance the transformation underway during times in which a reduction in defense spending appears to be expedient.

Concern, too, is warranted regarding the status that will be accorded Christmas Island and the Cocos Islands group, Australia's remote northeast Indian Ocean territories. Though both are thought defensible in terms of the Dibb *Review's* recommendations, there are, as Ross Babbage has argued, several "direct consequences" of their status as a defense asset:[53]

> In low and medium level contingencies, Christmas and the Cocos Islands have the potential to serve as a shield or forward line of defence on Australia's north-western approaches that would complicate an opponent's operations and channel his lines of approach to the mainland. Perhaps more importantly, these territories also have the potential in many circumstances to distract the opponent and force him to fight initially far offshore, rather than on the continent itself. In a period of crisis, this could buy Australia substantial time to cover national mobilization and provide opportunities to exact a heavy toll on the opponent's high technology units.[54]

Accordingly, until such time as the defense of these islands is given detailed consideration, a serious lacuna will exist in an otherwise improved Australian Indian Ocean strategy.

Implicit in the question of Christmas and Cocos Islands is the parallel question of how to reconcile what is, for Australia, an ends-means mismatch. Stated simply, Australia has scarce defense resources, acutely so when it is realized that the *closest* of these territories (Christmas Island) is over 1,400 kilometers from the nearest point on the Australian mainland and both islands are closer to Indonesia, Christmas Island significantly so.[55] In recognition of the fact that national efforts alone were insufficient to fasten the required level of regional security, Australia sought to extend the deterrent role of the alliance with the United States to cover the country's western approaches as well as its Pacific environs. Though technically the centerpoint of this alliance, the ANZUS Treaty of 1951 was not applicable to the Indian Ocean; a form of words was agreed upon between the signatories in February 1980 that permitted admission of the region to future treaty activities.[56] When, in July 1983, Minister for Foreign Affairs Bill Hayden unilaterally but without demur narrowed the geographic scope of ANZUS to the Pacific area and the defense of Australia, the Indian Ocean appeared once more to be excluded.[57] But even this is probably not irrevocable: as Thomas D. Young concluded, the origin of a threat to Australia "would make the geographic parameters of the Treaty esoteric, since it would be in all the parties' interest to meet an opposing force at the Alliance's most advantageous place and time, event if this were in mid-Indian Ocean."[58] The relevance of the treaty to the Indian Ocean is therefore contingent, although the extent to which the United States is facilitated in its Indian Ocean operations by Australia would appear to give the lie to this.[59] The United States and Australia are close allies with common interests in the region; the former can only welcome and encourage developments to date even if they do reflect a radical departure from traditional perspectives or security.

CONCLUSIONS

This chapter was conceived as a corrective to a liberal-optimistic wisdom that a closer defense relationship between Australia and New Zealand was possible in the aftermath of the breakdown within ANZUS of U.S.-New Zealand relations. It was conceived, moreover, as a corrective to the view that the conflict within ANZUS was an aberration and that, because of a history of comfortable accommodation within the alliance up to 1985, it was only a temporary dysfunction; that a path exists, in rational diplomacy, to the restoration of the *status quo ante* in trans-Tasman defense cooperation. This view is, however, rejected because to posit any such optimism of outcome requires a blinding of the analysis from all the factors that gave the conflict meaning—even to deny the existence of the factors in the first place.

In relation to the broader dimensions of this question, what needs to be understood, if the ANZUS conflict is to be given any meaning outside the immediate dimensions of a mere diplomatic breakdown, is that the alliance has failed the test of historical development in *trilateral* terms.[60] ANZUS was founded in a period of anxiety, in a period when there existed a harsh bipolar world and a Manichaean vision. As long as both were vital, the alliance could, and did, grow in complexity. This was not fatal in itself because, though signifying a transformation from unanimity to multiplicity and eventually conflict, there was for some time a remnant of the vision that was shared and a sense of generosity that held that differences could be tolerated and might even be a basis for creativity. But inasmuch as the alliance was predicated on a static vision and set of values, this proved to be a forlorn expectation.

The admission of this process, moreover, questions whether the advent of New Zealand's non-nuclear policy was and is as dislocating as is believed. Certainly, it catalyzed events since 1985; it accounts for New Zealand's marginalization within ANZUS and, indirectly, its rejection of a dependent defense relationship with Australia. Within the bilateral relationship with Australia, it must also be regarded as instrumental in the deterioration that has ensued. Yet the fact remains that the structural or material developments in Australia's strategic planning and policy, especially those relating to the country's west and northwest, were independent of New Zealand's initiatives. In time, moreover, they will increasingly inhibit (if they do not do so already) any political willingness to engage in a defense relationship as close as that which traditionally existed or significantly closer than that which now exists.

NOTES

1. *Defence Review 1983* (Wellington: Government Printer, 1983), p. 17.

2. Desmond Ball, ed., *The ANZAC Connection* (Sydney: George Allan and Unwin, 1985), p. 37, 38–52.

3. *Defence of New Zealand: Review of Defence Policy* (Wellington: Government Printer, 1987), hereafter cited as *Defence of New Zealand.*

4. For the Australian government's views, see *Uranium, The Joint Facilities, Disarmament and Peace* (Canberra: Australian Government Publishing Service, 1984).

5. Transcript of Post Cabinet Press Conference held by Rt. Hon. David Lange, prime minister, 25 November 1985. I am grateful to Peter Jennings of the Department of Politics, University College (Australian Defence Force Academy), University of New South Wales, for bringing my attention to this source.

6. *Mercury,* 22 February 1986.

7. *Age,* 12 December 1986; *Sydney Morning Herald,* 12 December 1986; and *Canberra Times,* 12 December 1986.

8. *Sydney Morning Herald,* 12 December 1986.

9. *Defence of New Zealand,* pp. 12–17.

10. *The Bulletin,* 12 April 1988.

11. For a full and well-researched discussion of historical differences between Australia and New Zealand on selected defense issues, see David Campbell, *New Zealand and the Nuclear Issue: A Comparative History.* Unpublished seminar paper prepared by the author as part of his Honours program of study in the Honours School, Department of Political Science, University of Melbourne, 1985. See Also, "New Zealand and the Vietnam War: A Retrospective Analysis," in John Henderson, Keith Jackson, and Richard Kennaway, eds., *Beyond New Zealand: The Foreign Policy of a Small State* (Auckland: Methuen, 1980), pp. 58–59.

12. *Australian*, 16 July 1987. Note: "Design" is the operative word according to Prime Minister David Lange who, on announcing this decision, denied that any decision had been made to actually *buy* such vessels.

13. In this context, New Zealand might also consider taking advantage of the upcoming Australian helicopter replacement program since it too will need a utility helicopter replacement in the same period.

14. *Age*, 12 December 1986.

15. Interviews.

16. *Newcastle Herald*, 9 February 1985.

17. For example, see, David Campbell, *Australian Public Opinion on National Security Issues*, Working Paper No. 1 (Canberra Peace Research Centre, Research School of Pacific Studies, ANU, 1986), hereafter cited as Campbell, *Public Opinion*; Ross Babbage, "The Prospect for ANZUS and Broader Alliance Cooperation Down Under," paper presented to the Eighth Annual National Defense University Pacific Symposium, Honolulu, 26–27 February 1987, pp. 13–14 (hereafter cited as Babbage, "Prospects") and Andrew Mack, "The Pros and Cons of ANZUS," a 1985 paper (Peace Research Centre, ANU).

18. Babbage, "Prospects," pp. 13–14.

19. Hyam Gold, "Australian Attitudes to New Zealand: Mass Patterns and Elite Variations," *Political Science* (NZ) 39: 2 (December 1987), p. 127.

20. *Ibid.*

21. Campbell, *Public Opinion*, p. 19.

22. *Australian*, 6 November 1987.

23. *Review of Australia's Defence Capabilities: Report to the Minister for Defence by Mr. Paul Dibb* (Canberra: Australian Government Publishing Service, 1986), hereafter cited as Dibb, *Review*; and *The Defence of Australia 1987* (Canberra: Australian Government Publishing Service, 1987).

24. Andrew Mack, "Australia's Defence Revolution," Working Paper No. 150 (Canberra: Strategic and Defence Studies Centre, Australian National University, 1988), hereafter cited as Mack, "Australia's Defence Revolution."

25. "Statement by the Minister for Defence on the Review of Defence Capabilities conducted by Mr. Paul Dibb," 3 June 1986, issued by the minister's office, p. 16.

26. *Ibid.*, p. 17.

27. Mack, "Australia's Defence Revolution," p. 24.

28. *Ibid.*, p. 18.

29. *Ibid.*, p. 16.

30. *National Times*, 30 March – 5 April 1984, pp. 24–30.

31. *Dominion*, 3 December 1986.

32. Babbage, "Prospects," p. 13.

33. *Australian*, 6 December 1985.

34. *Defence and Security: What New Zealanders Want: Report of the Defence Committee of Enquiry*, July 1986 (Wellington: Government Printer, 1986), letter from the prime minister to the chairman of the committee of 4 August 1986 (n.p.); pp. 71–90; and Addendum III.

35. *Canberra Times*, 7 August 1987.

36. *West Australian*, 25 March 1988.

37. Ross Babbage, "The Future of the Australian-New Zealand Defence Relationship," Paper presented to the Seminar on New Zealand Defence Policy, sponsored by the Institute of Policy Studies, Victoria University of Wellington, 9 December 1986, p. 16 (hereafter cited as Babbage, "Future"); and Babbage, "Prospects," p. 13.

38. *Sydney Morning Herald*, 21 February 1987.

39. *Age*, 12 December 1986.

40. Babbage, "Future," p. 13.

41. *Canberra Times*, 9 August 1987.

42. *Mercury*, 13 November 1987.

43. *Ibid.*

44. Interview.

45. For a fuller account of this aspect of Australia's security, see Michael McKinley, "Australia and the Indian Ocean," Chapter 14 in F.A. Mediansky and A.C. Palfreeman, eds., *In Pursuit of the National Interest: Australian Foreign Policy in the 1990s* (Sydney: Pergamon, 1988), hereafter cited as McKinley, "Australia and the Indian Ocean."

46. Iqbal Singh, "Indian Ocean: A Zone of Peace or Power Play?" Working Paper No. 64 (Canberra: Strategic and Defence Studies Centre, Australian National University Press, 1982), pp. 1–7.

47. T.B. Millar, *Australia in Peace and War* (Canberra: Australian National University Press, 1978), p. 357.

48. Department of Defence (Navy Office), "An Analysis of Trends in Trade and Shipping," Department of Defence, Canberra, November 1985.

49. J.O. Langtry and Desmond Ball, eds., *A Vulnerable Country?: Civil Resources in the Defence of Australia* (Canberra: Strategic and Defence Studies Centre, Australian National University, 1986), pp. 114–218, hereafter cited as Langtry and Ball, *A Vulnerable Country?*

50. Speech by the Minister for Foreign Affairs, Mr. Bill Hayden, MP, on the subject of the Indian Ocean, delivered to the Australian Institute of International Affairs in Perth on 20 June 1984, p. A3. The full text of this speech is found in the Department of Foreign Affairs, *Backgrounder*, No. 436, 27 June 1984, pp. A1–A15, hereafter cited as Hayden, "Indian Ocean" Speech.

51. *West Australian*, 26 February 1987; and *'Courier Mail*, 25 June 1987, respectively.

52. See Dibb, *Review*, and "Tabling Statement, Defence Policy Information paper—19 March 1987" by Minister for Defense Mr. Kim C. Beazley, MP, issued by the National Media Liaison Service.

53. Dibb, *Review*, p. 15.

54. Ross Babbage, "Christmas and the Cocos Islands: Defence Liabilities or Assets?" pp. 41–42, draft of Part 5 of *The Defence of Northern Australia* (forthcoming). The writer is grateful to Dr. Babbage of the Strategic and Defence Studies Centre, Australian National University, for making this paper available.

55. *Ibid*, pp. 2, 16.

56. Braun, p. 121.

57. Ramesh Thakur, *In Defence of New Zealand: Foreign Policy Choices in the Nuclear Age* (Boulder: Westview Press, 1986), p. 99.

58. Thomas D. Young, "ANZUS in the Indian Ocean: Strategic Considerations," Memoir presented for the Diploma of the University Institute of Advanced International Studies, Geneva, 1982, p. 4, as cited in Henry S. Albinski, "Australia, New Zealand, and Indian Ocean Security: Perspectives and Contributions from Outlying American Alliance Partners," William L. Dowdy and Russell B. Trood, eds., *The Indian Ocean: Perspectives On A Strategic Arena* (Durham: Duke University Press, 1985), p. 359.

59. See McKinley, "Australia and the Indian Ocean," pp. 256–258.

Part 4
Future Prospects

11

The Prospect for Strategic Rivalry and Security Cooperation in Pacific Asia

LAWRENCE E. GRINTER
YOUNG WHAN KIHL

As we approach the twenty-first century and the new "Pacific Era," the geostrategic value of the Pacific Rim will increase, as will the need for trans-Pacific security cooperation. This chapter identifies emerging trends in the strategic environment, including the pattern of superpower rivalry; and draws some policy implications for the region as a whole and for the United States in particular.

CHANGE AND STABILITY IN THE PACIFIC RIM SECURITY SYSTEM

In the late 1980s the strategic environment in Pacific Asia is rapidly changing. This is a result of policy initiatives undertaken by the major powers in the region, more particularly by the Soviet Union and the United States. The Soviet Union, under president Mikhail Gorbachev, is determined to emerge as one of the key actors and potential power players in the central strategic arena of the region. The United States, as a major actor in the Pacific Rim, had reaffirmed its traditional role and posture of defense.

But after the November 1988 presidential election, the United States must adopt a new Pacific strategy which goes beyond a reaffirmation of America's traditional commitment to the region's security. The ascendancy of Japan and other Asia Pacific countries into a dynamic, growth-oriented, economic region will necessitate the formulation of a new Pacific strategy which would maximize the potential stability and welfare of the Pacific Rim nations. The U.S. Pacific strategy in the 1990s must build upon the infrastructure that has transformed the region into a dynamic growth region, while continuing to strengthen security-trade links into the twenty-first century and successfully confronting new challenges posed by shifting power balances and realignment.

The Pacific Rim security system, as contrasted with other world regions (such as Europe and the North Atlantic), lacks symmetry in alliances and force structures. No NATO- or WTO-like institutional structures exist to coordinate the security policies of the respective superpowers and their allies. Moreover, no neutral bloc or neutral nations exist to mediate conflicts between the superpowers in the region, such as those in Europe that initiated the process leading to the Helsinki Conference on Security and Disarmament in Europe in 1984.

A critical pattern of Pacific Rim security therefore remains the bilateral interaction between the two superpowers; the systemic factors of geopolitics played a role in evolving this structure, which in turn moulded the security policy and posture of each of the superpowers. Unlike Europe, where the force structures of the two alliances are more symmetrical, the pattern of the Pacific Rim force structure is asymmetric. The U.S. strength in the Pacific Rim is primarily maritime, while the Soviet Union is relatively weak at sea but strong on land—almost 90 percent of the Soviet land forces in Asia, for instance, is deployed against China, not against the United States. A change in the strategic balance in the region, and Soviet reductions of its force structure, is therefore likely to result more from an emerging agreement with China than with the United States.

Three regional trends visible in the late 1980s are:

- The new Soviet initiative toward Pacific Asia
- The dilemma for the United States in confronting the Soviet challenge (especially for the new administration of 1989)
- Regionalism and sustaining East Asia's economic dynamism

The momentum of the changes will no doubt carry beyond the 1980s to shape the pattern of the Pacific security system in the 1990s.

THE NEW SOVIET INITIATIVE TOWARD THE PACIFIC ASIA

Soviet leader Mikhail Gorbachev launched a second major political initiative toward Asia, going beyond his Vladivostok speech of 28 July 1986. On 16 September 1988, addressing party leaders at Abalakovo, near the Siberian city of Krasnoyarsk, Mr. Gorbachev reaffirmed his eagerness to strengthen Soviet ties in Asia.[1] Showing his diplomatic agility, the Soviet leader suggested that an under-construction, disputed radar installation in Siberia (which the United States considered in violation of the 1972 ABM treaty) be placed under international control for use in the peaceful exploration of outer space.

He proposed to remove the Soviet naval supply point at Cam Ranh Bay in Vietnam, if the United States closed down its military bases in the Philippines, in a gesture to woo Asian opinion—including China's—away from the United States. A mischievous motive of Gorbachev was to exploit the difficult ongoing U.S.–Philippine negotiations about U.S. military presence in the Philippines. He also reiterated his call for a Chinese-Soviet summit meeting in the near future, indicating Soviet willingness to pressure Hanoi to withdraw Soviet-backed Vietnamese troops from Cambodia. China makes talks on Sino-Soviet normalization conditional upon: (1) Soviet troop withdrawal from Afghanistan, (2) Soviet reduction of troops along its border with China, and (3) Vietnamese troop withdrawal from Cambodia.

Capitalizing on the mood of evolving détente on the Korean peninsula, and timed with the Soviet participation in the XXIV Olympiad in Seoul, Gorbachev said Moscow was ready to develop economic links with South Korea, which had earlier announced an exchange of diplomatic missions with Hungary. Gorbachev also proposed negotiations to limit naval forces in the Pacific, a freeze on the number of nuclear weapons in the region, and talks on reducing military activities in the Sea of Japan and the Yellow Sea.

By taking diplomatic and economic initiatives toward the Pacific Rim, the Soviet Union seems determined to consolidate its position of strength following the military build-up in the post-Vietnam War era, and also to participate actively in the geostrategic balance of power game in the region. "The Soviet Union's policy in Asia, like any other part of the world, rests on the principles of freedom of choice and peaceful coexistence," Mr. Gorbachev proclaimed. He also said, deploring the alleged failure of the United States and the Soviet Union over ways in which to cooperate in the Pacific and Asia, that "there is no evident conflict between Soviet and American interests; the Soviet Union is for broad participation of the United States in the affairs of the Asian and Pacific region, worthy of its position and its political and economic potentialities; but it should be equal, without great-power manners and power-politics tricks."[2] (The U.S. response to Gorbachev's moves has been to probe Soviet motives and intentions.)

Since Shevardnadze's January 1986 trip to Tokyo, followed by Gorbachev's July 1986 Vladivostok speech, Soviet diplomacy in Asia has been vigorous. At the same time, according to U.S. ambassador to Indonesia, Paul Wolfowitz, there has been "a whole new series of personnel changes in the Soviet Foreign Ministry—not only Gromyko's replacement by Shevardnadze, but also a new deputy foreign minister for East Asia, Igor Rogachev, and a number of able new ambassadors. [These people] have radically altered the tone of Soviet diplomacy in the region from the heavy-handed, bullying style which helped gain them enemies in the past."[3] Highlighted by Shevardnadze's and Rogachev's trips to Southeast Asia and Northeast Asia in 1988, respectively, a Soviet "breakout" strategy has emerged. Impressions of the new vigor and sophistication of Soviet diplomatic activities in East Asia and the Pacific were confirmed by recent discussions one of this book's coeditors had with East Asian officials.

The purposes of these new Soviet activities, as Leif Rosenberger and Marian Leighton write, "are to create a more benign strategic environment in Asia and the Pacific for Soviet strategic interests, to transform the USSR into a legitimate power player in the region, and to carve out a stake for Moscow in Asia's dynamic economy."[4]

With its military bases at Vladivostok and Cam Ranh Bay secure, Moscow has sought to couple military deployment and investment with a more appealing overall diplomacy, commensurate with its altered objective of being a major Asian-Pacific power. The capstone would be a Soviet-sponsored Asian security conference as the key step to forging a hoped-for "Comprehensive System of International Security (CSIS)." The bottom line for Moscow's new Asia policy seems to be an increase in its trade links with the region. Sino-Soviet trade has grown in recent years. Soviet-North Korean trade and technology transfer are larger in volume than Sino-North Korean trade, and although trade between Moscow and Tokyo remains limited, Soviet diplomats in Tokyo are hopeful that it will increase in the years ahead as the Soviets explore Siberian development.

In Southeast Asia, Soviet trade with Thailand, Indonesia, and the Philippines is also increasing. Moscow's policy toward Hanoi, however, is tightfisted, evidently seeking to tilt Vietnam away from militarism toward economic development. In the South Pacific, Soviets also take new initiatives—fishing agreements and hard currency payments are offered in return for port calls and ship replenishment; and Moscow identifies with local anti-Americanism with strong support for New Zealand's anti-nuclear policy, in conjunction with local peace conferences.

Skepticism about Soviet motives lingers in Asia, however, and obstacles are clearly evident regarding the Soviet version of region-wide security cooperation. Furthermore, little evidence now exists for a Soviet military disengagement from East Asia and the Pacific. The SS-20s will be removed from the Lake Baikal area, and, in accordance with the UN-sponsored Geneva agreement on Afghanistan, all Soviet regular units may have left Afghanistan by February 15, 1989. But Vladivostok continues to host Moscow's largest fleet, and there is considerable Soviet hardware advantage over China on the Sino-Soviet border. Cam Ranh Bay continues to host a major Soviet flotilla, and the southern Kurile islands, with their Soviet MiG 23s and airborne units, are not reverting to Japan. "The Soviets may worry about regional arms races," as Rosenberger and Leighton write, "but [in East Asia] they display no reluctance to participate."[5] Changes in economic policies and political image, while maintaining its military policies, will be Moscow's approach to the Pacific Rim in the 1990s.

DILEMMA FOR THE UNITED STATES

As the Soviets improve their image and exploit new opportunities in Pacific Asia in the late 1980s, the United States has a different kind of challenge: to maintain leadership in the area while redistributing security burdens among allies and making its economy more competitive in relation to its friends. The Soviets are just entering the East Asian economic game; the United States has to contain East Asia's economic impact on the U.S. economy before it becomes out of hand, thereby further jeopardizing U.S. politico-military leadership in the region.

How to cope with the new Soviet activism diplomatically, while sustaining defense-oriented security posture, will be a critical challenge confronting the U.S. administration in 1989. The new Pacific strategy must reflect these changes and find creative ways of accommodating them:

- Compensating for U.S. weaknesses with burden-sharing
- Restoring economic competitiveness of the U.S. vis-à-vis East Asian countries
- Checkmating Soviet inroads into the Pacific Asia region

The cold war-threat premises the United States used to maintain its defense posture vis-à-vis the Soviet challenge in the region are gradually eroding. In a variety of Asian countries—capitalist, socialist, or communist—government leaders no longer feel threatened by Soviet policy initiatives. The results are complicating to U.S. interests—as manifested already, for example, by New Zealand's nuclear allergy. The Philippines insistence on military rent payments (in lieu of strengthening its external defense ties) is another example. Japan and South Korea's reluctance to join in a bilateral (or, with the U.S., trilateral) alliance against the Soviets may be another example. Although diplomats in China and Southeast Asian capitals often encourage the United States not to lose basing rights in the Philippines or in Northeast Asia, the rhetoric is not backed with concrete acts, and there is little these countries seem willing to do to prevent those losses.

Even though Chinese, South Korean, and ASEAN diplomats are quick to point out that of all external powers they want to play a stabilizing role, they feel most comfortable with the United States, ambivalent security policies and nostalgic expressions of good will do not build regional security. While the Soviets currently wage peace offensives around Pacific Asia, they also carry out clandestine activities and continue to modernize their military deployments in the region. U.S. military resources in the region are thin, covering a line from the Sea of Japan to the South China Sea and into the Indian Ocean. With about 160,000 U.S. combat forces now on shore and afloat in the Western Pacific, the United States is a relative military lightweight. The USSR has about 700,000 troops in the region, China has 3 million, and Vietnam and North Korea keep 1 million and 700,000 men under arms respectively.

How should the United States and its allies cope with these security trends? One answer is to promote burden-sharing and a gradual redistribution of security functions among U.S. allies. Where the Soviet navy is most vulnerable—in the Sea of Japan and in the South China Sea—allied naval and air alliances and pooled missions would make logical sense. An integration of Japanese, South Korean, and U.S. naval and air assets in the Sea of Japan, and combined ASEAN and U.S. forces in the South China Sea would also add logically to deterrence. However, the political will to do this does not yet exist, and Gorbachev's new policy initiatives are creating further havoc and more ambivalence.

One of the few officials in Southeast Asia who thinks about new kinds of politico-military burden-sharing in the ASEAN region is Philippine Foreign Secretary Raul Manglapus. Although he has been rebuffed so far by other ASEAN governments, Manglapus's ideas of a partial reconfiguration of U.S. military facilities elsewhere in the region ought to be pursued by U.S. diplomats in Southeast Asia. Why should the choice for the United States and Southeast Asia be absolute—to have U.S. military facilities solely in the Philippines or not have them anywhere in the region? This "all-or-nothing-at-all" approach is dangerous, and not in the best interests of the region. Burden-sharing ought to be a major U.S. policy in Southeast Asia (as well as in Northeast Asia) in the 1990s.

REGIONALISM AND SUSTAINING EAST ASIA'S ECONOMIC DYNAMISM

A new regionalism is on the rise in the Pacific Rim that reflects not only the global-regional interaction, such as the continuing U.S.-Soviet rivalry, but also intraregional interactions. The Pacific Rim as an economic region is moving away from the days of a communist-capitalist confrontation into a new era of diffusion of power among many Asian-Pacific nations. These emerging regional forces are sustained by the dynamics of growth-oriented economic activities and their promises built in the structure of maximizing economic policy incentives and expectations in Asian countries.

East Asia's regional economy has varied patterns and problems, which can be divided into four classes of participants:

- Japan: the global giant and premier Asian economic power, able to deploy massive amounts of capital, services and goods throughout the region
- The NICs: South Korea, Taiwan, Singapore, and Hong Kong,

investing throughout Southeast Asia and other regions of the world
- The ASEAN countries (Philippines excepted), Australia, and China: all generally showing good growth and productivity flexibility
- The Indochinese states, Burma, North Korea, and the Philippines: all recovering from or still suffering the effects of stifling central planned economies.

Pacific Asia will continue its drive toward the 1990s as the world's most economically dynamic region, led by Japan and the East-Asian NICs of South Korea, Taiwan, Singapore, and Hong Kong as the region's most dynamic export entities. Although they differ considerably in their internal economic structure, they are equally aggressive in expanding their overseas markets. Except for Hong Kong, all East Asian countries have pursued "protective" import policies.

Japan, benefiting from the rise of yen value, is now providing aid packages to Asia's less developed countries and other Third World regions. Japan wishes to increase its aid package commensurate with its newly acquired global status. Capital and investment flows within the Pacific Asia region are also showing new flexibility; NICs and Australian resources, for instance, flow into Thailand and the Philippines. Gradually, Japan, South Korea, and Taiwan are beginning to open their protected domestic markets and to reduce their non-tariff barriers.

The U.S. economic relationship with the Pacific Asian countries is also changing. While the recent weakness of the dollar has allowed some resurgence of U.S. exports, U.S. deficits with the region continue. U.S. pressures are mounting on Japan and the NICs to carry out import liberalization programs, such as opening protected domestic markets for U.S. agricultural items. Although the absolute levels of the U.S. trade deficit have levelled off recently (at about $100 billion out of a $235 billion two-way trade level) the United States continues to find itself at a competitive disadvantage with East Asia. This trend, unfortunately, is not likely to change in the foreseeable future.

NEW PATTERNS AND REQUIREMENTS
FOR SECURITY COOPERATION

East Asian trends with global manifestations that require new security cooperation are of three kinds. First, many Asian countries have abandoned the socialist model of development, whether Stalinist or Maoist. Instead, the market economy approach to development and economic growth has been adopted by both capitalist and socialist Asian countries. Second, domestic policy reforms, not only for economic growth but also toward greater openness and democracy, are also occurring in many

Asian nations. Third, the superpower strategic rivalry has moderated, as a result of U.S.-Soviet cooperation following the Reagan-Gorbachev summit in 1988.

Assuming that these regional trends will continue into the 1990s, the security requirements of the Pacific Rim countries will alter. The 1988 report of the Ikle-Wohlstetter commission identifies six trends in the security environment in the decades beyond 1987:[6] (1) the rise of Japan and China, (2) Soviet economic difficulties, (3) changes in military technology, (4) the worldwide diffusion of advanced weapons, (5) deteriorating U.S. access, and (6) the emergence of new threats in the Western Hemisphere. If these assumptions on emerging global and regional trends are valid, future military conflicts, including the ones in the Pacific Rim, will take the following configurations:[7] They will be

- conflicts of low intensity,
- predominantly in the Third World,
- on the Soviet periphery;
- the roles of "offense" and "defense" in wars with the USSR increasingly obscure; and
- military-technology decisive.

The Asian Pacific, as a dynamic, growth-oriented, economic powerhouse, must be protected from possible disruption emanating from these sources both within and without the region. Due to lack of collective security alliance structures in the Pacific Rim, like NATO or WTO in Europe, the prospects of multilateral security cooperation are not good. Yet, new bilateral and some trilateral patterns of diplomacy and security alignment are emerging. Signs of diplomatic accommodation are visible not only for the Soviet-led bloc but also for the U.S.-led group of nations. These entail possible normalization of Soviet-Chinese relations, Soviet-Japan relations, Soviet-South Korea relations, and Soviet-ASEAN relations. Likewise, the prospects of strengthening U.S.-China relations and U.S.-Mongolia relations are good, as are the possible trends of a breakthrough in U.S.-North Korea relations and U.S.-Vietnam relations. This is also true with the possible opening and improvement in Sino-South Korean relations and Japan-North Korean relations. In short, economic interdependency is gradually replacing ideological hostility.

On a multi-level, or trilateral basis, security cooperation is being promoted—on an informal basis—along the U.S.-Japan-South Korea front and also the U.S.-Japan-China front. U.S.-ASEAN-Japan security cooperation is now openly discussed, although the pattern has thus far been limited largely to the possibilities of economic assistance and trade/investment partnerships.

U.S. POLICY OPTIONS AND RESPONSES

The United States must respond to the challenges posed by Gorbachev's new Asia initiatives and by the emergence of the Asia-Pacific Rim into a dynamic, growth-oriented, economic bloc. U.S. Pacific strategy in the 1990s must first define the national purposes of U.S. policy in the Pacific Rim, and then specify concrete measures to cope with emerging security challenges with a view to containing regional conflicts.[8]

Several countries in the Asian-Pacific region are still torn by indigenous insurgencies, such as those in Cambodia, Burma, and the Philippines. These internally based conflicts tend to spill beyond territorial boundaries and to increase tensions with neighboring countries. Moreover, unlike most other world regions, the Asia-Pacific Rim is still plagued by unresolved border disputes—for instance, the Soviet Union and China, the Soviet Union and Japan, North and South Korea, Thailand and Laos, China and Vietnam, and China-Vietnam-the Philippines (over islands in the South China Sea).[9] So long as these territorial disputes remain unresolved, tensions and arms buildups will increase. Under these circumstances the danger of military conflict is real, and plans for deescalation and demilitarization of the entire region will be set back.

Future U.S.-Pacific strategy must take bold actions to provide leadership. The main policy objective should be to deescalate regional conflicts and thereby sustain peace and stability in the Pacific Rim. To achieve this objective, the United States must pursue specific Pacific programs on issues such as (1) the arms control regime, region-wide or sub-region-based (e.g., the Korean peninsula or the Indochina); (2) ASW (anti-submarine warfare) measured in specific seas (e.g., in the Sea of Japan); (3) nuclear-free zones (e.g., in the ASEAN subregion); (4) CSBM (Confidence and Security Building Measures) on both conventional and nuclear weapons, such as those adopted in the 1984 Helsinki-Stockholm CSDE (Conference on Security and Disarmament in Europe); (5) ground- and land-based force reductions in the Pacific Rim, such as the MBFR (Mutual Balanced Force Reduction) talks in Europe; (6) a Conference on Comprehensive Asian Security and Disarmament, such as the CSDE in Europe; and (7) the possible creation of the International Commission on Pacific Rim Security.[10]

The strategic planning and management of Pacific Rim security in the future must be bold and imaginative, going beyond mechanistic application of geostrategic tactics and moves of the past. Instead, the new U.S. Pacific strategy must actively seek to identify, shape, and direct the emerging security environment by positive adaptation and anticipatory response behavior. The United States must lead the movement toward a Pacific Rim security community, by uniting those nations already allied with or friendly toward the United States. Articulating common objectives and nurturing policy consensus among the U.S.-led Pacific Rim nations will be the first step in founding and evolving such a security community. Creative diplomacy, market economics, liberalized political systems, and a new realism in security responsibilities will be the essential ingredients in fulfilling the promise of a U.S.-led security community for the 1990s and beyond.

NOTES

1. Gorbachev's speech to Workers, at Abalakovo, 16 September 1988, as reported in Foreign Broadcast Information Service (FBIS) *Daily Report: The Soviet Union*, 19 September 1988, p. 59. Also, The *New York Times*, 17 September 1988.

2. As quoted in the *New York Times*, 17 September 1988.

3. Paul Wolfowitz, "Southeast Asia—Deferring Hard Choices," *The National Interest*, Summer 1988, p. 121.

4. See Chapter 3 by Rosenberger and Leighton in this book.

5. *Ibid*.

6. Fred C. Ikle and Albert Wohlstetter, cochairs, *Discriminate Deterrence: Report of the Commission on Integrated Long-Term Strategy to the Secretary of Defense*, January 1988, Washington, D.C.: Government Printing Office, 1988, pp. 5–11.

7. *Ibid*.

8. On some of these possible measures for containing and deescalating regional conflicts in East Asia, see: Lawrence E. Grinter and Young Whan Kihl, eds., *East Asian Conflict Zones: Prospects for Regional Stability and Deescalation*. New York: St. Martin's Press, 1987, pp. 116–118, 206–220.

9. *Ibid*.

10. Andrew Mack, Pacific Report on "Problems and Prospects for Arms Control in the North Pacific," *Defense and Disarmament Alternatives*, Volume 1, No. 6 (September 1988).

Appendix

Table 1   Growth in Soviet Armed Forces Deployments in the Far East

Element	1968	1973	1978	1983	1987	1988
Divisions	25	45	44	56	57	
Tanks			11,450		14,900	
APCs/IFVs					17,300	
Field Arty					13,000	
Combat A/C[a]					1,714	
Nuclear missiles[b]	100	100	100	350	1,250	
Carriers		0	0	0	1	2
Submarines[c]	105	110	120	126	145	
Other major combatants	55	60	67	88	98	

[a]Strategic bombers included.
[b]MR/IRBM warheads only.
[c]Strategic (SSB/SSBN) submarines included.

Source: International Institute of Strategic Studies, *The Military Balance* (London, annual); U.S. Department of Defense, *Soviet Military Power* (Washington, D.C., annual).

Table 2   Soviet Far Eastern Theater Forces

Naval Forces	*Ground Forces*
110 missile and attack submarines	7 armored divisions
2 aircraft carriers	45 motorized rifle divisions
14 cruisers	1 airborne divisions
17 destroyers	4 artillery divisions
22 frigates	14,900 tanks
30 corvettes	17,300 APCs/IFVs
200 other surface combatant vessels	375 surface-surface missiles
19 amphibious craft	4,000 surface-air missiles/AAA
98 auxiliaries	13,000 artillery pieces
Naval Air Forces	*Air Forces*
160 bombers	735 attack aircraft
26 carrier attack aircraft	815 fighter aircraft
1 naval infantry division	265 recon/ECM/tanker a/c
Naval Air Defense Forces	*Forces Deployed in Vietnam*
SA-5	5 submarines
SA-10	10 surface combatants
Early Warning Systems	18 auxiliaries
	14 fighter aircraft
	24 reconnaissance/ASW aircraft
	7,000 personnel

Source: U.S. Pacific Command.

Table 3   Highlights of U.S. General Purpose Forces

FY	1980	1984	1986	1987	1988	1989
Land Forces						
Army Divisions:						
Active	16	16	18	18	18	18
Reserve	8	8	10	10	10	10
Marine Corps						
Divisions:						
Active	3	3	3	3	3	3
Reserve	1	1	1	1	1	1
Tactical Air Forces						
(PAA squadrons)[a]						
Air Force						
Attack/Fighter						
Active	1,608/74	1,734/77	1,764/78	1,812/81	1,762/79	1,746/79
Reserve	758/36	852/43	876/43	900/44	894/43	876/43
Navy Attack/						
Fighter						
Active	696/60	616/63	758/65	752/67	758/67	792/70
Reserve	120/10	75/9	107/10	101/10	120/10	118/10
Marine Corps						
Attack/Fighter						
Active	329/25	256/24	333/25	331/25	334/25	341/25
Reserve	84/7	90/8	94/8	96/8	94/8	96/8
Naval Forces						
Strategic Forces						
Ships	48	41	45	43	42	42
Battle Forces						
Ships	384	425	437	445	439	443
Support Forces						
Ships	41	46	55	58	61	65
Reserve Forces						
Ships	6	12	18	22	28	30
Total Deployable						
Battle Forces	479	524	555	568	570	580
Other Reserve						
Forces Ships	44	24	21	21	20	18
Other Auxiliaries	8	9	7	5	5	5
Total Other Forces	52	33	28	26	25	23

[a]PAA—Primary Aircraft Authorized

Source: Annual Report to the Congress for Fiscal Year 1989 by U.S. Secretary of Defense Frank C. Carlucci, February 18, 1988. Washington, D.C.: U.S. Government Printing Office, 1988, p. 314.

Table 4   U.S. Military Personnel in Foreign Areas[a]   (End-Year, In Thousands)

	FY 1976[b]	FY 1979	FY 1980	FY 1981	FY 1982	FY 1983	FY 1984	FY 1985	FY 1986	FY 1987
Germany	213	239	244	248	256	254	254	247	250	250
Other Europe	61	61	65	64	67	70	73	75	75	73
Europe, afloat	41	25	22	25	33	18	25	36	32	31
South Korea	39	39	39	38	39	39	41	42	43	45
Japan	45	46	46	46	51	49	46	47	48	50
Other Pacific	27	15	15	15	15	15	16	16	17	18
Pacific, afloat (including Southeast Asia)	24	22	15	25	33	34	18	20	20	17
Miscellaneous foreign	8	11	42	39	34	41	38	32	38	40
Total	460	458	489	502	528	520	511	515	523	524

[a]Numbers may not add to totals due to rounding.
[b]September 30 data used for consistency.

Source: Annual Report to the Congress for Fiscal Year 1989 by U.S. Secretary of Defense Frank C. Carlucci, February 18, 1988. Washington, D.C.: U.S. Government printing office, 1988, p. 306.

Selected Bibliography

This selected bibliography reflects recent items published in English only that are readily available in the United States. The bibliography covers only book-length monographs published since late 1985. For items published between approximately 1981 and 1985, see Young Whan Kihl and Lawrence E. Grinter, eds., *Asian-Pacific Security* (Boulder, CO: Lynne Rienner Publishers, 1986), pp. 267-272.

The bibliography is grouped into three broad categories: (1) global and region-wide focus, (2) subregions (Northeast Asia, Southeast Asia, South Pacific, and South Asia,) and (3) specific countries and/or issues (the United States, the Soviet Union, China, Japan, Korea, Vietnam/Indochina, and the Philippines/ASEAN countries). References to other Asian countries, such as Mongolia and India, have been listed under the subregional categories to which the specific countries belong.

GLOBAL AND REGION-WIDE FOCUS

Aikman, David. *Pacific Rim: Area of Change, Area of Opportunity*. Boston: Little, Brown & Co., 1986.

Alagappa, Muthiah. *The National Security of Developing States: Lessons from Thailand*. Dover, MA: Auburn House Publishing Co., 1987.

Asian Issues 1985. New York: The Asia Society/Washington, D.C.: University Press of America, 1986.

Bell, Coral. *The Unquiet Pacific*. London: Center for Security and Conflict Studies, 1987.

Buss, Claude A., ed. *National Security Interests in the Pacific Basin*. Stanford: Hoover Press, 1985.

Brzezinski, Zbigniew. *Game Plan: A Geostrategic Framework for the Conduct of the U.S.-Soviet Contest*. Boston: Atlantic Monthly Press, 1986.

Cline, Ray S., James Arnold Miller, and Walter Arnold, eds. *Asia in Soviet Global Strategy*. Boulder, CO: Westview Press, 1987.

255

Diamond, Larry, ed. *Democracy in Developing Countries: Asia.* Boulder, CO: Lynne Rienner Publishers, 1988.

East Asia, the West and International Security: Prospects for Peace. Adelphi Papers 216-218 (Spring 1987). London: International Institute for Strategic Studies, 1987.

Gilbert, Stephen P., *Security in Northeast Asia: Approaching the Pacific Century.* Boulder, CO: Westview Press, 1988.

Grinter, Lawrence E., and Young Whan Kihl, eds. *East Asian Conflict Zones: Prospects for Regional Stability and Deescalation.* New York: St. Martin's Press, 1987.

Hayes, Peter, and Lyuba Zarski. *American Lake: Nuclear Peril in the Pacific.* New York: Penguin, 1987.

Heynes, Terry L. *American and Soviet Relations Since Détente: The Working Framework.* Washington, D.C.: U.S. Government Printing Office, 1987.

Keith, Ronald C., ed. *Energy, Security, and Economic Development in East Asia.* London: Croom Helm, 1986.

Kim, Chan W. and Philip K.Y. Young, eds., *The Pacific Challenge In International Business.* Ann Arbor, MI: UMI Research Press, 1987.

Kim, Roy, and Hilary Conroy, eds. *News Tides in the Pacific: Pacific Basin Cooperation and the Big Four.* Greenwood, CT: Praeger, 1987.

Linder, Staffan B. *The Pacific Century: Economic and Political Consequences of Asian-Pacific Dynamism.* Stanford: Stanford University Press, 1986.

McIntosh, Malcolm. *Arms Across the Pacific: Security and Trade Issues Across the Pacific.* London: Printer, 1987.

Morley, James W., ed. *Security Interdependence in the Asia Pacific Region.* New York: East Asian Institute of the Columbia University/Lexington, MA: Lexington Books, 1986.

————, ed. *The Pacific Basin: New Challenges to the United States.* New York: Academy of Political Science, 1986.

Morrison, E., ed. *Asia-Pacific Report, 1987-88: Trends, Issues, Challenges.* Honolulu: East-West Center, distributed by the University of Hawaii Press, 1987.

Nathan, K.S., and M. Pathmanathan, eds., *Trilaterialism in Asia.* Kuala Lumpur: Antara, 1986.

Nishihara, Masashi. *East Asian Security and the Trilateral Countries: A Report to the Trilateral Commission.* New York: New York University Press, 1985.

Olsen, Edward A., and Stephen Jurika, eds. *The Armed Forces in Contemporary Asian Societies.* Boulder, CO: Westview Press, 1986.

Pacific Regional Security: The 1985 Pacific Symposium. Washington, D.C.: U.S. Government Printing Office, 1987.

Park, Jae Kyu, and Byung-Joon Ahn, eds. *The Strategic Defense Initiative: Its Implications for Asia and the Pacific.* Boulder, CO: Westview Press, 1987.

Sakamoto, Yoshikaza. *Asia: Militarization and Regional Conflict.* Atlantic Heighlands, NJ: Humanities International, 1987.

Scalapino, Robert A. *Major Power Relations in Northeast Asia.* New York: The Asia Society, 1987.

Scalapino, Robert A., and Chen Qimao, eds. *Pacific-Asian Issues: American and Chinese Views.* Berkeley, CA: University of California Institute of East Asian Studies, 1986.

Scalapino, Robert A., Seizaburo Sato, and Jusuf Wanandi, eds. *Asian Economic Development—Present and Future*. Research Papers and Policy Studies No. 14. Berkeley, CA: University of California Institute of East Asian Studies, 1985.

Scalapino, Robert A., et al., eds. *Asian Political Institutionalization*. Research Papers and Policy Studies No. 15. Berkeley, CA: University of California Institute of East Asian Studies, 1986.

Scalapino, Robert A., et al., eds. *Internal and External Security Issues in Asia*. Research Papers and Policy Studies No. 16. Berkeley, CA: University of California Institute of East Asian Studies, 1986.

Segal, Gerald, ed., *Arms Control in Asia*. Basingstoke: Macmillan, 1987.

Simon, Sheldon W. *The Future of Asian-Pacific Security Collaboration*. Lexington, MA: Lexington Books, 1988.

Solomon, Richard H., and Masataka Kosaka, eds. *The Soviet Far East Military Buildup: Nuclear Dilemmas and Asian Security*. Dover, MA: Auburn House Pub. Co., 1986.

Stephan, John J., and v.P. Chichkanov, eds. *Soviet-American Horizons on the Pacific*. Honolulu: University of Hawaii press, 1986.

Stuart, Douglas. *Security in the Pacific Rim*. Brookfield, VT: Tower Publishing Co., 1986.

U.S. House of Representatives, Special Subcommittee on U.S.-Pacific Rim Trade, Committee on Energy and Commerce. *Hearings, June 18, 1985. the Soviet Role in Pacific Rim Trade: U.S.-Soviet Environmental Cooperation*. Washington, D.C., 1985.

Vickery, Michael. *East Asian Security and the Trilateral Countries: A Report to the Trilateral Commission*. New York: Columbia University Press, 1986.

West, Philip and Frans A.M. Alting von Geusau, eds., *The Pacific Rim and the Western World*. Boulder, CO: Westview Press, 1987.

SUBREGIONS

Northeast Asia

Ambroz, Oton. *Peking's Strategic Deterrence to Soviet Imperialism: A New Perspective on Global Strategies of War and Peace*. London: Pika, 1987.

Berger, Peter L. and Michael Hsia, eds., *In Search of an East Asian Development Model*. New Brunswick, N.J.: Transaction Books, 1988.

East Asia: International Review of Economic, Political, and Social Development. Boulder, CO: Westview Press, 1987.

Hart, Thomas G. *Sino-Soviet Relations: Re-examining the Prospects for Normalization*. London: Gower, 1987.

Huan, Guo-Gang. *Sino-Soviet Relations to the Year 2000: Implications for U.S. Interests*. Washington, D.C.: The Atlantic Council of the U.S., 1986.

Kelly, Ian. *Hong Kong: A Political-Geographic Analysis*. London: Macmillan, 1987.

Kendall, Harry H., ed. *The Changing Security Environment in Northeast Asia: Problems and Prospects*. Report of the IEAS. Berkeley, CA: University of California Institute of East Asian Studies, 1986.

Kim, Ilpyong J., ed. *Strategic Triangle.* New York: Paragon House., 1987.

Kiyohara, Michiko. *China watching by the Japanese.* Palo Alto, CA: Hoover Institute Press, 1987.

Low, Alfred D. *The Sino-Soviet Confrontation Since Mao Zedong: Dispute, Détente, or Conflict.* New York: Columbia University Press, 1987.

Scalapino, Robert A. and Masataka Kosaka, eds., *Peace, Politics and Economics in Asia.* Washington D.C.: Pergamon-Brassey's, 1988.

Segal, Gerald. *Sino-Soviet Relations After Mao.* Adelphi Papers. London: International Institute for Strategic Studies, 1985.

Sino-Soviet Conflict: A Historical Bibliography. Santa Barbara: ABC-CLIO Information Services, 1985.

Stolper, Thomas E. *China, Taiwan, and the Offshore Islands.* Armonk, New York: Sharpe, 1985.

Taylor, Robert. *The Sino-Japanese Axis: A New Force in Asia?* New York: St. Martin's Press, 1985.

Southeast Asia

Buszynski, Leszek. *Soviet Foreign Policy and Southeast Asia.* New Yorks: St. Martin's Press, 1986.

Chanda, Nayan. *Brother Enemy: The War After the War.* San Diego: Harcourt Brace Jovanovich, 1986.

Chang, Pao-min. *The Sino-Vietnamese Territorial Dispute.* new York: Praeger Publishers, 1986.

Crouch, Harold. *Economic Change, Social Structure and the Political System in Southeast Asia: Philippine Development Compared with the Other ASEAN Countries.* Brookfield, VT: Dover Publishing Co., 1986.

Domes, Jurgen and Yu-ming Shaw, eds., *Hong Kong: A Chinese And International Concern.* Boulder: Westview Press, 1988.

Johnson, Dion W., *Bear Tracks in Indochina: An Analysis of Soviet Presence in Vietnam.* Maxwell AFB, AL: Air University Press, 1987.

Kriangsak, Kittichaisaree. *The Law of the Sea and Maritime Boundary Delimitation: With Special Reference to Southeast Asia.* London: Oxford University Press, 1987.

Morrison, Charles E. *Japan, the United States and a Changing Southeast Asia.* New York: The Asia Society, 1985.

Pauker, Guy. *Government Responses to Armed Insurgency in Southeast Asia: A Comparative Examination of Failures and Successes and Their Likely Implications for the Future.* Santa Monica: Rand Corporation, June 1985.

Rambo, A. Terry, et al *Ethnic Diversity and the Control of Natural Resources in Southeast Asia.* Singapore: Center for South and Southeast Asian Studies, 1987.

Robison, Richard, Kevin Hewison and Richard Higgot, eds., *Southeast Asia in the 1980's: The Politics of Economic Crisis.* Sydney: Allen and Unwin, 1987.

Ross, Robert. *The Indochina Tangle: China's Vietnam Policy, 1975-1979.* New York: Columbia University Press, 1988.

Sanders, Alan J.K. *Mongolia: Politics, Economics, Society.* London: Pinter, 1987.

Valencia, Mark J. *Southeast Asian Seas: Oil Under Troubled Waters*. London: Oxford University Press, 1985.

Weatherbee, Donald E. *Southeast Asia Divided: The ASEAN-Indochina Crisis*. Boulder, CO: Westview Press, 1985.

The Oceania and South Pacific

Albinski, Henry S. *ANZUS, The United States, and Pacific Security*. Washington, D.C.: University Press of America, 1987.

Camilleri, Joseph A. *The Australia, New Zealand, United States Alliance: Regional Security in the Nuclear Age*. Boulder, CO: Westview Press, 1987.

Thakur, Ramesh. *In Defence of New Zealand: Foreign Policy Choices in the Nuclear Age*. Boulder, CO: Westview Pres, 1986.

South Asia and the Indian Ocean

Ashok, Kapur. *Pakistan's Nuclear Development*, London: Croom Helm, 1987.

Bannerjee, Brojendra N. *Peace, Friendship and Cooperation*. Delhi: BR Publishing Corporation, 1987.

Baxter, Craig, et al *Government and Politics in South Asia*. Boulder, CO: Westview Press, 1987.

Buzan, Barry, and Gowher Rizvi, eds., *South Asian Insecurity and the Great Powers*. London: macmillan, 1986.

Cohen, Philip, ed. *The Security of South Asia: American and Asian Perspectives*. Urbana, IL: University of Illinois Press, 1987.

Jayaramu, P.S. *India's National Security and Foreign Policy*. New York: ABC Publishing House, 1987.

Joeck, Neil, ed. *Special Issue on Strategic Consequences of Nuclear Proliferation in South Asia*. London: F. Cass, 1986.

Malik, Hafeez, ed., *Soviet-American Relations with Pakistan, Iran and Afghanistan*. London: Macmillan, 1987.

Rais, Rasul B. *The Indian Ocean and the Superpowers: Economic, Political, and Strategic Perspectives*. London: Croom Helm, 1986.

Saksena, K.P. *Cooperation in Development: Problems and Prospects for India and ASEAN*. Beverly Hills, CA: Sage Publications 1986.

Taylor, Jay. *The Dragon and the Wild Goose: China and India*. Greenwood, CT: Praeger, 1987.

Thomas, Raju G.C. *Indian Security Policy*. Princeton, NJ: Princeton University Press, 1986.

SPECIFIC COUNTRIES/ISSUES

The United States

Brown, Harold. *U.S.-Japan Relations: Technology, Economics, and Security*. New York: Merrill House, 1987.

Collins, John M. *U.S.-Soviet Military Balance 1980-1985*. New York: Pergamon-Brassey's International Defense Publishers, 1985.

Nicholas, J. Bruce. *The Uneasy Truce: Religion, Refugee Work and United States Foreign Policy*. London: Oxford University Press, 1988.

Palmer, Norman Dunbar. *Westward Watch: The united States and the Changing Western Pacific*. Washington, D.C.: Pergamon-Brassey's, 1987.

Rostow, W.W. *The United States and the Regional Organization of Asia and the Pacific, 1965-1985*. Austin: University of Texas Press, 1986.

The USSR

Bok Tan Eng Georges. *The USSR in East Asia: The Changing Soviet Positions and Implications for the West*. Paris: The Atlantic Institute for International Affairs, 1986.

Horn, Robert, *Alliance Between Comrades: The Dynamics of Soviet-Vietnamese Relations*. Los Angeles: Rand/UCLA Center for The Study of Soviet International Behavior, 1987.

Niiseki, Kinya, eds., *The Soviet Union in Transition*. Boulder, CO: Westview Press, 1987.

Rees, David. *The Soviet Seizure of the Kuriles*. New York: Praeger Publishers, 1985.

Rosenberger, Leif. *Soviet Union and Vietnam: An Uneasy Alliance*. Boulder, CO: Westview Press, 1986.

Rozman, Gilbert. *A Mirror for Socialism: Soviet Criticisms of China*. Princeton: Princeton University Press, 1985.

Thakur, Ramesh, and Garlyle A. Thayer, eds. *The Soviet Union as an Asian Pacific Power: Implications of Gorbachev's 1986 Vladivostok Initiative*. Boulder, CO: Westview Press, 1987.

China

Barnett, A. Doak. *The Making of Foreign Policy in China*. Boulder, CO: Westview Press, 1985.

Hamrin, Carol Lee. *China and the Future: Decision Making, Economic Planning, and Foreign Policy*. Boulder, CO: Westview Press, 1987.

Harding, Harry, *China and Northeast Asia*. Washington D.C.: University Press of America/New York: The Asia Society, 1988.

Joffe, Ellis. *The Chinese Army After Mao*. Cambridge, MA: Harvard University Press, 1987.

Lampton, David M. and Cathrine H. Keyser, eds., *China's Global Presence*. Washington D.C.: American Enterprise Institute, 1988.

Lardy, Nicholas R. *China's Entry into the World Economy*. New York: The Asia Society/Washington, D.C.: University Press of America, 1987.

Lovejoy, Charles D. Jr., and Bruce Watson. *China's Military Reforms: International and Domestic Implications*. Boulder, CO: Westview Press, 1986.

Medvedev, Roy. *China and the Superpowers*. New York: Basil Blackwell, 1986.

Perkins, Dwight H. *China: Asia's Next Economic Giant?* Seattle: University of Washington Press, 1986.

Wortzel, Larry M. *China's Military Modernization: International Implications*. Greenwood, CT: Praeger, 1988.

Japan

Drifte, Richard. *Arms Production in Japan: The Military Applications of Civilian Technology*. Boulder, CO: Westview Press, 1986.

Ellison, Herbert J., ed., *Japan and the Pacific Quadrille: the Major Powers in East Asia.* Boulder, CO: Westview Press, 1987.

Kiatamura, Hiroshi, Ryohei Murata, and Hisahiko Okazaki, eds., *Between Friends.* New York and Tokyo: Weatherhill, 1985.

Lincoln, Edward J. *Japan's Economic Role in Northeast Asia.* New York: The Asia Society/Washington, D.C.: University Press of America, 1987.

McIntosh, Malcolm *Japan Re-armed.* London: Frances Pinter Publishers, 1986.

Okimoto, Daniel, and Thomas P. Rohlen, eds. *Inside the Japanese System: Readings on Contemporary Society and Political Economy.* Palo Alto, CA: Stanford University Press, 1987.

Olsen, Edward A. *U.S. Japan Strategic Reciprocity.* Stanford: Hoover Press, 1985.

Shiraishi, Masaya, *Japanese Relations with Vietnam: 1951-1985.* Ithaca, NY: Cornell University Press, 1988.

Tsuchiyama, Jitsuo. *Japan's Alliance Policy: Past, Present and Future.* Boulder, CO: Lynne Rienner Publishers, 1988.

Yasutomo, Dennis T. *The Manner of Giving: Strategic Aid and Japanese Foreign Policy.* Lexington, MA: Lexington Books, 1986.

Korea

Bridges, Brian, *Korea and the West.* Chatham House Papers: 39. London: The Royal Institute of International Affairs, 1986.

Clough, Ralph N. *Balancing Act: The Republic of Korea Approaches 1988.* FPI Policy Briefs. Washington, D.C.: Foreign Policy Institute of the Johns Hopkins University School of Advanced International Studies, 1987.

———. *Embattled Korea: The Rivalry for International Support.* Boulder, CO: Westview Press, 1987.

Han, Sung-joo, and Robert J. Myers, eds. *Korea: The Year 2000.* Washington, D.C.: University Press of America, 1988.

Harrison, Selig. *The South Korean Political Crisis and American Policy Option.* Washington, D.C.: The Washington Institute Pres, 1987.

Kim, Ilpyong J., and Young Whan Kihl, eds. *Political Changes in South Korea.* New York: Paragon House, 1988.

Koo, Youngnok, and Sun-joo Han, eds. *The Foreign Policy of the Republic of Korea.* New York: Columbia University Pres, 1985.

Korea at the Crossroads: Implications for American Policy. New York: Council on Foreign Relations and The Asia Society, 1987.

Macdonald, Donald Stone, *The Koreans: Contemporary Politics and Society.* Boulder: Westview Press, 1988.

Nam, Joo-Hong. *American's Commitment to South Korea: The First Decade of the Nixon Doctrine.* New York: Cambridge University Press, 1986.

Olsen, Edward. *U.S. Policy and the Two Koreas.* Boulder, CO: Westview Press, 1987.

Polomka, Peter. *The Two Koreas: Catalyst for Conflict in East Asia?* Adelphi Papers No. 208. London: International Institute of Strategic Studies, 1986.

Scalapino, Robert A., and Sung-joo Han, eds. *United States-Korea Relations.* Research papers and Policy Studies No. 19. Berkeley, CA: University of California Institute of East Asian Studies, 1986.

Scalapino, Robert A., Sung-joo Han, and Hongkoo Lee, eds. *North Korea in a Regional and Global Context*. Korea Research Monograph No., 11. Berkeley, CA: University of California Institute of East Asian Studies, 1986.

Sneider, Richard L. *The Political and Social Capabilities of North and South Korea for the Long-term Military Competition*. Santa Monica, CA: Rand, 1985.

Sullivan, John, and Roberta Foss, eds. *Two-Koreas—One Future?* Lanham, MD: University Press of America, 1987. Copublished by arrangement with the American Friends Service Committee.

Wolf, Charles Jr., Donald P. Henry, K.C. Yeh, James H. Hayes, John Schank, and Richard Sneider. *The Changing Balance: South and North Korean Capabilities for Long-Term Military Competition*. Santa Monica, CA: Rand, 1985.

Vietnam/Indochina

Albin, David A., and M. Hood, eds. *Cambodian Agony*. Armonk, NY: M.E. Shape, 1987.

Chang, Pao-min. *Kampuchea Between China and Vietnam*. Singapore: Singapore University Press, 1985.

Dommen, Arthur Jr. *Laos: Keystone of Indochina*. Boulder, CO: Westview Press, 1985.

Fforde, Adam, and Suzanner H. Paine. *The Limits of National Liberation: Problems of Economic Management in the Democratic Republic of Vietnam*. New York: Methuen, 1987.

Pike, Douglas. *PAVN: People's Army of Vietnam*. Novato, CA: Presidio Press, 1986.

Shaplen, Robert. *Bitter Victory*. New York: Harper & Row, 1986.

Vickery, Michael. *Kampuchea: Politics, Economics and Society*. London: Francis Pinter Publishers, 1986.

The Philippines and ASEAN

Bonner, Raymond. *Waltzing with a Dictator: The Marcoses and the Making of American Policy*. New York: New York Times Books, 1987.

Bresnan, John, ed. *Crisis in the Philippines: The Marcos Era and Beyond*. Princeton: Princeton University Press, 1986.

Clutterbuck, Richard. *Conflict and Violence in Singapore and Malaysia, 1945-1983*. Boulder, CO: Westview Press, 1985.

Gedney, Willaim J. *Selected Papers on Comparative Tai Studies*. Bangkok: Center for South and Southeast Asian Studies, 1988.

Gregor, James, and Virgilio Aganon. *The Philippine Bases: U.S. Security at Risk*. Washington, D.C.: University Press of America, 1987.

Hawes, Gary. *The Philippine State and the Marcos Regime: the Politics of Export*. Ithaca, NY: Cornell University Press, 1987.

Lande, Carl H., ed., *Rebuilding a Nation: Philippine Challenges and American Policy*. Washington, D.C.: Washington Institute Press, 1987.

Leviste, Jose P., Jr., ed. *The Pacific Lake: Philippine Perspectives on a Pacific Community*. Manila: Philippine Council for Foreign Relations & SGV Foundation, 1986.

Martin, Linda G., ed. *The ASEAN Success Story: Social, Economic and Political Dimensions*. Honolulu: The East-West Center, distributed by the University of Hawaii Press, 1987.

Osborne, Robin O. *Indonesia's Secret War: Guerrilla War in Irian Java*. Boston: Allen and Unwin, 1985.

Preston, P.W., *Rethinking Development: Essays on Development and Southeast Asia*. New York: Routledge and Kegan Paul, 1987.

Snitwongse, Kusuma, and Sukhumbahnd Paribatra, eds. *The Invisible Nexus: Energy and ASEAN;s Security*. Singapore: Executive Publications Ltd., 1985.

Sopiee, Noordin, ed., *ASEAN at the Crossroads Obstacles, Options and Opportunities in Economic Cooperation*. Kuala Lumpur, Malaysia: Institute of Strategic and International Studies, 1987.

Tilman, Robert. *Southeast Asia and the Enemy Beyond: ASEAN perceptions of External Threats*. Boulder, CO: Westview Press, 1986.

Turley, Willaim S., ed. *Confrontation or Coexistence: The Future of ASEAN-Vietnam Relations*. Bangkok: Institute of Security and International Studies, Chulalongkorn University, 1985.

Weatherbee, Donald E., ed. *Southeast Asia Divided: The ASEAN-Indochina Crisis*. Boulder, CO: Westview Press, 1985.

Index

264

About the Book

Asian-Pacific security requirements in the late 1980s and beyond are changing, along with the shifting security patterns and strategic environments in the region. A variety of contradictory—even paradoxical—trends are emerging, with continuing force acquisition offset to some extent by discussions on force withdrawals and the reduction of tensions. This fully revised edition of *Asian-Pacific Security: Emerging Challenges and Responses*—"an **excellent overview of the region and its problems of strategy and security**" (***International Journal***)—brings the discussion of regional security policies up-to-date.